THE KENSINGTON BATTALION

The 22nd Battalion Royal Fusiliers arrayed for duty at Tidworth, November 1915. Colonel Barker is in front, with his Adjutant Captain Phythian-Adams at his right hand, and just behind them the four company commanders, with the men on foot (*Phythian-Adams papers*)

THE KENSINGTON BATTALION

'NEVER LOST A YARD OF TRENCH'

G. I. S. Inglis

Pen & Sword
MILITARY

"The 22nd Battalion Royal Fusiliers never lost a yard of trench or failed their comrades in the Day of Battle. Such is your record and such a record of you will be handed down to posterity."

Farewell of Brigadier-General Barnett Barker
2nd February 1918

First published in Great Britain in 2010 by
Pen & Sword Military
an imprint of
Pen & Sword Books Ltd
47 Church Street
Barnsley
South Yorkshire
S70 2AS

Copyright © G. I. S. Inglis, 2010

ISBN 978 1 84884 247 2

The right of G. I. S. Inglis to be identified as author of
this work has been asserted by him in accordance with
the Copyright, Designs and Patents Act 1988.

A CIP catalogue record for this book is available from the British Library.

Printed and bound in England
by CPI

Pen & Sword Books Ltd incorporates the imprints of
Pen & Sword Aviation, Pen & Sword Maritime, Pen & Sword Military,
Wharncliffe Local History, Pen & Sword Select, Pen & Sword Military Classics,
Leo Cooper, Remember When, Seaforth Publishing and Frontline Publishing.

For a complete list of Pen & Sword titles please contact
PEN & SWORD BOOKS LIMITED
47 Church Street, Barnsley, South Yorkshire, S70 2AS, England
E-mail: enquiries@pen-and-sword.co.uk
Website: www.pen-and-sword.co.uk

Contents

Foreword
By Gary Sheffield

The 22nd Battalion Royal Fusiliers (Kensington) is very close to my heart. I first came across the 22nd RF in 1981. As a history undergraduate at the University of Leeds, I was fortunate to take a special subject on 'Britain and the First World War' under the genial supervision of Dr Hugh Cecil. I already knew what I wanted to write my dissertation on. Having read Martin Middlebrook's *The First Day on the Somme* I was keen to research something to do with the raising of Kitchener's Army in 1914. Hugh advised me to go to speak to Peter Simkins, then Senior Historian at the Imperial War Museum, who was then finishing his magnificent study *Kitchener's Army* (eventually published in 1988). Peter, with typical generosity towards a completely obscure twenty year old student, took the time to discuss my project, gently corrected some of my naive assumptions, and steered me in the direction of the collection of material on the 22nd RF at Kensington Library. On visiting the library I was seated at a desk and boxes of documents arrived. I can still remember the thrill I got from handling these original sources - letters, orders and newspaper cuttings – a thrill which every historian worth their salt will recognise, and which no matter how blasé one becomes, never entirely vanishes. The result was my BA dissertation on the raising of the 22nd RF.

In 1983 I began work on an MA by Research, once again at Leeds. I had become fascinated by the officer-man relationship in the British Army during the First World War. It was an obvious step to study the 22nd RF (my dissertation had stopped when the Battalion crossed to France in 1915). As he relates in this book, it wasn't long before I came into contact with Geoff Inglis and we carried out our research in parallel, sharing sources, visiting surviving 22nd RF members and their families together and just talking about the Battalion, its personalities and doings. It made the lonely business of postgraduate research much more fun. In 1985 I got my toe on the ladder of a scholarly career as the lowest form of academic life in the Department of War Studies at RMA Sandhurst. Inevitably, my focus drifted away from the 22nd RF although Geoff and I edited a selection of Major Christopher Stone's letters, eventually published in 1989. Geoff began to write the history of the battalion but, deep into a part-time Ph D at King's College London, I could only cheer from the sidelines. For the reasons that Geoff gives in the book, he didn't finish it.

Fast forward a ludicrously long period of time and I received an e-mail from Geoff, who I hadn't heard from for some years. The book was back on – and would I write a foreword? The answer was of course 'yes', and you are reading the result. Apart from anything else, it is a small gesture of thanks for his generosity and help all those years ago.

Reading the text of *The Kensington Battalion 'Never Lost A Yard of Trench'*, I am carried back a quarter of a century to postgrad days. Memories of pub lunches with Geoff and Roland Whipp, our 93 year old mentor; visits to the Public Record Office to go through war diaries and after-action reports; 'field trips' to Horsham, where the battalion was stationed in 1915, and the Western Front to visit Boom Ravine and other places where the 22nd RF fought that were well off the usual battlefield tourist track. And the names: Bill Alley, Olly Berrycloath, H.E. Harvey, George Challis and of course Christopher Stone and Randle Barnett Barker. The 22nd RF was more than just a military unit. It was a community, a family even. It is that evocation of this aspect of the Battalion's history that, for me, makes Never Lost A Yard of Trench such a fine achievement.

We are not short of modern histories of First World War infantry battalions but this is undoubtedly one of the best I have read. The sheer depth of research (and of course the richness of the available sources) set this book apart from most of its peers. Of course, in-depth research needs to be interpreted but Geoff Inglis has a real 'feel' for his material and has produced an extremely readable, as well as scholarly book. The 22nd RF did not take part in the first day of the battle of the Somme, and so there was no chance that this book would fall victim to the 'First of July' syndrome suffered by so many battalion histories by modern writers, that is concentrating on the beginning of the Somme and treating everything else as a coda. Geoff Inglis has been careful to give due weight to the 22nd RF's entire history. His treatment of Miraumont and Oppy sheds light on episodes in British military history which remain obscure. I was pleased that he chose to continue the story right into the 1980s, because in a very real sense the Battalion only came to end with the death of its last member.

I am very glad that Geoff Inglis finished the project he began two decades ago. *Never Lost A Yard of Trench* is a fine work of military and social history. It is also a very fitting tribute to a remarkable group of men and women – the members of the 22nd Battalion Royal Fusiliers, the Kensington Battalion, and their families.

Gary Sheffield
Professor of War Studies
University of Birmingham

April 2009

Preface

I was drawn towards the Great War by the poets: first by the feverish patriotism of Rupert Brooke then by the grim images of Owen and Sassoon. I read Lyn McDonald's *They Call It Passchendaele* in horrified fascination. Almost at the same time the excellent series *Testament of Youth* (about Vera Brittain's war, with its effective use of her fiancé Roland Leighton's haunting verse) was playing on TV.

But were all Great War battles as apparently futile as Passchendaele, and was everyone as hard hit by the War as Vera Brittain? Investigating the Great War became a passion. I devoured book after book, went to lectures, began a modern history degree and began visiting the battlefields of France and Flanders in 1981, courtesy of the excellent Major and Mrs Holt's Tours. I realised that although intellectual curiosity inspired my visits, the rewards were emotional. I might have gone to France to discover Boom Ravine, but the most fulfilling experiences would arise from being part of the anticipation and the actuality of someone else's special visit – perhaps arriving at a relative's grave for the first time.

I wanted to have a story to tell, something I could identify with, but my immediate family was too old or too young to be involved in the Great War.

A chance meeting with the then Local Studies Librarian at Kensington Central Library, Brian Curle, led to him suggesting that I look at the Broughshane Collection: seven boxes of files, letters and documents particularly concerned with the raising and deeds of the 22nd Royal Fusiliers in 1914-18. Within a short time I knew that this was my story, so I abandoned the degree to devote my attention to researching it.

As I moved though the archives in one direction, a young man called Gary Sheffield was researching the same battalion from a different direction. We both contacted the same 22nd Royal Fusiliers veteran for an interview. In fact Gary was two weeks ahead of me, and it was the veteran, ex-Sergeant Roland Whipp, who brought both of us together. Gary and I met afterwards and decided to pool all our discoveries. Our aims overlapped and were non-competitive: Gary seeking material on officer-man relationships and morale for his MA, me looking just for the overall story.

By the end of 1985, we had explored just about all of the major archival material, and I had five chapters written. Gary, now lecturing at Sandhurst, obtained a commission for us to edit the letters of Christopher Stone (who rose to become second in command of the Battalion). I put the book aside and concentrated on editing my half of the letters.[1]

My father had an accident which meant that the time spent researching had now to be devoted to family affairs. The half-written book and piles of source materials lay under my bed collecting dust for twenty years. I was embarrassed not to have finished the job but unable to draw a line under it. Two years ago another researcher, Tom Thorpe, enquired whether I might have any material relevant to his study of both Kensington regiments (the 13th Kensingtons and the 22nd Royal Fusiliers). I handed over what I had, including the 90-odd typed pages written in the nineteen-eighties. To my surprise he kept urging me to finish the story.

As a historical Rip Van Winkle I had to spend months getting my general knowledge of the war back up to scratch before starting anything specific to the Battalion, but fortunately, the historiography of the First World War has gone through a revolution in the last twenty years. Evidence-based history, gained from thorough study of primary archives, is much more common now, whereas many older studies seemed to be based on pre-existing assumptions such as A the war was totally futile, B all the generals were bone-headed, and C life in the trenches was continuously horrendous.

Compton Mackenzie described such a pressure to conform to the dominant view in his Foreword to the paperback edition of his memoir of the Gallipoli Campaign:

Gallipoli Memories *was published in 1929 when the mood of the moment regarded with suspicion any book about the war that even hinted at a lighter side of it.*[2]

Another example is in *Testament of Youth*, written in the early nineteen-thirties. She said she had been strongly affected by Haig's 'backs to the wall' message of April 1918, but then hastily qualified herself by saying that his reputation had not been stripped of much of its glories by official 'revelations.'[3] Many of the 'revelations' emerging in the nineteen-twenties and nineteen-thirties can now be seen as self-serving distortions which it simply made it harder to get at the truth.

This is the story of one service battalion in the Great War. Its members did not view their experiences though a futile lens, or reinterpret their experiences though fashionable pacifism and they often had fun, in or out of the trenches. They believed in loyalty, duty and in each other.

Their final commanding officer Lieutenant-Colonel WJ Phythian-Adams, who had taken up a religious career after the war and was now Canon Phythian-Adams, powerfully expressed their views at a Service of Remembrance in November 1935:

'As the anniversary [Armistice Day] *comes round again,' he said, 'it will do our younger generation no harm if we remind them of one or two things.*

'We are a little tired, we who fought in the great war, we who were told loudly and constantly that we were heroes – although we had sufficient sense of humour to know that that was not true – of being told now that we were doing the devil's work out there and that we were the instruments of the powers of evil in Europe.

'That is a charge which we ought not to pass by in silence, for it dishonours not only the living, but the dead…

'We gave up,' he continued, 'our jobs, our joys, our ambitions, our homes and our families for something bigger than ourselves, for the honour of our country and the freedom of mankind; and because we made that sacrifice, God gave us in return His

exceedingly great reward of comradeship… which everyone treasures as one of the greatest prizes to be won in life.'[4]

The Battalion was raised in the early days of the war by the then Mayor of Kensington, William Davison,[5] a passionately patriotic Ulsterman. It arrived in France in late 1915 and performed with great distinction in 1916. Although starved of reinforcements after some very costly battles in the spring of 1917, contributing to it being one of the battalions disbanded in February 1918, the Battalion had a unique spirit, which came to the fore again after the war.

Many battalions had reunions for some considerable time after the war, but the 22nd Battalion Old Comrades Association not only held annual reunions in London, it held Remembrance Services in London and Horsham; it did its best to look after those members who had fallen in hard times by trying to get them jobs or at least making grants of money; and it had once or twice-yearly Children's Parties. Above all, it published its excellent little magazine *Mufti* until the late nineteen seventies, when there were only a handful of veterans still alive. 13 Platoon additionally held its own reunion of original members from 1915 to 1971 (broken only by the Second World War).

This spirit derived in part from its mixture of Londoners (from clerks and bankers to dockers and labourers) and irreverent, adventurous Colonials, but particularly from the man who blended their personalities, created a Battalion both happy and efficient, and then commanded it throughout almost all of its wartime service in France: Lieutenant-Colonel Randle Barnett(-)Barker.[6] Without exaggeration, 'BB' was loved by his men as the father of the Battalion, and although he perished in 1918, his example set the tone for the creation of an Old Comrades Association after the war.

For the current study there is very good source material: the *Broughshane Collection and Battalion Cuttings Book* at Kensington Local Studies Unit, local newspapers particularly the *West Sussex Gazette* (whose cub reporter became a lifelong supporter of the Battalion and its Old Comrades Association), Major Christopher Stone's short but data-rich *History of the 22nd Battalion* and *B.B.*, the Old Comrades Association magazine *Mufti* running from 1919 to 1977, interviews with veterans and/or their surviving families in the 1983-85 period, War Diaries of the Battalion, Brigade etc at the National Archives in Kew, Major Barton William-Powlett's diaries, and Colonel Phythian-Adams's letters. Above all, the richest sources derive from the daily letters written by Colonel Barker (carefully transcribed by his wife to remove private family material; from going to France in November 1915 to April 1917) and Major Christopher Stone,[7] (from leaving Horsham in 1915 until he returned home in March 1919). As both reflect the view from Battalion HQ, I have tried not to let the latter material dominate the story. Fortunately *Mufti* contains many reminiscences from NCOs and private soldiers.

I am most grateful for everyone's assistance in contributing material, first in the nuneteen-eighties and more recently, and I would especially like to thank Henry Phythian-Adams and Gwen Stokes (daughter of Fred and Edie Keeble) for making their picture collections available.

The style adopted here has been to make extensive use of direct quotation from contemporary documents to more readily capture the flavour of the period. In the last ninety years written English has changed considerably; then it was much more formal, with more punctuation and capitalisation of nouns. I have retained the original spellings inside direct quotes, but preferred modern usage outside it. Thus inside a direct quotation someone might be described as D.S.O., M.C., while outside it I would write DSO MC. I have written out Army ranks in full so Corporal, Sergeant and Major, but I have used RF and KRRC for Royal Fusiliers and Kings Royal Rifle Corps because they occur so often.

Composition of Battalion, Brigade, Division

It will be useful to describe the composition of common Army units. An Infantry Battalion circa 1915 consisted of about 1000 men and 30 officers. It was divided into four Companies (eg A, B, C, and D, about 200-240 each), plus Headquarters, which included specialists like Signallers, Transport etc. It would be commanded by a Lieutenant-Colonel, with a Major as a Second-in-Command. Within each Company (generally led by a Captain) there were four Platoons, each around 40-50 men led by a Platoon Officer (often a Second Lieutenant). Thus there were 16 Platoons in a Battalion, numbered 1 through to 16.

Four Battalions made up a Brigade, and three Brigades (plus a Pioneer Battalion) generally made up an Infantry Division. Two or more Divisions made up an Army Corps, while two or more Corps made up an Army.

A Battalion tended to be a stable unit that stayed within the same Brigade and same Division, but Divisions were quite often moved between Corps and even between Armies. Thus an average private soldier would know his Brigade and Division, eg 99 Brigade, 2nd Division, but not necessarily any of the units higher than this.

The Coming of War in 1914

If Britain was to be involved in a European war the likely enemy was no longer France, but resurgent Germany. Since the turn of the century there had been a plethora of publications in Britain imagining wars in which Germany was the invading enemy. The best known was Erskine Childers' 1903 *The Riddle in the Sands*, but the prolific William Le Queux's works were widely available, notably *The Invasion of 1910* (published in 1906)[8]. In 1913 Saki (the famous short-story writer), wrote a novel called *When William Came* which described life in Britain after a lightning war won by the Germans, in which the new ruler was described as 'King of Prussia, Great Britain and Ireland, Emperor of the West.'[9]

Ever since Kaiser Wilhelm had imposed his arbitrary and unpredictable authority on German foreign policy, suspicion had increased in both countries about the ambitions of the other, resulting in the Dreadnought-building race and many international crises. Somehow each one was defused, but it was probably just a matter of time before one side elected not to step back from the abyss.

The story of how the assassination of Archduke Franz Ferdinand in Sarajevo on June 28th 1914 began a chain of events that led to Britain declaring war on Germany on the 4th August is too well known to be covered here in detail. What started as a dispute between the Serbians and Austrians soon became Germany and Austria-Hungary against Russia, France and Serbia, with the British rather hovering on the fence until the German invasion of Belgium gave them a *casus belli* that they could rally the nation behind: gallant little Belgium, whose borders had been guaranteed by Britain since 1839 on 'a little piece of paper'.

And then there was Lord Kitchener, and his lighthouse gaze into a future that involved years of warfare and millions of men, in contrast with the quick war so many people anticipated. And that recruiting poster for the new Army he believed Britain would need.

1 *From Vimy Ridge to the Rhine, The Great War Letters of Christopher Stone DSO MC*, Crowood, 1989, Eds GD Sheffield & GIS Inglis, henceforth *Sheffield & Inglis*
2 Compton Mackenzie, *Gallipoli Memories*, Panther Edition 1965, p9
3 Vera Brittain, *Testament of Youth*, Fontana edition, 1979, pp 419-420
4 *Mufti*, Xmas 1935, 16, No 4, pp 3-6
5 William H Davison, 1872-1953, a native of Ballymena, County Antrim, educated at Shrewsbury School and Keble Collage, Oxford, Mayor of Kensington 1913-1919, Conservative MP for Kensington between 1919-1945, knighted (KBE) in 1918 and then created 1st Baron Broughshane of Kensington in 1945. His first wife was Beatrice Mary (a daughter of Sir Owen Roberts, and hence a relative of Randle Barnett Barker), divorcing her in 1929 to marry Louisa MC Marriott. *ThePeerage.com; Ballymena Observer*, 1914 (nd: in *Broughshane*, II, 88); *Mufti*, June 1953, 33, No 121, pp 2-3
6 Later Brigadier-General R Barnett Barker DSO and Bar, four times Mentioned in Despatches; 1870-1918. Educated at Sedbergh School 1882-8 where he was a keen sportsman, he was gazetted into the 3rd Battalion Royal Welch Fusiliers in 1889, then was Adjutant of the Volunteer Battalion of the RWF at the time of the Boer War. An excellent rider of a horse, he was second in the Grand Military Point to Point Steeplechase in 1904. He left the Army as a Captain in 1906, became Brigade-Major of the Cheshire Infantry Brigade until 1913. Was briefly Commandant of the POW Camp at Frimley in August-September 1914, before becoming second in command of the 22nd Royal Fusiliers, then its commanding officer in 1915. He remained its CO until he was promoted to command 3 Brigade in November 1917, then 99 Brigade in January 1918. (Biographical information: *Sedbergh School Register* 1882, *Rouge Et Noir*, 7/1888, 3/1889, 11/1890, *The Sedberghian*, November 1918, *The Times* 5/4/1918, *Morning Post* 5/4/1918, *Abergavenny Chronicle* 5/4/1918, *West Sussex County Times* (hereafter *WSCT*) 6/4/1918; private communications from his son Philip Sankey-Barker 29/2/1984, and Colonel ROF Prichard [ex-RWF], 14/1/1984)
7 Christopher Stone, 1882-1965, educated at Eton and Christchurch College, Oxford, where he met his lifelong friend, future brother-in-law and co-founder of *The Gramophone*, EM Compton Mackenzie. Teacher, private tutor, novelist, he became the first Disc Jockey on BBC radio in 1927, with a wonderfully relaxed and informal style. (See his sister Faith Compton Mackenzie's autobiography, *As Much As I Dare*, 1938; the Introduction to *Sheffield & Inglis*; obituary in *The Times*, 24/5/1965, obituary in *Mufti*, June 1965, 44, No 145, p3)
8 See John Ramsden *Don't Mention the War: The British and the Germans Since 1890*, Little, Brown, 2006, pp 56-90; also Niall Ferguson, *The Pity of War*, Penguin, 1998, pp 1-11
9 Available online at http://haytom.us/showcatpicks.php?thiscat=10

Chapter One

A Kensington Battalion
of Lord Kitchener's New Army

ON SEPTEMBER 10, 1914 a packed public meeting was held in a school playground in the London Borough of Kensington, where a huge wagon bedecked with flags formed the platform, on which were Mayor William Davison and eleven local dignitaries.[1] Mayor Davison began proceedings with a passionate speech:

Why is this meeting being held tonight? So that there may be no one within the borough who shall not know the reason why we are at war, who shall not be assured of the righteousness of our cause, and who shall not have occasion to ask himself whether he is doing everything in his power to help.

Why are we fighting? The German Chancellor gave the true reason to our Ambassador. 'You are going to fight,' he said, 'for a little piece of paper.' Yes, we are fighting for a little piece of paper, but by that little bit of paper England's honour was pledged. To what? To protect the weak against the strong. To protect right against might. (Cheers.) What would have been our position to-day if we had stood aside and withdrawn from our bond for fear or greed of gain? What would have been our feelings if we had looked at gallant heroic Belgium, laid waste by barbarian hordes? ...As the Prime Minister said, 'It were better that our country were blotted out from the page of history.' (Cheers.) Assuredly our cause is righteous. We strove for peace and we were given a sword. And now we must see his thing through. (Cheers.)

...Kensington has done splendidly so far.

The original call to arms.

In two days at The Town Hall the Kensington Territorial Regiment was raised to full strength (1,000) and 100 over. Then we got leave to have a second battalion, and in two more days 1,300 more had given in their names. The War Office asked me if I could help them with their new army. I said, 'Yes, if you will let me have a Kensington Battalion where those who know one another

Kensington High Street at the turn of the 20th Century, featuring the Town Hall and Public Library. Factionpress

William Davison, Mayor of Kensington 1913-19, and raiser of the Battalion.

can be trained and serve together.' They said, 'If you can raise a battalion of 1,100 strong you shall have the honour of calling it the Kensington Battalion.'…You have got time to join, you who are left. I could not bear to think that any Kensington lad should not have his chance, that any in after life should feel the pathos and regret of this verse that was written the other day:

'How will you fare, sonny, how will you fare
In the far-off winter night,
When you sit by the fire in an old man's chair
And your neighbours talk of the fight;
Will you slink away, as it were from a blow,
Your old head shamed and bent?
Or say – 'I was not with the first to go,
But I went, thank God, I went.'

And should it be that some of you who go forth shall be added to that great Roll of Honour of those who do not return, still I say to you:
Haste Ye! Enrol!

'For how can man die better than facing fearful odds
For the ashes of his fathers, and the temples of his gods?'
(Prolonged cheers.)[2]

After the other speakers had stoked the fires of patriotism still further, the reporter commented: 'A fairly large number of recruits was then enrolled for the Kensington Battalion of Lord Kitchener's Army.'

The recruitment poster described the conditions of entry:

Age on enlistment 19 to 35, ex-Soldiers up to 45, and certain selected ex-Non-Commissioned Officers up to 50. General service for the duration of the war. Height 5ft 3in and upwards. Chest 34in at least. Medically fit. Pay at Army Rates. Married Men or Widowers with children will be accepted, and will draw Separation Allowances under Army Conditions.

Another paragraph was heavily underlined:

Special arrangements will be made for men working together, or who know one another, to be enrolled in the same Company so that they may serve together.[3]

It owed something to the recently-developed Pals concept, and while a number of groups of men – from Notting Hill Rugby Club or William Whiteley's store for example – did join together *en masse*, central London in mid-September 1914 wasn't quite the same sort of tight-knit community as in say Hull or Accrington.

By the time the next week's *Kensington News* came out, recruiting was 'proceeding slowly – too slowly.' Recruitment drives were carried out in different parts of the borough, then extended to the neighbouring borough of Hammersmith and to Northampton Polytechnic in Regent Street,[4] all without a great deal of success, although some willing men were being pinched by recruiters for an infantry battalion for Colonials. The problem was that the initial surge of volunteers had reached its peak nationally between the end of August and the first half of September, with the peak week 30/8-5/9, when news of the BEF's stirring retreat from Mons reached the newspapers. This had undoubtedly helped the second Kensington Territorial Battalion (whose recruitment started on August 31st), become full up so quickly, as well as giving an impression of considerable unfulfilled demand.[5]

The first recruitment meeting for the new Kitchener Battalion had occurred the day that numbers started to decline, when many men who had given some sign of interest earlier had found somewhere else. This difficulty in achieving its establishment of 1,100 men[6] would, however, lead to the formation of a battalion with unique characteristics.

The same Colonial Infantry unit mentioned earlier was also struggling for numbers. Initially it had advertised for 'Colonial and Overseas men resident in this country.' Later ones softened this to 'having resided in the Colonies,' and then 'having had any association with the Overseas Dominions and Colonies.' Major-General Sir Francis Lloyd, the GOC London District, suggested to Mayor Davison that the Kensington Battalion should merge with it. The Colonials would make up A and B Companies of the new unit, with the Kensington battalion becoming its C and D Companies. The target market for the Colonial Infantry was men who happened to be in Britain at the declaration of war, like HC Lissiman, who had come to Britain for a short working holiday in 1914 (his fiancée back in Australia wouldn't see him for another five years), rather than those who had specially travelled to Britain to offer their services, but some did: thus JDF Tilney came back from Argentina in August 1914 on the Royal Mail Steam Packet Company SS *Andes*, while WB Boulter came back hotfoot from Chicago.[7]

AS Rose remembered it being built on the left-over remnants of 2nd King Edwards Horse, also for Colonials:

> *How many of you …can recall the first officer we had? Captain Cunningham of the Bengal Lancers, left behind by the 2nd King Edward's Horse, who had left the morning I arrived at the White City.*
>
> *The remnants were a miscellaneous collection including Jim Carson, son of Lord Carson, very much in everyone's mind at that time; a disconsolate figure sitting on the shafts of a local grocer's cart (which had been commandeered) who turned out to be 'Saki' of the Morning Post, afterwards Sgt Munro of 'A' Company...*[8]

As recruiting became more difficult, the recruiters had used all their wiles:

> *He was a very amiable recruiting sergeant, the day was a Sunday in September 1914, the date 13th, and the place was the White City, Shepherds Bush.*
>
> *There had been a war on for a month or so, but the doctor did not think my chest measurement quite good enough for the Army. The recruiting sergeant asked me as I was leaving how I had got on and seemed very surprised at my fate. He requested*

The famous author Saki, otherwise H H Munro, and later a Lance-Sergeant.

17

Colonel Archibald Innes, the first CO of the Battalion, with a DSO from the Boer War

me to wait, and after he'd had a few whispered words with the recruiting officer, I was invited to try my luck with the doctor again. By some chance or other, my chest measurement was by then satisfactory and I was then returned to the recruiting officer who kindly asked me what regiment I would like to join. I replied that any old lot would suit me.

'We have a very fine regiment of Colonials in formation at the White City,' he said, and I was invited to join them. I could hardly claim to be a Colonial, but I was assured that, being anxious to become full-strength as quickly as possible, this regiment was willing to take a few other than Colonials on holiday in England, of which it was proposed to form the regiment.[9]

Fred Keeble (a local man, born in Hammersmith, who worked at the Times Book Club in Oxford Street) and his running pal Albert Greenwood joined together at the White City on 11th September. They both had early regimental numbers (95 and 96), were exactly the target market the Mayor was looking for, but as they were allocated to A Company, it is possible that they initially joined the Colonials.[10]

There was no doubt, however, about the 'Whiteleys Boys': Whiteleys – a big department store in Queensway north of Kensington – was very patriotic and invited its young men to enlist. HV Harrington, JW Lawrence and SJ 'Claude' Upton (all in the Gents Outfitting Department) and WW 'Baby' Clark (Jewellery Department), were four friends who wanted to join up together.[11]

Upton and co waited a week or two for 'Baby' Clark to return home from his holiday, then they all took a day off to join up. By this time Clark and Lawrence had done some investigation: at this time people under 5 foot 6 inches in height, people with false teeth, and people with glasses were being rejected. This ruled out Upton (glasses), while Lawrence had already failed a medical. They had eight rejections in the morning, then:

Second Lieutenant Christopher Stone (centre, front) and the Signallers. Corporal Fred Keeble is next left of him, and Lance-Corporal EM West is next left of him. Keeble papers

> *We finished up at the Regent Street Polytechnic…and we were examined by a doctor…We were worried about Claude but he had learnt most of the letters on the thing [optical chart]. He went first, cos if he didn't get passed, we wouldn't go in…The doctor, who was writing, said 'One of you come and read this card' and Lawrence said 'After you Claude' – his name wasn't Claude at all but the name stuck. We all passed and we found we were in the Kensington Battalion of the Royal Fusiliers.*[12]

Later the brothers Hughes, and Stone from the Wine Department, also joined up to make seven from Whiteleys all in the same platoon, all of whom would survive the war. Clark and co then celebrated in the local pub. This was where bank-worker LB Comerford had gone for a quick beer and sandwich after a futile attempt at trying to join up had taken up most of his lunchtime hour:

> *Hardly had I savoured the ineffable taste of my foaming tankard when in marched a body of men in single file, in Mufti, but with tickets in their lapels. They looked a lovely lot – happy, carefree and upstanding. They must have been hand-picked by Kitchener. Summoning up courage I approached the obvious leader of the gang who they called Claud, and asked what regiment they belonged to. Proudly he answered 'Kensington*

Battalion of the Royal Fusiliers.'

So he decided to join them. He reported to the White City, where:

A Sergeant looked me over with a practised eye and secretly conferred with a gentleman in a bowler hat. He then looked disapprovingly at me and barked, 'Report to 13 Platoon.' It sounded as though he was relegating me to the Foreign Legion.

"*When I contacted the platoon I was overjoyed to find that same bunch of chaps I had met in the pub, and I lived with them ever after...*[13]

Personal relationships and recommendations were more important in the recruiting of officers. Major JA Innes formerly of the Rifle Brigade, with a DSO from the Boer War, was offered command of the Battalion via one of Mayor Davison's Aldermen recommending him. Captain Randle Barnett Barker, a relative by marriage to Mayor Davison and formerly of the Royal Welch Fusiliers, was offered the post of Second-in-Command.

Some of the officers, plus Regimental Sergeant-Major (henceforth RSM) LC McCausland, the General Secretary for Kensington General Hospital, came via the National Reserve (for whom Davison had raised money in May 1914). Four officers from the Inns of Court included WJ Phythian-Adams, Captain Alan MacDougall and Captain BG Godlonton, an over-forty South African with Boer War service.[14]

Barton William-Powlett was an Abergavenny neighbour of Captain Barker's. He had written off on the 14th September to join the 3rd Lincolns. But the latter had not given him a quick answer, while Captain Barker sent him a wire on the 22nd offering him a Captaincy in the new Kensington Battalion. The next day, Powlett went down to London to meet all the senior personnel in the Battalion, but he was still unsure what to do. He agonised over his decision, but eventually:

Barton William-Powlett
(pictured as a Major)

Major Barnett Barker, second in command of the Battalion.
This portrait hangs in Sedbergh School

> *Have heard from W Stewart that 3rd Lincolns are the Reserve & I should [only] go out as a draft so think I should join Kensingtons and go out with pals I know.[15]*

On the 29th September, the recruits from the Polytechnic in Regent Street marched over to join those recruited at the Town Hall. They in turn met the former Colonials (now A and B Companies).

JM Greenslade was very impressed by the bearing of the Colonials:

> *And as we stood patiently enduring the shuffling of the numbers, and the pinning on of temporary badges, and so on, we had a glimpse of swarthy, strenuous, shirted men marching past in rhythmic step and with faces set. It was just what we wanted to make us realise that was how we should be presently – human automata to be moved at the will of one man…and if there was any friction in the amalgamation of the two half-battalions, it was short-lived. But friendly rivalry in efficiency survived for a long time.[16]*

The White City was the site of the great Franco-British and Japan-British Exhibitions of 1908 and 1910, with the protective white cladding on what had been 20 palaces and 120 exhibition buildings giving rise to the name. JM Greenslade again:

> *Amid the fading and shabby glories of 'marble' palaces, in surroundings in which many of us had enjoyed rollicking evenings in Venetian or Japanese imaginings, we formed up shoulder to shoulder in platoons and companies.*

There was not enough room for everyone to live in, so some like Roland Whipp who lived in Finchley, North London, arrived in the morning and went home at night.

Some attempt had been made at recruitment to group together men with others of similar background. Thus D Company generally, ie Platoons 13 through 16, but 13 and 14 Platoons particularly, were very middle class units. We saw how Comerford, a bank worker, was cycled into 13 Platoon, which he saw as his sort of people. Roland Whipp made a similar comment about 14 Platoon. We don't have much direct evidence for Platoons 15 and 16, although Private Farnsworth said his 16 Platoon were 'liquorice all sorts.'

C Company (Platoons 9-12), on the other hand, was much more likely to be staffed by local working men from (then) downmarket areas like Notting Hill, plus some recruits from the east end of London. Thus Private

Berrycloath said that many of his colleagues in 12 Platoon were stevedores and dock-workers from the East End. Notting Hill Rugby Club was one source: Chris Wakelin (10 Platoon), and his friend Bill White (who both worked for Kensington Council as sweepers) came from there, and probably also the Smith brothers (Albert, Tom and one other, in 12 Platoon).[17]

Second Lieutenant Godlonton, a South African, liked his 13 Platoon men so much that he invited twelve of them to a night out with champagne, brandy and a floor show, but 12 Platoon had little respect for their weedy (5' 3") little officer.[18]

One question was: what should the new combined unit be called? It was time for some 'democracy':

> Our new C.O. rode onto the parade ground one fine day and said what a fine lot of fellows we were.
>
> 'Now,' he asked, 'what do you want to be called?'
>
> He very considerately left it to us after telling us that it was a choice between 'Imperial' or 'Colonial' or 'Kensington.'
>
> He revealed his view when he suggested that if we were called 'Kensington' we should be adopted, so to speak, by the Royal Boro.
>
> It was an historic moment, for we couldn't very well go into the fray without a name, and A and B were dying to be called 'Colonial.'[19]

The answer came back that A and B Companies wanted 'Colonial' (or 'The Colonial

The Adjutant and the Sergeants – they look tough, experienced hombres. Phythian-Adams papers

Infantry'), while C and D Companies preferred 'Kensington,' although the D Company officer said it mattered little to them as long as they got out to France. Colonel Innes seized on this answer as representing the 'right spirit' and announced that they were to be called the Kensington Battalion. His decision had been the only one, given the help that the Borough of Kensington and the Mayor in particular, would give to the Battalion all through its life. Colonel Innes did not, however, increase his popularity with A and B Companies by telling them 'to put that in your pipe and smoke it'.

It was time for the Battalion to be acquainted with RSM McCausland. He had first joined the army as a boy soldier in 1880 (making him not far short of fifty in 1914), retiring in 1898. His was a subtler way than the 120-decibel shout:

> *…The great little man. You remember, there was not much of him: short, stocky and smiling, he was the most loved Sergeant-Major in the British Army…Can't you hear him now 'Why do you worry me so?' as we tried our damnedest to look and drill like soldiers back in 1914.*[20]

Another of his favourites was to say plaintively:

> *There are nine hundred and ninety-nine men doing their best – and one man spoiling the whole Battalion – why will you punish me?*

'Lad Broke' (obviously a D Company man) explains:

Colonel Barker, the Adjutant and the Non Commissioned Officers.

As I became a seasoned warrior instead of 'season' holder from suburb to City, I found that Mac was not addressing me solely, but was directing his conversation to the other 999 as well, and I became less embarrassed.[21]

Drilling and parading were done in Wormwood Scrubs, near the prison, but there were no rifles and no uniforms in the early days – it even took some time for broom handles to be issued for guard duty. As for the appearance of the soldiers: Second Lieutenant Phythian-Adams had a bowler hat and a brown suit. Private Bill Alley, on the other hand, had a bowler and a navy-blue suit, so type of clothing was no guide to rank. Indeed Private 'Dad' Grover used to turn up to training in his chauffeur-driven Rolls Royce. And if decorations were worn, these could be for some very obscure wars – for example Newberry had a 1906 Zulu Rebellion medal – or might seem to be inappropriate for the wearer. Seventy years later Private Farnsworth still took great delight recalling seeing a sergeant-major with whom he had a challenging relationship, taken down a peg. It involved someone, Lord(?) Rowland(?), who had joined up as a private soldier, wearing a DSO ribbon (only awarded to reasonably senior officers). Sergeant-Major Rose put him on a charge and took him to Colonel Innes. When Colonel Innes looked up, he was flabbergasted:

'Rowland where the hell have you come from?' – Rowland was Innes's Colonel in the Boer War and the two of them then went off and got full in the Officer's Mess. It put Rose where he was meant to be![22]

The time came to march up to the Tower of London and collect rifles. These were old

Frank Gee and his Troubadours. Later *Fusiloils* was the name used to describe the Battalion Concert Party.

style drill rifles, covered with vaseline:

> *And when the order was given to 'Slope Arms' one young soldier refused, saying he was not going to get vaseline all over his new army raincoat.*

If this had been regular army, the young man would have complied with the request pronto, and his ears would have been ringing for some time to come. This was the new army:

> *And the sergeant in charge obtained some newspapers and proceeded to wipe off the vaseline, and the lads marched back to the White City feeling almost like 'real soldiers.'* [23]

On 8 October the Battalion was inspected by Major-General Sir Francis Lloyd, General Officer Commanding (hereafter GOC) London District. The general praised them publicly, but privately, according to Captain Powlett's diary, he 'cursed our Co. awful' and sent Powlett (who had dismissed his first parade only two days earlier) and some of the other officers back to Chelsea Barracks for extra training.

The Mayoress's Concert for the Kensington Battalion was held 14 October. Much of it was sketches, lectures and stories, but the musical items were the highlights, especially those provided by the beautiful Phyllis Dare. She sang the famous recruiting song '*Your King and Country Want You.*' This has the famous refrain beginning: 'Oh, we don't want to lose you but we think

The beautiful Phyllis Dare sang to them and won their hearts.

you ought to go,' and ending with the adaptation of the original words to

> We shall cheer you, thank you, kiss you
> When you come home again.

The Kensington News went on:

> The song was received with tremendous enthusiasm, the audience joining wholehearted
> in the chorus. Miss Dare was recalled several times, and her efforts were heartily
> applauded.[24]

After the war, many a man remarked that they were still waiting for the kisses.

Despite such events, the White City had many drawbacks as a headquarters. In particular, the catering was poorly managed (the providers would end up being sued for providing bad meat), while the whole area was now full of Territorials (some 20,000 recruits were quartered there by 13th of November).[25] The rough and ready accommodation for the men may have helped accelerate the process of 'stirring and mixing up.' D Company's Maurice Drake wrote a series of articles in the (London) *Evening Standard* about the progress of the Battalion. He found a positive voice:

> In one corner of a great bare shed in the White City twelve straw mattresses lie in a row
> upon the concrete floor against the wall. On them sleep a
> shoemaker, a baker, a coalminer, a surveyor, an ex-
> Guardsman, a glass-painter, a motor-body builder, an

The Adjutant in the garden of 8 Wimblehurst Road after receiving his captaincy

8, Wimblehurst Road where the Adjutant Captain Phythian-Adams was comfortably billeted

Pte Mitchell and his wife and children – the very salt of the earth. Edith was seven at the time and her younger brother three. (courtesy Edith Parsons)

electrician, a carter, a bank clerk, and two gentlemen of leisure, one from Canning Town and one from Half-Moon Street. They are a community. The bank clerk provided the family looking-glass, the shoemaker and collier blacking and brushes, the glass-painter a clothes brush, and the idler from Half-Moon Street a box of cigarettes.

This is a thing that some of us have prayed for – that the best men of Hoxton and Mayfair should rub shoulders and learn to like each other. And to think we have done it without compulsory service![26]

The other problem was to identify the few who would become non-commissioned officers. Some men, like Claude Upton and Fred Keeble, stood out as having natural ability, and were promoted very early. Traditional ways to make up the numbers of NCOs were to ask if anyone had been a soldier before, or in any sort of uniform.

EC Rossell (B Company) told a story that was a subtler version of this:

We were 'fallen in' by the acting S.M. Dunlop who said, "Step out in front anyone who knows anything about soldiering"… No one stepped forward… "Alright dismiss".

Rossell and Jenkins made the mistake of right-turning: obviously they had drilled before and they were made NCOs on the spot.[27]

Maurice Drake again:

Promotion is easy enough – it is pressed on you, even. The question is, can you keep twelve men obedient and in good temper? Yes? Then take charge of a section and let us see what you can do with them. A ready, well-behaved section means quick promotion for its leader: he is corporal, lance-sergeant, platoon sergeant quicker than the company tailor can sew the stripes on his sleeve.

Even in this short time there were signs of gelling. Thus Private Frank Gee wrote the words for the first marching

Private John Mitchell was a local man, living five miles from Horsham. Here he is looking proud as punch in his first uniform (courtesy Edith Parsons)

The Transport Section (Roffey) stables.

A platoon-sized group of men, probably in Horsham from the look of the houses and the way the uniforms are being worn, with the man on the extreme right believed to be Private Richard Burnard (A Company). (Courtesy Esther Ratcliff)

Happy on the march: looks like the flute is accompanying some singing. The mounted officer on the left is believed to be Captain Adams. (Phythian-Adams papers)

Adjutant Phythian-Adams, relaxed on manoeuvres. (Phythian-Adams papers)

song for the Battalion – lustily sung to the tune of '*The Battle-Hymn of the Republic*':

We are the Kensington Battalion of the Royal Fusiliers,
We said goodbye to all the girls and kissed away their tears.
We get a bob a day and if we saves it up for years
We'll all be millionaires –

So to hell with the Kaiser and his Bosches,
We'll make set for Belgian losses,
And tell him where to stick iron crosses
When we get to Berlin.[28]

Mayor Davison had to make a quick decision about whether to find other winter quarters or not. Colonel Innes came forward. He owned land in Roffey about two miles north of the town of Horsham which he was prepared to hire out. Mayor Davison put the idea to Major-General Sir Francis Lloyd, whose response was that if it was to be done it should be done immediately. Frantic negotiations were put in train for the temporary billeting of troops in private homes in Horsham and Roffey until such time as the Mayor could have a proper hutted camp built in Roffey Park. Meanwhile the Mayor was struggling to kit the men out:

> The War Office held me responsible, though unable to provide any assistance except by giving me a list of Government Contractors, all of whom I found were already fully engaged with Government orders for more than a year ahead. I accordingly turned to various Kensington firms to assist me in my difficulty.[29]

By 'various Kensington firms' he meant some of the biggest retailers in Britain: names like Harrods and Derry & Toms. Here is the list of items that the Mayor was asked to supply, with his chosen supplier in brackets.

List of Articles Required For Kitchener Battalions

Item (Supplier)	Quantity	Price/person (£. s. d)
Greatcoats (Harrods Ltd)	1100	1. 5. 6
Boots & Laces (Harrods Ltd)	2200	1. 5. 0
Caps (Harrods Ltd)	1100	0. 2. 6
Drawers (Harrods Ltd)	2200	0. 5. 0
Suits (= battledress; Harrods Ltd)	2200	2. 14. 0
Puttees (Harrods Ltd)	1100	0. 2. 6
Shaving Brushes (Harrods Ltd)	1100	0. 0. 5 1/4
Hairbrushes (Harrods Ltd)	1100	0. 1. 3
Spoons (Harrods Ltd)	1100	0. 0. 4 3/4
Chevrons (Harrods Ltd)	1100	0. 0. 7 1/4
Jerseys (Spiers & Pond Ltd)	1100	0. 4. 6
Holdalls (G Groom Ltd)	1100	0. 0. 5
Braces (Derry & Toms)	1100	0. 0. 9 1/2
Combs (Derry & Toms)	1100	0. 0. 1 3/4
Hussifs (= 'Housewifes'; Derry & Toms)	1100	0. 0. 5 3/4
Razors (Derry & Toms)	1100	0. 1. 2 1/2
Shirts (Derry & Toms)	2200	0. 9. 0
Knives (Derry & Toms)	1100	0. 0. 5
Forks (Derry & Toms)	1100	0. 0. 4 3/4
Toothbrushes (Rylands & Son)	1100	0. 0. 2 3/4
Socks (Scotch Wool & Hosiery Stores)	3300	0. 2. 6
Kit Bags (Waterproofing Ltd)	1100	0. 3. 3 1/2
Cap Badges (4; Firming & Son)	1100	0. 0. 2
Title Badges (6; Firming & Son)	2200	0. 0. 8
Towels (John Barker & Co Ltd)	2200	0. 1. 3 1/2
Added later:		
Marching Equipment (Lillywhite Frowd)	1100	2. 16. 8
Entrenching Equipment (Thomas & Son)	1100	0. 3. 0
Total:		£10. 2. 4 1/4[30]

AT—TEN—TION !!!

D for our **Down**-right deep-breathing proclivities.

Corporal (later Sergeant) Downs, in charge of PE.

The cost overall, including the two late additions, was £11,129. 11. 7 or £10. 2. 4¼ per person.

First was the knotty problem of getting the men into proper boots. He signed a contract with Harrods. By 8 October 265 men had received boots but there were problems with the quality. Accusations and counter-accusations were levelled and the issue rumbled on for some time.[31]

On the other hand, Harrods had managed to find for the Battalion some of the last khaki cloth available in London, so the Battalion were able to wear khaki battledress when many other battalions were still in blue or grey substitutes. Suppliers of equipment inevitably delivered it late due to the huge pressure on manufacturers from all sides: because of great competition for raw materials and skilled workers (some of whom would have joined the Forces), and because of the difficulty of scaling up from small quantities into bulk orders. Thus Spiers & Pond, with the contract for 1100 Jerseys at 4/6d each, and supposed to have been delivering 240 a week beginning on the 10th October, were forced to write on the 29th October that they only had 214 Jerseys ready, while their manufacturers now refused to guarantee more than 180 Jerseys per week.

Sometimes great creativity was shown, thus Lillywhite Frowd managed to adapt their normal manufacturing of items like cricket bags into making marching equipment (like canvas packs). In fact Walter Frowd made products so good that the

The Battalion had two excellent cartoonists. One was Aussie Pte Percy Cannot (a typically modest self-portrait).

The fierce Corporal Fraser's bayonet lessons were legendary. This was drawn by the other Battalion cartoonist, Henry Lea (who was also a mad inventor).

F Sergeant Fraser who taught us the bayonet.

A for our Artist who **Cannot** be matched,

company received further orders from the War Office.

Occasionally a great bargain was obtained, such as the top-quality razors (made by Krupps of Germany, and therefore in lower demand as Christmas presents), gained for half price from Derry & Toms. The latter also made excellent khaki shirts, but even they had problems delivering on time, as this letter from Colonel Innes shows:

At the time of writing I have only received 708 shirts.

These shirts are very urgently required. There are 350 men who have not received one; and many of those issued have already been in wear 10 days and it is quite time they were washed.[32]

High time indeed.

The Mayor may have thought his financing of the Battalion was over. Not so! Besides the building costs and obvious items like beds (he insisted on supplying iron bedsteads with expensive sprung mattresses, to the dislike of the War Office), there was a 10-page schedule of requirements that listed precise requirements of furniture, items for Ablution Rooms, Quartermaster's Stores, Officers Mess, weighing machines and so on, right down to sets of chess and draughts.

On the morning of October 27th 1914 cheering crowds followed the column of 'nearly marching' recruits as it made its way to Addison Road Station in Kensington. Two long trains took the Battalion down to Horsham.

Miss Marjorie Edwardes was the cub reporter for Horsham affairs with the *West Sussex Gazette*. She was there to watch the men arriving. Of course they were a motley crowd, but there was *something* about them, and she would remain actively interested in the Battalion all of her life:

The scene outside the railway station on the day of their arrival was full of interest. Every type and class of man seemed to be represented, and every conceivable and inconceivable variety of clothing. There was a good sprinkling of khaki, but the greater number of men appearing to be at present without uniform. Here and there a genuine 'cow boy' with his knotted scarf and black felt hat, and easy rolling gait, attracted attention, some lay about on the grass by the roadside, others stood around in little ill-assorted groups, talking and joking. Many carried the heavy rifle, some were hatless, a strange mixture of civilian attire: but all presented a dogged, serious, and purposeful air, as though the work in hand was all-absorbing.[33]

Another local resident, Bob Green, watched the billeting of the men:

Round the corner of the road where I lived, came the most unusual sight of a long double line of shuffling humans, Colonials and Cockneys, Burghers from the Transvaal and barrow boys from Bermondsey, some quite smart and others not so smartly attired. Here and there a muffler and obviously untailored clothes hiding the slouching frame, rubbing shoulders with the contrasting touch of the higher-priced product of Kimberley or J'burg. Little otherwise to attract attention except the occasional order 'Halt! Two over here. Next two in No. 7' and 'Afternoon missus. Ere's a couple of lodgers for you,' and so on down the street until the long double file became disintegrated – dispersed into the homes of Horsham folk.[34]

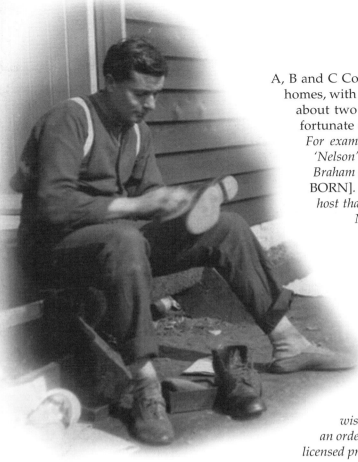

A, B and C Companies were billeted in Horsham homes, with D Company in the village of Roffey about two miles away. Some men were even fortunate enough to be billeted in pubs:

For example, five of us were billeted at the 'Nelson' Sergts Brown, Elgie, Wild, Cpl Braham and myself [B O'Reilly Nugent, or BORN]. *We could not have wished for a finer host than Mr Street – a true son of Sussex. Nor could there have been a more motherly hostess than Mrs S. Then of course there were their daughter and Bertie, their son – lovely kids.*

They had beer with dinner and beer with singsongs, but it couldn't last:

Like everything else in the old days of Kitchener's Army they decided that we were enjoying ourselves and that this was no way to make soldiers. They got wise to the joys of 'The Nelson,' issued an order that no troops should be billeted on licensed premises, and that was an end of it. So we were posted to other billets, happy enough in their way, but I never forgot Mr. Street and his family.[35]

WW Clark, affectionately known as 'Baby', cleaning his boots outside his hut (courtesy WW Clark)

The Nyes, the Potters (whose daughters sang in Battalion concerts), the Jarretts and the Hancocks were all remembered with great affection by PA Emmerson for their hospitality.[36]

LG Lewis, the local golf pro before joining the Battalion, brought his new pals back to the house for tea, as his daughter Hilda recalled:

Vividly do I remember Frankie Gee, Darky Woods & others playing our piano, seating myself and sisters on same, and teaching us to sing 'Ten Dirty Little Fingers on Two Dirty Little Hands'.[37]

Not every billeting arrangement worked flawlessly. The future Mrs Wally Soffe, then just three years old, remembered that one of the two C Company men billeted in her house was frequently drunk, and they had to fetch an MP to him once.[38]

News that lots of young soldiers were in town (there were also a few hundred men from the 4th Reserve Battalion of the Royal Sussex Regiment) didn't take long to get around. Miss Edie Lacey was doing a sewing and tailoring apprenticeship at the well-

Baby Clark and pals (presumably from 13 Platoon) at their Roffey hut. (courtesy WW Clark)

known retailer Chart & Lawrence in West Street. One lunchtime she was out strolling with a friend and they thought they would investigate the new arrivals: 'You know what girls are like [chuckle] – make a beeline for the boys'. She came across this attractive soldier (Corporal Fred Keeble) standing reading a newspaper in the Carfax, so she poked the newspaper and thereby caught his attention. This was to be the man she would marry, although they had to overcome stern parental disapproval and could only meet in groups with her friends or sisters as chaperones.[39]

On 28 October, the pattern of events was set: the men drilled in the morning in Springfield Park and went off for a route march in the afternoon. Next day it was drill in Denne Park and a mock battle in Roffey Park. Captain Powlett admitted that they lost their way in the route march and: 'Awful muddle we were in attack'. D Company, the enemy, disconcerted their opponents by continually howling 'D'.[40] They hadn't had much time for extra training before they were inspected by the GOC Eastern Command, General Woolcombe, 6th November, but they did put on a good show:

> The inspection took place in beautiful Denne Park, just now a veritable fairyland of fallen gold. For some time before the appearance of General Woolcombe the troops were drawn up in two very long serried ranks along the wide avenue of lofty trees, and the air was rent by the sharp orders coming from the officers, and responded to with very creditable smartness by the men. There was a quiver of bayonets, almost suggesting the quiver of slender reeds by the river's side. The battalion, after only two months training, presents a very smart appearance.[41]

Hard but fair characterised the new officers at this time. Thus Major Boardman, D Company Commander: 'A severe disciplinarian, but a marvellous company

Roffey Camp huts. This is hut 5, alias 'The Jolly Boys', for 3 Platoon. Private Mitchell, who worked in the cookhouse, is fifth from left in the back row.
(courtesy Edith Parsons)

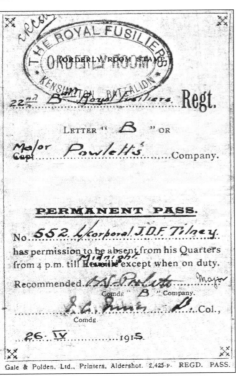

L-Cpl Tilney's pass, signed by Major Powlett his B Company commander and Colonel Innes.
(Courtesy Arturo E Goodliffe)

commander. A tall, well-built man. Very military stance,' while Second Lieutenant Willie Murray:

> Was a strict disciplinarian, but at the same time, kind and gentle; he always had the care and welfare of every men at heart... was an excellent leader, an inspiration to us all in A Company; we would have followed him anywhere.[42]

Sergeant Charles Downs, the PE Instructor, put the men through their paces:

> Vehicles and pedestrians along the King's Road of a morning find entertainment in watching the physical exercises practised by the men. The sinuous bending and swaying is rather fascinating to watch. Coats have been flung down under the trees, and shirt sleeves have been rolled up high above the elbow. Now and then, in the course of the drill, there seems to be a veritable forest of bare arms held up high and twinkling in the sunlight.[43]

Major Boardman used to take the 22nd Battalion

over to Christ's Hospital every week for musketry practice. It was not the only thing the 22nd Battalion and the 4th Royal Sussex shared in common: the old Corn Exchange was turned into a Recreation Room for both units, which soon held the first of many Battalion concerts that did much to cement relations between the town and soldiers: 'It is only necessary now in Horsham to announce that the Royal Fusiliers are giving a concert to ensure the hall being filled to its uttermost limits.' The showstopper on this and many other occasions was Private Teddy Rutland (Rutherford): '…in his ridiculous song, 'I do like a nice mince pie!' and the singing lessons to the audience which accompanied it.' A week later it was the mixture as before at the Corn Exchange, this time with ladies present and the Misses Potter assisting with their singing and piano playing. Amid the familiar names, were one or two new ones including Corporal (Claude) Upton doing an amusing recitation and Private Jimmy Markie doing a humorous song. The concert performers now became known as 'Fusiloils.'

During the daytimes, however, the Battalion was hard at work; there were plenty of route marches, often with an enterprising 'Orange-Woman' following behind them in a pony and trap. There was lots of singing with *We are the Kensington Battalion of the Royal Fusiliers*' used by everyone, of course, but if 13 Platoon were in the lead, they had their own song, *'Tee Latsi Bah,'* led off by the powerful voice of Claude Upton:

Tee latsi bah, Tee latsi bah fah,
Cora Bella, Core Bella
Keching, keching a shingle,
That shall be our chorus, a chorus, a CHORUS.[44]

Saki (Corporal Munro, A Company) said he had recently done a march of twenty-three miles: 'most of it at a very quick rate and a lot of it over difficult ground,' but 'was not stiff or tired the day afterwards.' By the end of November Saki had refused offers of a commission in another regiment because he felt he would make a reasonable soldier but an indifferent officer.[45] Whereas Colonel Innes was the man at the centre of affairs in Kensington, the emphasis subtly moved over towards Captain – now Major – Barker. He was the one who took them training and with whom they practised attacks.

On 14 December Christmas leave began for the men, with first choice of Christmas week given over to married men. Captain Powlett was fortunate enough to get Christmas week off also. On the 28th he returned from Abergavenny to Horsham with Major Barker. His year-end comment to his 1914 diary was: 'I am glad to say I finish the year with the best Company (B) in 22nd Royal Fusiliers'.

Mayor Davison sent a briar pipe and Christmas greetings to every man. Such a gift required acknowledgment. RSM McCausland knew the form, you addressed your letter to the Battalion CO:

I have the honour to respectfully ask, at the unanimous desire of the Warrant, Non-Commissioned Officers and men of the Kensington Battalion, that you will be good enough to convey to his Worship the Mayor of Kensington…

In comparison, Privates Gerald Rees and Frank Paddon – Canadians from B Company – felt no such inhibition and wrote off their heartfelt thanks directly to the Mayor:

> *I understand that we, as a Battalion, are indebted to you for the Xmas gifts we have received today and I also understand that, thanks to your good offices, we have been otherwise equipped far quicker and better than many Battalions.*[46]

There was something quite magical about late 1914/early 1915 in Horsham. Perhaps it was simply days of innocence. Perhaps social habits newly acquired had had sufficient time to acquire a legendary status without getting stale, such as the Sergeant and CSM who hawked their talents for beer:

> *The one at the piano the other one with a violin, and when the beer ceased to flow how they departed to their next port of call – they certainly earned their free drinks.*[47]

The weather helped too; on the 22nd January there was a heavy snowstorm. Private Harriss had a very vivid picture of that time:

> *When we went to Horsham in billets it was a great adventure to me really living in the country and that winter when the whole countryside looked like something out of Switzerland, and then that wonderful spring, and the woods full of primroses and all the flowering trees and shrubs and hearing the cuckoo for the first time in my life, and then there were the bluebells, vast expanses of them in places and the flocks of curlews.*[48]

Even magistrates contributed. Sergeant Curtis and the indefatigable PC Burningham visited the Star Inn at Roffey at 10 pm – well after licensing time – and saw:

> *…several soldiers sitting round the fire in the Club room at the rear of the premises, while another soldier was singing at the piano, with the landlord's daughter as accompanist. On the table was a half-filled bottle of ale, and several glasses containing the same, one having froth on the surface.*

It was surely an open and shut case. Instead, the magistrate dismissed the case, no actual consumption of the beer after hours had been proven, while the beer could have been bought before 9:30 pm.

Musical evenings flourished. Over thirty years later an anonymous Horsham resident ('a pretty 17 year old girl at the Carfax Hotel' in 1915) recalled:

> *Frank Sinatra wasn't in it when Sgt. Abbey sung 'Absent', or when Sgt. Heffill sang 'Songs of Araby', and Teddy Rutland sang (if he was sober enough), 'I do like Snice Smince Spies.' Salome waltz was usually played during the twilight dance, and usually the lights failed at intervals. Happy days. We swooned at Sgt. Hunt's violin solos.*[49]

Second Lieutenant Christopher Stone joined the Battalion early in 1915. Stone, a novelist who lived at Field Place, Horsham, had initially joined the Public Schools Battalion as a private, was not happy there, and had been negotiating since before Christmas to take a commission with the 22nd Battalion. He would become one of its most influential members.

Sport was the other element that flourished in the winter and spring of 1915. Matches between the Battalion and local teams began to crowd other contests out of the pages of the local newspapers. There was football of course (captained by Lance-Corporal 'Jock' Martin), golf (including the local professional LG Lewis, while Second Lieutenant Murray was an outstanding player), rugby union (the Battalion had several internationals), miniature rifle range shooting and cricket in the summer.

The Battalion was rich in writers and journalists. It was no surprise therefore when it began to produce its own *22nd Batt. Royal Fusiliers Fortnightly Gazette*, with the first edition out on 15 February. Second Lieutenants Stone and Murray were the men initially begging for contributions: Saki (eventually) contributed articles rather than his trademark stories, Frank Gee produced amusing pieces, Corporal Fred Pignon commented on the sport, JMG (Jack Greenslade) wrote pen-portraits of Battalion personalities, while specialists like Corporal Downs (PE) and the fierce Sergeant Fraser (bayonet) were roped in to write about their specialities. The magazines featured splendid cartoonists in Australian Private Percy Cannot and South African Private Henry Lea.[50]

A major change occurred on Saturday, 6 March, when A and B Companies moved in to the new huts at Roffey, with C and D Companies following a few days later. As Bob Green said, the move was 'Generally to the regret of their landladies who had come to look upon them almost as sons – and here and there to the regret of daughters too.'[51] On the other hand, the Battalion could grow together more as a unit, rather than being day-boarders.

Colonel Innes and the Mayoress at the May 1915 Battalion Sports Day.

There was more drudgery required in the huts, but there was still a soupcon of the School Camp:

> *Yesterday I found that I was hut orderly (there are thirty of us to a hut) and I found that drawing rations, cleaning the hut, washing plates, cups etc., kept me busy from a quarter to 6 a.m. till 5 30 p.m. with hasty intervals for meals. We have a good deal of fun, with skirmishing raids at night with neighbouring huts, and friendly games of footer; it is like being man and boy at the same time.*[52]

Frank Gee would play the schoolboy trick of leaving the outer door a bit ajar, with a pan of water precariously balanced on it, just waiting for some incautious latecomer such as Sergeant Marshall who was reputedly very fond of his drink.

RSM McCausland was finally persuaded to take a commission with C Company,[53] and this enabled Sergeant-Major Dunlop to become RSM for the Battalion. Some weeding of the four by now over-strength companies was done to create E Company, which Captain Godlonton, 13 Platoon's officer, also joined. This would in turn become part of the Reserve Battalion, the 27th Royal Fusiliers, which the 22nd would share with the 17th Royal Fusiliers (the Empire Battalion).

Manoeuvres in the nearby countryside increased. A mock attack at Plummers Plain and Mannings Heath in early March in front of Major-General Drummond MVO was widely reported in the local press. There was not much for onlookers to see initially, then:

One caught a glimpse through a crack in the fragrant green of a pine wood. In single file, close on one another's heels, they passed stealthily into the dim fastness of the forest, and the next moment the pines seemed to have completely engulfed them, like the green waters of a mighty wave. Hardly a sound could be heard as they slid into their green haven. Presently there came a loud note from a bugle, taken up immediately by bugles all over the country-side, and then one knew that it was The Charge, for with a wild yell of triumph the men rushed up the step hillside in a long closely-formed line from where they had lain hidden under the ridge, and the attack was finished. Nothing more to do then but form up and presently make the four and a half miles march back to the town.[54]

This may have been the legendary assault on Mannings Heath that Mrs Innes was reputed to have enjoyed so much she asked her husband if the men could do it again.

The men soon realised just how good the food was in camp, with many a comment in the *Fortnightly Gazette* about becoming a 'Battalion of Falstaffs.' Major Barker was in overall control of 'what' – of making the 5 1/2 pence per day per person go around – and Sergeant-Cook Fowles (head chef of the Great Central Hotel) of 'how'. A sample menu shows how impressive it was.

Sunday
Breakfast: Coffee, Porridge and Milk, 1/2 Coy Brown Stew or 1/2 Coy Bacon & Eggs, Bread butter and Marmalade
Lunch: Pea Soup, Meat Pie, Greens, Jam Tart
Dinner: Tea, Bread & Butter, Salmon
Monday
Breakfast: Coffee, Porridge and

Their final Horsham number: which sold out almost immediately.

Colonel Barker reading the lesson at the last church parade in Horsham, with Captain McDougall the bowed figure at the right. The air seems to crackle with excitement and trepidation. (Phythian-Adams papers)

Milk, ½ Coy Steak and Chipped Potatoes, ½ Coy Bacon & Sausages, Bread, Butter and Jam

Lunch: Carrot Soup, Meat Pie, Potatoes, Rice and Mixed Fruits

Dinner: Tea, Bread & Butter, Sardines, Jam

Tuesday

Breakfast: Coffee, Porridge and Milk, ½Coy Bacon & Sausages, ½Coy Steak and Chipped Potatoes, Bread, Butter and Jam

Lunch: Lentil Soup, Irish Stew, Potatoes, Jam Roll

Dinner: Tea, Bread & Butter, Bloaters, Jam

Wednesday

Breakfast: Coffee, Porridge and Milk, ½ Coy Brown Stew, ½ Coy Bacon & Tomatoes, Bread, Butter and Jam

Lunch: Pea Soup, Roast Beef & Yorkshire Pudding, Baked Potatoes, Greens, Ginger Pudding

Dinner: Tea, Bread & Butter, Tinned Herrings, Jam[55]

Weekends were more relaxed, and lady visitors welcomed. For family-man Private John Mitchell, whose home was in Plummer's Plain only five miles away, the lady friend was his seven year old daughter Edith,

We [Edith and her three year old brother] *often walked into Horsham to meet him, we either had tea at Wakefields tea shop in West Street (alas no longer there) or back at Camp sitting on Dadd's bed, our tea was served in 'basins' no cups or mugs in those days.*

Private Lacretelle, pals and dog mascot. Lacretelle is third from right, back row. Looks more Tidworth than Horsham, but very 'tents in the garden' (Courtesy Miss P Lacretelle)

However the fellows in Dadd's hut were a wonderful lot. One fellow I still remember we called 'Curly Peter' he made a fuss of my Brother & I. Poor chap never came back.[56]

Weekend passes were organised. Most men were keen to get away, but less so once they realised how much spare food was available then, particularly the famous Sherry Trifle (an occasional Sunday treat). Not all of the designated bottles of sherry actually went into the Trifle, but enough did to make the Trifle almost always the first item of food to be recalled, along with 'steak for breakfast.'

The road between Horsham and Roffey was heavily frequented late at night by young soldiers desperate to get back to camp before final roll call. A few cunning men managed to persuade the engine drivers of the non-stop late train to halt at Roffey Station just long enough for them to hop out, but others walked, ran, or used bicycles. A new crime began to be mentioned in the Petty Sessions pages: driving a bicycle at night without lights. The burly Captain Godlonton was fined two shillings and sixpence for this crime. He had come up against the determined PC Burningham and had come off second best:

> Defendant refused to stop when requested by P.C. Burningham, remarking that it was 'rot' to expect him to carry a lamp on such a moon-lit night, and a chase ensued, the constable eventually overtaking defendant near the camp.[57]

In mid-April the Battalion soccer team beat the cup-holders Horsham Trinity in the final of the Horsham Charity Cup, but particularly of interest was the fancy dress of some of the Battalion supporters from D Company (and especially 13 Platoon):

> Brilliant striped blankets hung about their shoulders, gaudy turbans adorned their heads, and ornaments of startling kinds were disposed about their persons. These included fearsome looking bones, garish feathers, and in one case a festoon of bright tin lids. Whenever a goal was scored they cast themselves upon the ground in front of the pavilion in true native fashion, making deafening sounds of joy…With their dubbin-darkened faces they presented a most engaging appearance, and many were the coins that they charmed out of the onlookers as they took round the collecting boxes in aid of the hospitals.[58]

The Battalion Sports was held at Roffey Camp 26 May in brilliant sunshine. The latter was a very well-attended affair – over 2000 according to the *West Sussex County Times*. The sporting highlight was the Inter-Company competition won by B Company, particularly from the effort of men like CSM Rossell and Private Gray. CSM Rossell, a wonderful all round sportsman, won the individual championship. Seventy years on,

The Battalion Football team that won the Charity Cup.

43

Baby Clark at the Horsham Charity Cup Final
(courtesy WW Clark)

Roland Whipp still had a sharp memory of the fluidity of Rossell's actions in the High Hurdles: how he seemed to just glide along smoothly, while the other contestants jerkily ran-and-jumped, ran-and-jumped.[59]

Amidst all the jollity, there was one event that seemed out of place, which reminded everyone that we were at war, and these were soldiers:

The Bayonet-Fighting contest was won by Brown, D, [probably Sergeant Micky Brown] second being Taylor, B. This was a grim sight, seeming to strike an incongruous note with all the gaiety and good humour of the afternoon. It was a breath of grisly war that stole in upon the light-hearted festivities, the joking and the cheers. A queer hush came over the spectators who crowded round to watch, half repelled, half fascinated. The combatants, protected by a sort of padded armour, and helmets from which they peered as if from a cage, rushed at each other at the signal, and it was a case of quick thrust and parry, and then the whistle went, and the dealer of the vital lunge was awarded a point. The spring bayonets used have a round cap at the end, but so fiercely are they used that one can well believe the queer padded armour is not superfluous.

News came through that the Battalion were due to go to Clipstone Camp near Mansfield in Nottinghamshire in

Some members of 13 Platoon who dressed up to collect for local hospitals. They rushed out on the field at half time and played a game on their own, but rather hampered by their long robes (courtesy WW Clark)

June for Brigade and Divisional training. E Company would be staying behind.

In the Souvenir edition of the *Fortnightly Gazette* was a wistful poem (*Le Dernier Cri* by M.K.T.E.) from someone representing the young women of Horsham. It began:

> *The last farewells we now must say,*
> *The parting words of sorrow speak;*
> *The Fusiliers are going away!*
> *They're going away this very week!*
> *Small wonder that we feel forlorn –*
> *Think of it! Going! Going! Gone!!!*

And ended:

> *It doesn't really seem quite right*
> *That we should have it all to bear,*
> *Our sky so grey and theirs so bright –*
> *Oh, Fusiliers, it isn't fair!*
> *For you the joys of northern gals:*
> *For us, – the Editorials.*[60]

There was a last flurry of concerts, in which the powerful voice of Adjutant Phythian-Adams was seen to particular advantage on songs like Land of Hope and Glory and then it was farewell:

> *The town had a very desolate appearance after the train had puffed out of the station and the crowd had dispersed. It was a cold, grey, sunless, windless morning, and there was a feeling of very real depression in the air. The Fusiliers have made some very good friends in Horsham, who very sincerely regret their going.*[61]

A typically slow, roundabout journey followed. The camp was a shock, as Major Powlett confided to his diary: 'The Camp is not half finished – no lights – no roads – no ranges. It is built on a heather forest – awful lumpy parade ground.'

Arriving that weekend were a number of other Royal Fusilier Battalions they would to know very well in the future: the 17th (the Empire Battalion), 23rd (1st Sportsmen's) and 24th (2nd Sportsmen's), as these were their three companion battalions in 99 Brigade. Other units in their Division, the 33rd, were 98 Brigade (the University and Public Schools Battalions (UPS): composed of the 18th, 19th, 20th and 21st Royal Fusiliers), and 100 Brigade (made up from the 16th and 17th Middlesex, 13th Essex and 16th Kings Royal Rifle Corps).

Life in camp was made more bearable by the YMCA, who had built a huge marquee where concerts were held in the evenings. A few days after arrival, at least one of the Battalion had made a name for himself: 'The Kensingtons have with them a violinist whose performances on the instrument are very fine.'[62] There was one very important difference between this YMCA and the one back at Roffey:

Oh! Roffey Camp, we miss you!
Our hearts are sad and sore;
Your canteen charged 2d per pint,
But here it's a penny more.[63]

A few managed to make their way to Mansfield (three miles away) on a Saturday evening. Enterprising local businesses charged steep prices to convey the soldiers to and from the camp. Corporal JH Richardson, formerly an ambulance attendant at Hammersmith Workhouse, was killed on this road in the most unlucky of fashions: he stood off a narrow pavement to let a lady pass at the exact moment that a car came charging around the corner.[64] The Coroner recorded a verdict of manslaughter and Richardson was buried on the 5th July with full military honours.

There was a certain seepage from the Battalion in Clipstone, as impatient men sought other units promising earlier action. Private Brunton (the Rugby international) joined the Northumberland Fusiliers, while 'Baby' Clark and Hugh D Hughes joined the Cyclist Corps. Meanwhile, someone decreed that the efficient and popular RSM Dunlop was too old to go out to France.

On the 20th the Battalion, plus the 17th and 23rd battalions, took part in the first Brigade manoeuvres, involving about four hours of outpost and picket work, extended order practice, and ending in an attack on an imaginary stronghold attack over Strawberry Hill.

The men did not have long to wait for another move: the whole Division decamped to Tidworth on the Salisbury Plain at the beginning of August. Half the 22nd men were housed in huts (Bhurtpore Barracks) and half were in (sodden) tents.

Bhurtpore Barracks, Tidworth, with A Company men in residence (some of the others were in sodden tents). (courtesy DC Bone)

In mid-August E Company in Horsham had been reinforced and was now the 27th Royal Fusiliers. Colonel Innes moved over from the 22nd Battalion to take command of it, with Major Barker becoming the CO of the 22nd.[65] From our position of hindsight we can see this was the right move. Without Colonel Innes there might not have been a 22nd Battalion, and there certainly wouldn't have been a 'Horsham.' There was no doubting his patriotism, and his ability to solve the initial problems, but in Major Barker this odd mixture of Londoners (with sprinklings from all over Britain), Colonials, clerks and stevedores had found its mentor.

On the 14th August the men had their first 'proper' shooting practice, albeit with Mark III rifles and 'mainly Yankee ammunition'. As Major Powlett said: 'We are to race through after months of marking time.'

Practice makes perfect, but Buff Whitehouse from B Company remembered some less than proficient moments:

The idea of leaving Horsham was an unpleasant bombshell. The text went as follows:

The Major: 'Did you get a message sent to you?'
Private: 'Yes, sir.'
The Major: 'What was it?'
Private: 'That the 22nd Battalion Royal Fusiliers were leaving Horsham.'
The Major: 'Then why, in thunder, didn't you pass it on?'
Private: 'Please, sir, I thought it was a joke!!!!'

> The Sergt blew his whistle to advance. [By the time he] blew the halt, my bayonet had stuck in the boot heel of Bill Bailey in front, by now I was in a fearful sweat. I tugged to get it out. Just behind me was Charlie Austin. He wanted to know what was up. Sorry to relate as I pulled the rifle back, I hit him on the chin with the butt of the rifle. Poor Charlie went quite pale. I thought these two would set about me when we got out, but a pint each squared it.[66]

They became accustomed to going out on long manoeuvres, sometimes overnight, as Private Harriss recalled:

> On Salisbury Plain, waking up from sleep, lying on the ground in a ploughed field and everything, and us too, covered in white frost, then getting up and looking at a most awe inspiring spectacle, sunrise. The whole sky in the east was blood colour and in movement like a titanic fire, and then golden streaks rose up like an enormous fan, truly a sight never to be forgotten.[67]

On 29 September the Battalion celebrated its anniversary. In the evening the Mayor and the battalion officers visited the Sergeants Mess for dinner. It was a time for eulogies and the Mayor waxed eloquent:

Their first anniversary: dinner at the Sergeants
Mess with the Mayor.

*The excellent spirit of this body of
men through a gruelling training
is almost entirely due to Lieut.-
Col. R. Barnett-Barker. There is
not a man in the battalion who
does not rejoice at the idea of
placing his life in the hands of
such a capable officer and man.
He is loved as indeed few officers
are loved, and the men would not
exchange him for the world.[68]*

Colonel Barker responded that his
heart was in the Battalion and it had
been the proudest day of his life
when he was given command of it.

By early November 1915 the
Battalion's departure to France was
'imminent.'

The local traders put up prices
while 'the barber braced his wrist to
make as many fourpences for No 1
clips as he could.' Their cavalry
neighbours took 'souvenirs,' while
the final indignity for many men
was to open their newly issued
paybooks and find out that they
were in debt![69]

On 16 November the Battalion

left for France.

1 *The Kensington News And West London Times* (hereafter *Kensington News*), 11/9/1914, p5; poster in the Broughshane Collection and Battalion Cuttings Book at Kensington Local Studies Library (hereafter Broughshane for both: the first has a volume and item number, eg II:62 for the poster, the second has just an item number (eg 2590)

2 *Ibid*; The first one from Harold Begbie's *Fall In*, the second one from TB Macaulay's *Horatius*

3 Poster loose in *Broughshane*, II

4 *Kensington News*, 18/9/1914; the Mayor was a Governor of it : *Broughshane*, 2: 88

5 *The Nation in Arms* by Ian FW Beckett, in *A Nation in Arms*, p7, 1985, Eds Ian FW Beckett and Keith Simpson; *Call To Arms*, by Charles Messenger, p96, W & N, 2005

6 The Mayor blamed the War Office delaying approval, but only 5-6 days elapsed between the second battalion of Territorials being complete and recruiting starting for the 22nd

7 His fiancée waited patiently and they were married for around 60 years; information from his daughter, 14/8/84. I am most grateful to Arturo E Goodliffe of Buenos Aires, Tilney's brother-in-law, for giving me, in October 1984 a great deal of useful information about Tilney (B Company). Boulter information from Katharine Ehle, 20/6/84

8 *Mufti*, June 1950, 30, No 115, p2. Others say the officer's name was Conningham and his regiment was the 33rd Punjabis.

9 CE Fidler, *White City Memories*, *Mufti*, Summer 1933, 14, No 2, pp 6-7

10 Information from his widow, Mrs Edie Keeble, 1984.

11 1984 interview with WW Clark, plus *Mufti* (June 1965, 44, No 146, pp 11-12)

12 WW Clark interview, 1984

13 *How I Joined The Army*, *Mufti*, Xmas 1965, 44, No 146, pp 10-11

14 *Mufti*, Christmas 1943, 24, No 103, pp 6-7

15 Diary of Barton William-Powlett, henceforward *Powlett Diary*, 25-26/9/1914

16 *History*, p17

17 Interview with Mrs Rawly, daughter of Chris Wakelin, in June 1984

18 Interview with Ollie Berrycloath, 1984, who said the 'weedy' officer was gone in under a fortnight

19 *Mufti*, July 1921, 2, No 13, p2: *Mufti*, Christmas 1960, 40, No 136, p10

20 Obituary, in *Mufti*, Xmas 1947, 27, No 110, pp 10-11: by Fred Pignon; also *Mufti*, Summer 1935, 16, No 2, pp 7-8 and Christmas 1962, 42, No 140, p1

21 *Mufti*, July 1921, 2, No 13, pp 7-8

22 Interview with Mr Farnsworth, 1984, whose voice was hard to make out; there was a Lord Ronald Bateman and an Oswald Rowland. Both were was killed, still as privates, on 17/2/1917: *Soldiers Died in the Great War, Part 12 The Royal Fusiliers*, 1921, p132 and p135

23 *Mufti*, Christmas 1964, 44, No 144, p2

24 *Kensington News*, 16/10/1914

25 *West London Observer* 15/1/1915, and 12/3/1915

26 *Evening Standard*, 19/10/1914; others are 9/10, 27/10 and 7/11/1914

27 *Mufti*, Summer 1963, 43, No 141, p5, also see *Mufti*, Xmas 1967, 47, No 149, pp 12-13

28 Using a combination of Roland Whipp's and 'Baby' Clark's versions told us in 1983, which scan better than the version in *Mufti*, Summer 1960, 40, No 133, p4

29 *History*, p11

30 *Broughshane*, 8177, 8147, 8148

31 *Broughshane*, 8100, 8101

32 *Broughshane*, 7912, Innes to Davison

33 *West Sussex Gazette* (hereafter *WSG*), 5/11/1914; Miss M. K. Tickner Edwardes was her full name

34 *Mufti*, Summer 1963, 43, No 120, pp 14-15, also *Mufti*, Summer 1964, 44, No 143, p5

35 *Mufti*, Xmas 1955, 35, No 126, pp 12-13

36 *I Remember a Few Horsham Friends*, *Mufti*, June 1958, 38, No 131, p12

37 Personal communication with Hilda Marshall, 3/6/84

38 Interview with Mr and Mrs Wally Soffe, November 1983. The two men were JH Brackenbury and EJ Kelly

(the less sober one), both killed in 1916

39 Interview with Mrs Edie Keeble, 26/5/1984; interview with her daughter Mrs Gwen Stokes 19/4/09

40 *Powlett Diary*, 27 & 29/10/1914; 'D' howling from WJ P-A, *Mufti*, December 1919, <u>1</u>, No 2, p2

41 *WSG*, 12/11/1914

42 Interview with WW Clark, September 1984. Boardman was from Christ's Hospital as were Captain Goodwin and 2nd Lt 'Pussy' Wood; *Mufti*, June 1953, <u>33</u>, No 121, p6

43 *WSG*, 5/11, 3/12 and 10/12/1914; *When We Were Young – II, Mufti*, Christmas 1934, <u>15</u> , No 4, p7

44 Interview with Roland Whipp, 18/11/1983. He said that 13 Platoon were the best at singing as they were at almost everything else

45 Saki, *The Square Egg and Other Sketches With Three Plays*, letter dated 29/11/1914, p84, hereafter *Biography* (reprinted by Kessinger Publishing as *The Biography of Saki*, n.d); he was also reluctant to share his knowledge of German, probably for a similar reason

46 *Broughshane*, <u>3</u>: 17-18, 18

47 *Mufti*, Xmas 1963, <u>43</u>, No 142, p2

48 FJ Harriss, *More Memories, Mufti*, Christmas 1960, <u>40</u>, No 136, p15

49 *Mufti*, Xmas 1946, <u>26</u>, No 109, p11

50 *Mufti*, Autumn 1939, <u>20</u>, No 94, p3

51 *WSG*, 6/3/1915, *Mufti*, Summer 1963, <u>43</u>, No 141, pp 14-15

52 Saki, *Biography*, p 85, letter dated 5/3/1915 – a misprint for 15/3/1915

53 *Mufti*, Autumn 1935, <u>16</u>, No 3, p8

54 *WSG*, 11/3/1915; also see *Mufti*, Autumn 1939, <u>20</u>, No 94, p5 for Drummond's confidential report

55 *Broughshane*, III: 53-54; w/c 13/4/1915, the other days were of similar quality

56 *History*, p19; Personal communication with Edith Parsons, 6/1/84

57 *WSG*, 6/5/1915

58 *WSG*, 22/4/1915, also *Mufti*, Spring 1935, <u>16</u>, No 1, p4; WW Clark was one of the supporters

59 *Mufti*, May 1920, <u>1</u>, No 7, p4, According to his widow, Rossell was: 'was athletic champion of all India & captained their hockey team at the Olympic Games in Stockholm in 1912. He was a 'natural' at all sports he has played tennis at Wimbledon, shot at Bisley & has his Leicestershire County cricket cap!' – letters 1984 & 1985. *WSCT*, 29/5/1915. Interview with Roland Whipp, 18/11/1983

60 *Fortnightly Gazette*, 26/6/1915; it was of course Marjorie Edwardes

61 *WSG* 1/7/1915

62 *The Mansfield and North Notts Advertiser*, 2/7/1915; possibly Sergeant Hunt

63 Originally in the first Clipstone *Fortnightly Gazette*, but reprinted in *The Mansfield and North Notts Advertiser*, 23/7/1915

64 *The Mansfield and North Notts Advertiser*, 9/7/1915.

65 *WSG*, 26/8/1915, also Broughshane, IV: 19, 17/8/1915

66 *Memories*, H Whitehouse, Mufti, Xmas 1965, 44, No 146, p4

67 *More Memories*, FJ Harriss, Mufti, Christmas 1960, 40, No 136, p15

68 *The Kensington News*, 15/10/1915; Broughshane, IV, 31-2

69 *Mufti*, November-December 1920, 2, No 6, p6; due to their Christmas 1914 leave being unofficial

Chapter Two

France at Last:
Christmas in the Trenches

A T FIRST LIGHT 6 NOVEMBER it was cold, grey and damp; the sort of weather the Scots call dreich. As the main party of the Battalion made themselves ready, snow began to fall. A couple of hymns were sung and a prayer said, and around 7 am they were on their way at last, with the countryside now draped in white. A cavalry band led them on their march to Tidworth Station, serenading them with popular songs like *Keep The Home Fires Burning*.

There was quite a crowd at the station to see them off. The Brigadier of 99 Brigade,

The Battalion's officers in November 1915, just before they left for France.
Front, on the ground: Second Lieutenant HJ Thompson and Captain Trower RAMC.
First row: Captain RE Banbury, Captain FS Goodwin, Captain A McDougall, Major TH Boardman, Lt-Colonel R Barnett Barker, Major RW William-Powlett, Captain GW Daman, Captain LC McCausland, Captain WJ Phythian-Adams.
Second row: Lieutenant A McIntyre RAMC, Second Lieutenant GC McEntee, Second Lieutenant CR Stone,Lieutenant Fenton-Smith, Second Lieutenant EAS Gell, Second Lieutenant CJ Fowler, Lieutenant RL Roscoe, Second Lieutenant EC Rossell, Second Lieutenant EWP Gibson, Lieutenant WH Tomkins, Lieutenant J Walsh.
Back row: Lieutenant JHE Woods, Second Lieutenant GS Warren, Second Lieutenant WA Murray, Second Lieutenant CG Moore, Second Lieutenant CB Grant, Lieutenant CDA Black, Lieutenant TH Evans, Lieutenant FJ Merrell (Quartermaster).   (Phythian-Adams papers)

Brigadier-General Kellett, was there, while Mrs Barker (wife of the CO), Mrs Powlett and Mrs Banbury (wives of B Company officers) gave out morning newspapers to the men.

Sergeant Gilbert Varley, a shy man of great hidden depths (amongst other things he swam in the Serpentine on Christmas mornings), who would become a tower of strength to the OCA after the war (Mufti)

Eventually the emotional farewells were over and the first of the two trains set off at 8:28 am to the strains of *Auld Lang Syne*. The great adventure had begun. Relief was probably the dominant emotion, not least for the servant of Major Rostron (the new second in command), who had staggered onto the platform under 'the largest green canvas kit-bag ever'.[1]

It took some twelve hours for the train to travel from Tidworth to Folkestone, with about half the time being spent at Ashford Station due to some embarkation problems ahead.[2] The Battalion arrived at Folkestone at around 8:30 pm, detraining onto a darkened platform. Their transportation orders sounded very scary:

No Smoking in the precincts of the Port of Embarkation is to be permitted. On arriving at the Pier, absolute silence must be maintained. [On the voyage]...no talking (except Whispering), or striking of matches, is to be permitted.[3]

Some noticed that there were not enough lifebelts to go around, but all was well. The voyage, across a flat sea in bright moonlight, with a destroyer on both sides, was uneventful and only four men were ill.

Claude Upton was summoned by his (D) Company commander, Major Boardman, shortly before they arrived at Boulogne. He was told that he was to be first off the boat and act as 'guide.' He was flabbergasted: 'When I enlisted and was asked whether I'd been abroad I told them I'd been to France, but forgot to add only for a 'day-trip'. How then was I to act as guide?'[4] But the order hinged on a different meaning of the word 'guide: Upton was to be the right marker, or 'guide,' for his company to formate upon when marching.

It was late in the evening when the Battalion marched through the deserted streets of Boulogne, with the cobblestones muddy and slippery and occasional deep puddles awaiting incautious feet. Their destination lay at the top of the long hill, a frozen, windswept plateau where the snow still lay four inches deep in some places. This was the notorious K-Camp.

The welcome at the camp made for little improvement:

A British supply convoy in the streets of Boulogne. Factionpress

> *The curses of the innumerable battalions which had rested there had fallen upon it; and no one to greet us at midnight but a drunken man in the QM* [Quartermasters] *Stores, who was prepared to issue as many damp and lousy blankets as was required. It was a vile welcome to France.[5]*

Upton, again on orderly duty, was called away on a task just when the men were getting into their sodden tents. When he returned:

> *I discovered that there were eight men already asleep* [in it] *but they had left a space for me. It was where the water dripped in from the top of the tent.[6]*

The next morning dawned bright and frosty. Most of the snow had disappeared overnight and the sun succeeded in drying up the ground. The cheerfulness of the men had largely returned, but they were disappointed that they were not to be allowed 'sight-seeing'. Around midday on the next day, the 18th, the Battalion set off on the four mile march to the railway station at Pont de Briques, their first experience of the famous pavé roads. On the way Frenchwomen and young girls accompanied them, attempting to sell them small cakes and chocolate. There were also:

> *Little boys running beside us advertising their big sisters at one franc. Did they really think we would break ranks? I suppose they did but looking at these tiny boys one wondered what they knew about that sort of thing.[7]*

At the station an enormous train awaited them. They entrained about 2 pm with the thirty officers in eight dilapidated first-class carriages and the men in the famous '8 chevaux/40 hommes' cattle trucks. In fact they were squashed in 44-45 to a truck, which meant that few saw much of the French countryside unless bold enough to get up on the roof. The journey took about six hours to get to Steenebecque, where a guide awaited them to show them the way to their billets in the darkness. He was much vilified in the men's memories. As Claude Upton put it:

...the long weary march through the night with the sound of the guns in the distance. We must have marched some twelve miles only to find next morning that the station was still in view. It was indeed a circular tour.

The fearless Brigadier-General Kellett, commander of 99 Brigade and beloved by the men. (Mufti)

The next three days were fairly quiet ones of settling in and organising systems. The men were able to write home, meaning that the officers were required to begin what Major Powlett described as 'the charming experience' of censoring the men's letters. The Colonel was particularly amused by one man's flight into fancy that began 'I am writing this on the back of a dead German'.[8]

Seeing the lack of an Army cigarette issue for the men at this time, Colonel Barker wrote asked his wife to 'send some out'. Mrs Barker started sending the equivalent of one pack per man per fortnight, ie about 1,000 packets per fortnight. A few days later, when there was still no sign of either Army issue or those being sent by his wife, he went out himself and bought £5 worth for the men, which would have supplied a goodly proportion of the Battalion with a packet each. Later the Army cigarette issue would arrive more regularly, if not quite featuring the highest quality brands:

What an assortment they were – 'Three Witches', 'Red Hussars', and others never heard of before or since.[9]

Christopher Stone described a typical scene in the officers' mess:

A cosy day, though it's cold outside and freezing hard. The Colonel, [Major] Powlett, [Captain] McCausland and [Lieutenant] Walsh are playing bridge. Major Rostron, the Second in Command, is sitting over the fire and the Adjutant [Captain Phythian-Adams] *has gone off to Brigade HQ for orders about our move...Rostron is excellent and improves greatly on acquaintance, a brigand by instinct, an MFH and Cavalryman. He knows the ropes out here thoroughly and is invaluable in looking after our comforts. He has a terrific stammer which adds a great deal to his humour and ferocity. He has given me half a pack-saddle, about the size of a large haversack, for my kit, which will help. I am getting on splendidly at HQ and everyone is very considerate and kind. The C.O. now calls me Christopher.*

I repeat that you needn't worry about my comfort, I have all that I want and more, except you; and of course I don't wash as much as I should at home. As Powlett says, 'One day you wash as far down as possible; and the next day you wash as far up as possible, and you wash possible about once a fortnight'.[10]

The next day, 22 November, the men marched what turned out to be twelve miles to Neufpre Thiennes, but unfortunately the Colonel's horse stumbled while trotting fast and he came off:

My first thoughts were, fancy doing thirteen months hard work and then to miss the result by a broken leg. My leg and ankle are jolly sore and I shall doubtless be very stiff tomorrow but thank goodness I haven't broken anything.[11]

The next day they moved again, to Cantraine:

It was a perfectly lovely morning – hard frost, ground hard – we stepped out like young stags; we were marching on our own and had only about seven miles to do.

They were moving closer to the front, passing other troops (Indian and British), and motor vans on the way. The sound of the guns was of course the key element, impressing Paul Destrubé amongst others: 'We can hear the distant rumble of the guns, and the long continued roar makes you realise the dimensions of this tremendous struggle.'[12] Little war damage could be seen yet, although the Germans had passed though Cantraine in the early days of the war. One persistent rumour that had been with them since they arrived in France was now about to become fact: their brigade (99 Infantry Brigade) was about to swap with 19 Infantry Brigade from 2nd Division (Regular Army). Further exchanges would be arranged within the brigades of 2nd Division such that each brigade would now contain two New Army and two Regular battalions, the purpose being to leaven the raw recruits of Kitchener's [New] Army with the experienced Regular troops. For the 22nd Battalion there would be the honour of joining one of the original Regular Divisions 'out' since 1914.

Men of a Regular Division behind the lines in the winter of 1915-1916.

Naturally the high command of 2nd Division wished to evaluate what they had inherited, so it had been to the 22nd Battalion's advantage that they had strolled out like young stags on their march to Cantraine, as they had been watched all the way by staff officers from 2nd Division. The Colonel described the consequences:

> *The Brigadier* [Kellett] *sent for all Colonels* [of 99 Brigade battalions] *at 6 pm. My 2nd-in-command went* [because of the Colonel's ankle, now greatly swollen]. *There appears to have been a terrific strafeing and Battalions were called rotten etc – <u>but</u> – none of these remarks were to apply to the 22nd Royal Fusiliers and the Colonel was to be congratulated on commanding such a magnificent and well-disciplined battalion. Isn't that nice?*

On 25 November the Battalion marched to Bethune, that most British of towns on 1915-16. The men (almost one thousand of them) were all billeted in a very large College des Jeunes Filles. This was a place high in the memories of the men, usually prefaced by a remark about the absence of the 'jeunes filles'. Christopher Stone described it thus:

> *We* [HQ] *are in a girl's preparatory school and the whole battalion is just up the road in a huge college for young girls; many sleeping all over the floors of the classrooms and so on: it looks so funny. I have been over there to have my first bath since leaving England. It was underground and very nice, a hot shower bath. The girls have great fun there in peace time: there are rows of cubicles each* [with] *a bath. Now it is used chiefly for men when they come back from the trenches, they strip and bathe and their clothes are handed up through windows into the courtyard (now the scene of fires and cookers) and ironed.*[13]

Stone was also responsible for provisioning the Officers' Mess:

> *It's a biggish town and I have been out shopping for the mess, buying eggs, bread, butter, Brussels Sprouts, Quaker Oats, Graves and Perrier and plates etc …and some sausages for my signallers breakfast.*[14]

Because Stone was out marketing, he may not have been aware of the other reason why the men of the 22nd Battalion particularly remembered the College des Jeunes Filles. Major Powlett's discreet and cryptic diary gives one a clue:

Bethune Cathedral - a familiar landmark to many British soldiers in 1915-16

The men had been paid and were not allowed out of billets. There was some noise – Hell in the battalion. Other regiments were out. It was bad luck.

Indeed there was talk of a near-mutiny, with fixed bayonets being required. Claude Upton left behind a full account of the story:

The powers that be decided to pay the troops, and as we were all 'broke', we were delighted. But our joy was short-lived as an order was issued that no man was to leave the school.

Pandemonium set in. Men with money in their pockets and with no chance of spending it! They all crowded into the main hall and every time the R.S.M. came into sight they hooted. The whistle came for orderly sergeants. I was the first to arrive and was told, 'Go out and quell that riot'.

Being fairly well known in the Battalion they listened to me. I told them that if they would disperse and return to their classrooms I would see that arrangements were made that some of each platoon were allowed out to purchase anything they might require –

The College de Jeunes Filles at Bethune – source of much regret that the young girls were not at home. (Keeble papers)

but if they continued to demonstrate nothing could be done.

My words had the desired effect, but I discovered later that the 'old soldiers' had – to use an army term – 'used their initiative' and gone out the back way without waiting for permission.[15]

The men might well feel aggrieved, having been confined to billets continually since they had arrived in France. New experiences for the men were, however, just a few days away. Next morning, the 26th November, the Battalion marched off in rain turning into the familiar snow, via Beuvry along the straight La Bassée road with its poplar trees lining the way, towards billets at the ruined village of Annequin South. On the way they met a battalion of 98 Brigade (from 33rd Division which had arrived France two days before them). These men were just returning from trench duty and when one of the 22nd Battalion men (J.M. Morton) visited this area six years later, the image of this battalion 'their eyes heavy with sleep, their faces stubbly and scarred with mud'[16] came immediately to mind.

The next morning D Company paraded for physical drill, but was soon dispersed by German shells, one going through the butcher's shop where 13 Platoon was billeted. Private Bill Alley was standing guard outside the billet, but was 'afraid to leave his post in case he was "shot at dawn".' He only abandoned it when his Company Commander Major Boardman arrived to tell him to 'get under cover, you damn fool'.[17]

2nd Division now consisted of 5, 6, and 99 Infantry Brigades. In 99 Brigade 17th and 24th Royal Fusiliers (which had gone off to 5th Brigade) had been replaced by two regular battalions (1st Royal Berks, 1st Kings Royal Rifle Corps – alias the KRRC) and, temporarily, the 5th Kings Liverpool Regiment, a territorial battalion.

The next step for the new battalions was training in trench warfare: six days in the trenches under instruction from experienced troops and six days of trench construction and maintenance also under the instruction of experienced units. The 22nd and 23rd Battalions came under the instructions of 6 Brigade for this purpose. On 27 and 28 November the officers and NCOs of the 22nd Battalion were taken up to the front line trenches just beyond Cambrin (further along the La Bassée road) in small parties for a 24 hours instructional visit. On the first day the right half of the officers and NCOs went there, on the next day the left half. While the officers and NCOs were in the front line men from 6 Brigade gave instruction to the men in their billets, and when the officers and NCOs returned they reported to the men their experiences and what they had learned about trench warfare. On the third and fourth days the men were taken up to the trenches in small parties of platoon size for 24 hours front line duty, being interspersed among experienced platoons from the Royal Berks and the KRRC.

On the fifth and sixth days the officers and men were taken up to the trenches in larger parties, this time of company size, and this time each company was sandwiched between regular companies from the Royal Berks and 5th Kings Liverpools (the KRRC having been relieved meantime).

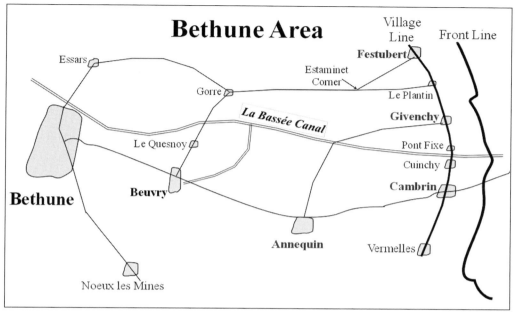

Bethune Area

Essars
Festubert
Village Line
Front Line
Estaminet Corner
Gorre
Le Plantin
La Bassée Canal
Givenchy
Le Quesnoy
Pont Fixe
Cuinchy
Cambrin
Beuvry
Bethune
Annequin
Vermelles
Noeux les Mines

Where the Battalion first went into the trenches; showing the little umbrella of villages from Festubert to Vermelles just behind the front trenches and the 'stalk' beginning at Bethune and going along the La Bassée Canal

The 5th Kings Liverpools were due to leave 99 Brigade shortly but left an indelible impression on Sergeant Fred Pignon:

We arrived at last [at the front line] *and I was shown into a sort of dugout, or was it a 'dug-in', and introduced to a sergeant and corporal of the 5th Battalion King's Liverpool Regiment. This battalion had been on active service for some time and they were indeed 'old soldiers' and grand fellows at that. My hosts had received Christmas parcels in which I shared, my first meal in the front line and I enjoyed it as we talked, not about their own exploits but about how easy and comfortable it was holding a front line. I don't think they were putting on a show for my benefit but I am sure they wished to give me confidence in myself when it came to my turn to take charge of the trenches. Having timorously ventured to put my nose over the trench I was encouraged to take a better view of the barbed wire and devastation lying between the British and German trenches. Gaining confidence from my King's Liverpool friends I began to look around without ducking every time some Hun aimlessly fired an occasional shot. 'What about a walk over the top?' asked my sergeant friend. I wanted badly to say 'No thank you', but hadn't the courage to do so, so instead 'if you like'. So off we set, scrambling through our wire and actually walking upright – I thought we ought to have been crawling as we used to do on the peaceful countryside around Horsham. But I couldn't very well crawl when my instructor was not only standing up but also actually smoking his pipe; my mouth was too dry to think of smoking.*

Up went a Verey Light from the German lines. It came towards us and I was about to scramble into a nearby shell hole when the Sergeant in a peremptory and distinctly audible order, commanded 'Stand still!' I froze where I stood; I probably closed my eyes and contemplated a very short life in the front line. The light fell a few yards away and fizzled out. 'There you are, there is nothing in it; if you stand quite still it is unlikely you will be seen', he said with soothing Lancastrian reassurance. We went more than half way to the enemy lines, dropped into a shell hole and he offered me a cigarette. 'It's quite all right as long as you keep the end out of sight'. But even with this encouragement I felt this would be tempting providence too much and declined.

Well, we were out there for about half an hour, I suppose – I felt I'd been there all night, but I wasn't scared anymore. I talked as we walked back to our trenches and I felt as though trench warfare was a simple experience. Of course we learned better later on. But shall I ever forget the night when some grand fellows of the King's Liverpool Regiment took me under their wing, and with complete understanding and generous kindliness, smoothed away my initial terrors of the Front Line. [18]

For PEG Green, an NCO from D Company, the problem with the first night was that you thought of yourself just as a tourist. He and a colleague were sharing a small sodden dugout in their first night in the trenches and:

Suddenly the groundsheet which covered the entrance was roughly pulled back and an NCO of I believe the 1st Berks, with whom we were doing our 'first tour of trench duty', bellowed out this order ['Stand To'] to us in the first light of a dreary November 1915 dawn.

Half awake I replied, 'We are the 22nd Battalion Royal Fusiliers', to which came the quick retort, 'I don't care who the hell you are, you will "stand to" just the same'. [19]

Christopher Stone's first experience was full of mounting anxiety:

At 8:15 (28 November) …we were guided in a zigzag course for an hour up to an absolutely ruined town [Cambrin] in which a good many men managed to live in dugouts etc. Thence for some obscure reason our guide led us forward still in the open, although there was a communication trench close by. I got rather nervous as we gradually approached the German lines in full view of a village which I knew was full of snipers. At last I ran forward to the Major [Boardman] and guide who were walking in front and suggested it would be healthier to get under cover. The guide said he always went this way. At that moment there was a whizz and a shell hit the ground not twenty yards from us! I was the first into the trench of them all! [20]

PEG Green takes up the story:

…the first shell fired at us burst just in front. The party halted, everyone seemed surprised at the sudden course of events.

Major Boardman gave one order 'Advance', but as we moved forward the second shell burst much closer, someone ran. Then all ran, except one man left standing, the others had disappeared into a trench.

The one man went to see where they had all gone and began to laugh saying, 'You are a fine lot of soldiers!'

The third shell came much, much nearer. That one man fell into the trench, whilst the others laughed, saying, 'What is the matter, chum, you are a fine soldier.'[21]

By 2 December the Colonel's ankle had recovered sufficiently for him to visit the front line, where he experienced heavy shelling and saw the man standing next to him hit in the forehead by a splinter. He must have written off a vigorous description of his adventures to Mayor Davison, as the latter wrote back to him full of anxiety:

You really must be more careful of yourself and not take risks…I consider you owe it to the Battalion to stay unwounded.[22]

On 2 December it grew warmer and then poured with rain, causing great damage to the trenches:

The men came back from the trenches today…the thaw has done awful damage and the trenches were falling in all night. They were building [them] up with sandbags all that time. In spite of every precaution most of the rifles got choked up with dirt. The men were mud from head to foot and wet through up to their waists, I never saw such a forlorn lot. I had tea and rum with bacon, bread and jam waiting for them on return; their feet were all washed then they turned to the breakfast. I visited them all and found them most cheery and delighted. I love them all, they are all splendid.

In this first spell in the trenches the Battalion suffered its first 'active service' casualties. Private Melton appears to have been the first on the 28th November, being wounded in the neck and leg by a shell splinter. This was while standing guard over the Colonel's billet, with the dubious honour of the first casualty actually in the trenches going to Lieutenant WA Murray (the golfer). This (a shell splinter in the wrist) would be the first and least serious of his four wounds. Meanwhile, Private Glinwood had a most remarkable escape from death. Back in billets, C Company's cooker (field kitchen) was hidden behind a wall, with Private Glinwood happily sitting on it. A shell plunged earthwards at a steep angle and blew the cooker to pieces. Apart from being blown off it, Glinwood escaped with nothing more serious than a splinter in his knee – and the good fortune to have Christmas at home. Tonsley, the Colonel's servant, had an unusual self-inflicted wound. Shells were falling about sixty yards from the Colonel's billet and:

We got the splinters of a shell against the house. Tonsley rushed out and picked them up and of course got jolly well burnt, as they were red hot.

For the next six days (the second half of the twelve-day training period) the Battalion remained in billets, sending up working parties to the trenches, which remained in a parlous state because of the continuing wet weather. Despite the issue of new clothes more suited to the situation: 'thick leather fur-lined waistcoats, also mackintosh capes and gumboots up to the waist,' being in these working parties must have been a really unpleasant experience: 'just as if you stood in a duckpond with a wall of mud in front of you which continuously fell on top of you'. Even the Germans were observed in early December to be baling water out of their (supposedly better drained) trenches.[23]

On 5 December the new padre, the Reverend EP St. John, whom the Colonel seems to have wangled for the Battalion after hearing that he was working with an ambulance unit only fifteen miles away, held his first service. The Colonel was well satisfied with it and wrote a few days later:

[He] *is a real man, not a canting rotten sort of parson. I fancy he will reform half the Battalion. We are all rather a lot of sinners.*[24]

After seeing him share the hardships and dangers of the men, Colonel Barker gave the padre some practical help: '5,000 cigarettes to touch up the men's religion.' One of B Company's platoons (No 5) seems to have had more than its fair share of deeply religious men, who had their own choir under Sergeant Stevens and according to Major Powlett often had a billet by themselves so that they could sing hymns each Sunday wherever possible. One suspects, however, that the views of the majority of the men were nearer those of Major Rostron: 'There's only one religion [out here] – not to let the other fellow down.'[25]

The Colonel was taken to the 'holy-of-holies':

This morning I went up to a gunner's observation post in a ruined building. It was most interesting; they [the Artillery] *are so frightened of getting them* [the observation posts] *discovered that you begin to go into all sorts of cellars and trenches commencing about 100 yards behind the post… Eventually you climb stairs and reach the top of a chimney stack. Certainly this class of war is most weird, you look over miles of absolutely flat dreary desolate country, not a sign of life anywhere* [but] *shells exploding everywhere. The trenches are so flat that it is difficult to see our lines and the Germans.*

Eric Stevens, of B Company, believed to run the excellent church choir that impressed Major Powlett so much

It might seem impossible to identify targets, let alone transmit their exact positions in conditions as devoid of landmarks as those described here, but the Colonel became more convinced of the value of good observation posts after his next visit to one a few days later (on top of a slag heap), when he saw the first shell requested by the observer burst among a party of Germans who had rather foolhardily been doing their washing in the open.[26]

British guns were fairly continually in action near to the Battalion's positions. Because there was such little retaliation from the enemy in early December, some of the new arrivals were led to believe that the German artillery had been mastered. The alternative, of course, was that the Germans were saving up their shells for an especially nasty bombardment.

On 5 December the Germans had an observation balloon exactly aligned with the La Bassée road,[27] which, one assumes, spotted a working party of twenty men from B

Company returning unawares to their billets. German artillery fire was brought down on the party and a whizz-bang burst in the centre of the them, killing Private Edgington and wounding ten others.

One of the early casualties was Sergeant Downs of B Company, the former Battalion PE Instructor and rugby football player. He was taken down the line then transported by hospital barge to Calais where he was placed in the No 4 Field General Hospital. He was informed that he was to be evacuated to England on the 10 o'clock boat and a red wooden label was hung on his stretcher. Next to him was a slightly wounded man on whose stretcher hung a white label. Downs dosed off and when he awoke the next morning his companion was gone, presumably evacuated, and now he had a white label instead of a red one. Only later did he find out what his wilier companion must have been aware of, that a red label meant 'evacuate' while a white one signified 'retain in hospital'.[28]

On 9 December the Battalion moved off in soaking rain for a few days respite at a friendly little village called Fouqueril, south-west of Bethune. On the next day the Battalion underwent gas drill for the first time. After a lecture given by the Chemical Adviser 1st Army, each man (wearing a gas mask) was required to go through a tent filled with chlorine in a wet sports field just outside Bethune. The aftermath was rather more popular; a bath in the great underground baths at the College des Jeunes Filles in Bethune and a change of clothing. Some men appeared to have been 'allowed out'; a pass exists enabling a Private Rowland of C Company to visit Bethune on 10 December, to return to billets by 11 pm.[29]

On 15 December the Battalion moved back to their old billets at Annequin South in preparation for their first solo sojourn in the front line trenches at Cambrin on the 16–20 December.

For those officers at Battalion HQ (unlike the Company and Platoon officers), the night of 16 December represented their first night in the trenches. On his first sight of the twelve-foot square dugout where he would live and sleep for the next four days along with Major Rostron, the second in command, the Colonel called it the worst in France. By the next morning he discovered other terrors:

Our supply department broke down utterly yesterday as regards Headquarters: no water, no coal… It's extraordinary how little one minds about these things; discomforts like mud, rain, dirty plates etc seem nothing. The one thing I cannot and will not get used to are the rats. I am terrified. They are bold, fearless, terrible creatures which don't mind a torch being flashed at them.

Rostron woke with a gall – the rat jumped off his head onto my face – I was panic-stricken and to my disgust saw him by the light of my torch on my blanket. I fairly leapt up and shook everything; all night long I had them round me.

The other Battalion HQ officers, the Adjutant (Captain Phythian-Adams) and the Signalling Officer (Lieutenant Stone) had their own small (ten feet by five) dugout nearby which was of similar construction and relatively secure against all but the largest shells. As Adjutant, Captain Adams would spend much of his time there:

British Tommy on sentry duty in the trenches.

It is of course quite dark and one sits like a mole all day or most of it with a lantern burning beside one and a phone handy. At one's back behind a galvanised iron screen which blocks the other entrance sits an invisible orderly who receives messages through a small hole. A terrific bump and thud announces the entry of our mess waiter who has probably fallen downstairs. Another, duller and more terrific, announces a 'whizz-bang' from the cheerful Hun.[30]

Christopher Stone left behind a vivid account of a tour around the front line trench system:

It's a lovely warm night with a bit of moonlight; light enough to see your way without a torch. Most of the trenches have footboards laid down in them which keep them fairly clean but greasy. I go up a communication trench, first of all up the centre of our section and pass C-Company Headquarters where [Captain] Black is asleep. [Captain] MacDougall is said to be out in front by himself examining the wire. I go on to the fire trenches and then turn right-handed. It's all zigzag work of course: a bay and then a traverse, a bay and then a traverse, endlessly from the North Pole to the Swiss frontier without a break! In about every third bay there are two sentries standing on the parapet. At the corners of the bays there are often glowing braziers and men sleeping round them or half-asleep: and you pass the entrance to dugouts and hear men murmuring inside and the hot charcoal fumes come out. On and on: sometimes I clamber up beside the sentries and look out. There's little to see, rough ground, the barbed wire entanglement about fifteen yards away, the vague line of German trenches. If a flare goes up it lights the whole place for thirty seconds and is generally followed by a good deal of rifle fire. You see the flash at the muzzle of the rifle…In my wanderings I come to a sap and go along it – very deep mud here, that nearly pulls off my boots – 100 yards out towards the Germans, and at the end I find three or four bombers on guard in case a Bosche tries to come across.[31]

On 18 December the new Divisional General, Major-General W B Walker, paid a surprise visit to the Battalion. He told Colonel Barker: 'Colonel, your men have the right spirit, they have been trained the right way and they go the right way about things.' C Company, said the General, was the best one he had seen in France. Of course, General Walker might have been thinking about the unexpected lecture he had received in trench war weaponry from the young and diminutive Private Harriss:

I was alone in a communicating trench, when along came General Walker. He stopped and I asked him if I could have a talk with him; he agreed.

I began by telling him that I thought the war was being fought all wrong and the method was too costly in human life. I said it takes over a year to train a good infantryman, and then to have them mown down like corn before the reaper, was all wrong; if we went on like that we should lose the war through shortage of man-power. I went on to say the enemy had, so we were told, a machine gun to every twenty men, while we had only one machine gun crew to a company [around 200 men]. I added that what we needed was some contrivance on wheels, which could go ahead of us. Have it armed with a pair of heavy machine guns, and a quick firing gun, which could knock out the enemy machine gun nests. By pushing down gaps in the barbed wire, this armoured car could go ahead, and we could follow up and reach the enemy trenches, with only small casualties. The General asked how I thought the car was going to get over the trenches. I replied, I should have to leave that problem to the R.E.s [Royal Engineers].[32]

Two days later Christopher Stone was prowling around in the trenches when:

One of my old No. 10 Platoon men was hit at about 4 in the morning and I happened to be prowling about, so went and held a torch while he was bound up [by Sergeant Varley]: you can imagine that I didn't enjoy it but I must get used to these horrors and free myself to look at them, especially when they are minor casualties. He was shot through the face (cheeks and nose) just under the eyes which was lucky for him.[33]

This was Private Harriss. He wasn't quite so lucky: the shot had blinded him.[34]

A particular problem for the first few trench tours for the Battalion was their rations; these usually arrived raw and the men had nothing to cook them with (later they would acquire some Primus Stoves). Claude Upton describes how they often arrived:

Loose tea and sugar thrown into a sandbag with bread – four or five men to one loaf – and cheese dumped on top. By the time it arrived most of the loaves were broken, the bags were wet, the tea and sugar sticking to the bread and cheese.[35]

Sometimes all that could be eaten were crumbs of bread and cheese as in the case of Paul Destrubé's 'repast':

Your letter reached me when I was in the middle of a repast, or well, would you call a dog biscuit and a piece of cheese a repast. Prior to the arrival of your epistle misfortune had been fast overtaking me. Three times the piece of cheese had been brushed from my hand and had fallen, half burying itself in the mud at the bottom of the trench; and three times it was subjected to a cleansing process on the seat of my trousers.[36]

In the front line trenches uncooked bacon and dry (or even moist) tea and sugar was of limited value, because to light a fire was to bring down enemy fire upon it. Claude

Upton was nothing if not resourceful:

Instead of dishing out the bacon and tea, I got hold of a clean petrol tin, cut off the top and made a frying pan.

I managed to get hold of a charcoal brazier and in the support line got a fire going. I filled the petrol tin with water and made the tea, cut the loaves in slices and fried the bacon.

I had L.-Cpl. Curtis standing by and then sent him along to each man with the hot bacon between two slices of bread and with the tin of hot tea.[37]

And there was rum, the famous 'SRD', remembered with great favour. Claude Upton, as Platoon Sergeant, was responsible for its distribution among his platoon:

One or two of the men told me they were tee-totallers. I explained to them that it was not given to them because the Army was fond of them but that it was an order that they should drink it…Within a short time of my first issue most of the men wanted to go 'over the top', so after that I used to issue it in small tots during the night, every time I relieved a sentry.[38]

A raid was planned for 15 December, along with an artillery bombardment and the release of gas. On that date wind conditions were unfavourable for the release of gas and continued so for the next few days. Just before the gas was eventually released on the 21 December a voice was heard from the German lines:

For goodness sake, Tommy, let it off tonight as we have been standing-to now for four days and I suppose you've been doing the same.[39]

Despite an effusive report on the success of the gas by the officer in charge of releasing it, those regimental officers from the different battalions in the line at the time were much more sceptical.[40] Indeed, because of the alertness of the Germans in responding to its release – with the sky rapidly full of flares and lights and prepared fires lit on the German trench parapets to drive the fumes upwards – the raiding party did not in the end go out.

As the Battalion was due to go back into the front line trenches for 23-26 December, one of the problems experienced by some of the men when they were out of the front line in the 20th-23rd was just how much of the edibles they had received from home for Christmas they should scoff while they had the chance, and what amount they should leave for the 'official' Christmas celebrations after they had come out of the line again. As one man put it:

At the risk of injuring yourself you must eat as many cakes as possible because if you don't, the noise of the rats using their toothpicks will keep you awake all night.[42]

On 23 December the Battalion moved back into their former front line trenches, relieving the 5th Kings Liverpools. This relief was heavily shelled and relations were again strained between the two battalions, with Colonel Barker not a little displeased that the outgoing battalion had not ordered immediate artillery retaliation. It must be said that the Liverpools, 'out' since early 1915, expressed more of a live-and-let-live mentality. They were 'old soldiers,' grown sceptical of actions likely to lead to needless loss of life. When Colonel Barker attempted to contact the artillery to order retaliation, he found that all the wires were down, cut by the shellfire. Within half an hour Lieutenant Stone and his signallers, under heavy fire, had located and repaired the breaks. Fortune favoured the brave and none of them were wounded. Indeed the rest of the Battalion survived the day without casualties, all excepting the old pioneer sergeant, who fell down the dugout steps.

On Christmas Eve there was great consternation as an experienced miner in C Company claimed he heard the sound of an auger-drill about twenty yards away, suggesting that the Germans were mining underneath them. There had been a history of mining in this area by both sides. Fortunately, the summoned mining experts said it was merely the sound of running water, 'enlarged by vivid imaginations'.[42]

For men aware of the famous 1914 Christmas Truce there must have been intense curiosity to see what 25 December 1915 would bring. This time, however, there were strict orders passed down from GHQ against any fraternisation at Christmas or New Year: any Germans who showed themselves and attempted to fraternise were to be fired upon. In the event, Private Vango was shot dead by a sniper in the early hours of Christmas morning while non-stop rain overnight had left the trenches in an atrocious state, so the priority became trench maintenance.

Paul Destrubé said that the men around them broke into 'song and merriment' after the 'drying and brightening sun' had raised spirits, so machine-gunner AJL Tottenham's memories of the Germans singing patriotic songs like '*Gloria Victoria*', '*Die Wacht am Rhein*' and '*Gott Strafe Englandt*' probably referred to later in the day.[43]

The Battalion's 'official' Christmas Day became 27 December, after they had returned to their old billets at Annequin South, and when all the retained edibles from home could be put to use. Their gifts included for each man: plum puddings from Colonel Barker's wife; fifty cigarettes and a half-pound of chocolates from the Mayoress of Kensington; a cigarette holder and six more cigarettes from the Mayor; and two fat carriage-lamp candles from a family of children (thought to be seven nephews and nieces of Colonel Barker) who had given up all their Christmas presents in order to buy something for the men.[44] Not every gift arrived in peak condition. There was the pork pie that a woman had specially made for the CO. Unfortunately, 'it arrived in a pulp after a fortnight's travels and had to be buried'.[45]

Christopher Stone's signallers had an impressive celebration:

The CO and I went round just now and found them all in the kitchen of the house where they are all billeted, sitting at a log table (whence procured I don't know) covered with food; the sideboard elaborately built up with beer bottles, fruit, cigars and so on; and the men festooned with some of the things that I stole from HQ for them: paper flowers and lanterns. They are a cheery bunch of men and drank our health and made speeches in the best style.

On the 28th they marched further behind the line to Annezin, on the other side of Bethune, and on the 29th reached L'Écleme-Robecque, which was to be their home for the next fortnight. SIGMA wrote an interesting account of the Battalion's progress so far to *The Kensington News*:

I do not know how to convey to you at home the mixture of monotonous routine and of interesting episode that makes up the usual time in the trenches. The work on fatigue parties, clearing communication trenches knee-deep in mud; building up parapets and traverses that the wet weather had demolished; trudging back through miles of trench to fetch rations in sandbags or water in petrol cans; cleaning rifles all the time, on sentry-go hour on, hour off, trying to keep wet feet warm, boiling pannikins on charcoal braziers for the tea in the cold night watches, 'standing to' at dusk and dawn – all the details of the endless round of duties are very fatiguing to the normal year-trained man. But more fatiguing than life in the trenches is the encumbered march into them and out of them, to and from billets that are perhaps a mile in rear of the firing line as the crow flies, and considerably more when you have to scramble and push and crouch and be delayed by blocks and tripped by telephone wires through tortuous communication trenches often deep in mud; and then, once in the open, to follow chosen routes over rough ground more often than not harried by shellfire.[46]

Ratting season lasted all year round in the trenches. Factionpress

But best of all was the spirit of the men:

…the amazing spirit of the men. You wouldn't believe it unless you saw it actually under your eyes. Cool, cheerful, laughing, grousing, covered with mud, drenched to the skin – they are the finest fellows in the world; every day a little more knowing and self-reliant, and able to extract comfort from apparently impossible situations and billets. They pick up things quickly! Kensington has every reason to be proud.

The planned Divisional and Brigade manoeuvres were cancelled because of the wet weather and soaking ground, so the men had a real rest for a fortnight. Divisional HQ provided several entertainments that seem hardly out of place three or four generations later:

But they are mad keen on diversions – there's a pantomime, several

cinemas and music halls, roller-skating rink, football, boxing etc, all run by the Division, which also does coffee stalls in every billeting area.[47]

In early January Major Powlett was given two reasons to repay his faith in his B Company. First they were being picked out as best Company in the New Year's Day parade, then on the 9th he was very pleased with the singing of Sergeant Stevens' choir at the Battalion church service.[48] Meanwhile higher authority came up with a novel solution to the rat problem: ferrets! 99 Brigade was to have been allocated 500 ferrets, meaning that over 100 would come to the 22nd RF. The idea caused much mirth:

> *Of course the plague of ferrets will be far worse than the rat plague. Once you put the ferret in you will never see him again as the whole place is honeycombed with rat runs... How the men will laugh and enjoy it. They will all get bitten. They are all so delightfully cheery and boyish.*[49]

Unfortunately, the ferret solution seems to have been shelved as no more was heard about it. Major Rostron brought back from leave a more personal solution to the rats plaguing Battalion HQ; a spotty fox terrier called 'Romp', which, in his short career with the Battalion, did become a champion ratter, laying the basis of his reputation by killing at least eight rats in the HQ billet at Essars.

Notes: Much of the material in the above (and following) chapters has come from the Barker and Stone letters. Footnotes referring to direct quotations from them have been minimised where these sources are obvious.

1 *History*, p27
2 70 years on, ex-Private 'Olly' Berrycloath could still remember that interminable halt; interview, 15/1/1984; it was probably War Council members being rushed through
3 Embarkation Order, 16/11/1915 – *Phythian-Adams Papers*, henceforth 'PAP'
4 *Mufti*, June 1960, 40, No 135, pp 8-9 and June 1965 44, No 145, p6
5 *History*, p27
6 *Mufti*, June 1965, 44, p6
7 Interview with ex-Sergeant Roland Whipp, 18/11/1983
8 *Mufti*, November-December 1920, 2, No 6, p6 and Summer 1960, 40, No 135, p9
9 *Ibid*, 19/11/1915; *Powlett Diary*, 19/11/1915
10 *Mufti*, 1970, 49, No 154, p7 and 1965, 44, No 145, p8; and Christopher Stone asked *his* wife to send his 30 signallers a packet each every week
11 *Stone Letters*, hereafter *CRS*, 21/11/1915; MFH = Master of Foxhounds
12 *Barnett Barker Letters*, henceforth *RBB*, 22/11/1915
13 *Broughshane*, Destrubé letters, 2534, 22/11/1915
14 *CRS*, 25/11/1915, *Sheffield and Inglis*, p33
15 *Ibid*, not *S and I*
16 *Mufti*, June 1965, 44, No 145, p7
17 *Mufti*, Summer 1924, p2
18 *Mufti*, June 1965, 44, No 145, p7 (Claude Upton)
19 *Ibid*, June 1956, 36, No 127, pp 12-13
20 *Ibid*, June 1962, 42, No 139, p2

21 *CRS*, 28/11/1915
22 *Mufti*, Summer 1962, <u>42</u>, No 139, p2
23 *Broughshane*, <u>8639</u>, 6/12 and 9/12/1915
24 *RBB*, 5/12 and 13/12/1915; *National Archives (PRO), WO 95*/1288: 2nd Division Tactical Progress Report, 10/12/1915
25 *RBB*, 12/12/1915
26 *Powlett Diary*, 6/1/1916; *CRS*, 6/12/1915
27 *RBB*, 6/12/1915 and *Broughshane* <u>8638</u>: Davison to RBB, 13/12/1915
28 *WO 95*/1288: 2nd Division Tactical Progress Report, 5/12/1915
29 *Mufti*, Autumn 1935, <u>16</u>, No 3, p3
30 *Broughshane*, Battalion Souvenir Book
31 *PAP*, WJP-A to his sister 22/12/1915
32 *CRS*, 17 and 18/12/1915, fuller version in *Sheffield and Inglis*, p36
33 *Mufti*, June 1954, <u>34</u>, No 123, p iii
34 *CRS*, 21/12/1915
35 *Mufti*, Spring 1938, <u>19</u>, No 88, pp2-3. Christopher Stone broadcast an appeal for Wireless for the Blind, citing Harriss as an example, then Harriss came forward and told his story to *Mufti.*
36 *Mufti*, June 1965, <u>44</u>, No 145, pp6-7
37 *Broughshane*, Destrubé Letters, <u>2534</u>, 22/12/1915
38 *Mufti*, Summer 1970, <u>49</u>, No 154, pp 6-7
39 *Mufti*, June 1965, <u>44</u>, No 145, p8
40 *RBB* 22/12/1915, also *CRS* 22/12/1915 with slightly differing words
41 *WO 95*/1288 and *WO 95*/1360 (5th Kings Liverpools), 1372 (22nd RF), 1371 (1st KRRC)
42 *Mufti*, Xmas 1934, <u>15</u>, No 4, p2
43 *CRS*, 25/12/1915
44 *Mufti*, Christmas 1928, <u>9</u>, No 44, p1
45 The machine gunners waited until 8/1/1916 from Percy Cannot's dated menu in Broughshane.
46 CRS, 3/1/1916
47 *Kensington News*, 14/1/1916: almost certainly written by Christopher Stone, because of Sigma indicating a signaller; and it's his style
48 *CRS*, 7/1/1916
49 *Powlett Diary*, 1/1 and 9/1/1916
50 *CRS*, 7/1/1916 and RBB, 1/1/1916

Chapter Three

Festubert, Givenchy and Souchez

FESTUBERT WAS IN THE SAME GENERAL AREA as their previous trench location, Cambrin, but north of the La Bassée Canal. In fact one could think of the six villages just behind the front line as the edges of an umbrella with Bethune as the handle and the La Bassée Canal as the spine: from north to south the villages were Festubert, Le Plantin, and Givenchy (-les-la-Bassée), then the canal, then Cuinchy (with its famous smokestacks), Cambrin and Vermelles.

The reserve line ran just outside the village. It consisted of breastworks built up of sandbags up to about six feet in height; the countryside had become too boggy for the construction of trenches since the Germans had diverted the course of the La Bassée Canal. Some 350 yards further ahead, in even boggier conditions, was the firing line,

A Company officers at Festubert. From left to right: Tomkins, Roscoe, Bede (later Sir Bede) Clifford and Murray. Clifford, the first man to cross the Kalahari Desert in a wheeled vehicle, would go on to a glittering diplomatic career, while Murray was a very successful golfer. (from Sir Bede Clifford's memoir *Proconsul*)

which consisted of fifteen or sixteen separate 'islands' (or 'grouse butts'), quite devoid of any communication with each other. Here the men would spend only twenty-four hours in the front line, then be taken to dry out. Because the area was overlooked by the Aubers Ridge (the target of unsuccessful British attacks in 1915) no movement up to the firing line was possible by day, and it was hazardous at night, as Sergeant Downs described:

> *The road from the old British front line through Cove Trench* [at Festubert village] *to one section of the islands was formerly christened by the French Quinque Rue, but with the lively adaptability of the Tommy to any foreign tongue, was better known as 'Kinky Roo'…Quinque Rue was sprayed nightly by two German machine guns familiarly known as 'Blighty Albert' and 'Kinky Roo Jimmy'.[1]*

The breastworks provided only a fragile defence that could easily have been destroyed by shellfire and probably were not even bullet-proof. Nevertheless, during the Battalion's stay there, hostile shellfire was not heavy and tended to be concentrated further behind the lines. Good dry weather plus the freedom to walk about in the open air behind the breastworks rather than being cooped up underground in a smelly, rat-infested dugout, made life much more tolerable for the officers at least. Christopher Stone grew quite lyrical about life in the reserve line outside Festubert in his 19 January letter, written from 'The most charming spot in France':

> *My darling it is perfectly lovely here. A glorious fresh sunny morning – sunlight everywhere; on the pools of water, on the wings of aeroplanes, on the ruined redbrick houses of the village behind us. We live behind a thick wall of sandbags about six feet thick and have light shelters erected against this breastwork. All is in the open air – that is what is so refreshing. I am sitting in our headquarters dugout writing at a good solid table; our food is on shelves above me, and at my side are two bunks, the upper one the Colonel's, the lower one mine.[2]*

The Padre, the Reverend St John, had been living up to the high expectations held of him. Sergeant Downs commented that:

> *He had cemented once more the bond that had so thoroughly been established with the rank and file, by looking after a platoon in the islands when their officer (Captain Goodwin) had become a casualty.[3]*

There was only one death during this tour, with Private

Festubert terrain showing how water-logged it was.

72

Edwardes becoming the first fatal casualty among the machine-gunners. 'One of the gunners' [AJL Tottenham] remembered the incident:

> *Poor Edwardes, one of the cheeriest of souls, was 'sniped' in the throat while whittling up wood for the firepot about nine o'clock in the morning. The body had to lie there all day, because in that exposed position his comrades dare not bury him until dark. His death cast a gloom over the whole section, and we felt sorry for his widow and four small sons.*[4]

Edwardes was a hefty six-footer and bringing in his body for burial from No 9 to No 5 island caused not a few problems. Sergeant Downs watched the Padre perform the last rites when night fell:

> *He had barely commenced when a flare went up and a German machine gun began traversing. With the exception of the Padre the funeral party flattened themselves to the ground, whilst he remained standing until the service was complete.*[5]

Colonel Barker, Major Powlett and Christopher Stone were among those fortunate

enough to obtain seven-ten days' leave in the last third of January. Major Rostron took over the Battalion. He had to try a case involving a private who had lost a lot of equipment:

> *Major Rostron's stammer was historic, and it took him just about five minutes to read through the charge, how: 'While on active service, etc, etc, Private —, Number —, was deficient of the following articles', all of which was painfully but faithfully enumerated. Then he asked the culprit 'W-w-w-w-ell, wh-wh-at, have you g-g-g-ot to say?'*
>
> *Hoping for the best, but rather too pertly, the prisoner answered, 'N-n-n-nothing, sir.' 'W-w-ell, I have', was the reply. Facial muscles were badly strained that day.[6]*

Later Major Rostron would have to try one of the few genuine stutterers in the Battalion. The mutual exchange of question and answer took a very long time and Major Rostron took exception to what he interpreted as insolence, giving the unfortunate victim ten days CB rather than the two he might have expected.

After coming out of the front line on the 22nd the Battalion moved to four days in billets in Festubert and Epinette, sending up working parties to the front line. They then went further back to Hingette (a few miles north of Bethune) for a week when the whole Division was in Reserve. Here they received their first drafts of men from their feeder battalion, the 27th Royal Fusiliers, and this was also where Barker, Powlett and Stone encountered the Battalion when they returned from leave. One's first leave was so much yearned for, yet once home in the UK, one could feel very out of place.

On his first day home in Abergavenny, Major Powlett commented to his diary:

The village of Festubert.

It is a curious feeling to be out of it all – such a stillness. Home looked lovely. Had a good feed and went to bed.

And on the day after (a Sunday):

Put on mufti and went to church. It is nice to be in this armchair again plus walking about in mufti, but it seems awfully strange.[7]

As the days ebbed away, depression would strike. Major Powlett spent his last two days in London visiting shows as was the custom, but was 'not in the humour to enjoy anything much'.

For Colonel Barker it set in immediately he had arrived back in France;

I was very depressed last night, I didn't know it would be so hard coming back again – when you get back here it seems as if the war would go on for ever and really, from the soldier's point of view, viz. the actual fighting, there is no reason why it should ever finish.

New adventures were in store at their next location which would drive away some of these low moods. On 3 February they moved off for four days in the trenches at the infamous hotspot of Givenchy. This was the next village south of Le Plantin, and home to the decidedly unhealthy Windy Corner, where several roads converged.

A Company were in the line at the Duck's Bill only thirty yards from the Germans. Fortunately the latter were 'Saxons' (ie peaceable, the opposite of 'Prussians' or 'Guards'). Major Powlett, commanding B Company, was in support at Gunners Siding, a trench running along the back gardens of a row of ruined houses. Just in front of Gunners Sidings was the Marie Redoubt, whose squeaky Givenchy Pump had been immortalised in the famous Bruce Bairnsfather cartoon. The recently returned Sergeant Downs was there and so was the platoon ventriloquist:

'The Fatalist' by Bruce Bairnsfather.

A sentry, the ventriloquial one, was posted at night at the junction of the communication trench and the keep, and another one was doing duty at the bomb store a short distance further on.

I visited the first one at midnight and dished him out with his rum ration and then made my way to the second sentry with what was left. We exchanged a few words and to my surprise next morning received a complaint that he had received no rum.

Of course I was very mystified, but during the day happened to hear, around the traverse a chuckling account from the mimic of how he hopped over the top and met me again just in front of the bomb store and got a second helping. I left him out of the ration that night and when he complained in the morning I told him that we apparently had two impersonators in the platoon, and that in my judgment the second one was the superior.[8]

There were new dangers at Givenchy. The 'rumjars' (*Minnenwerfers* or 'Minnies'), were

Large quantities of German stick grenades awaiting delivery to the front line.

Grenade throwers in action.

Opposite: Sniper working along with a spotter.

German trench mortars that threw:

> *A big thing like a football that comes lobbing through the air quite slowly and goes off with a tremendous explosion. The sentries have to stand and look upwards and blow a whistle* [once for left, twice for right] *when they see one coming and then everyone dives for shelter and dodges the damned thing.*[9]

Another peril was rifles grenades. They were: 'like a tin of salmon and turn over all the time. They will kill you all right within five or six yards but don't damage the trench.' Trench mortars would do a great deal of damage to a trench if they landed in one, but it was much more difficult to see the rifle grenades coming.

German rifle grenades did claim a handful of lives in this trench tour and there were frustratingly few British rifle grenades with which to reply to them. Despite these dangers this was a tour with a certain amount of fun. There was for example 'Payne the firework man's' invention of a new type of flare, which was fortunately let off during the day time:

You fire it from an enormous huge pistol and I fired one off this morning in daylight from the trenches, it was awfully funny! It went high in the air and suddenly a linen parachute opened with a light attached to it, which burned brightly. The wind was blowing against us so it sailed over our lines for nearly a mile.[10]

The Colonel produced a cunning plan to gain revenge on the Germans for their Minnies and grenades:

We got the artillery to give the Hun a great strafeing and then opened rapid fire on their front line. We then gave three cheers, they thought at once we were charging and filled their trenches. Meanwhile our men slipped back into dugouts and we opened artillery fire on their crowded trenches. I hope we collected a few. It's really all delightful work, all the men and officers are splendidly keen.

Captain Clifford's men had located a sniper's post and were particularly interested in potting a ginger-moustached officer who frequented it. Unfortunately Clifford missed his target and the Germans were also shown to be able to devise cunning plans:

That silly ass C. missed the ginger moustached German officer and then, more foolishly, asked the gunners to blow up the post. I arrived on the scene just as they were starting, we had to clear our front line trenches as the sniper's post was only about forty yards from them. They put 100 high explosives at it. It was impossible to observe the effect or even direct the fire. After this about seven of us went down to the sap and looked over with a periscope and found that they hadn't even touched it. Suddenly they sent over

trench mortar bombs at us. They are so cunning as of course they knew what we were up to – that we would go down after the bombardment to have a look down the sap.

You can see these bally footballs in the air. C. called out, 'Here one comes', 'Keep still' and then 'Run like blazes'. They all dashed around another sap. I pursued and found C. hadn't left enough room for us all to get in. I jumped on the top of the others and buried my head in a private's legs. We were all screaming with laughter. The bally thing burst about fifteen yards away and covered us all with soil. You have to count to ten after the burst before you get up. No sooner we were up than Sergeant-Major Stackpole yelled out, 'Here's another one right at us.' Off we dashed again to another place where the same thing occurred.

On the next day the Germans were understandably 'lively.' One of those injured by trench mortar was Private H Tweedy of 13 Platoon. Both Colonel Barker and the Mayor of Kensington wrote immediately to his mother so that by the time the official War Office notification arrived, her anxieties had been considerably allayed.[11]

During tour of the trenches Mayor Davison was among a party of VIPs connected with the raising of battalions being shown around selected trenches. He managed to see the other Kensington Battalion (the Territorial 13th London Regiment), who were in a rest camp at the time, but he was not allowed to see the 22nd Battalion because they were in the front line.[12]

During the Battalion's stay at Givenchy Captain (Doc) Miller arrived – the fourth medical officer of the Battalion (two had been sacked). He arrived with a reputation for bravery, having served with the 1st KRRC amongst others and went on to become one of the Battalion's most loved and most respected characters. After he had died in 1925, Christopher Stone wrote the following words about him:

More than anyone else – I am not exaggerating – W.A.M [Miller] educated the Battalion for the ordeals which were still untasted when he first took us in hand.[13]

The Battalion moved back into the Givenchy front-line trenches from the 11th to the 15th. As they moved in via Windy Corner, one man from B Company was shot dead – not a good omen – but he was to be B Company's only fatal casualty during the four days and one of only three in the whole Battalion. The Battalion began to feel a significant shortage of officers at this time. Some were on leave, some were injured and some were on courses. In fact the Divisional Fighting Strengths Summary for this time shows fifteen officers – half of their strength – as 'included but not with unit.'[14] Some honourable exceptions were Major Boardman (on loan to the KRRCs and shortly to command the 8th Royal Irish Fusiliers) and Captain McCausland, who at fifty was finding trench life rather too much for him and who was to be sent to the IV Corps Trench Mortar School. There were one or two others who managed to be on courses almost permanently.

The Mayor of Kensington made representations for the Colonel, all the way up to the Adjutant General. The official view was that the number on the establishment of the Battalion (thirty) was the correct number. Nothing could be done until the absentees had been permanently struck off it. Over the next couple of months several officers – unfit, unable or unwilling – were culled from the Battalion's establishment, but this did not solve the current problem, with the remaining officers: sick, overworked or both. Christopher Stone took over the adjutancy when Major Adams was on leave, then volunteered to take over a platoon officer's duties for a night from Captain McDougall who was 'seedy'. Nor was Major Powlett well:

Poor old P. looks a hundred and is as white as a polar bear. I am afraid he won't be able to stick this sort of life much longer. He is so splendid and conscientious. I don't know

The Destrubé brothers: George, Paul and Guy – always getting into trouble in the UK, but doughty fighters in France. (Broughshane Collection 8369 and online at http: //www.vac-acc.gc.ca/remembers/sub.cfm?source=collections/virtualmem/photos&casualty=593455)

what I shall do without him if he cracks.

The day after Colonel Barker wrote this Major Powlett was much chirpier, having sniped a German officer from an observation post (much to the chagrin of the Colonel), but a few days later he was recording in his diary the diagnosis of sciatica which would eventually lead to his evacuation to England in April.

Paul Destrubé, one of the three famous Canadian brothers, wrote an exquisite description of life in a Givenchy dug-out:

This trip in the trenches I have been quite fortunate in securing a dug-out with six others. Of course it is exceedingly small, measuring no more than 5 ft by 4 ft, but then I must bear in mind that beggars are not choosers...

I have not long been from my post, and I am writing this in the aforesaid dug-out, huddled up in the corner. This sand-bag abode is feebly illuminated by a candle dimly burning. My neighbour who is yet more uncomfortably cramped up, is falling off to sleep, and his muddy, unshaven and jam smeared face is resting on my shoulder. Occasionally he grunts vigorously, making the paper I am writing upon flutter. I have just removed an open tin of jam from under the mud-clotted boot of the fellow opposite me. A fair-sized piece of cheese is pinned to the sand-bagged wall by means of a cartridge. The bread has been devoured, but a few pieces of hard tack biscuits lie scattered somewhere on the ground beneath this living, semi-sleeping entanglement of men. A bayonet thrust into the wall serves as a candlestick, and the candlegrease is slowly but persistently dripping on the fellow's forehead who is sleeping directly underneath. With one finger I could swing the bayonet to one side – but I am not going to do so, because it would be a pity to destroy such a charming situation. I'm almost hypnotised as I watch the grease slowly dripping – drip, drip, drip – and still he sleeps!

And so we are here, huddled and interlaced together, strangers all, until we met in the common cause; in this circle of six we once represented such a different type, but now all gradually approaching the same – the man in his primitive stage.

Firing a trench mortar: sketched by Henry Lea, who was transferred to the 99th TMB.
From Henry Lea's *A Veld Farmer's Adventures*

French troops using a catapult to lob grenades into the German trenches.

But my reflections have been disturbed; my neighbour is responsible for more grunts and furthermore he's tried to stretch himself. There! – I thought so – he's kicked the fellow opposite in the stomach, and now they are both grunting. All is quiet again, the dirty unkissable face is in its old position again – on my shoulder.[15]

On the night of the 13-14 February the Germans made several vigorous bombing attacks on A, B and C company positions; or did they? The Colonel tells the story, tongue in cheek:

Quite exciting last night when I got up about 12:50 am to the trenches. A Coy was full of a bombing attack the Germans had made on them. According to their account they had inflicted the most appalling losses on the Huns and had heard them all yelling etc. Of course I had to go down the sap and congratulate the gallant bombers. I had just come out when I heard they were attacking B-Company. Powlett turned the machine-guns and rifles on them. Same stories of awful losses inflicted. I was there at the time looking over the top of the parapet and I must say I didn't see a single German but I'm stupid at night [he had slight deficiencies of night vision and hearing]. *Again at 5 am they attacked McDougall's* [C-Company] *with bombs and were easily driven off. The men loved it all.*

The sequel, the next day, suggested more sound and fury than peril:

Clifford's [A-Company] *bombers told me they had killed two Germans at the head of their sap so I told them to fetch in the bodies. They found two logs of wood. The other company bombers are having great fun about it.*

Quite possibly they were genuinely being probed by enemy patrols, which slipped quietly away, but one man's comments on his first experiences in the trenches at Cambrin seem appropriate here:

Then up to the trenches beyond Cambrin, there to stand on the firestep watching for Kaiser Bill on his white charger, and seeing in a broken tree-stump or other derelict object many a Heinie who never existed at all.[16]

During this spell (11-15 February), two companies of the 6th Royal Irish Rifles (under the famous Major Willie Redmond) joined the Battalion for trench instruction. These were not the most disciplined of troops:

But their RSM accompanying Colonel Barker on his nightly rounds used to plead for them, 'Don't be too hard on the bhoys, sir, – don't now'.[17]

The machine gunners of Sergeant Brierley's team at the Marie Redoubt found their hospitality somewhat abused by the newcomers:

The first night was decidedly frosty, and we made ourselves cosy in our shelter of waterproof sheets and curtains. The firepot glowed temptingly and one Irish guest after another ventured in and made himself at home. Soon we were out in the cold, while our shelter was full of snoring Pats.[18]

Another hazard of this second tour of the Givenchy trenches was the British trench-mortars, then in a rather primitive stage (it was a month or two before the arrival of the reliable and effective Stoke Mortars). The operatives of the early mortars were not very popular due to the

Major Willie Redmond.

German retaliation that nearly always followed their firings. The Colonel tells of a typical incident:

> Yesterday our trench-mortar which is cracked I am told, was fired by a dashing young boy of the battery who had twenty small grenades. What happens is this. The boy fires his twenty rotten grenades most of which are badly turned and burst in the air. The peaceful Hun then turns on his grenade throwers and his 'Minnies' and we get an awful time. Our men spend an hour or so of intense nervous activity, dashing about the place. Eventually we have to get the heavy and field artillery batteries to stop the Germans. Cost to the country £300. This usually occurs twice a day and sometimes at night. I told (-) it was all bally nonsense. Of course they reply, 'You must keep on worrying the Hun.' I am all for grenading the Hun till he's silly if you have the tools to kill him with. But for our cracked mortar under a cracked boy to take on the best 'Minnies' in the world – and always to be knocked out by them, is giving no one worry but yourself.

The Trench Mortar Battery appeared to be a dumping ground for some of the more difficult men like Henry Lea (the latter, besides being one of the Battalion cartoonists, was forever creating unlikely inventions and writing off to the authorities about them). The Battalion ventriloquist seems also to have been sent there as Henry Lea tells:

> One cold morning he couldn't get near the brazier, to fry the bacon, because of Sappers. (They were big chaps). Presently calls were heard 'Sappers to the front. Hurry up.' Out bundled the Sappers and in glided the ventriloquist and the rest of us who had been frozen out. Stout fellow.[19]

On the 15th the Battalion moved back to Ham-en-Artois (several miles north-west of Bethune) for Divisional Rest via two days each at Le Quesnoy and Gonnehem. They were fortunate that heavy snow and frost prevented the sort of brigade manoeuvres that had been planned, making the spell at Ham from the 19th to the 27th much more of a real rest period in fairly comfortable conditions.

Sergeant Fowles (formerly head chef at the Great Central Hotel) returned to enhance the reputation of the Battalion HQ mess as one of the finest in the Division. In fact the morale of the Battalion as a whole seemed to have peaked around this time: when Brigadier-General Kellett visited it on the 20th, he announced to Colonel Barker that 'In all his service he had never seen a happier battalion or one in which everyone worked in so much harmony.' The Divisional General was similarly impressed, particularly with the Battalion bootmakers shop, where each man's spare pair of boots was repaired by the Battalion 'snobs' and stored.[20]

Because of the German attacks on the French at Verdun, the British had agreed to take over more of the line. On 27 February the Battalion set off southwards to take over French trenches in the Souchez area (just north of Vimy Ridge). They took a train from Lillars to Noeux-Les-Mines opposite Lens. They walked for a few miles through what seemed to be one long mining village to Petit Sains, where Lieutenant Fowler had been sent ahead to billet the Battalion. As the Colonel said: 'The great thing was to find Fowler! However, he is a priceless officer and met us exactly where I expected him.'

The officers and men were soon billeted in miners' cottages. Although only a few

The village of Souchez when the Kensingtons arrived to take over from the French.
Factionpress

miles from the front line, Petit Sains was a complete contrast to the ruined villages the Battalion had encountered further north. It was full of a great muddle of mixed French and British troops and furthermore:

> *To add to the entanglement the mining civil population has never moved out as the pits are still working. Although we are only five miles from the Fire Trench this place has never been shelled. The* [Mining] *Companies are all owned by German capitalists, also the houses.*[21]

This was a most curious situation, but no more curious than the type of warfare the Battalion would soon encounter. The next day, the Battalion received abrupt orders just before dinner to move four miles to the rear to Barlin and exchange with the 23rd RF, as it was due to go into the trenches the day after and the exchange would cut four miles off their march.[22] Needless to say, this was not a popular move, although Colonel Barker postponed it until 9:30 pm to give the men time to eat first. Soon the rain came down in torrents, with snow for good measure. Initially the men retained their good humour:

> *They sang 'Raining, Raining, Raining, Always —— Raining' etc to the tune of 'Holy, Holy, Holy'…However by the end of five miles they were pretty well fed up… Can you picture arriving in a downpour of sleet at midnight in a mining village with every light out and 1,000 men to find lodgings for? Really, my officers are absolutely priceless.*

Barlin was remembered by many 22nd RF men as the least welcoming of places. Yet some of its residents were very pleased to see them, queuing up to make their acquaintance in fact:

> *One chappie and I went up to the first floor of our cottage and spread out our things …* [on] *the plank floor…He was kneeling on these boards. I suddenly said 'Good Lord!' – And I told him* [why] *– the lice were marching up the back of his shirt in solid columns.*

It was from this time onwards that lice began to be mentioned. 'Chatting' was of course the ritual scourging of the lice in one's clothing or on one's body:

> *That was the worst part of the war these lice – they got into the sewing parts of your clothing then they got into your skin and as they fed and got into the difficult parts of*

you to get out. We used to run along our seams with a flame, but you had to do it quick enough not to burn the fabric. Some were black and smooth when they hadn't had a feed, but when they had fed they had red spots on them.[23]

On the early hours of 3 March the Battalion relieved the 135th French Regiment in the Bois des Noulettes – a wood on the side of a hill. The timing of the relief became mixed up. First the Battalion was ordered to relieve the French at 5 pm on the 2nd. The French replied that they were not being relieved until 5 am on the 3rd. Colonel Barker agreed to the French time and sent forward an advance party – to find the French leaving at 3 am. Sergeant Downs was shocked by the lack of French march discipline:

Pipes fully charged in usual haycock fashion, cries of 'Bon chance', 'Allez, toute suite', lamps flashing, no semblance of fours by the right, and every man carrying some type of walking stick and leaving in his wake a tantalising odour of 'rhum' and 'vin du pays'.[24]

There was one blessing to this: the huts had been left in such a foul and verminous condition that they had to be thoroughly cleaned first. Sergeant Downs described the huts:

[They] looked and smelt as if they had been occupied by some species of human rabbit. They were deep in decayed straw and this was soon bundled outside.

The straw was also full of French cartridges, which caused some fun later, as they exploded when the straw was burned. On the other hand, French dugouts were impressive:

The Bois rises out of a valley almost precipitous to about sixty feet. They have cut steps all up the hill amongst the trees and cleared out places, where the six huts are built, all most beautifully made; where the huts aren't, there are dugouts like caves. On the top of the hill they have burrowed in and made more dugouts. It's an absolute rabbit warren and the men from a distance look like rabbits coming out of their holes. The engineering feat is really marvellous.[25]

There was a strange truce in operation in this area. Colonel Barker heard an explanation for it:

We hear a Hun Regiment has been sent out here for sixty days punishment so are most annoyed with their authorities. The French had an arrangement with them that no one ever fired at each other. As we are in the most impossible conditions with trenches only covering our waists, we propose carrying on the same arrangement. The islands at Festubert were a picnic compared to this. The only difference is that no one shoots at you so it's like working with a problem on your own with an icy bath waiting for you if you take a false step. The – [Berks] were most disturbed as two bullets came over today! and the Germans deny firing them.

Last night they were all outside their trenches and quite happy till the – [Berks] took up a coil of wire. A burly Hun told them to stop as it belonged to them![26]

Next day (5 March) the Battalion relieved the Royal Berks and went in to the Souchez trenches for a four-day stint. The trenches were in an atrocious state from the rain and snow and there were still many corpses lying around from the French-German battles earlier in the war. The relief became a severe test of stamina and good humour, with many stops and starts. Gumboots had just been issued before the march, and while most people had a left and a right, they weren't necessarily the same size, or related to the size of their feet.

Roland Whipp nearly lost a stripe here:

We were at Souchez then – trying to get into it. We were mixed up with some KRRs, the guide lost his way and the fairy lights went up showing us up so clearly. And there we were standing around not knowing what to do, waiting for the guide or somebody to do something about it. It was deep snow or deep rain – a horrible position – and suddenly I was nearly flung off my fee by a chap rushing through. He nearly spun me off my feet. I just called out to his retreating form, 'Bollocks to you'. He turned round and came back – he turned out to be a Lieutenant in the KRRs I think – and asked me for my name and number which I gave him but smiling very sweetly at him this time. But when our stint in the line was over I was taken to the Orderly Room (to answer the charge) by Phythian-Adams the Adjutant. 'BB', a very nice man, asked me what happened. I told him exactly as it was. He then asked for the report from this Lieutenant, but when the Adjutant was handed this – he was quite a religious man and later became Canon of Carlisle – and told to read it out, when he got to the word 'bollocks', everybody exploded except Phythian-Adams who was probably blushing. And 'BB', who had a moustache like Harry Tate [the famous music hall performer],

Harry Tate and his famous moustache.

French troops leaving the Souchez area to take part in the fighting in defence of Verdun.

and was looking down at the papers in front of him, when it came to the word 'bollocks' his moustache started bobbing up and down just like Harry Tate's! When he had got himself and his moustache quietened down he asked me (I was an unpaid Lance-Corporal at the time – one stripe up and no pay): 'If you had known he was an officer would you have said that?' And I said 'Oh, no, sir, of course not, sir. He didn't look like one and he didn't speak like one.' (More howls of laughter). And so he didn't know what to do after that one! But his moustache quietened down then he said 'Case explained', and that was the end of it, and I kept my one unpaid stripe.[27]

Moving into trenches where, despite their discomfort, there were 'friendly' Germans nearby (sapheads probably twenty to fifty yards apart) was extraordinary. Firstly, the men were welcomed by a German shouting 'Hello Royal Fusiliers,' which then started a pattern of 'hearty good-mornings' each day with 'our friend the enemy'.[28]

Some of D Company's trenches were knee deep in water but close to some very friendly Germans. Here there were rumours of a snowball fight with their German counterparts and there are many tales about exchanging tins of bully beef for German sausage. Sergeant Fred Pignon was invited by the Germans to make up a fourth at bridge, with his return guaranteed.[29]

Syd Rogers was one of the D Company bombers occupying the front sap. He saw a German soldier fling something – possibly an envelope – into No Man's Land:

Next morning most of the Germans including an officer – who spoke excellent English, it appeared that he had lived in Cardiff before the war – were standing on their 'firestep' grinning at us across 'no man's land'.

The officer suggested that we exchanged newspapers. I told him that I would get some, but I was only allowed some magazines. I returned with those to the 'Sap head' and showed them to him. He threw some papers into our 'Sap head', but I purposely threw the magazines into 'No Man's Land' to where I thought the envelope lay. He laughed and said I was a poor thrower for a bomber.

I told him I would crawl through our wire and get them for him, if he would come and meet me. This I did but he did not leave his trench – however I was lucky enough to find the envelope, so I threw the magazines to him and returned to our sap head.

The envelope contained a letter from a French girl who had been taken prisoner at Lens, but her father and mother had escaped and were living in Paris. She appealed to whoever got the letter to send it to her parents to let them know she was alive and safe. There was no doubt she had given the letter to the German soldier who, being unable to post it, threw it over to us hoping we could get it through.[30]

Those whose mindsets were inclined towards sniping, like the Colonel, a noted sportsman, also had some difficulty in holding back:

I saw more Germans than I have seen in four months, they were strolling about in front of their wire. It was just like looking at some big salmon in a pool which you long to catch and it fairly made my mouth water. They have a white flag tied up on a wrecked tree. The only thing you must not do is to walk about in daylight, or expose yourself, then they shoot. This is the etiquette at present.

B Company bombers near Souchez:
Back row: E Holston, G Morton, LW Humphries, R (Buff) Whitehouse, SB Boyce
Front row: CJ Douglas, HG Hallett (sitting), D Colbeck. *(Mufti)*

Captain Gell got lost when exploring a communication trench in broad daylight. Eventually he decided the only way home was over the top. As an exposed figure he was fair game; he had a horrendous time dodging from shell-hole to shell-hole, being fiercely sniped the whole time. He ended up unwounded but encrusted in mud.

The Battalion would end up staying in the Souchez area for two months. There is agreement that the front line troops became less peaceful with each other, but there are no convincing reasons why and when. We counted up the number and type of shells fired by 2nd Division artillery, but this gave no clues. It's possible that the type of targets might have changed, or maybe moving from aiming-to-miss to aiming-to-hit, but we have no direct evidence for this.[31] The most romantic of the theories involved

The strange truce at Souchez: Henry Lea (cap reversed to avoid identification) looking over at a German watching him through binoculars. From Henry Lea's *A Veld Farmer's Adventures*

the pacific Saxons opposite coming to the end of their sixty days of punishment and being replaced by aggressive Guards troops, with notice of the ending of the truce given by the British throwing over the usual tins of bully beef to the enemy, but stick grenades rather than sausages being the reply. But ex-Private Berrycloath did tell us this with a twinkle in his eye.[32] There was a complication. A German sniper from *another* front (the Vimy Ridge on the right of the Battalion front) was taking great delight in the juicy targets on the 22nd RF front. A favourite target of his was the latrines (then open on the German side), which thereafter could not be visited during daytime until the entrance was turned around. The sniper was eventually trapped by his own greed:

> A papier-mâché representative of a soldier's head was brought to the trenches and was incautiously raised above the parapet. Immediately a clean hole was drilled through the forehead by the sniper's aim. A careful bearing along the line was thus given, then the mask was taken around the corner to another spot where the same thing occurred. This gave us a second line, and at the point of convergence there seemed to be a little mound on the side of the ridge, clearly the sniper's lair.
>
> The Artillery had an 18-pounder in the support line, and an observer came down to correct the bearing. He phoned back the range and elevation and with the first shot the sniper was blown up.[33]

On 9 March the Battalion, still in the same ill-fitting gumboots, moved out of the line in pouring rain to what turned out to be pleasant billets in a ruined village called Bouvigny. There were few casualties due to enemy action in the present tour, but poor weather and very unhealthy conditions had had their toll on the overworked line officers: half a dozen officers were reported as being very seedy.

Bouvigny's ruined church, with its crumbling buttresses and blown-open graveyard, created much awe, but there were other attractions in Bouvigny; in the words of Major Powlett: 'Madame Constance looks hot stuff'.[34] One presumes this is the same lady who also impressed Sergeant Downs:

> Standing in an isolated position at the fork of the road leading into the village was an estaminet where the main attraction was a beautiful damsel with the silkiest stockings and the highest heeled shoes seen out of Paris.[35]

During March steel helmets were given out to the men, gradually, rather than all at once. Sergeant Downs remembered reading in a fortnight-old newspaper that every man in France had one, at a time when there were perhaps two steel helmets in the whole of B Company. The men were suspicious of them at first, and it would take some instance involving the stopping power of the helmet before a man would grudgingly admit that they might have some value. 'Olly' Berrycloath could remember exactly the moment when he first had faith in steel helmets. He was in a party of six and they had one steel helmet between them that they would pass around like a piece of unwonted baggage:

> It came to my turn to carry it. We were always arguing whether to carry it or wear it. I decided to wear it. My mate 'Knobby' Knowles was behind me. He nudged me in the dark – there was a dent in the steel helmet where a bit of shrapnel had hit it. That's the best of having lucky 999 for a [Regimental] number.[36]

According to Colonel Barker, Christopher Stone and Major Powlett were thinking of setting up a 'Battlefields Ltd' company after the war:

> They will take a trace of this battlefield, or Cambrin, and make it more realistic. Parties will come up at night and be shelled with puff-balls and have 'Very Lights' on. American millionaires will pay £100 for a night in a dugout, with people thumping on top for shells. Of course the corpses etc will all be there and men wounded etc. Conversation of this sort of foolishness passes the time well.

The Battalion was relieved on the 17th by the Royal Berks without being disturbed by shellfire. Indeed the enemy's behaviour seemed most odd: 'We hadn't a single shell, the machine gun fire seemed to choose the wrong moments.' One wonders whether the front line troops had been ordered to fire but had deliberately elected to miss.[37]

Back at the Bois de Noulettes they found the huts improved. Even so, Major Powlett was suffering from his sciatica, while Colonel Barker had picked up a persistent cough that was threatening to prevent him going on leave. He struggled away four days later, but spent the first five days of his leave in bed. On the 21st the Battalion moved back to Hersin for 'rest', which included sending up working parties to the trenches. Captain Black, censoring or otherwise hearing about a witty letter by Saki, could not resist quoting it himself:

> We are now out of the trenches having a 'rest'. It is reported that some of the men, hearing that Heaven is a place of eternal rest, have renounced their religion.[38]

A real rest was near: Divisional Rest at Ourton, lasting almost a fortnight, began on 27 March. Ourton, just outside the mining belt, became one of the Battalion's most favourite spots. Some fifteen years later, during an Old Comrades Association tour of the battlefields, ex Corporal (of the Signallers) Ernie 'Mac' West found its atmosphere coming back to him:

> *Ourton, that quiet village with its old stone church standing up in majestic glory on the top of a hill and watching with ceaseless care on the collection of humble dwellings, defying the tumult of war to wreck its quietude. Stop here and rest you awhile, it seemed to whisper; enjoy my hospitality and drink deep of my charm but leave your guns and bitter feeling for other places… The stream running between banks coated with spring flowers is as joyous as ever and it brought back to my memory those pleasant hours spent on its bank with Robeson, where we shared the contents of several novels by reading aloud one chapter each.*
>
> *Joyous, peaceful Ourton, the healer of tired nerves, may we ever remember you as such.[39]*

Roland Whipp recalled Ourton and its inhabitants as fondly, but it was where he went swimming in the stream and forgot to take his favourite watch off. Needless to say it never went again. The only creature that seemed unhappy at Ourton was Romp, (lacking rats and bitches).

On the 5th Colonel Barker returned from leave only to find that, owing to Brigadier Kellett's illness, he had to take over temporary command of the Brigade. He did not enjoy it initially, but warmed to some of the advantages, such as being able to billet himself in the biggest chateau he had seen and having a car to drive him around, yet he appears to have made every excuse to go back to the Battalion mess for his meals.

The Battalion meanwhile had made the long journey to Bomy (four miles march to station, train to Aire, then another march of about ten miles) on the 9th, all in baking heat, with Lieutenant Fowler (commanding 6 Platoon, B Company) distinguishing himself by:

> *…carrying rifles and packs of two other men as well as his own. Yet before he attended to himself at Bomy, he inspected the men's feet and saw the cooks about a meal for the chaps. His men would have followed him through fire and water.[40]*

The Battalion machine-gunners were split up at this time. A new Brigade Machine Gun Company (99) was formed which would use the (heavy) Vickers Gun, the aim being to concentrate the firepower of these guns rather than have them divided into penny-packets between the battalions. Lieutenant Grant would move over to command the unit, which would also include Sergeant Jock Martin and twenty-four of the former Battalion machine-gunners. The remaining Battalion machine-gunners, using the (light) Lewis Gun, would become the Battalion Machine Gun Section under Sergeant Lawton.

On 13 April, in the thirteenth hour of the day, Sergeant Downs attempted to go off on leave with twelve others. As he said: 'the coincidence of the numerical strength of the party and the day of the month aroused the gloomiest forebodings'. They spent

Vickers heavy machine gun and Lewis Light Machine Gun.

two frustrating days at Boulogne before being turned back.[41]

The Battalion enjoyed a pleasant few days at Ourton in good weather before going back to the trenches on the 17th. The weather broke while they were on their way. Hurricanes and squalls of rain and hail combined with traffic jams everywhere made this an appalling journey. The only bright spot was the considerateness of the (2nd) East Lancs Battalion whom they were relieving. The latter had improved and even managed to pump out the deep HQ dugout, they had started a library, had left

behind not only candles but also spare ones, plus cans full of water. The Colonel commented:

> *You have no idea how these small things add to our comfort on arrival. You can never find your candles, matches etc and the old candles burn out ten minutes after the departing people. Also the water is always about two miles away so it means sending some poor wretched tired men.*

The Battalion lost about twenty casualties (one killed) in the present tour, the majority being due to a very nasty bombardment on 18/19 April with 4.2" and 5.9" shells on the trenches occupied by C Company.

At Bouvigny 1,000 pipes and 1,000 pairs of socks arrived as presents from Kensington, but Romp 'conqueror of a thousand rats' disappeared – perhaps stolen by gunners.

The Colonel had been greatly distressed by the loss of the twenty or so of his men. He set to work devising schemes in their next tour to cause a few casualties among the Germans opposite (who had been openly working on their parapets at night) by having the guns fire at irregular intervals on the enemy trenches. He did this on the 24th and the German retaliation came back on the night of the 25th/26th (when the 22nd Battalion was spending its first night back in the trenches again) as follows:

> *For some reason the Germans opened a furious bombardment and put a barrage fire behind our line. I have heard nothing like it since the old days at Cambrin. Real big heavy stuff. The barrage often means an attack is coming and it is to stop our reinforcements coming up. My own Regt got it all, but the Hun shooting was hopeless and all the shells fell onto empty fields behind. Not a single casualty. Thousands of pounds worth of shells wasted.*

From hindsight one can see the events as part of a sequence. A Live-And-Let-Live situation was in existence, with specific rules like no firing on front line trenches. There had been transgressions on both sides. This bombardment could be seen as a warning, designed to deter not to kill. At this time 'truce' activities were still continuing on the front of the Royal Berks next door.

While Colonel Barker was away at Brigade HQ, Major Rostron made nightly inspections of the 22nd Battalion trenches:

> *Not to be forgotten was his tall gaunt figure; his very creamy breeches, his almost saturnine cast of features surrounded by a French casque which gave him an almost Mephistolian appearance, with head high trench staff; as he furiously strode though the trenches on his tour of inspection.*[42]

The first DCM won by a member of the Battalion occurred around this time, but as he (Frank Baker, a farmer from New Zealand) had been seconded to the Trench Mortar Battery (forthwith TMB), which left no War Diary of consequence, the incident is not well documented.

Frank Bull also served in the 99th TMB at Souchez. His weapon of destruction was not the reliable Stokes Mortar but 'a French aerial torpedo gun in a dilapidated state' which was situated in an isolated sap between the front and second lines:

This is a frightful weapon of destruction, firing a sixty-pound torpedo which entered the ground to a depth of twelve feet before exploding and made a hole like a small crater. Its chief purpose was the destruction of machine gun posts instead. Naturally Fritz would immediately start searching for it with high explosive shells and eventually they put paid to it, and nearly to us.

Only two were allowed on the gun at a time and I, with an old regular, had just fired at a target that had been given us by an observer, when reprisals begun. Just by the gun was a small dug-out where a store of torpedoes was kept.

The first shell of this particular strafe went over the top. It is surprising how after a time one can sense a 'nasty one' coming. With one jump my pal and landed down the dug-out on our backs and the second shell landed right on top and blew the lot in.

Fortunately one of the beams across the entrance held. We could see daylight and clawed a hole big enough to crawl through, but our gun was out of action for good.[43]

Henry Lea, Baker's previous partner on the gun, believed that Baker won the DCM for digging out Frank Bull.[44]

The Battalion won its first MC at this time and we have much better evidence for this. Lieutenant EC Rossell went out with a patrol of two men on 26 April to reconnoitre a German saphead. It was occupied, a flare went up and he was spotted when he was seven to fifteen yards away from it. The party crept into the nearest shell-hole, which was rather small to accommodate all of them. Christopher Stone was at the Aid Post, the billet he shared with Doc Miller, when Rossell arrived there in the early hours of the morning of the 26th and heard the story first-hand. After the first German grenade had exploded just outside the shell-hole:

The next [grenade] *fell on the edge and rolled down inside; Rossell could only pick it up with his left hand and lay it outside – not throw it, owing to his cramped position and it went off just as he withdrew his hand and laid the back of his hand open very nastily. Of course the hand is extraordinarily painful, always full of nerve centres. He certainly saved his own life and those of his men by his promptitude.*[45]

Stone later received word that Rossell had lost one finger and might have to lose two others, but in a photograph taken when Rossell was celebrating his 99th birthday at his home in South

Lieutenant (later Colonel) Rossell, winner of the Battalion's first MC, pictured here on his 99th birthday. The wound he received to his fingers on 26 April 1916 can clearly be seen

Africa in February 1984, he can clearly be seen to possess all the fingers of his left hand except the index finger, although his wife added that his second and third fingers in that hand were useless to him.[46]

The Battalion only suffered five casualties apart from Lieutenant Rossell during their tour from 26th-29th. One of them was one of the famous Destrubé brothers, shot through the chest and right lung:

> It occurred before sunset and as soon as it was dusk my brother and I carried him back over the top (there being no communication trenches to the firing line). It was for four hours that we struggled along with him before we finally reached a place of safety where we handed him over to the R.A.M.C.
>
> It was with a weary and heavy heart that we retraced our footsteps to the front line. The question of whether he will live or not haunts us day and night, and how will the home folk take it? How strange this all is, this ceaseless conflict. To think that the day my brother was hit I had seen and spoken to a German from the sap end and he had thrown a packet of tobacco over to me in exchange for some cigarettes.[47]

At Brigade HQ Colonel Barker was becoming acutely frustrated by the passive warfare. He could order up the occasional artillery strafe, but infantry action was out of the question. When Brigadier-General Kellett returned on the 30th, Colonel Barker stayed on at Brigade HQ owing to Kellett having to command the Division because of General Walker's illness.

On the 29th Colonel Barker had his hair cut by a private from the 23rd RF; nothing special in this one might think, but: 'He is the head hairdresser at the Savoy and does Phyllis Dare's hair, and all the theatrical people.' Phyllis Dare was of course the famous singer who in 1914 told the Battalion at the White City 'We don't want to lose you but we think you ought to go'.

On 3 May the First Army Commander General Munro presented Private Baker with his DCM at Sains-en-Gohelle, with one officer and thirty other ranks from the Battalion present at the ceremony. On 5 May Colonel Barker received word that he was to stay in command of 99 Brigade for the three weeks it would take General Walker to recover – a signal compliment; as such a long period would normally have been filled by a brigadier-general brought in for the task.

The Battalion returned to the Souchez trenches for what would be their last tour there from the 3-7 May. This was a fairly uneventful stint, with only a handful of casualties, none killed. General Kellett was celebrated for his insatiable curiosity and absolute fearlessness. Both combined to the peril of others accompanying him on his 'rambles' though the trenches. On the 7th he phoned Colonel Barker to request a meeting with him at 9:30 am in the Bois des Noulettes. Bolting down his breakfast, the Colonel dashed off to the rendezvous. An exhilarating if hair-raising experience was in store for him:

> Of course I knew what I was in for when I started my ramble with him, and I took the precaution to send my orderly on, so he would be handy to attend to our corpses. I had to show him the route I had reconnoitred for bringing up the reserve battalion to the

front line to avoid the Barrage [barrage fire on the usual route of reinforcement] *…I told him before we started that he must do as I advised or I wouldn't be responsible for his or my safety. He behaved beautifully, ran when I told him, ducked his head and even crawled. Eventually we got safely into the communication trench. We then went up to the line to visit one of the battalions. From there for the last two months we have been cutting a communication trench on the right and left, to the front line, as at present we can only go over the top at night. We went a long way up the trench on the right as far as had been repaired but he insisted on going to where there was still a sort of trench, which covered half your body. I shouted at him to stop. He said, 'I suppose that trench is our front line', looking at a trench 300 yards away. It was the <u>German</u> front line and I told him that luckily the snipers post had been blown up yesterday by our artillery or he would be dead. He then consented to return. Nothing daunted, he said he would go up the left communication trench, we got up this to within about thirty yards of the support line when it abruptly ceased. I showed him the new support line and explained how splendidly it was getting on etc. He then said, no matter what I advised, wild horses wouldn't stop him going there. It meant a run across the open within 350 yards of the Germans. I told him he must jump up suddenly and go first. He got across all right without a shot being fired. I knew of course if I followed him they would be alert and have go at me, so I waited five minutes and went right back to where the trench took a bend, it meant a longer course but a safer one, as they would naturally have their rifles laid on the course he took. I got almost to safety when some blighter fired and missed me by about five yards. Altogether it was a ripping morning and I feel as fit as a flea after it.*

The Battalion, meanwhile, left Bouvigny for billets at the Tile Factory on the 10th and moved back via Brouay to Cambtain Chatelaine, and on the 15th they began six days at their favourite Ourton. Saki wrote:

We are at the moment in a very picturesque hill-top village where we have been twice before; I had a boisterous welcome from elderly farm-wives, yard dogs and other friends.[48]

Brigade manoeuvres were organised there by the Colonel. Sir Henry Wilson, the Corps Commander, met Colonel Barker while watching one of the battalions practising. The two made a favourable impression on each other, with General Wilson sending the Colonel's name in on a special list of recommendations for promotion to brigadier. The manoeuvres, held on 20 May were: 'a glorious success – quite surpassed anything I had hoped for… If only I could have sold the scheme as race cards it would have provided drink for us all.' The Corps Commander in turn congratulated him: 'Barker, I

Sir Henry Wilson, the Corps Commander.

am very pleased with the show, I don't think it could have been done better'. Colonel Barker then admitted he was now: 'Purring like a pussy. What rot it all is.'

On 21 May the Battalion moved off to Hersin. The men's packs were issued, mail from home was given out and the Padre held a well attended service. Within an hour there was considerable gunfire in the distance, coming from Vimy Ridge on the Battalion's right. Orders were issued for the Battalion to make itself ready to move off in two hours time. Then it was one hour's readiness, then everyone relaxed when the all clear was given. The process was repeated a few times, so that when the real emergency occurred everyone was caught at sixes and sevens. Sergeant Downs had gone off to watch the by now spectacular bombardment, and very pleasant to watch it was for those sufficiently distant from it. He recalled:

> In the darkness it was a deluge of flame mingled here and there with such a variety of coloured signals as to outshine any 'Brock's Benefit' that had ever been staged.[49]

When he returned, new orders for collecting warlike stores had been given, and he was in trouble:

> There was I with no candle, and equipment to find and piece together in the required fashion – and worst of all – late on parade into the bargain.

Of course his absence hadn't been noticed with so much going on.[50] The Battalion paraded in full battle equipment in the by now darkened streets of Hersin. They came across a strange and yet very familiar sight, London buses:

> A fleet of hearse-like motor buses came up, all black and boarded, and with jocular cries of 'Fares Please', 'Pass right along', 'Change here for the Bank', we clambered aboard and jolted off. Whither we knew not, but the bombardment on Vimy Ridge appeared to be consistently drawing nearer. As usual that cheery soul, Dave Cohen, was the life of No.8 Platoon and his flowing mimicry of the cockney bus conductor kept everyone in good spirits. Just as dawn broke the buses unloaded their cargoes and their companies filed into a wood [Bois de la Haie], on the left of the road. Orders were given that no one was to touch his water-bottle, and after a brief respite we moved out in artillery formation to Villers-au-Bois.[51]

There had been a great deal of mine warfare in the northern part of the Vimy Ridge and recently the British had achieved the upper hand. The opposing German commander had evolved and executed a brilliant scheme to capture a few hundred yards of the British front line trenches, affecting the 47th and 25th Divisions, with the British mine shafts as his particular targets. It involved overwhelming firepower: Eighty batteries firing perhaps 70,000 shells on a frontage of about a mile.[52]

Colonel Barker dashed off a note:

> I very happy. Don't worry, all may go well. We are off to the Vimy Ridge. Things there are in a bit of muddle.

1 *Mufti*, Spring 1936, <u>17</u>, No 1, pp-5
2 *CRS*, 19/01/1916, *Sheffield and Inglis*, p41
3 *Mufti*, Spring 1936, <u>17</u>, No 1, p5
4 *Mufti*, Spring 1928, <u>9</u>, No 1, pp 2-3
5 *Ibid*, Spring 1936, <u>17</u>, No 1, p5
6 *Mufti*, Xmas 1935, <u>16</u>, No 4, p10
7 *Powlett Diary*, 22/1 and 23/1/1916
8 *Mufti*, Summer 1936, <u>17</u>, No 2, p8; the cartoon can be found at p21 of *Best of Fragments of France*, Eds T and V Holt, Milestone Publications, 1978
9 *CRS*, 6/2/1916
10 *RBB*, 5/2/1916
11 *Mufti*, Xmas 1941, <u>22</u>, No 99, p7 and Xmas 1942, <u>23</u>, No 101, pp 2-3
12 *Broughshane*, <u>8623</u>, Davison to RBB, 8/2/1916
13 *Mufti*, Autumn 1925, <u>6</u>, No 3, pp 2-3
14 2nd Division War Diary, *WO 95*/1289, Fighting Strengths Summary of 12/2/1916
15 *Broughshane*, Destrubé letters, <u>2534</u> (referring to this or the first tour of duty at Givenchy; the letter simply says 'February 1916')
16 *Mufti*, June 1957, <u>37</u>, No 129, p12
17 *History*, p30
18 *Mufti*, Spring 1928, 9, No 1, p4
19 *Mufti*, Xmas 1936, <u>17</u>, No 4, p11: There Saki (Corporal Munro) and a few kindred souls formed the 'Back Kitchen Club,' whose rules codified the comradeship of the trenches, *Mufti*, Summer 1936, <u>17</u>, No 2, pp 8-9 and Saki, *Biography*, pp 98-100
20 *RBB*, 20/2/1916; JW Wood and Rowe were the two 'snobs' or shoemakers, *Mufti*, Spring 1930, <u>11</u>, No 1, p5
20 *RBB*, 28/2/1916
21 99 Brigade War Diary, *WO 95*/1368, Movement Orders 28/2/1916
22 Interview with ex-Sergeant Roland Whipp, 18/11/1983
23 *Mufti*, Spring 1937, <u>18</u>, No 84, p2
24 *RBB*, 3/3/1916
25 *RBB*, 4/3/1916; Hun regiment: in a later letter he says this is for not being sufficiently aggressive. Also see *PAP* for 'wire' story, WJ P-A to Grace, 6/3/1916.
26 Interview with Roland Whipp, 18/11/1983
27 *Mufti*, April 1920, <u>1</u>, No <u>6</u>, p4, and Summer 1937, <u>18</u>, No 85, p7
28 *Mufti*, February 1921, <u>2</u>, No 8, p3
29 *Mufti*, Xmas 1963, <u>43</u>, No 142, p16; Syd was invited to Paris by the grateful parents, but not able to take up their offer
31 Figures from CRA 2nd Division, March and April 1916, *WO 95*/1317
32 Interview with Olly Berrycloath 15/1/1984
33 *Old Soldiers II* (ex-Sgt Charles Downs, B Company), *Mufti*, Summer 1937, <u>18</u>, No 85, p8
34 *Powlett Diary*, 9/3/1916
35 *Mufti*, Autumn 1937, <u>18</u>, No 86, pp 8-9
36 Interview with Olly Berrycloath, 15/1/1984
37 *RBB*, 18/3/1916; See T Ashworth, *Trench Warfare 1914-18: The Live and Let Live System*, 1980
38 *Mufti*, February 1920, <u>1</u>, No 4, p2
39 *Mufti*, Summer 1931, <u>12</u>, No 2, pp 6-7
40 *Mufti*, Summer 1928, <u>9</u>, No 2, p2 'One of the Machine Gunners' (ie AJL Tottenham)
41 *Mufti*, Xmas 1936, <u>17</u>, No 4, p8
42 *Mufti*, Xmas 1935, <u>16</u>, No 4, p10
43 *Mufti*, Spring 1939, <u>20</u>, No 92, pp 2-3
44 *Mufti*, Summer 1939, 20, No 93, p3; the *London Gazette* citation does mention digging out two men under heavy fire, and bandaging their wounds, despite being wounded himself.

45 *CRS*, 26/5/1916 – a longer version in *Sheffield and Inglis*, p50. See also Colonel Barker's account, *RBB*, 26 and 27/4/1916, in which he says he has recommended him for the DSO and Rossell's own account in the *West Sussex Gazette* [hence WSG], 13/7/1916.

46 Information about Rossell, who died 8/6/1985, from his delightful widow: letters 1984 and 1985. Rossell also appeared on ITV on 4/6/1984 on *This is Your Life*, as the godfather to WW2 fighter hero, Wing-Commander Johnnie Johnson.

47 *Broughshane*, Destrubé Letters, 2534, 30/4/1916.

48 Saki letter, 20/5/1916, *Biography* p92.

49 *Mufti*, Summer 1938, 19, No 89, p9.

50 *Mufti*, Summer 1938, 19, No 38, p 8-9 and also 1920, 2, No 5, p7.

51 *Mufti*, Autumn 1938, 19, No 90, p9 and Autumn 1936, 17, No 3 p 5.

52 General von Freytag-Loringhoven's account in *British Official History, Military Operations, France and Belgium, 1916*, pp 224-226; Nigel Cave, *Vimy Ridge* (Battlefield Europe series), Pen & Sword 1996, Jack Sheldon, *The Germans at Vimy Ridge 1914-1917*, Pen & Sword, 2008.

Chapter Four

Excitement at Vimy Ridge

C URIOUSLY, BOTH SIDES were temporarily commanded by former sub-chiefs of their respective General Staffs: Lieutenant-General Sir Henry Wilson commanded IV Corps, while the German IX Reserve Corps was commanded by General Freiherr von Freytag-Loringhoven.[1]

Von Freytag-Loringhoven's assault began at around 7:45 pm.[2] By all accounts the British defenders hardly knew what hit them. At 9:38 pm 99 Brigade was ordered to go forward as soon as possible by bus and motor lorry to the Bois de la Haie – as we have recounted. An hour later the Brigade was placed under the orders of 47th Division. Gradually it emerged that in the Berthonval Section of the line held by the 47th Division the enemy had taken their front, support and reserve trenches, as well as a small section of line held by the 25th Division in the adjoining Carency section. Counter-attacks launched by these units had failed to drive out the enemy.

Lieutenant-General Sir Henry Wilson.

General Freiherr von Freytag-Loringhoven

Early on the 22 May the Commander of IV Corps, XI Corps and the 47th and 25th Divisions held a conference which resolved that 142 Brigade (the reserve Brigade of 47th Division), 99 Brigade and 25th Division should attempt to regain the ground lost. The attack was to be launched just after the rising of the moon at 1:30 am on the 23rd.

On the early evening of 22nd, Sir Charles Munro (First Army Commander) insisted that the attack be postponed until after dark on the 23rd as there had been insufficient artillery preparation and the delay would allow new troops to familiarise themselves with their surroundings, while the later hour would permit greater consolidation in darkness and extra guns being brought forward. Instead 99 Brigade simply relieved 140 Brigade. Despite Sir Henry Wilson's misgivings about the postponement also giving the Germans more time for consolidation of their gains[3], the counter-attack was re-timed for 8:25 pm on the 23rd. On the 99 Brigade front, the 22nd Royal Fusiliers were due to attack on the left and the Royal Berks to attack on the right, with the 1st KRRC in support and the 23rd Royal Fusiliers in reserve.

We left Colonel Barker in temporary charge of 99 Brigade, with General Kellett having taken over 2nd Division because of the illness of General Walker. General Walker returned late on the 22nd freeing General Kellett. This created a dilemma: where should Colonel Barker best be situated? He was left betwixt and between:

> Gen. K [Kellett] *turned up late night just as we were moving up. He is now in command of the Bde as the Div. Commander has returned, so I am in rather a hopeless position as my orders etc and scheme are to be carried out and I am to remain at Bde Hdqrtrs and to be consulted about any alterations.*[4]

The Germans opposite were doubtless aware of the British reinforcements coming forward and of the new trenches hurriedly dug at night (standing out in daylight because of the disturbed chalk). They would be anticipating a British attack. Their foreknowledge of its time and place was speculated as being due to deserters or spies. It was probably due to good German intelligence work.

The KRRC diary described what happened on the 23rd:

> *The Bosch made a very good 'guess' as to what our intentions were and began an extremely heavy bombardment with heavy percussion shells. They had been shelling fairly heavily the whole afternoon and so had our Artillery, but this was a different kind of bombardment line – they really meant business.*
>
> *Just before we* [i.e. the 22nd RF and Royal Berks] *were due to attack the Germans changed their shells and fired high explosive 6" shrapnel at us, as if they knew to the minute the time of the commencement of our attack. This was the heaviest bombardment of all and one could not see for 200 yards for the whole of our rear was a mass of smoke from the shells.*[5]

One of the 22nd Battalion men described just what it felt like to be in this bombardment:

> *Well, talk about Dante's Inferno, or hell with the lid off: either description would fit. For about an hour or so it simply seemed as if the heavens had opened and were raining pieces of iron, lead etc like a tropical thundershower. In fact, it was not at all unlike one, the roar of hundreds of guns, the bursting of shells of all sizes, taking the place of the thunder, and the showers of bits of metal – the place of rain, and making a constant swishing noise which one could hear about the roar of the explosives. There was a valley* [Zouave] *with one rather steep side near where we were, and high explosive shells simply rained onto it until all one could see was a fog of smoke, with dull red flashed lighting it up all over the place. The ground trembled and rocked from the concussions of the big 'Black Marias' and 'Coal Boxes'.*[6]

All the communications between Brigade HQ and further forward had been down since the 21st. Despite constant attempts by 99 Brigade Signallers to restore wired communications the constant German bombardment meant that this was never achieved. Visual signalling was useless because of the dust and smoke. Wireless contact was valuable to some extent, but the forward wireless masts were continually shot down meaning that although the forward units could sometimes send virtually instant messages to headquarters, Brigade HQ could only send messages to the front by means of runners – who might take up to an hour to get there, if at all. Control of the battle would therefore devolve to the Battalion commanders who, by another unfortunate coincidence, were both second-in-commands taking over temporarily.

Let us return to 99 Brigade HQ. A message, timed at 8:15 pm, came through there and reached General Kellett, after it had been decoded, at 8:22 pm. It was from the acting CO of the Royal Berks and it contained disturbing news: 'Will not attack. Enemy has made barrage on our position. We are suffering heavy casualties.' General Kellett at once attempted to send back a reply to the officer that 'You must capture position.' But worse was to follow. Three minutes later he was handed a message from Major Rostron commanding the 22nd RF saying: 'Will not attack. Shrimp [code for Royal Berks] informs us they will not attack. Enemy are putting barrage on their position.'[7]

Both his attack battalions had apparently refused to advance and the message he sent them: 'Stand fast a short time. Directly barrage lifts arrange with [22nd RF/1st Royal Berks] to attack' – never seems to have been received. It was obvious that little influence could be exerted on the battle from Brigade HQ so Colonel Barker volunteered to go to the front to clear things up. General Kellett gave him full power to deal with the situation as he saw fit. The way forward, of course lay through the inferno. General Kellett commented later on his decision

> …which I directed him to do <u>with great reluctance</u> as at the time he left my Headquarters the hostile barrage was such that it appeared most improbable that he would live to arrive at the Zouave Valley.[8]

Northern Vimy Ridge May 21-23/1916 (from a drawing in the Barnett Barker papers)

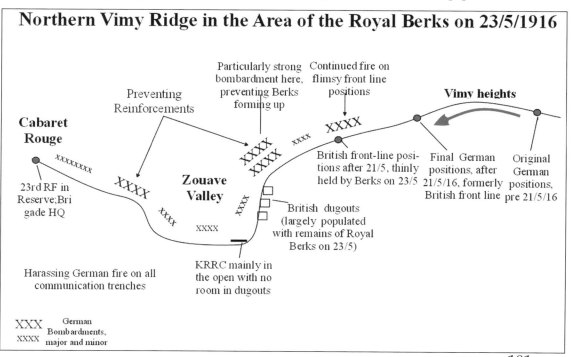

Colonel Barker did survive the bombardment, sending back news of his arrival at 10:30 pm, and later commented that he 'wasn't a bit frightened,' attributing his calm to the effect of his favourite liver pill, Haemoglobin. As to the effect of the bombardment on his companion, Captain Kane:

> There was nothing but the pitiable condition of his companion to show from what an appalling experience he had just emerged.[9]

On their way forward through the communication trench, Barker and Kane encountered a variety of frightened human debris – 'all sorts of parties, ration carriers, wire carriers, pigeon carriers, Brigade bombers etc lying flat on the floor' – who were meant to have reached the front line hours earlier. He arrived at the Zouave Valley in no mood for compromise: the mess <u>was</u> going to be sorted out. He found that the Royal Berks had not left their trenches – had been unable to form up, in fact, because of the barrage – nor had the 22nd RF except for one company (B), which had not received the 'cancel' instruction.

His anger would appear to have been principally directed towards Major Sharpe, the temporary commander of the Royal Berks. His logic may well have been: if the Berks would not or could not attack he would replace them with a unit which would attack, so he pulled the Royal Berks out of the front line and replacing them with the KRRC who were in support, and then reorganised the time of attack to 1:30 am, this time with the 22nd RF and the KRRC attacking.

Later he realised he had been over-hasty, particularly as the strength of the German bombardment seemed to have died down some time after 9:40 pm: if he had left the Berks in place then perhaps the reorganised attack time could have been earlier and that might have changed the course of events.

At Corps HQ the messages coming in were still confusing: units of the 47th Division had apparently attacked successfully at the appointed hour, but with less success at their right, where they adjoined 99 Brigade's attack frontage. 99 Brigade seemed not have launched their attack, but on their right the 25th Division seemed to have got to their objective.

The question was how long 99 Brigade's attack could be delayed for it still to stand a chance of success; the Chief Staff Officer (BGGS) at 47th Division advised that the attack could go in up to the rising of the moon at 1 am, but no later, and if they could not make all of their objectives they were to attempt to occupy the old French trench partway.

At 12:30 am another message was sent off to Colonel Barker that: 'If troops had not started attack by receipt of this message, then they were not to attack.'

Fortunately for all concerned Colonel Barker then received the 12:30 am message and managed to cancel the attack. In order to thin out the front line before daylight he relieved the 22nd RF by the Royal Berks, with the relatively fresh 23rd Royal Fusiliers being retained for carrying parties. He then returned to Brigade HQ, reaching it at 2:30 am and was kept there for some twelve hours going over the events of Friday. Later it was learned that the 47th and the 25th Division attackers had been driven out of their gains – the only people who had captured ground and left it without the enemy ejecting them was one company of the 22nd Royal Fusiliers, but we shall come to their story in a moment.

While the German Corps Commander, von Freytag-Loringhoven was able to return to his desk at the end of May with a notable success under his belt, the whole affair had been a rather humiliating one for Sir Henry Wilson. Troops under his command had lost perhaps 300-600 yards in depth along a front of around three quarters to a mile in length; the attacks made by the troops under his command had failed. A certain amount of Wilson's anger was directed at General Munro for his 'interference' on the 23rd (postponing the time of attack) and on the night of the 23rd/21st (stopping any further attempt by 99 Brigade). He was also annoyed with General Kellett for keeping Colonel Barker (in whom he had, from his diary, a good deal of confidence) back at Brigade HQ, and a great deal of his venom was directed at both Sharpe and Rostron. Indeed his diary – no doubt written at the height of his anger and disappointment –

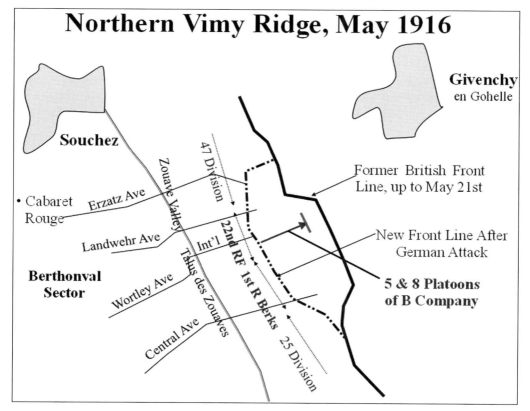

Where two platoons of B Company attacked on the 23rd May, unsupported on either side

uses the word court-martial in their regard.[10]

Major Sharpe explained he had held the front line with only a few men and sent the rest back under cover of the side of the hill just east of the Talus Des Zouaves earlier in the day in order to reduce casualties. Unfortunately, this meant he had stranded most of his men the wrong side of the German curtain fire. His company commanders made two attempts to form up, but after having the attack platoons almost wiped out, the company commanders personally came back to him and begged him to call off the attack, as it would be sheer murder.[11] Major Sharpe's decision certainly affected the 22nd Royal Fusiliers as, although the Brigade orders specified that 'the 22nd R.Fus. to direct,' Major Sharpe was senior to Major Rostron and thus Rostron may have felt obliged to conform to Sharpe.

With the benefit of hindsight, we can see that Rostron's decision was a blunder: the

Sergeant Downs (the Battalion's PE specialist) was involved in the Vimy Ridge attack with 5 and 8 platoons. Here he is with some of his B8 men.

Royal Berks were prevented from advancing on one side of the 22nd Battalion, but equally important was what was happening on the *other* side. Unfortunately, the lack of effective communications with Brigade HQ deprived him of any other guidance. Rostron seems to have been suffering from nerve strain at the time and was gassed sufficiently badly to be taken to hospital the next day. He therefore fades gradually from our story, remembered with affection to his terrific stammer, his great help to the Battalion in the early days in France, his dog Romp and his air of dignified urgency as he strode through the trenches on his tours of inspection.

The greater irony was that after the 8:25 pm attack was cancelled, runners took the message to each of the 22nd Battalion's companies; that going to B Company was wounded and gave his message over to a Lewis gunner (believed to be Corporal Starling of D Company). H E Harvey of 8 Platoon dramatised it as follows:

'What the ___? Who's that? Are you hit chum?' The reserve Lewis gun Corporal stooped down to the huddled figure.

The wounded man, a runner from Brigade HQ, slowly raised a blood-soaked arm, his hand tightly clenching a crumpled and besmirched scrap of paper.

'Rush it along chum,' he pleaded. 'O.C. B Coy – Stop 'em. Attack's off.'

He dropped back unconscious.

The gunner dashed off with the written message and reached the newly made trench. Save for some poor torn corpses, it was empty.

At the top of the ridge he yelled 'B Coy – Retire.' It was a forbidden word, but the shriek and crash of missiles drowned his voice.

He must fetch the boys back. But a Boche bullet found a precious billet and the gunner dropped. The only line of communication with B Coy had snapped.[12]

So 5 and 8 Platoons of B Company, with no support on the right (where the Berks would have been), or on the left (where the other company of the 22nd Battalion would have been), went forward alone. Sergeant Downs was Platoon Sergeant of 8 Platoon. He recalled getting his orders from Captain Banbury at around 8:00pm. Downs returned to his platoon:

Magazines were recharged with 'one up the spout', equipment was readjusted to allow a spade or a pickaxe to be thrust behind the haversack, handshakes were exchanged, a few jokes cracked and then 'zero' hour, 8:25pm.

'Over you go', came the command; someone said 'God loves you all' and B Company rose over the pitifully low parapets and

sailed off into the blue.

Simultaneously the crash of the German barrage fell on the newly vacated trenches and spraying machine guns swept the lines as the ridge was topped.

There was a little bunching which was corrected by a warning shot, the line straightened out still bearing half right, it thinned and bore on.

The first trench, pounded almost level, was crossed and then the objective, lit up by the flashes of detonating shells and the multi-coloured rockets, became visible in the quickly gathering gloom.

The last few yards were covered with a rush and the handful of survivors leaped into the enemy's trench only to discover that their foes had withdrawn.

The first task of the attackers was to prepare for an immediate counter-attack by the Germans:

The task of consolidating was begun, blocks were established right and left, fire-steps hastily recovered and a count of the garrison was taken. It was twenty-six all told. Anxiously they waited for support. None was forthcoming.[13]

Undoubtedly a great number of others been driven into shell holes partway over, eg Sergeant Walker, 5 Platoon:

Contact was lost. I found myself in a prepared position in the side of the ridge which offered fairly good cover from the main barrage. The night was pitch black – I could not see any other living soul. When I saw a reflected dim light coming up from a dugout, armed with a Mills Bomb I was relieved at a friendly answering call from those down below, where I found Captain Banbury, together with some of No.5 and 6 [8] Platoons and some poor devils from the London Regiment.[14]

Captain Banbury had been wounded about half way over. Lieutenant Fowler, who had taken over command from him, had suffered a very severe wound further on – a letter from Colonel Barker to his parents stated that it was 'almost within thirty yards' of the German trenches, while 'his conduct was most gallant and his leadership perfection.'[15]

The command at the front therefore devolved on Lieutenant Gregg. Signaller Dodson was sent back to get support and to report on their progress. On his way back Dodson encountered Captain Banbury and was instructed to tell Company HQ, according to Sergeant Downs, 'I have obeyed orders. There is nobody on my right or left.'[16]

When Dodson reached Company HQ he found 'Doc' Miller there. According to his orderly Lance-Corporal Metcalfe, Doc Miller:

Went berserk for a little and when he recovered barked at me, 'Get a rifle and bayonet, Metcalfe, and come with me.' I obeyed, and we trudged over to the German line and there was B Coy.[17]

Miller and Metcalfe safely – but not without hazard – reached the captured section of the German trench where Lieutenant Gregg was in command. Miller and Gregg then had a 'long and acrimonious discussion,' according to Metcalfe, the essence of which is easy to deduce: Gregg was not at all keen to retire from a captured position while Miller was undoubtedly telling him that he would get no support and the position was therefore hopeless. Eventually Gregg was convinced of the good sense of withdrawal and he ordered the party back to the British lines.

Miller and Metcalfe then began wandering No Man's Land succouring the wounded. Metcalfe's own rendering of it is typically modest and self-belittling:

He [Miller] barked, 'Come on Metcalfe', and we began to trudge back in the same direction – but our attention was claimed by numerous wounded men, for whom we did what we could, patching them up and getting them away on stretchers…

On the way back, Doc Miller's language to German troops, who could not possibly have heard it – every time a bullet went by – had to be heard to be believed.

Miller, Metcalfe and their other helpers managed to account for all missing men – a feat rarely achieved in a major action under fire and made more hazardous by the approaching dawn.

Sergeant Walker's account continues:

We returned in sections (very depleted sections) through that inferno, taking shell hole cover, we came across Lieutenant Fowler fatally wounded and stayed with him for a while. But our orders were to retire and it was every man for himself with a run like hell to the next shell hole. My attempt resulted in being blown back into the hole with a shattered right leg and a bang in the shoulder. I shall always be grateful to L/Cpl Dunkley who stayed and did what he could for me.

Dunkley got back and made his report. In due course the stretcher bearers came and carried me back – although we were a sitting target we were not fired on.

The Battalion was then relieved by the Royal Berks and sent to the rear; to the Bajolle-Maistre support line. Many of the men, exhausted after three nights of little or no sleep:

…fell asleep on the floor of the firesteps just as they were, without bothering even to eat – now of course it is raining and the poor dears will be soaked through. It's heartbreaking what they have to put up with.[18]

Later on the 21st they moved further back to billets at Villars au Bois, on bare boards in their clothes, and to Camblain L'Abbé on the 25th.

Harry Van Tromp was one of those who lost their lives in the Vimy Ridge affair

Colonel Barker was most proud of his boys. On the 21st he reported to his wife:

The rest of the regiment was in a state of mutiny after not being allowed to go after B Company. Weren't they all splendid? I knew they would be. We lost about 130 men. The doctor behaved in a most gallant manner and I have recommended him for the VC. Tell…[presumably Major Powlett] about my splendid B's. We were the only regiment in any of the divisions who got there [a pardonable exaggeration – some of the other units had reached their objectives only to be driven out again] and if only – I won't put it down, it sickens me, we should probably have cleared about 700 yards of German trench and kept it…I then arranged to attack it again at 1:30 a.m. We should have been absolutely successful as the doctor returned from the German trench at 1.00 a.m. with our wounded and said they were unoccupied but – to my bitter, bitter disappointment – I got a wire from the Corps to say I wasn't to advance. Doubtless they were right as dawn is about 3.00 a.m. so we mightn't have had time to consolidate. Anyway my gallant regiment has come out of it splendidly and everyone is talking about them, fellows arriving up from 20 miles behind the lines.

L-Cpl Harry Rosewarne, the OCA's printer after the war. Loyalty and conscientiousness streams from every pore. *(Mufti)*

General Kellett told the Battalion on the 21st that it had saved the honour of the Brigade and General Walker also had some kind things to say about them. When Colonel Barker returned to the Battalion after his grilling at Brigade HQ later on the 21st, he 'led them out company by company' and 'had a good talk with all of them.' 'Lad Broke' recalled that talk:

Some of us saw him weep at Vimy Ridge. He was acting Brigadier on that ill-fated occasion. He was 'BB' when, his voice vibrant with pride, he told us some of the secret history of that day, and what <u>his</u> battalion had achieved.

'Everyone knows the 22nd Battalion,' he declared and we did not cease to thrill even when some ignorant soldier was heard to enquire the following day as we marched by 'what blinking mob's that?'[19]

The Battalion had indeed won its spurs, but at what cost? The Colonel's original estimate of 130 was revised downwards and the final tally seems to have been three Officers wounded (one fatally), seven other ranks killed and seventy-eight wounded. The officers were Captain Banbury (leg), Major Rostron (gassed) and Lieutenant Fowler (who was to last only a few more days). Among the wounded were

Sergeant Downs and Sergeant 'Bully' Stadden (their old drill Sergeant).[20]

As far as the casualties of the other units in 99 Brigade were concerned the Berks were originally thought to have 110 but this was later reduced to seventeen killed, fifty-eight wounded and three missing for the week ending 27 May, while the KRRC had two officers wounded, seven other ranks killed and forty-three wounded up to and including 21 May, the 226th Field Company RE (some of whom went over with B-Company) had suffered about forty casualties and there were a small number from the Machine Gun Company and Trench Mortar Battery.[21]

Other men in the Battalion had been casualties, however, but had not wanted to miss any action, as the Colonel related:

> *Did I tell you that fourteen of our men concealed their wounds for two days till they were absolutely sure there would be no more fighting? Wasn't it splendid of them? A special report has to be made on it, as I believe there has been no similar case in this war.*

Doc Miller did not get his VC but instead received a well-earned DSO, with Lieutenant Gregg receiving the MC. The Colonel was also put forward for the DSO. Four DCMs were awarded to B Company men for their exploits: to Sergeant Fisher (for organising a defensive flank in the enemy line and for guiding back his party by the stars) and Sergeant Charles Wheeler (for carrying out two risky reconnaissances after gaining the enemy line and for guiding Captain Miller around until all the wounded had been brought in). We have already described Lance Corporal Metcalfe's exploits and the fourth DCM was won by Private George Webb who remained with his wounded Sergeant (probably Walker), dressed his wounds under fire, and despite being himself wounded in the chest went off himself to seek stretcher-bearers for his sergeant, refusing all medical attention until he had been attended to. Details of MMs won here are less readily available but Lance-Sergeant Freddie Gent and Private Percy Cannot (the Cartoonist) were both awarded the MM around this time.

In the following days both Sir Henry Wilson and Colonel Barker were still keen to regain their honour. GHQ decided that it was not worth the effort, particularly as the guns which would have been required were needed elsewhere, as part of the artillery build-up for the major British attack on the Somme.

The Battalion moved back into the same trenches on 26 May for a four-day stint. It was a quiet time, in dry warm weather, with only about a dozen casualties in all from the continuing artillery duel, but the loss of the mine shafts and the skimpy nature of the new trenches created considerable uneasiness. Colonel Barker described the atmosphere as charged with electricity, adding that it was like living on top of a volcano. The men worked like Trojans, he said, on consolidating their position. On the evening of the 27th, for example: 'Everyone but the sentries are digging and wiring'. Lance-Corporal Rosewarne was one of those guarding the nightly working parties. He left a memorable impression

> [He] *would attire himself in his ground-sheet draped over this shoulders in the form of a Cavalier Cape, fastened in front with a bit of string, and always wore his tin hat at a most rakish angle. I enjoyed the sight of him thus presented, through many a night."*[22]

During the stint in the line the Battalion was at last reinforced with officers (twelve – plus 150 other ranks). The new officers were a mixture of the young and green – and the not-so-young. Some doubts were cast on the stamina of some of the older ones for trench warfare. The latter were encouraged to show their mettle by volunteering for the more hazardous assignments. One of the new (older) officers was Ralph Durand. He tells the story of his initiation with the Battalion:

I was sent out with Captain Gell [D Company Commander; Durand was to command 13 Platoon] stomach-crawling to inspect the German wire on Vimy Ridge. The enemy spotted us and in the darkness that followed the Very Light we scuttled into a big shell-hole and stayed there until Jerry had tired of slinging bombs at us. I had kept my eye on the North Star all the way across no Man's Land and as it was I who guided the patrol back to our front line, Gell could not conscientiously say, as 'BB' had hoped, that I was too old for my job. That is why I was allowed to stay with the Battalion.

Barnett Barker told me this himself one night at dinner.[23]

Most of the Battalion casualties had been on the last day, due to German retaliatory fire for a bombing attack carried out by the brigade on their right. Captain GDA Black of C Company, one of the originals from the White City, described the horrifying results of this German retaliatory bombardment. Two of the three men to die were killed instantly but:

I went up to the place and found this chap with an arm nearly off and a huge hole in his side. He was perfectly wonderful in his cheerfulness. Although he must have been suffering agonies, he never lost consciousness and talked and laughed away all the time. His first words to me were 'Oh, I am all right sir.' When the Doctor was taking the remains of his arm off he said, 'Oh yes, chop it off, it's no good to me? Our medical officer, Miller, has been out here since the beginning of the war and said he had never seen anything like the bravery of this man, Whitlock in C Company. They took him out of the trenches but he died later in hospital.[24]

Meantime Lieutenant Fowler had lost his struggle against his wounds and had died 1 June. As he had been the first of the Battalion's officers to die, his death cast a gloom over the officers and the men of his company. In a letter six years later, his mother wrote movingly about him:

I heard from many men in my son's company after he died by they told me very little news. They chiefly said how much they loved him and what a splendid officer he was. I knew he would be, as whatever he did, he did as well as he possibly could. He did not like the Army, but from what I've heard from Col Barnett Barker (as he was then), plus Captain Banbury, he was a good soldier. He was a Schoolmaster by profession, would never be anything else and loved his boys and they loved him.[25]

On 30 May the Battalion moved back to the support line and then on 2 June the Battalion moved off for eight days rest at a village called Estrée Couchie. ('Extra Cushy'), but it was all too soon back to the front line on the 10th (at Carency, where the Royal Berks were on the 23rd). Colonel Barker, paying an early visit on the 6th, was particularly unimpressed that the Colonel of the battalion they were due to take over from did not seem to know where the Germans were:

> I shall now have to send out at least three officer's patrols when we arrive so as to locate his wire and his position. It's perfectly beastly for those wretched subalterns going out on patrols, I know my nerves would go in a couple of nights. Gell, Roscoe and young Black say they thoroughly enjoy it. They should really all get decorations. They carry their lives in their hands every time and have to be awfully cunning. Their reports too are absolutely reliable. As they are about the only three old officers left in the regiment I can't risk them now.

The Battalion had a miserable time going into the new line in a violent thunderstorm with the ground turned to chalky mud, with the steep slope making progress very difficult. As was often the way, the anticipation was worse than the actuality, and the trench stint was a relatively uneventful one apart from bitterly cold weather and the Battalion moved back to billets at Villers-au-Bois where Captain Black was disgusted at the accommodation which awaited the men:

> At the end of April they took away one of their two blankets, which was fairly sensible, but now they have taken away both. I do wish the men on the Staff who gave these orders had to do like our fellows. Fancy coming in dead-beat and soaking wet after four days in the trenches to come back to sleep without any covering in an absolutely empty hut with a mud floor, not even any straw! Yet we officers are allowed to take about as many blankets, clothes, food etc as we want to.[26]

Saki managed to get on leave, which his sister remembered as 'delightful' and as 'passing with lightning speed'. She recalled her parting words to him at Victoria Station as being 'kill a good few for me'.[27] Alas, these words only showed the great divide in attitudes to the enemy between those at the front and those on the home front. Roland Whipp remarked to us: 'The safer you were, the more you hated them'.[28]

On the 17th the Battalion returned to the front line Carency trenches for five days. The weather was very warm and pleasant and both the Battalion and the Germans opposite appear to have opted for enjoying the sunshine rather than for more martial pursuits – at least for the first day or two. Claude Upton:

> It was sometime after the fiasco of 23 May, we were doing normal trench duty, the weather was very hot and in the valley a mine crater had filled with rainwater forming a very inviting lake for a hot day.
>
> It was very peaceful as 'Jerry' was possibly dozing in the afternoon heat. Someone suggested a bath – it seemed an ideal opportunity for a good wash.
>
> With cries of 'mind the wire' the crater was soon filled with naked figures. It may have been the noise that wakened 'Jerry', or just a routine 'straffe', but suddenly over came the shrapnel – the pool emptied and every man rushed for his 'tin hat'. There they were, everyone felt perfectly safe with his 'tin hat' on – although otherwise in the nude.[29]

The trench tour was however to end in tragedy. On the 21st Captain Black was hit and killed by a rifle grenade on an otherwise quiet day. For Black, who had many times risked his life on raids or wiring parties and had survived because of his own skill and cunning, to be killed almost at random, minding his own business so to speak, seems difficult to accept even now.

Black's company commander Captain McDougall, who had been standing in as second in command of the Battalion until Major Harman arrived, was numbed by the event:

> My best subaltern, as fine a boy as every breathed was killed ten days ago. I haven't quite realised the fact yet, he was unconscious throughout – which was sad. His expression was more pure and serene than any dead man's I have seen – touched as it were with immortality. We buried the boy quite close to the line amongst the men and I think all is well with him and the Bosch gave us about fifteen minutes for the service and then the machine guns spattered all around and we had to get off.[30]

The Battalion moved back to support trenches at the Talus des Zouaves from the 22nd to 27th June (where they received their new machine gun officer, Lieutenant Pimm), then moved back to not very comfortable billets in Maisnil Bouche where, on the 30th June, Sergeants Wheeler and Fisher were awarded their DCMs. Meanwhile Colonel Barker had learned that his recommendation for an immediate DSO had been rejected.

Christopher Stone, now promoted full Lieutenant, had been looking forward all June to leave, only to have his hopes dashed just a day or two before he was due to go. As he had suspected, all leave had been cancelled due to the imminence of the big push: the Battle of the Somme. On the 1st July, the first day of the battle, Colonel Barker wrote:

> Another lovely day, by now you will have heard that the 3rd and 1st armies have broken the German line on about a ten mile front. They appear to have taken the front line and are held up on what we call the village line. They have penetrated about 1,000 to 2,000 yards. This is very good news but of course one know nothing of the intention. It may only be to create a diversion to take the pressure off Verdun and also to prevent the Huns sending any troops from here to Russia. Or – it may be the Big Push. I can't somehow think it is unless the Hun is very much weaker than we thought. In the meanwhile our job is to hold the Germans on our front and stop them sending any of their troops to resist our main attack.

On the 2nd Colonel Barker had heard more news, but the full picture was still not clear:

> They seem to be hung up a bit in the big attack. The reports are so complicated that it's difficult to understand the exact situation. We have gone to Montauban and from there have thrown out a defensive flank to join up with the French. Apparently we are held up at a very strong position at Thiepval so the Montauban lot are attacking due north now to capture the place in flank.[31]

Nowadays we view 1 July as one of the largest setbacks ever suffered by the British army; there were 57,000 British casualties on this day, one third of them killed, against perhaps 8,000 German.[32]

Only on the right wing of the British attack (around Montauban and next to the French) did the assaulting units gain (and keep) their objectives. Almost everywhere else along the line there was a tale of disaster: of uncut wire despite the nine day bombardment, of the Germans emerging from unforeseen deep dugouts to mow down the advancing British, many of whom had been told that they would merely have to stroll over and occupy the German lines as the artillery would have destroyed all resistance. Now we can see that the tactics were inappropriate, the enemy's strength and resilience underestimated and the intelligence faulty.

On 4 July, perhaps having heard more about some of the setback on the 1st, Colonel Barker was feeling pessimistic. At this time, however, the Somme was a battle far away for the Battalion, which moved into Berthonval Trenches on 5 July, 1916, amid thunderstorms, with heavy rain creating a quagmire in the trenches.

The Colonel's spirits were soon restored by a priceless practical joke played by Stone and Doc Miller on the Padre:

Did I tell you about S.J. [St John] and the hedgehogs? We are always pulling his leg and S.[Stone] and the Doctor with whom he lives are constantly playing practical jokes on him. Most nights he finds a hairbrush in his sleeping bag. The Doctor found two of the most priceless hedgehogs I have seen, almost as big as cows. He bought them to my headquarters so I suggested SJ's bed was the place for them. On coming to bed he sat heavily on one of them which squeaked. He turned back his blankets and in the dim lights thought it was a hairbrush and put his hand in to pull it up. The result is obvious. He was frightfully cross, saying he had come back for eight days rest and this was what happened night after night etc. He then got into bed and put his toes on the other one at the bottom of the bag. This was the limit. The Doctor and Stone were sympathetic and said that evidently the female hog had somehow got into his bed and the male had followed. Curiously enough he more or less believed the story!

On 6 July a party of 22nd Battalion men went out on patrol; not being allowed to raid the enemy, they contented themselves with cutting the enemy wire and gathering information – otherwise 'stirring Fritz up a bit' – leading to Captain Gell, in charge of the party, being recommended for the MC as his efforts had been seen by the Colonel:

He was on patrol with about twenty men and the Hun opened a very heavy machine-gun and rifle fire. I happened to be in the fire trench about fifty yards away and just met him coming in from No Man's Land – the firing certainly was very heavy. Two of his men were hit, so he made all the rest crawl back and saw them safely home. He then went back with a Sergeant to the wounded men. One he found horribly hit, so he and the Sergeant tried to carry him back. The man was hit twice on the journey and killed. This is really only in the ordinary day's work, and if I hadn't happened to be there, should never have heard about it.

General Walker then sent Colonel Barker a letter of thanks for his valuable information and patrolling in the vicinity of Angel Avenue.[33]

On the 11th they attended a concert arranged by Sergeant Jamison. News of it reached the *West Sussex Gazette*: 'The old 'Fusiloil' khaki concert party that delighted many Horsham audiences during the 'Fusilier' period is still going strong in France.' It included songs by Captain Adams, Corporal Jack Jones and Reverend St. John amongst others, while Corporal Markie received an ovation for his Lauder-esque ditties. Sergeant Claude Upton was well to the fore with a monologue, while Lance-Corporal Jackson and Pivate Tremayne scored with an amusing sketch, but:

> *Private Horrocks gave a demonstration what a tough proposition a 'Royal Fusilier' must be to his enemies by allowing himself to be trussed up with strong cord by a member of the audience and placed in a sack, and successfully escaping from this trifling embarrassment within five minutes. So, dear old Horsham, your 'Boys' are keeping their battle cry well to the fore, 'Always merry and bright.'*[34]

At Camblain L'Abbé the Lewis Gun Section was reorganised with two extra guns being added, Brierley becoming a full Sergeant and Hennessy a Lance-Sergeant. Eight of the gun-commanders who were still privates were made (unpaid) Lance-Corporals. The two Destrubés after having been snipers and bombers at one time, were now Lewis Gunners and one of these two popular rebels had to take a stripe. Their response was characteristically unconventional. First there was the matter of who should get the stripe:

> *The Colonel one day on his rounds in the line noticed the L/Cpl and said, 'Hello, Destrubé. Splendid! I see you have a stripe,' and knowing what one did the other did too, added*
> *'Has your brother also a stripe?'*
> *'No sir,' replied Destrubé.*
> *'How is that?' asked 'BB'.*
> *Destrubé said: 'Well Sir, it was like this, a circumstance arose whereby it was essential that either my brother or I took the stripe, so we tossed for it'*
> *'Ah!', exclaimed 'BB', 'and you won?'*
> *Destrubé answered in a very mournful tone: 'No sir. I lost!'*[35]

Guy was the one who had been obliged to take the stripe so his brother Paul kept a close eye on him:

> *Each day I marvel at his change of attitude towards promotion and a smile flickers across my 'mug' when my eyes catch sight of his coat sleeve. My brother and I are with the machine guns and the stripe on his arm only really designates him as a gun commander and not as a red tape artist.*[36]

On the 13th it rained, of course, as this was the day that the Battalion were due to go back into the Berthonval trenches, but there was some compensation in the arrival of 1,000 new shirts from Kensington.

More important, however, from the point of view of the war, was the exciting news of the success further south. This was General Rawlinson's bold pre-dawn attack (3:20 am) on 14 July, carried out after only the briefest of bombardments, which surprised the Germans almost along the whole attacked front. The troops were able to cross No Man's Land before the Germans had risen out of their deep dugouts, while support troops followed up closely behind the initial attackers to prevent them being shot from behind. Many lessons had been learnt since 1 July.

Although the British had pierced the German second line over a wide front, High Wood was still controlled by the Germans. Fierce attack and counter attack continued on the right wing of the British lines at Longueval and Delville Wood, where the 9th Scottish Division could not quite hold onto the village and the wood. Part of the 9th Division was the South African Brigade. Obeying an instruction to take and hold Delville Wood at all costs, they captured all but the north-western corner on 15 July. For the next few days there were constant attempts by many German units to recapture the wood and by the South Africans to capture the whole of it. Gradually the South African numbers were whittled away and a fierce counter attack by the Germans on the 18th drove them back to the southern parts of the wood. When the South Africans were at last relieved late on 20 July and the roll-call was called next day, only twenty-nine officers and 751 men remained from an original strength of 121 officers and 3,032 men before they went into the wood. The South Africans could not have done more, but other hands would have to pick up the torch.

On 13 July the 22nd Battalion began an abbreviated stay in the Berthonval trenches, then started moving backwards on the 15th, arriving in Dieval on the 18th.

On the 20th the Battalion caught a train for Longeau (south-east of Amiens), then a sixteen mile route march awaited them to take them to their destination, Morlancourt. The march was a most gruelling affair on a baking hot day as Colonel Baker wrote:

> Think of the poor men after seventeen [actually nine] *months of trenches to take on a march with soft feet etc etc. It was a bit of a nightmare. It was horribly stuffy hot. I have at last realised what a big battle is* [like]. *The main road we marched along was never for one moment free from motor lorries, ambulances, motor cars. I assure you, for the sixteen miles I never once breathed a breath of God's good air. It was one dust cloud. Poor poor men. They struggled on most gamely…we sha'n't be fit to fight for 48 hours.*

The Battalion arrived at 9 pm and only four men had fallen on the march – a fine performance and one that was praised by General Kellett. Doubtless stout fellows like 'Saki', who had carried other men's rifles, had aided the men.[37] Morlancourt was just a few miles behind the old British front lines in the Somme area. They were now in the area of XIII Corps, commanded by Lieutenant General W N Congreve VC[38] a well-respected commander notable for careful husbandry of his troops, and the most successful Corps Commander on the 1st of July. The South African Brigade was under his command, and some of the 22nd Battalion remembered seeing the remnants of them returning after their bitter sojourn in Delville Wood. The 'Devil's Wood' as it was called, was a tough nut, and it was to be 99 Brigade's next major task.

1 See Keith Jeffery, *Field Marshal Sir Henry Wilson: A Political Soldier*, OUP, 2006, pp 162-7 for a very fair summary of the politics and the damage done to reputations on the British side

2 IV Corps War Diary, 21/5/16, *WO 95/713*

3 *Diary of Sir Henry Wilson*, IWM, 21/5/1916, thereafter *Wilson Diary*

4 *RBB*, 23/5/1916 (~4.00pm)

5 KRRC War Diary, 23/5/1916, *WO 95/1371*

6 *WSG*, 20/7/1916: author not specified but probably a B company man

7 99 Brigade Narrative from 8 30 pm 22nd to Noon 24th May 1916, *WO 95/1368*: The original message before coding and decoding was somewhat less peremptory: *"Royal Berks inform me, they cannot attack owing to shellfire. I am therefore standing fast."*

8 *RBB* Papers, General Kellett's DSO recommendation for Colonel Barker

9 'B.B.', Christopher Stone, p29

10 *Wilson Diary*, IWM 23/5/16 et seq.

11 99 Brigade War Diary, 24/5/16, *WO 95/1368*.

12 *Mufti*, March 1920, Vol 1, No 5, p7 This was Harvey's first rendering of the story. He elaborated it slightly for his book *Battle Line Narratives* published in 1928

13 *Mufti*, Summer 1939, 20, No 93 pp 6-7

14 *Mufti*, Summer 1962, 42, No 139, pp 6-7

15 *WSG*, 20/7/1916

16 *Mufti* Summer 1939, 20, No 93, p 6-7.

17 *Mufti* Summer 1962, 42, No 139, pp 7-8. Miller had also armed himself with a rifle.

18 *CRS*, 24/5/1916; longer version in *Sheffield and Inglis*, p52

19 *Mufti*, Oct-Nov 1921, 3, No 2, pp 7

20 *Mufti* Spring 1939, 20, No 62, p6, Spring 1937, 18, No 84, p10, Summer 1942 23, No 100, p6.

21 Casualties from the 2nd Division A&Q War Diary, *WO 95/1307*, KRRC Diary *WO 95/1371*, 22nd RF War Diary *WO 95/1372*, 99 Brigade Diary *WO 95/1368*.

22 *Mufti*, June 1956, 36, No 127, p11

23 *Mufti*, Xmas 1938, 19, No 91, p5

24 *Ibid*; Black had come fresh from Bradfield College, where he had played Apollo in *Alcestis* because of his Greek God looks

25 Letter written 15/2/1922. *Documents concerning the Writing of the History of the 22nd RF Battalion* – IWM, Dept of Printed Books. Fowler, in his 29th year, from Oatlands Chase, Weybridge was an Assistant Master at Sandroyd School; *The Times*, 10/6/1916, *The Surrey Herald*, 9/6/1916 and 7/7/1916

26 *Mufti*, February 1920, 1, No.4 p2, Black letter 6/6/1916

27 *Saki*, Biography p93

28 Interview with Roland Whipp, 18/11/1983

29 *Mufti*, Summer 1966, 45, No.147 p8

30 From McDougall's last recorded letter in the *Victory University Review* 10th July, 1916, *PAP*; also see *CRS*, 22/6/1916, *Sheffield and Inglis*, p57

31 *RBB* 2/7/1916; hard to tell if and how much he was censoring his letters

32 Martin Middlebrook, *The First Day of the Somme*, p264

33 Probably referring to Captain Gell, but also to the work of other officers and men in the Battalion

34 A J L Tottenham remembered the sketch as: 'Pte Jackson as a waiter and Teddy Rutland [otherwise called Rutherford] as the chorus girl customer' – *Mufti*, Autumn 1928, 9, No 3, p4; *WSG*, 3/8/16; *Mufti* May 1921, 2, 11, p4 and July 1921, 2, No.13 p3

35 *Mufti*, Autumn 1933, 14, No.3, p iii

36 *Broughshane*, 2534 Destrubé Letters, 20/7/1916

37 Saki, Biography p100 (Spikesman's memoir)

38 General Congreave's son Billy (also a VC) died on 20 July, the day that the Battalion arrived in Morlancourt. See Terry Norman's The Hell They Call High Wood, p 151

Chapter Five

The Devil's Wood and Hebuterne

O N SUNDAY 23 JULY the 22nd Battalion moved forward to the Sandpits (alias Happy Valley). Colonel Barker explains:

Here we are, bivouacked on the battlefield… We are just below the crest of a slope and if you walk about 300 yards you can see the battle in full glory. That is to say as much of a modern battle as there is to see. I don't know, nor does anyone when we move up to do an attack. It might be this evening or not for a day or two. We are just handy, on the premises for any eventuality.

Many men looked back on these days at the Sandpits with great affection. It was the quiet before the storm. Sergeant Claude Upton left this description:

You remember the old order to 'scatter', well without any orders the Batt. scattered in every direction and in a very short time the place looked like a huge 'ant-hill' with men running about with boxes, doors, sandbags full of sand, sheets of iron, lumps of wood and everything with which it was possible to make any kind of shelter. In less than an hour a fair size village had sprung into existence, the men having formed into parties. My party had a 'bon little shanty', the sides of full sandbags supporting the roof and ground sheets. The back was made up of boxes, one making a fine cupboard, another we used as a table and he inside we made more homely by decorating with picture postcards. Here for two days we spent a very enjoyable time.[1]

On the previous day, all the battalions in the brigade had been given an inspiring pre-battle speech by Brigadier Kellett whose theme was that they were the British Bulldog, which, when it fastened its teeth into anything, would never let go again.[2] Many of the men were taken by his other metaphor, that the NCOs were shepherds and the men sheep, and that if the shepherd was killed then the men should seek another leader, so many of the Signallers' shelters had names like Sheep Pen and Shepherds Rest.

On the evening of the 23rd Padre St John preached an excellent and well-attended service, using two packing cases for an altar and a blanket to shield the candle from the wind. Christopher Stone described it thus:

The Padre in cassock and surplice moving around the crowd of nearly 100 men. It was rather moving and I was glad I had the chance of going.

Colonel Barker couldn't wait to examine the trenches taken from the Germans on the first of July: why were the British successful here, in particular? It did not seem as if the trenches had been bombarded any more efficiently – which meant that the success was down to something else:

One read in the paper of the marvellous effect of our bombardment but it didn't seem to me anything approaching what the Germans did to our front line at Souchez and Vimy Ridge. There they absolutely levelled the ground. The deep German dug outs seem quite to have escaped, but I suppose our advance was so quick after the bombardment lifted that the Hun was caught down there.

Ever the professional, he looked forward to the challenge: 'You know how I hated not being in this big battle and now I have got my wish.'

On the 24th at 8 pm the Battalion moved forward again. They were now occupying trenches just beyond Montauban, recently wrested from the Germans. Battalion HQ appeared to have been a German general's dugout, and it was complete with wallpaper, muslin curtains, mirrors, bookshelves and even a sleeping room with its own air vent to the surface. Unfortunately, one or more heavy shells burst among C Company men, killing five with nineteen wounded. At a stroke that company lost four of its best sergeants, including Sergeant Wiles and Sergeant Farley. Sergeant Wiles's father had only recently heard about the death of another of his sons, serving with the

The area between Montauban and Delville Wood
(From Frank Mumby's 1917 publication: *The Great World War*, part xvii)

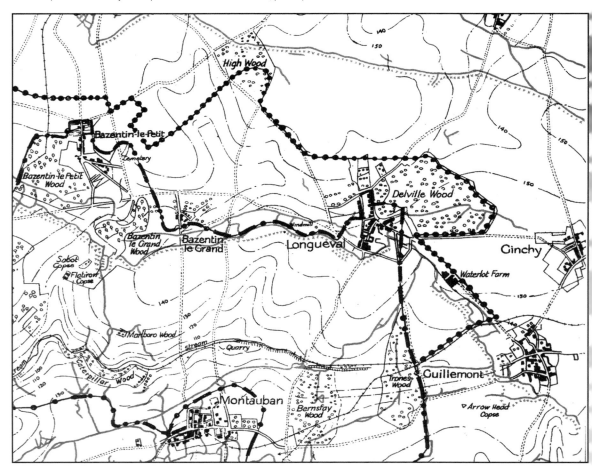

Ruins of Montauban Church following its capture 1 July 1916. Men of the Kensington Battalion passed through this village on their way to Delville Wood. (Taylor Library)

South African Brigade at Delville Wood, when he received the following letter from Captain Alan MacDougall:

> I regret, more than words can express, that I have to tell you of the death of your son, Sergeant G. B. Wiles of the Royal Fusiliers. He was killed on July 25th, near the front line, and death was instantaneous. Your boy was one of the bravest men I have ever met, and showed an utter disregard for his personal safety when his duty was to be done: and his example of coolness heartened up men in countless times of danger and hardship.[3]

Sergeant Bob Farley was one of those mortally wounded. On the 31st Captain MacDougall told his father:

> I liked your boy from the moment he joined my company and I did my best to promote him. Lately as you probably know I made him a Sergeant; and no one deserved promotion better. He was always cheerful, always willing and his ability was above what one looks for in an ordinary sergeant. He was one of those rare NCO's who have ideas of

Two French casualties from the 1914 period buried by the Germans in Delville Wood.
(From *An Der Somme*, courtesy EB Furmston)

> *their own and good reason for having them. The officers liked and trusted him, the men loved him.*[4]

The letters are an eloquent testimony to the personal characteristics of all three men – Wiles, Farley and MacDougall.

On the 25th the Battalion's second in command, Major Harman, was sequestered to command the defences of Montauban, while A and B companies moved forward to relieve a Scottish battalion from the 35th (Bantam) Division, for men smaller than the army's minimum height requirement of five foot three inches. Claude Upton found them rather wild:

> *The trench we finally got into was very narrow and was then held by a lot of untamed Scotch Bantams whose language it was impossible to understand, and after about 10 minutes we gave up the attempt and were glad when they cleared out and left us in complete charge…During the visit of the Scotch gentlemen they had cut in the side of the trench shelters for themselves, and although they had offered fair cover for them, they were of course too small for we big Englishmen, and it was owing to this fault that we had our first [13 Platoon] casualty, Sid Rogers, who had crawled into one but found it too small and started to make it larger, a lump fell on him and broke his collar bone. This of course meant a Blighty for him.*[5]

Gunfire was incessant and was not confined to high explosive: on the 26th the

Germans sent over a nasty combination of tear gas and phosgene gas shells. Gas delivered by shells was still a novelty for the Battalion, as Claude Upton tells:

> It was a very dark night with heavy damp mist and a fairly strong cold breeze, and exceptionally quiet. Suddenly we heard a shell coming. It landed with a dull thud. We both remarked 'That's a dud'. They continued to come and we both wondered what they were, they could not all be duds. Were they something new? that might send us to sleep, or would the last one explode them all? ...It was absolutely silent, except for the hissing sound made by the shells.[6]

Fortunately the wind was strong enough to keep the gas moving on.

The 26th was also the day Colonel Barker got news of the big operation. The plan was simple. Delville Wood and Longueval village (to its left) were to be taken – and held – 'at all costs'. All the artillery from two Corps (X111 and XV) were to be made available for the task. 5th Division (from XV Corps) would attack Longueval village and the western outskirts of Delville Wood. On their right, 2nd Division was to take almost all of Delville Wood.

Within 2nd Division, 99 Brigade had been selected to take the wood, with 15 Brigade doing the honours in 5th Division. Within 99 Brigade, 23rd RF (on the left) and the KRRC (on the right) would do the initial assaulting, beginning at 7:10 am the next morning, with the Royal Berks following up in support.

Each of the two assaulting battalions would attack in two waves, with each wave involving two companies side by side. The first wave would go over at 7:10 am and take their first objective (along the ride called Princes Street, about midway through the wood), while the artillery lifted to pound the second objective and the second wave formed up in the old British front line. An hour later the artillery would lift onto the third objective, while the second wave passed though the first wave to advance to the second objective (about as far ahead as the first objective had been from the original front line). This second wave would then pass onto the third objective, close to the northern edge of the wood, thirty minutes later, when the artillery lifted to the northern approaches to the wood, to try to prevent any reinforcements from the north. At each stage troops would work feverishly to strengthen their positions and defend them against counter attack. To aid them, all four companies of the Royal Berks would advance with the second wave, along with three sections of the 99th Machine Gun Company, two sections of the 1st East Anglian Field Company RE and a section (four guns) of the 99th Trench Mortar Battery.[7]

The 22nd RF had a much less glamorous role: A and B companies were to be used as carrying parties at the behest of Staff Captain Allfrey, while C and D companies would be kept back at Bernafay Wood as Brigade Reserve under Colonel Barker, along with a section (4 guns) of the Trench Mortar Battery.

An overwhelming bombardment of every gun that could be brought to bear – 369 of them – started promptly at 6:10 am on the 27th. Philip Gibbs dramatised the event only slightly in the *Daily Telegraph*:

> I am told that the concentration of guns for this morning's bombardment secured the

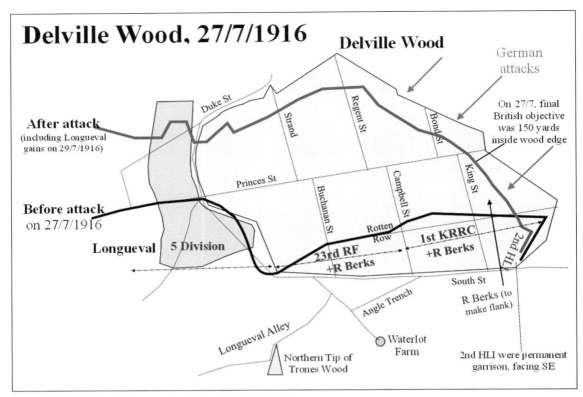

Delville Wood, 27/7/1916

Delville Wood

German attacks

On 27/7, final British objective was 150 yards inside wood edge

After attack
(including Longueval gains on 29/7/1916)

Duke St

Strand

Regent St

Bond St

King St

Before attack
on 27/7/1916

Princes St

Buchanan St

Campbell St

2nd HLI

Longueval   **5 Division**

Rotten Row

1st KRRC +R Berks

23rd RF +R Berks

South St

R Berks (to make flank)

Angle Trench

Longueval Alley

Waterlot Farm

2nd HLI were permanent garrison, facing SE

Northern Tip of Trones Wood

Delville Wood: the attack of the 27th July 1916.

most intense series of barrages upon one position since the battle of Picardy started twenty-seven days ago. …Our batteries over an area of several miles, from the long-range heavies to the 18-pounders far forward, flung every size of shell into this 'Devil's Wood' and filled it with high explosives and shrapnel, so that one great volume of smoke rose from it and covered it in a dense black pall.[8]

The leading battalions in 99 Brigade moved out into their jumping off positions a few minutes before 7:10 am, in order to keep a straight alignment along their lines.

Then the barrage lifted and the troops were off. The barrage had done its job only too well: they encountered horrific scenes of dead and dying Germans, with others pitifully coming forward to surrender, or fleeing off northwards. A few showed some resistance, but not enough to hold up the attacks. Both battalions had reached their first objectives by 7:15 am (KRRC) and 7:19 am (23rd RF).

The next waves set off for the second objectives just before the artillery lifted at 8:10 am. The KRRC again stormed ahead. Because resistance had been light on their front, they pushed onto the third objective at 8:38, reaching it at 8:50, and began to dig in to make a line 150 yards inside the northern edge of the wood to defend against attacks from the north and north-east. Meanwhile one of the duties of the Royal Berks company in support on the right wing of the KRRC was to make a defensive flank to defend against attacks from the east. This flank was also about 150 yards from the (eastern) edge of the wood.

The 23rd RF encountered problems, however. A machine gun firing over from Longueval caused casualties. It was soon knocked out, but the big problem then became heavy fire coming from an unexpected redoubt right in front of them. It resisted their attacks until Colonel Vernon, the battalion commander, sent forward more men and two Lewis gun teams. The latter, plus some bombers, managed to work their way around the flanks of the redoubt. The 23rd then stormed the redoubt with the aid of a party of 1st Norfolks from the rightward attacking battalion from 15 Brigade. The redoubt turned out to be a sort of quarry concealing three machine guns and possibly a field gun (removed), with a considerable garrison, some of whom were killed in the assault, but somewhere between twenty and fifty were taken prisoner and sent back with the Norfolks.

The 23rd RF now moved on to take their second and final objectives around 9:40 am. They then began to consolidate fifty yards inside the northern boundary of the wood, before pulling back a little to conform with the KRRC line. They also had companies of the Royal Berks in support, the leftwards one of which prepared strong points to protect the left flank of 99 Brigade's advance.

On the left 15 Brigade had encountered much stiffer resistance, with many undiscovered machine guns and un-pacified strong points. They had made some good progress, especially on their right where they were in Delville Wood in contact with the 23rd Royal Fusiliers, but had not managed to complete the capture of the orchards at the northern end of Longueval.

99 Brigade's first task had been to occupy the wood. The second, and much harder task, would be to hang onto these gains, as Delville Wood was a position that the Germans were particularly reluctant to give up. It was a salient, a great boil jutting into the German lines, with the KRRC positions vulnerable from the north right around to the south-east. This second task would suck in almost all of the 22nd Battalion.

At 9 am the Germans swept the wood with heavy shell fire. Half an hour later the KRRC reported German forces massing for counter-attack north of the wood, with other forces dribbling up men to the edge of the wood on the eastern flank, looking for weak spots in the British line. They found a wide space between the KRRC lines in the north-east of the wood and the defensive flank set up by the Royal Berks. The Germans cleverly sneaked men between the defences and bombed in seventy yards of British lines. The KRRC counter-attacked and regained about forty yards of this, losing considerable men doing so.

Meanwhile the Germans attacked from the north, and much close-quarters (fifteen yards range) fighting and bombing went on for some hours, but the KRRC managed to hang on despite damp SOS rockets: a pigeon did get through to Brigade HQ with their request for more bombs. Help began to arrive from a variety of sources: the 23rd RF sent over bombers, the Royal Berks supplied bombers and discovered a cache of 100 boxes of bombs and thirty boxes of ammunition that had lain undiscovered since previous attacks in the wood, the 2nd HLI were generous with bombs and

Delville Wood, a little later than the July battles (20 September 1916), but showing the great devastation. (Taylor Library)

ammunition, 6 Brigade supplied a variety of materiel, while 5 Brigade commander sent along two companies of the 17th RF.

Carrying parties from the 22nd Battalion (originally A and B companies, but augmented by one of the two companies in Brigade Reserve at Bernafay Wood because of the increased demand for re-supply, amid the great difficulty of getting anything forward through the German bombardment) had also arrived by mid-afternoon. The last of the Brigade Reserve – about 100 men of C and D companies from the 22nd under Captain Gell – went up to reinforce the south-east part of the wood in the early afternoon. At one time even the engineers and sappers of the 1st East Anglian Field Company RE – there to help create strong-points and defences – were believed to be manning a section of the line. Colonel Barker was obliged to watch all the forces under his command sucked into the battle until no one was left.

Almost everyone had to go up Longueval Alley:

It was here you saw war in its most terrible aspect, it was one continual death trap. It

was here most men were lost; on all sides and at every yard, shells burst, and every shell claimed its toll. There were men alone, in twos and threes, even in larger parties. At times it was difficult to tell if they were sleeping naturally, or the sleep from which they will never awake. Added to this the smell was such that for days afterwards it was not possible to forget. Even when miles away you could still smell it. From beginning to end you were dodging shells of every kind and every minute you had to make way for S.B.s [Stretcher Bearers] both our own men and the R.A.M.C. At one point there was a wounded man on a stretcher with both the bearers dead. All along the trench were 'funk holes' and in many were men in the act of taking cover, gripping their rifles, their eyes wide open, but dead they looked like wax.[9]

Sterling service was also given by the 99th Machine Gun Company, many of whose guns were pushed right up into the front line, where they were very effective, but also very vulnerable – six of the 11 guns were put out of action during the day's fighting, while about 60% (82 out of 138) of its other ranks and 8 out of 9 officers became casualties. Its CO, Captain CB Grant, an ex-22nd RF man, and friend of Christopher Stone, was 'here, there and everywhere, helping everyone, unperturbed, and as cool as ever',[10] siting his guns and organising their firing, until he used up the last of his personal nine lives.

Many men have a premonition of doom before a battle. For Grant the premonition had been so strong that he had requested communion from Padre St John, who related the incident many years later as part of a sermon:

'You will remember,' he suggested, 'our machine-gun officer Lieut. Grant. He came to me in the field before we went into Delville Wood.

'He had just come out of the C.O.'s headquarters and asked me to celebrate the Holy Communion with his men.

'As we were walking across he said: 'This is my last. This is the end.' If you remember, it was the end.

'But I recall the way he said it. There was no cringing, no whining, no trying to escape or get out of it. It was his duty, and he was going to lead those men as he had led them so often before.'[11]

We can see where the focus of the attacks was from the scanty diary left by the

Pte. W. A. Darrington
25247. "C" Coy. R. Fus
-22nd
Missing 27th July /16. at
Delville Wood.

In February 1920 his mother was
still seeking information about
his death, but in Delville Wood
many a man was simply blown to
pieces and left no trace.

machine-gunners: the three guns in the centre of the KRRC line (No 1 Section) fired off 17,500 rounds (an enormous amount). No 4 Section, in reserve with its four guns, had been very quickly sent up to reinforce the KRRC on the right flank and appears to have been firing 'continually,' while No 2 section (just one gun) fired off 2000 rounds in support of the Royal Berks on the right wing, before running out of ammunition. In contrast, the three guns with the 23rd Royal Fusiliers (No 3 Section) fired off just 600 rounds.[12]

Major Lewis in the 23rd Royal Fusiliers' regimental history described how the 23rd was easily able to deal with tentative frontal attacks, but that casualties really became heavy later:

Then the Hun artillery got busy on the wood, which was of course, an ideal mark. For the rest of the day they simply poured heavy shells in. It was pretty terrible. Trees were torn up by the dozens, and fell blazing. By the end of the day there was nothing but shattered stumps.[13]

The German strategy on the 23rd Royal Fusiliers front was clear: wipe them out by shellfire.

The 23rd were eventually relieved by the 2nd South Staffs (6 Brigade) in the late afternoon. Legend has it that they strolled out jauntily smoking German cigars and feeling (justifiably) proud of themselves: perhaps this was true, but only after they had left Longueval Alley a long way behind!

Companies from the 17th RF (5 Brigade) and 17th Middlesex (6 Brigade) managed to get through in the early evening, albeit with heavy losses, and began relieving the exhausted KRRCs and their variegated bands of helpers.

We know much less about what happened to the 22nd RF on that day. We know that Captain Gell of the 22nd RF did good work with his 100 men from C and D companies defending a strong-point in the south-east of the wood. Some of those involved in carrying parties duty made several trips back and forth, while others were simply pressed into service in defence of the line as soon as they arrived. Later, Captain Walsh rounded up the last of them and took them into the line. This force probably also served on the eastern or south-eastern side of the wood. Only a few men of the Battalion remained at Bernafay Wood to stuff bombs and ammunition into sandbags. Because their deeds occurred in such widely dispersed areas, the achievements of these small groups were imperfectly recorded, as in the 99th Machine Gun Company, where there was no one left to put men forward for medals.

A number of Battalion 'characters' became casualties that day. Second Lieutenant WA Murray (the golfer) got his second wound, this time a bullet through the shoulder.[14] Corporal Jimmy Markie, one of the leading lights of the Fusiloil concerts, was killed by a bursting shell. One of his colleagues wrote:

> Poor Jimmy Markie, one of the cheeriest and best. It seems so hard to realise he has gone west. He used to sleep next to me in the hut and stood next to me in the Platoon, and we never met in the canteen without having one together and drinking to old B Coy.

Other well-known names included Corporal Harry Haddock (13 Platoon's first fatal casualty) and Lance-Sergeant Lawton and Corporal Wharton (with the 99th MGC) both killed.[15]

There was much unrecorded heroism by the ambulance drivers:

> They brought the cars up as far as they could and calmly waited for them to be filled, although shells of every kind were bursting around, more than one car came through hell, only to be blown to pieces when they reached their goal. The work done by the R.A.M.C. and our own stretcher bearers was wonderful. All day and all night they kept on backwards and forwards into the front line, they carried on their grand work treating friend and foe alike.[16]

Private Farnsworth, who served with the Battalion transport, recalled making six or seven trips up to the wood carrying materiel. His most vivid memory, however, was of finding hidden treasure in the wood: about a dozen Maconochies (tins of stew). He was shortly afterwards blown up by a shell 'near Waterlot Farm' and evacuated back to the UK.[17]

If one had a Blighty wound, and survived the journey back across the Channel, one could end up in a hospital simply anywhere. Private Farnsworth, for example, told them that he was a Londoner, but was sent to a hospital in Scotland. Private Jack Isaacs, on the other hand, couldn't believe luck when he ended up in a temporary military hospital right opposite his house in Horsham.[18]

The 22nd Battalion was relieved on the night of the 27th-28th, but not everyone got out then. Because the British lines in the wood were often no more than scattered holes in the ground in a landscape of tree stumps, it is little wonder that parties of men were undiscovered for days. This particularly applied to Lewis gun teams, thus Buff Whitehouse remembered that he went in with a Lewis gun and 10 gunners and came out two days later with just 4 men. HV Wilkinson, J Petchey and RH Rogerson were part of a group (from B Company) that spent two days without water – which included seeing a man come to bring them rum being blown up by a shell not 10 yards in front of them. The three mentioned above were later awarded MMs.[19]

HV (Jim) Harrington and George Guyatt turned up long after they had been marked down as missing. They had gone through a particularly gruelling time, without food or water for more than 48 hours:

> They had been on fatigue taking trench mortar bombs up the front line. The officer in charge refused to let them come back and they 'went over' in the 'first wave'. At one time

they were very hard pressed. The officer having been knocked out leaving only a corporal. He was on the point of giving up, but Private Guyatt took command. They were in an isolated position but managed to hold on, and in the end came out 'on top'. Both were recommended for decorations.[20]

Private Harrington added a few more details when writing a thank you note to Miss Peake of Horsham for one of her famous food parcels:

My pal and I got separated from our company and eventually found ourselves in a small advance post with a few of another batt. As they had suffered several casualties we had to stop and help them for 24 hours, and while there repulsed a counter-attack. A whole line of the Huns came for our position and tried to bomb us out. Thank goodness we managed to send them back by rapid-firing at them. It might interest you that my pal and I were recommended for Military Medals for this. All our pals had given us up as lost so were glad when we turned up again.[21]

AJL Tottenham, then aged 46, was finding trench life hard but determined to stay and do his bit with in the Lewis Gun Section. He had been given the slightly softer job of cook and 'Quarter bloke'. He was the star of the story of *Tot and the Tea*:

Tot conceived the idea of taking hot tea to 'the Boys' and having filled two petrol cans with the precious beverage, he started off with them slung across his shoulders with the ubiquitous sand-bag. All along his route he was hailed by thirsty men for a 'sup' but it was for his boys, and no one else had a look in. By sheer tenacity he found the different teams and delivered to each his just due, it was near daylight when he returned to his quarters having travelled all night. It was indeed a great exploit.[22]

Now in Tot's words:

When I reached my gunners at last and delivered my two cans, there was from all those recumbent figures a cheer that made the journey seem worthwhile.

One would never have guessed, to look at them lolling about there, that Gerry was barely sixty yards away and quite likely to counter-attack at any time.[23]

On the 28th, two companies of the 22nd Battalion were in the old British trenches in Delville Wood (later going all the way back to Montauban), while another was in support lines much further back (level with the northern tip of Trones Wood). The other company had drawn the short straw: Longueval Alley.

Ralph Durand had a pretty uncomfortable time there on the night of the 27th-28th:

For part of the following night we sat huddling against the side of the road dodging H.E. and wishing that the dead horses in the neighbourhood did not smell so high. Then we moved off to some newly-dug trenches, a hundred yards or so from the north-west corner of the wood [Trones Wood].

Soon afterwards the Huns got the range of our trench. The first news I got of it was that I was buried in loose earth. I found that a high explosive shell had fallen in the next bay smashing it flat, killing Sergeant Keene and five other stout fellows.[24]

The shell that killed Sergeant Frank Keen may also have been the same one that killed Private Cuthbertson.[25] He was one of those privates with an extraordinary background that the Battalion seemed to attract. Well educated, he did further engineering training in Hungary. Although the army made use of his engineering skills from time to time, and he taught the German language to volunteer classes of soldiers, it is extraordinary to see him still allowed to serve his time as a private. A few days later Colonel Barker was standing opposite a prisoner: 'Quite a nice Hun was captured last night. I wanted information from him very badly but no one could speak German.' Alas, no Private Cuthbertson.

On the 29th C and D companies went right back to Bund Trench (behind Montauban), while A and B companies joined Major Harman in the Montauban defences. There was one notable casualty. Everyone remembered (Private) 'Dad' Grover, a man of considerable age, turning up to training in the early days at the White City in his Rolls Royce and chauffeur. He could easily have found a cushy job, but stayed in the ranks as a stretcher bearer. While the others were only too glad to leave the Wood behind, Dad Grover volunteered to stay behind to help a wounded man. As 'Crippen' (probably Ralph Durand) commented later in *Mufti*:

> Thus a man who throughout his army career never looked like becoming a soldier, when the time came gave his life caring for his comrades.[26]

A Battalion roll-call was taken on the 29th. The Battalion was now down to eighteen officers and 400 men. A few days later it would be back up to eighteen officers and 449 men when stragglers came in. On the 27th it had lost one officer killed (Captain Grant),

A rather fanciful depiction of BB rearranging the defence of the Wood that appeared in the *Daily Sketch* in October 1916

and four wounded, with twenty-six other ranks killed, plus 143 wounded and twenty unaccounted for. This gives five officers and 189 men in total. As the total casualties in the brigade were forty-five officers and 1,119 men for all four battalions and other units like machine gunners and sappers, the 22nd had certainly contributed their fair share for a battalion that was supposed to be in reserve.

Nevertheless, because the 22nd had been in reserve, they would be the lead battalion in the next show. That was to come sooner than they thought: on the 31st Colonel Barker wrote:

> We go up into the wood tomorrow night, I am in command of it and don't relish it one atom. According to captured documents the Huns are massing for a strong counter attack. It's about due now. Of course if they want the Wood they will take it, they only have to withdraw their infantry from their trenches near the Wood and then turn on all the artillery they have and simply obliterate it. Hope the fancy won't take them during my tour there.

This would be for three nights, later reduced to two; meanwhile Captain John Walsh had gone down with a high fever after his exploits in the wood. The first thing that Colonel Barker needed to do was to go up to the Wood and do a proper reconnaissance of all of it. He spent all of the morning of the 1st August in there, at great personal risk. Sweeping changes were needed:

> The present dispositions of British troops in the Wood are to my mind nothing more than xxxx and if the Hun wants the wood he could walk into it, I am altering all this, I shall have the most anxious 48 hours of my life as I should feel it an everlasting disgrace to lose it.

Essentially he reorganised the defences so as to be:

a. Focused on firepower: (12) Lewis guns and (8) machine guns (the remnants of 99 Brigade Machine Gun Company were released to his command), with a minimum of vulnerable human beings (the 22nd RF, with the 23rd RF in support), and

b. A joined-up force, where the left and right flanks were in touch with each other rather than scattered remnants, randomly situated[27]

A and D companies were in the front line, with C Company at the south-east end of the wood and with B Company in support. The 23rd RF were back in Longueval Alley. Getting into the wood proved extremely difficult; first A Company were heavily shelled, then the relief of the 1st Kings Liverpools – apparently badly shocked by their experiences in the Wood – was not completed until dawn.

Corporal Roland Whipp recalled returning to the Battalion on this day, and having a torrid time:

> I got about a third of the way in…this wretched shell came over and absolutely 'puckered' us – that'll pay me for missing the first show, I thought … After it settled down the youngster opposite me – sitting as close as you are – was still sitting there, but I couldn't get a word out of him. He was shell-shocked.[28]

Whipp, who had the great benefit of being able to control his fear, tried to comfort the boy, only to receive the sudden retort: 'You don't feel anything anyway.' 'Didn't I, by George!' he responded and his account continued:

And then I found a miner from Clipstone way – probably recruited from there – who got his —— blown off – the details don't matter – and he got hold of me, strong in his death he was, yelling out for mother and yelling out for me, in turn…and I couldn't get away from him, I hadn't the heart to, he was holding me so tight. Of course he died – his insides were outside…

The people being relieved…it was almost panic. I mean they were going out the right way but rushing out… I saw a scoop the Germans had probably made. It went back probably eight feet into the side. I saw a young officer chap… at the farthest end, whimpering… I went up to him to try and get him out… He was tucked away in the corner and I was urging him, 'Pull yourself together' and suddenly I heard a charge like a herd of buffaloes coming along.

A German attack had intervened; this was beaten off by a party from the unit being relieved, a crowd of whom then crashed down in front of the scrape, trapping Roland Whipp and the terrified boy. Eventually the other troops left, but the boy still refused to go and Whipp had to leave him behind. He summed up his experience: '…All this had happened and I hadn't even been an hour back in the line.'

Next morning Colonel Barker spent another four hours touring dispositions in the wood. Despite the extreme peril he was in, he preferred this rather than being cooped up overnight in an overcrowded filthy dugout that had not been cleaned since the Germans had departed, listening to incessant shelling.

Indeed 'Shelling was more or less constant all day and night' was the understated comment in the 22nd RF's War Diary for the 2nd August (one officer, Lieutenant Holmes, wounded, seven other ranks killed and sixteen wounded). There had been attacks by the Germans:

They made a weak attack last night but covered it with tremendous artillery fire. Fifty Huns advanced shoulder to shoulder against our trenches. Doubtless they didn't exactly know their position. It was quite light, at 9.15 p.m. Our fellows waited until they got within fifty yards and then mowed them down with six machine guns and rifle fire. Another party crawled up at the same time to within fifteen yards, they were obliterated with bombs. At 2.45 a.m. another party of fifty came quite close up and shouted out. 'Don't shoot, we are "wirers".' We shot all right and got three prisoners and fifteen corpses.[29]

Sergeant Brierley, one of the Lewis gunners, was put forward for a DCM for his work in repelling one of these attacks. Tot asked him what he had done to deserve it. It was of course bad form to boast:

'Well, to tell you the solid, honest truth, old man,' he said, 'I'm hanged if I know. There was an alarm in the night that the Germans were counter-attacking and we all blazed away like mad. There was a deuce of a row and schemozzle, and we were supposed to have repelled a counter-attack. But not one of us saw a Gerry the whole time.[30]

In contrast, Delville Wood was where Saki (Lance-Sergeant Munro of A-Company) was gaining inspiration to write parts of his Birds on the Western Front:

At the corner of a stricken wood (which has had a name made for it in history, but shall be nameless here), at a moment when lyddite and shrapnel and machine-gun fire swept and raked and bespattered that devoted spot as though the artillery of an entire Division had suddenly concentrated on it, a wee hen-chaffinch flitted wistfully to and fro, amid splintered and falling branches that had never a green bough left on them. The wounded lying there, if any of them noticed the small bird, may well have wondered why anything having wings and no pressing reason for remaining should have chosen to stay in such a place. There was a battered orchard alongside the stricken wood, and the probable explanation of the bird's presence was that it had a nest of young ones whom it was too scared to feed, too loyal to desert.[31]

Meanwhile someone else had been prospecting every day in the wood: Christopher Stone. The incessant shelling meant that the telephone wires were constantly being broken. Stone was in there all day on the 1st repairing breaks, a job he could have delegated to more junior staff. He repeated this on the 2nd. When the big German attack came, the Colonel was able to get in touch with each of his companies. Colonel Barker put him in for an MC, explaining to Mrs Stone that:

He was out last night under a heavy artillery fire, so intense that a Regt which we had relieved wouldn't go back home, and waited until Dawn. He was careering about in the Devil's Wood with a coil of wire on his back amongst corpses and had a horrid time. He really is a very great success and is as brave as a lion.[32]

The 3rd August was a similar day to the 2nd; high in tension but with fewer casualties, just seven other ranks wounded. German artillery eased off from about 11 am. It seemed the Battalion had got off lightly.

There was just the small matter of getting through the relief. A and D companies were lucky to escape at midnight, but B and C companies did not manage out of the wood until 7 am. The problem was that a neighbouring unit was going to be attacking in Longueval at midnight. The enemy seems to have anticipated this attack and attacked the 22nd in Delville Wood at 9:20 pm, putting down a barrage on British rear areas, including Longueval Alley, that stopped many of the battalion's relieving units getting forward.[33]

Unfortunately the commander of C Company, Captain Alan MacDougall was killed by shellfire in the early hours of the morning when the Germans attacked again, and just after he had scrawled 'relief complete' but not yet added his signature, with CSM JE Evans[34] also killed by the same (trench mortar) shell. Altogether seven other ranks were killed and ten wounded during the night: a final reminder just how lethal the wood was.

The Colonel was very upset by MacDougall's death:

Oh this beastly, beastly war, MacDougall was killed three hours before we came out. He was absolutely my best officer and one of my best friends. It knocked me quite over and I can't get over it. I am trying to get his body brought down tonight... I hate to think of him lying amongst the carnage, so I hope they will succeed tonight. He somehow knew

The beginnings of the cemetery at Delville Wood. (IWM Q100768)

it and I found he had left a letter behind for me.

Teams were sent up to the wood three times to look for Captain MacDougall's body. Private Ollie Berrycloath remembered being on one of the unsuccessful missions (probably on the 4th August). On the 5th Doc Miller went back into the wood with a team of stretcher bearers and spent the whole night tending wounded and searching for MacDougall. At length he recognised a boot sticking out of the ground, and arranged for MacDougall's body to be brought back for a service on the 6th, attended by General Kellett amongst others.[35]

For the Adjutant, Captain Adams, who had served with MacDougall right from the Inns of Court Training Corps days in 1914, the loss of his friend had been a particularly bitter blow. He was delighted to be able to write to MacDougall's family to say the body had been found and properly interred.[36]

The Battalion moved back via Bund Support and Mine Trench to bivouacs east of the Citadel area (and west of Carnoy), well behind the lines and out of range of all but the largest guns. In the next few days they would move further and further from the lines.

A stack of mail was waiting for the men in their bivouac areas, as Lance Humphries describes:

Among the pile for the B Company Lewis Gunners was a parcel for Doug Colbeck, already on his way to Blighty and as usual this was divided among the gun team, but it contained a pipe which several of us coveted. A well-worn pack of cards was produced – highest cut first pick – and I cut the King of Clubs. Buff Whitehouse also cut a king so we shuffled and had another go. My King of Clubs came up again and I had the pipe.[37]

The pipe would have a charmed life.

Captain McDougall, a very conscientious officer, and great friend of Major Adams.
(detail from group photo in Phythian-Adams papers)

Despite Major Harman having returned to the Battalion, it was very short of officers. Sergeant PW Fisher and CSM GH (George) Evans were promoted from the ranks to become 'Subs,' while Captain BF Woods, last heard of in E Company, was loaned to the 22nd from his present placement in the 23rd RF. Reinforcements from the 27th RF (now based in Edinburgh) began to dribble in with the arrival of six non-commissioned officers, followed by drafts of thirty and forty other ranks.

The Battalion's total casualties for the period between 24th July and 6th August were one officer killed (not counting Captain Grant) and seven wounded, plus fifty-six other ranks killed and 203 wounded, a sizeable proportion of the Battalion, even if it had been at full strength. Such large numbers meant it was impossible for the Colonel to write off to the family of every man. A new post-battle system was begun whereby the list of casualties was sent as soon as possible to Mayor Davison. The latter then attempted to send a more humane letter than the official communication to the next of kin. In most cases Davison's letter would arrive in advance of the official one.[38]

We can see how it worked in the case of Private William Joseph Bascombe, who signed up when the Battalion was training in Horsham, and is commemorated in the Horsham Roll of Honour. Once his parents had received news of his death from Davison, they informed the local paper, which then published parts of their letter:

> You will already have received the sad news which has only just reached me of the death in action of your son, Private W. Bascombe, number 1432, of A Co. As the raiser of the Battalion I desire to express my deep sympathy with you in the great loss you have sustained. I trust the knowledge of your son's splendid patriotism and the fact that he has given his life for his king and country may do something to soften your grief.

The War Office notification arrived the morning after Davison's letter.[39]

Before the Battalion left the German guns completely behind, there was one slight scare at the Citadel. Colonel Barker wrote:

> My slumbers were rudely disturbed at 8 a.m. by the bursting of a huge shell near us…Meanwhile another one burst, so I skipped up and saw one of the Brigade tents

smashed to atoms. A few seconds after, K [Brigadier Kellett] came by in a car roaring with laughter in his pyjamas.

After their next move further away from the line, Colonel Barker was almost pining for familiar noises:

The distant roar of the guns is like soft music and quite soothing. You really can't imagine the absolute peace after ten days of ceaseless deafening noise.

On the 10th the Divisional General, Major-General Walker, came to see the Battalion to congratulate them (and Colonel Barker) on their part in taking and holding Delville Wood; the men 'cheered frantically at the finish' in response. Colonel Barker enthused about the atmosphere in the division:

He is such a dear and we all love him. All the divisions of the army envy us for the ideal gentlemanly way we soldier. We are all friends and pals and everything runs so well and smoothly. No wretched strafing over trifles. Red tape is unknown.

The Colonel was well-known himself for having 'no wretched strafing over trifles', as Corporal Howes recalled with pride:

On this particular night 'lights out' had gone and everyone had turned in. In out particular bivvy there were four gunners 'Schneider' Taylor, 'Pic' Godwin, Carrville, I think it was and myself, all of '13' [Platoon]. We were rather slack in putting out our candle and presently we were startled by the well-known voice of the R.S.M. ordering us to 'come outside,' instead of which we promptly blew out the glim and 'laid low.'

The order was repeated, accompanied by a repetition from the Adjutant, who, unknown to us, was accompanying the R.S.M. on his rounds.

Thinking 'discretion the better part of valour' we emerged and were made to understand that we were for orders in the morning.

The next day for the first time for each of us we were marched off by the police to B.B.'s tent. After the preliminaries of 'Caps off – right turn, etc,' the charge as read over, questions were asked, and answers given, after which B.B., looking straight at us, said, 'The Lewis Gunners did splendidly in Delville Wood. On that account the charge is dismissed. I, for one, stuck my chest out a little further.[40]

The Battalion then marched 7 miles to Méricourt L'Abbé where the Colonel sent them bathing:

I have sent the whole battalion off to bathe in the river about two miles away. They are all lousy and it's like a monkey house, seeing them stripping and killing the germs in their shirts. Poor fellows, they are wonderful.

On the 13th they had an early start (3 am) to catch the train to Saleux, followed by a 10 mile route march to Vaux-en Amienois, close to Amiens, where normal life resumed, if only for a short while. Indeed many rushed over the fields to see the new soldiers arriving, and gave roars of applause when they saw the pickelhaube helmets that some men had acquired as souvenirs.

Meanwhile Captain Adams, whom we remember being very moved about the loss of his close friend Alan MacDougall at the conclusion of the relief from Delville Wood, had written a poem about it. He gave it to Colonel Barker for an appreciation and the

Colonel in turn sent it off to Mayor Davison with instructions to send it to *The Times* for publication. It was published in many of the dailies.

To A. M.
3/8/16

[MacDougall was born in North Uist in the Hebrides, then went to Victoria University in New Zealand, before coming to Oxford as a Rhodes Scholar, where he obtained a double first in History and then became a university lecturer, latterly at Bedford College, London]

Relief Complete

Not where in grey surge of unnumbered miles
Rises the Coronach of the Hebrides;
Nor far away where molten sunlight smiles
On Southern Seas;
Not from the cloistered strife of Academe,
Spent with its subtle warfare, bowed with years
Of honoured labour, did'st thou pass, supreme
Among thy peers:
But in the blasting hurricane of the Fray,
Deaf to its roar, unheeding of its toll,
Humbly before the Altar did'st thou lay
Thy splendid soul.
So thou art gone, but who that lives can mourn
The promise of thy manhood, who by Fire
Tried and Accepted, did'st endure to scorn
The World's Desire?
Rather we pray that we who hold the Fort
May with equal courage pace our beat,
Till, unashamed, we can at last report
'Relief Complete.'
P.H.Y.
6/8/16[41]

As the Battalion moved back towards the Somme battlefield, the familiar organizational problems increased. It was a relief to go into well-revetted front-line trenches in Hebuterne on the 21st of the month. The much under-strength 22nd Battalion replaced a much stronger battalion of Scots Guards, resulting in some amusing episodes:

In one bay there were five Guardsmen standing on the fire step – but I only had one man to take over – Gerhold. 'Gerry who wouldn't hurt a fly.' At the signal they looked down and said, 'Where's the others?' Gerry replied, 'I can manage this bit.' The five got down – the one got up, and the word went around - relief complete.[42]

Colonel Barker was delighted to be back in the line:

It's the most delightful place I have ever been in and is a perfect rest cure. Beyond a lot of trench mortaring and sniping, at present it is absolute peace. After our recent 'rest'??? we would all like to stop in these trenches for a month without ever going out. My headquarters are in a wood with leaves on the trees and hardly knocked about....We have a most delightful open shelter against a wall...Fancy we drive our transport right up to this shelter, though we are only about 700 yards from the Bosch. The wood is very large and dense and on top of a slope, so everything for four miles behind us is out of sight of the Hun. We are too happy for words. Couldn't have believed there was such luxury in the trenches.

Alas, there a big explosion in a village four miles behind the line (Coigneux). A small explosion in an ammunition dump attracted lots of men to the place, when the whole dump went up. Among them was Brigadier Kellett's son – in fact father and son were due to dine together that night. At first his injuries were not thought to be fatal, but he died the next day. Brigadier Kellett left immediately for ten days leave, meaning that Colonel Barker was obliged to move to Brigade.

On the 25th they went back to Couin, having had only one officer casualty (2nd Lt 'Ernie' Hayes, wounded but at duty), plus one other rank killed and two wounded in their four-day tour. There they picked up fifty-two other ranks and sent men out on fatigue parties. Some of these involved 'Roger' fatigues – the carrying of bulky gas cylinders up to the front line – a very unpopular duty. According to HE Harvey, the 'five-foot steel cylinders of compressed 'cloud' phosgene' were 'a staggering back-breaking dead-weight of 175 lbs.'[43]

Some of the new drafts didn't seem up to it; twelve of the first batch of forty had been rejected as 'cripples', while in the new bunch of fifty-two there was a 'conchie':

A conscientious objector seems to have wandered into my last draft. On the way up to the trench he stuck the muzzle of his rifle into the ground and refused to go any further forward. He said, 'I object to killing anyone' you can imagine how most of the men roared. An officer explained to him that he would be shot all right after trial and that as it was a quiet part of the line he needn't shoot anyone. Of course he was terrified directly he heard a shell or two...In the Wood we would have shot him ourselves, during the present calm you are allowed to be frightened.

The next period of trench duty (29/8-4/9) was extended to six days because of the quietness of the line. Meantime, the weather had changed to wet, so trench duty was less pleasant. Privates G Guyatt, HV Harrington, HV Wilkinson, J Petchey and TJW Fitton were given MMs in 2nd Division Routine Orders for their work at Delville Wood.

It was obvious that this was a live and let live sector. This wasn't the 2nd Division way. Their first task was to achieve the strategic initiative, and the second was to dominate No Man's Land.

Colonel Barker and the other commanders were full of cunning ways of taking control of the initiative:

> Whenever he drops his trench mortars into our lines, we do nothing at all and pretend to like it. But when he misses the trenches and goes beyond them, we retaliate like blazes with all our artillery. For the last two days he has been plastering us in nice safe fields between the fire trenches and support lines…Certainly the regiments who had these lines for the last eighteen months must have had a lovely time. Of course we shall spoil it all I know as we always do…I sent one of my boys with thee men to get the particulars of a sunken road about 300 yards to our front in 'no man's land.'… They had a most exciting time and found that he had built up a machine gun emplacement and also had a light railway there. Doubtless he ran a trench-mortar up at night and fired from there.

That explained how German trench mortar shells were able to reach all the way to the British lines. Some days later British artillery blew up the railway line and the trench mortar strafes from that place stopped.[44]

On the 5th September the British finally let off the gas that had been the cause of so many groans carrying it up. The results were announced as a great success; quite why was a bit of a mystery: the enemy didn't seem to show much reaction to it. Now it was the small matter of rebuilding the parapets, and transporting most of the empty cylinders away again (although 230 of the 800-1000 had not gone off).[45]

Then it was back to bivouacs for six days with another turn in the Hebuterne trenches from the 10th to 16th September. This period was to be a particularly memorable one for a number of reasons. First it seemed as if the Royal Berks, whom they relieved, had been more pacific, allowing the enemy to chase away some of their working parties, for example. Some aggressive patrolling would help to sort that out. Unfortunately on the 12th September, the newly promoted Second Lieutenant Fisher DCM – Tot's old platoon sergeant – was shot dead by a sentry as his patrol pressed up against the German wire:

> He was a clever, well-read man who had travelled widely, and was one of the finest topographers in the battalion. He was a brave and fearless sergeant and a very promising officer. At Horsham, by the way, he dodged church parade by declaring himself a Buddhist.[46]

The saga of the Colbeck pipe continued. Lance Humphries had twice cut the King of Clubs to beat Buff Whitehouse for it. Lance continues:

> It was nicely broken in when 'Jerry' dropped a 5.9 in the trench just behind me and after a fortnight in an advanced operating station at Authie I found myself on a hospital train en route for Boulogne and 'Blighty' and minus a pipe.

Buff was left to look after the pipe. It would stay in his possession until a ceremonial hand-over after the war.[47]

Meanwhile Colonel Barker, back at Brigade due to Brigadier-General Kellett's illness, was requested at 1 pm on the 14th to put up a scheme for a sizeable raid on the German trenches 'tonight' – which did not leave much time for planning. In the event it was downgraded to a patrol, because the German wire was not thought to have been cut well enough. The purpose behind the raid and other schemes at this time was to draw German attention away from the big attack down in the Somme area that was to take place on the 15th, which involved a new weapon.

News filtered through of the successes of the attack in Flers-Courcelette. Now it could be named:

> They call our new invention 'The Tank.' I had better not tell you what it is, though the wire says there is one in F— [Flers] followed by a crowd of cheering soldiers.

A few days later, after news about them had appeared in *The Times*, it was time for the Colonel to describe to his wife just what these 'tanks' were:

> They are little steel forts on caterpillars and hold 2 machine guns and a 6-pounder gun. They climb up and down any mortal thing, they have great claws and are almost human. I believe they can almost climb a vertical bit of ground. Anything they don't like they knock down or crush. They waltz up and down the German wire crushing it and shooting into the trenches. Of course a shell knocks them out but nothing else.

Wonderful though the new weapon was, and although he wanted one 'for a regimental pet', there was a sting in the tail: 'I believe several of them broke down and probably by now most of them are out of order.'

Colonel Barker was also very bucked up by hearing that he was to be awarded the DSO for his defence of Delville Wood, especially as the number of decorations for Delville Wood had been slashed. He would have preferred to have received it for his actions at Vimy Ridge when his actions were voluntary, rather than at Delville when, he said, he had only done what any conscientious CO ought to have done. In fact he compared his own prospecting in the Wood unfavourably with those of Christopher Stone:

> I consider Stone's action as gold to copper compared to mine. Rather than risk a man's life he took on the job himself he gets nothing now but might pick up an MC in the quarterly list.

The Divisional General still wanted identifications of the enemy units opposite them, and so wanted the raid repeated on the night of the 15th, after more wire-cutting had gone on. It would be led by 2nd Lt WJR Martin, and 25 other ranks from B Company. The position to be raided was very close to that of the night before, but it would include a sap jutting out from the German line. The Stokes Mortar '1 minute rapid' barrage, to keep German heads down at zero hour, would be repeated as that had worked well. This time there would be one or two amendments. There would be more concentration on making sure that German working parties did not repair the gaps blown in the wire: the 99th Machine Gun Company was charged to do this. The artillery barrage would be even narrower around the area to be raided: there would just be enough room for the raiding party, and it would isolate them better from enemy reinforcements. This time the guns would simply concentrate on and around the area to be raided, but the raiders would only go out after the second of two all-arms barrages.

At 10:30 pm Second Lieutenant Martin and his men, in three parties with twenty yards between each one, stealthily made their way up to ten yards short of the head of the German sap (this was about another 30 yards from the German front line). As soon as the Stokes Mortar barrage stopped, one of the parties jumped into the sap. They then clubbed or bayoneted everyone in it and made their way to where the sap joined the enemy's fire trench. Meanwhile Lt Martin and his teams were running along the side of the sap, reaching the enemy line at 10:47 pm. He shot and killed one man at a yard's distance. His teams then spread out to left and right along the enemy front line and made blocks, held by bombers. They then completed their work. By 10:55 pm they were on their way home. They had killed at least 11 (for which they had evidence, but they claimed it was at least 20) and they brought back 10 unwounded prisoners with them (belonging to the 99th Reserve Regt of the 26th Reserve Division, according to the daily Intelligence Summary). None of the 22nd men were wounded.[48]

Major Harman suggested that the enemy must have withdrawn his front line troops because of the artillery bombardment, but had reinforced the garrison in the sap. Thus the troops captured in the front line had probably fled there from the sap. As acting brigade commander, Colonel Barker commented with grim satisfaction that: 'Every raider had blood on his club or bayonet', concluding:

> 11) I account for the success of the Raid as due to the fact that the Officer and men meant business, and were determined not to return without some spoil.
>
> 12) I account for the lack of casualties as due to:-
>
> The excellence of the Artillery fire. On the night previous, when the wire was found uncut, the reconnoitring patrol was fired on by Machine guns on right and left of the gap. By drawing the Artillery curtain closer to the point of entry, and in fact only allowing just sufficient room for the raiders to enter their allotted portion, any action from machine guns was entirely stopped.
>
> The excellent disposition of the Machine Guns, and their well-directed fire, which, continued to the last moment, entirely prevented the enemy from putting up their heads until the raiders were upon them.
>
> The effect of the 1 minute's fire of the Stokes guns - which was of a most intense and well-directed nature.
>
> The confidence the raiders had in the Artillery, Machine Guns and Stokes Guns. This enabled them to approach within 40 yards of the German trench under their fire, and so rush the Germans before they had time to man their parapet.[49]

Colonel Barker could not have been happier. Congratulation flowed in from all sides either for his DSO, or the raid, or both. Next day Brigadier Kellett returned:

> The dear old man took over from me after lunch. He was so delighted about the DSO and I thought he would never stop shaking my hand. When I told him about the raid he was in the 7th heaven. It is nice to serve under such a perfect gentlemen who has no axe to grind and can play the game.[50]

Meanwhile, the Divisional General had the whole raiding party paraded in front of him to receive his congratulations.

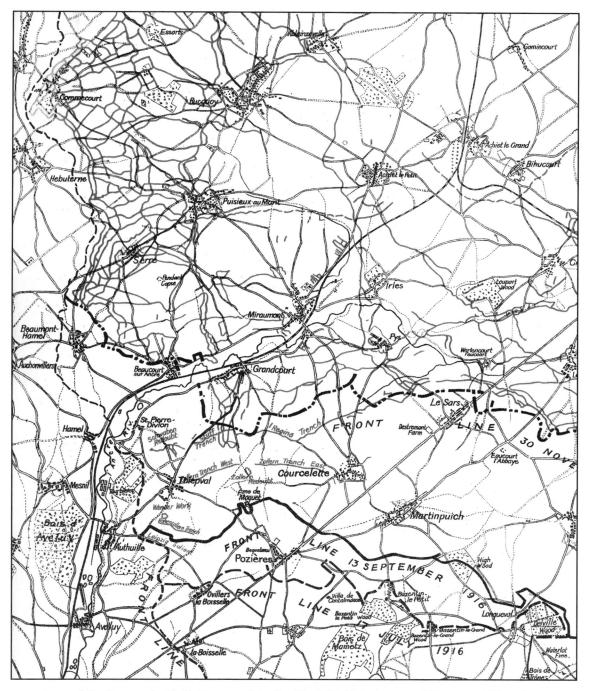

Area of the Somme battlefield covered by the 22nd RF. Hebuterne and Beaumont Hamel are top left, Montauban and Delville Wood are bottom right, while spring 1917 locations are top central. (From Frank Mumby's 1917 publication: *The Great World War, part xvii*)

When the Battalion was involved in serious fighting, Doc Miller was never far away, going well beyond the call of duty. Thus his MC citation reads:

> *For conspicuous gallantry and devotion to duty. He accompanied a raiding party with his stretcher-bearers, and remained in the enemy trenches until quite certain no raiders were left behind. Previously he had accompanied a patrol under heavy fire and tended the wounded. He has on many occasions displayed great gallantry and determination.*[51]

Quite **what** he did in the enemy trenches, was another matter. His assistant Sergeant Metcalfe gives another angle:

> *It was at Hebuterne, after one of those raids so dear to 'Dusty's heart. We had all been out in no man's land for a bit, 'Dusty' enthusiastically blazing away at the German line with a rifle, in the open…*
>
> *And what a soldier! The army lost a very fine soldier when 'Dusty' became a doctor, but then he would have been a serious loss to he medical profession had he been a soldier. Most of the battalion know of his qualities as a soldier, and most of them have met him at some time or another in extremely unhealthy localities.*[52]

The Battalion bivouacked in the Couin area between the 16th and 20th, then went to billets at Authie for ten days, where they were in Corps Reserve. On the 21st Captain Adams returned from leave to take over command of the Battalion from Captain Walsh, as Colonel Barker had departed on leave.

At Authie they celebrated the first of a series of 13 Platoon anniversary dinners that would go on until 1971. Claude Upton, then its platoon sergeant, recalled it:

> *On September 24th 1916, we had experienced the joys of trench warfare, having been in and out of the line several times, but on this very important date, we were out, to hold our first anniversary dinner, in France.*
>
> *Our dining room was the bedroom of a hospitable French woman, on whom we were billeted – being the largest room in the village. Thirty-five answered their names, including two Q.M.S., five Sergeants, four Corporals, seven Lance Corporals and seventeen Privates, all original members of the Platoon.*[53]

Cooks from D company provided 'a wonderful menu', while men from 14 Platoon volunteered as waiters. Claude continued:

> *As Platoon Sergeant I occupied the place of honour and proposed the toast to 'The Platoon,' saying among other things, 'That as a Platoon we were unique.' Little did I think that in those far-off days that forty years later I should again occupy the place of honour as Chairman to again welcome members of 13 Platoon.*[54]

On the 25th the Battalion had its Sports Day, reminding many of the famous time in 1915:

> *Flags bearing the Regimental colours, coloured bunting and khaki, marquees and tents, side-shows and amusement booths, were all there lending a holiday air, but Horsham friends were missing. Yes we really did miss them all, and although perhaps half the present population of the little French village turned out to watch us, they could not make even a little of that at home feeling existing at Roffey.*[55]

There were traditional footraces plus some unusual sports:

The Transport mules were coaxed rather than driven or ridden round the course in the Mule Races. The difficulty appeared to be in keeping them somewhere near the course, and it was a dangerous pastime even looking on.

Sometimes the right equipment was not available so one had to improvise: 'A cricket ball not being available, a throwing the bomb competition took its place'. Private Leadbitter, D company, launched a mighty effort of sixty yards to win the competition. He was said to be very disappointed with his throw; he had been aiming for the officers' enclosure a hundred yards away.

The day was brought to an end by a concert arranged by Sergeant Claude Upton. Sergeants Booth, Leonard and Pearson were awarded MMs, with Sergeant MR Brierley having been given his DCM two days earlier.

Down south more attacks were going on. The Battalion was placed on two hours notice to move. Some fortified villages (like Morval, Lesboeufs and Combles) and strong points, such as Thiepval (excellent work by 18th Division) and Mouquet Farm, had been captured in the latest attacks, but there had been no strategic breakthrough.

On the 28th the Battalion was ordered to stand down. It would now begin a spell of 'ordinary' trench duty beginning on the 30th September, but in a new area, a mile or two to the south: the Redan North sub-section. They would get to know this area rather well in the next six weeks.

1 *Mufti*, June 1965, 44, No 145, p9, also see Ralph Durand's autobiographical novel *The Steep Ascent*.
2 *Mufti*, Xmas 1929, 10, pp 4-5.
3 *WSCT*, 7/10/1916.
4 IWM, Farley file, letter dated 31/7/16.
5 *Mufti*, June 1965, 44, No 145, pp 10-11; (the 18th HLI or the 9th Royal Scots).
6 *Mufti*, Summer 1965, 47, No 150, pp 5-6.
7 Operational orders and narrative from 99 Brigade War Diary, *WO 95*/1368, also the unit diaries (1371, 1372) and divisional diary (1291). Also see *History of the Second Division*, pp 270-283, and *The Royal Fusiliers in the Great War*, pp 120-124.
8 Taken from a reprint in *The Edinburgh Evening Dispatch*, 29/7/1916, p3.
9 *Mufti*, Summer 1968, 47, No 150, p7 – almost certainly Claude Upton.
10 *WSCT*, 12/8/1916 His body was identified in 1928 from fragments of clothing and badges: *Mufti*, Xmas 1928, 9, No 4, p8. and Spring 1929, 10, No 1, p5.
11 *Mufti*, Spring 1931, 12, No 1, pp 2-3.
12 *WO 95*/1373, War Diary of 99th MGC.
13 *23rd RF History*, op cit, p87.
14 *Mufti*, Summer 1938, 19, No 90, p6.
15 AJL Tottenham, *Machine-Gun And Lewis Gun Section Roll of Honour*, also see *Mufti*, Spring 1929, 10, No 1, p5; Haddock: *Mufti*, Summer 1925, 25, No 106, p5; *WSG*, 16/8/1916 and 17/8/1916.
16 *Ibid*, p6.
17 Interview with ex-Private Farnsworth, 4/9/84. Sounds as if he was wounded going up Longueval Alley.
18 *WSCT*, 26/8/1916, p3.
19 *Mufti*, August 1920, 2, No 3, p2.
20 *Mufti*, Summer 1968, 47, No 150, pp 7-8. Guyatt went on to become Captain Guyatt MC MM. *Mufti*, Summer 1962, 42, No 139, p9 has the tantalising but unexplained comment about '*Much more could be written*

of the action. How Moberley brought D Coy out of the wood, handing over to Captain Gell by Trones Wood'. Presumably this was another small party of 'lost' men.

21 *WSCT*, 26/8/1916, p3.

22 *Ibid*, Xmas 1944, <u>25</u>, No 105, p8, by 'some of the gunners'.

23 *Ibid*, Xmas 1928, <u>9</u>, No 4, p7.

24 *Mufti*, July 1920, p6. Shortly afterwards Durand was sent back down to the transport.

25 Sgt FW Keen: *Chiswick Times,*18/8/1916; Pte FJ Cuthbertson: *Broughshane*, <u>V</u>, pp 71-72

26 *Ibid*, Summer 1968, 47, No 150, p6 and Xmas 1928, <u>9</u>, No 4, p7. Also see obituaries in *The Times*, 11/8/1916, *The Porthcawl News*, 10/8/1916, *Cardiff Times and South Wales Weekly News*, 12/8/1916.

27 DSO citation included in *Broughshane*, <u>V</u>, pp 91-92.

28 Interview with ex-Sergeant Roland Whipp, 18/11/1983.

29 *RBB*, 3/8/1916.

30 *Mufti*, Spring 1928, <u>10</u>, No 1, p2. The *History*, pp 36-37 has the phantom (?) attack on the evening of the 3rd, but there seems better evidence for the 2nd.

31 Can be found at bibliomania (www.bibliomania.com)

32 *Stone Papers*, RBB to Mrs Alyce Stone, *Sheffield and Inglis*, p64.

33 *RBB*, 4/8/1916.

34 *The Kensington News*, 1/9/16; letter dated 6/8/16.

35 Interview with ex-Private Ollie Berrycloath, 15/1/1984; *Mufti*, Autumn 1925, <u>6</u>, No 3, p3.

36 *PAP*, 8/8/16, also probably from the magazine of New College, Oxford.

37 *Mufti*, Summer 1961, <u>41</u>, No 137, p5.

38 *Davison to RBB*, 15/8/16, *Broughshane*, <u>8601.</u>

39 *WSCT*, 19/8/1916 –'received last Monday' in a newspaper dated Saturday the 18th and hence arrived on the 13th, (or 6th). Also see *Broughshane*, <u>8601,</u> op cit.

40 *Mufti*, August/September 1921, <u>3</u>, No 1, p6.

41 See *The Times*, 18/8/1916 and *The Evening News and Evening Mail* 18/8/1916, amongst others, in *Broughshane*, eg <u>V</u>, 74. Also see the *Victoria University Review* and the similar New College Oxford publication in *PAP*.

42 *Mufti*, Summer 1963, <u>43</u>, No 141, p12 and also Summer 1945, <u>25</u>, No 106, p5 – probably both Claude Upton.

43 *Mufti*, Summer 1929, <u>10</u>, No 2, p5; reviewing Harvey's *Battle-line Narratives*.

44 *RBB*, 24/8/1916. Also see KRRC War Diary for 6-7/9/1916, *WO 95*/1371.

45 See Report on Gas Discharge SE of Hebuterne on 15/9/16, *WO 95*/1292.

46 *Mufti*, Spring 1928, 10, No 1, p6, also see 22nd RF War Diary (*WO 95*/1372) for 12/9/1916 and *WSG*, 5/10/1916, p10.

47 *Mufti*, Summer 1961, <u>41</u>, No 137, p5.

48 See *WO 95*/1372, 1368, 1292 and 1318.

49 *WO 95*/1372, 1292; Major Harman then left the battalion to command the 14th Hampshire Regiment.

50 *RBB*, 17/9/1916. Congratulations for the raid went right up to the Corps Commander and 'best of all' the Army Commander.

51 *London Gazette*, 14/11/1916

52 Memoir by WH Metcalfe, *Mufti*, Spring 1926, <u>7</u>, No 1, pp 5-6

53 *Mufti*, December 1954, <u>34</u>, No124, pp 13-14. Also see '*13*': booklet for the 5th anniversary dinner 27/9/1919 at the Holborn Restuarant (and which said 45 attended, not 35)

54 *Ibid* and *Mufti*, Xmas 1945, <u>25</u>, No 107, 75 (also Claude Upton)

55 *WSCT*, 7/10/1916, p 4; also *WSG*, 19/10/1916

Chapter Six

On The Redan Ridge Anxiously Waiting

O N 30 SEPTEMBER THE BATTALION marched south-east from Authie to new – much less attractive – front line trenches at the northern end of the Redan Ridge. Hardly had they arrived *in situ*, but they were visited by bigwigs, and plots were afoot:

The Army Comdr [General Sir Hubert Gough], *Corps Comdr* [Lieutenant-General EA Fanshawe] *etc came up here and I had to take them to a certain spot to view a certain spot, with a mind to an attack some day. The Army Comdr is most charming. He makes it his business to know all about you before he arrives, he then makes you imagine that he has come miles just to see you personally. He said to the Corps Comdr 'We haven't had a single identification since Barker fetched those 10 Huns', altogether I spent a delightful hour with them, lying on our tummies in the open on the wet grass.*[1]

Meanwhile, despite the persistent attentions of the enemy trench mortars and unpleasant conditions caused by continuous heavy rain, the Battalion spent a reasonably casualty-free six days in the new trenches, moving back to billets in Mailly Maillet on 6 October. The latter was only about a mile behind the front line, but much of it was still standing: relative luxury!

On the 6th, MCs were awarded at Betrancourt by General Walker to Captain Gell (dating back to July) and Second Lieutenant Martin for his leadership of the successful raid of 15 September. Sergeant WH Metcalf also received the DCM (dating back to his work at Vimy Ridge in May).

Within a short period the wet and unhealthy conditions had greatly increased the number of men absent sick (Saki, ie Lance-Sergeant Munro, with malaria, and Claude Upton, with typhoid, were taken to hospital somewhere around this time), while a number of young 'subs' were struck off the strength because of persistent ill health.

On the 10th they did their first rehearsal in dummy trenches. They practised the same attack on the 11th, 12th and 13th (with aeroplane support). Colonel Barker hoped that he might be able to fight this battle with his Battalion and not away at Brigade, but he was not at all looking forward to his men having to attack in the face of enemy wire that was 'about forty yards deep and five feet high, in front of every trench for at least four miles'.

The attack was planned for the 14th, according to that most reliable of sources: German prisoners, but postponed because of the state of the ground and weather. Some games of football and *impromptu* concerts were possible, and there were hares, lots of them, leading to a novel use for the steel helmet:

> *This country is full of hares, our own bag today was five knocked over by steel helmets. Splendid thing the steel helmet, some of the men cook in them, drink in them and [now] kill hares in them.*[2]

At times, the hares provided a bit of light relief from the rehearsals:

> *We'd been doing all this practice – blue lines, green lines and all this sort of thing – we were behind the lines at Mailly Maillet... Suddenly a hare sprang out and, you know, the whole thing collapsed. They'd forgotten their discipline...and they were at the hare with their bayonets. They got the poor thing in the end...it just shows the awful sporting instinct of the British.*[3]

The spell in the Redan (left sub-section) trenches from the 17th-20th was characterised by lots of artillery but little infantry-to-infantry action. Both sides appeared to be leaving their front lines very lightly tenanted to minimise casualties, and both sides had very deep dugouts that were proof against all but the largest calibre shells.

Colonel Barker had no definite information about the size or date of their imminent attack. It kept being altered. German prisoners were now, however, pretty certain that the British were going to attack with thirty-one divisions on the 20th of the month.

True to their intelligence, the Germans ferociously bombarded the British lines on the 20th. This time they managed to score a direct hit on one of the deep British dugouts with a large calibre shell: three men were buried, two dead, and six dug out alive – and most of the latter were very badly shaken.[4] More disaster happened later to one of the Lewis Gun teams when a 5.9 shell landed right beside it. Lance-Corporal EJ Meyers was killed, with his brother (NF) and Jack Holliday severely injured, and all but Private Squibb injured to some degree.[5] The Battalion spent two nights in Mailly Wood, then marched further behind the lines to Acheux Wood, where they would stay until the end of the month.

Colonel Barker found out that a fanciful drawing of him directing the defences of Delville Wood had appeared in the *Daily Sketch*. His son at Eton had it framed and put on his wall, but he was more touched by a letter from a wounded private:

> *Will you kindly allow me to offer my humble congratulations upon your gallant deed and your decoration. I can assure you no one is more prouder than I am to know that my Commanding Officer has won such laurels for my late Battn and I am sorry I am no longer with you now, but that is impossible as the injury I received that night has left me with my left leg 1½ inches short.*[6]

It was almost impossible to find anywhere to exercise, but Colonel Barker found one:

> *After it [lunch] I waded through the slush and mud over your ankles and found one dry spot viz – the Railway Station. I walked up and down this place for an hour.*

He would continue using this spot daily, and the memory of the tall athletic Colonel marching up and down on his own along the deserted railway station platform (all twenty yards of it) would loom large in Christopher Stone's memory.[7]

The heaviest rain of all was at the end of the month. The persistence of the bad weather had a depressing effect on everyone, British and Germans – and the latter

This is the ruin of Beaumont Hamel station, but we would expect nearby Acheux Wood station (where the Colonel exercised on an untouched strip of platform) to look rather similar.

were suffering more shellfire.[8]

The men had hardly started on their five miles walk to the trenches on the 30th before the rain came down in torrents and continued to fall until they arrived at the front line. The trenches were in such bad condition that 'waders were worse than useless'. Water was knee-deep in some parts while the mud was so deep in others that 'on several occasions it was necessary to drag men out of it by the use of ropes'.[9] Colonel Barker sent out a patrol of twenty men under the recently-returned Captain Clifford to check the German wire, but the latter reported back that he could not get near the German line. No Man's Land was simply one long bog.

This spell in the trenches was reduced to three days, more than long enough. Thankfully casualties for the spell were only one other rank killed and two wounded, but the first sick parade out of the trenches at Mailly Maillet on 2 November numbered 103 other ranks – mostly for minor ailments like trench fever, high temperatures and boils. Next day it was up to 140 – including Captain Adams and Captain Gell – and all this out of about 400 effectives. On the other hand, Sergeant Leonard had won a Bar to his MM, presumably for his good work in the September raid, while Christopher Stone had got his MC after all.

In the next few days sixty-two reinforcements trickled in. Corporal George Challis was in the first batch to arrive, 3 November, at Mailly Maillet. He had had a devil of a job to find the Battalion, being sent repeatedly to the places the battalion had just vacated, and when he did catch up with them, it was when the exhausted Battalion had just come out of the trenches, so he did not get much of a welcome.[10]

After three days in Mailly Maillet it was back to the trenches again on the 5th, but this time the term of duty had been reduced to 48 hours. Then it was two nights on Bertrancourt, followed by three days at Acheux Wood. At least the continuing bad weather (some 12 mm of rain fell on 7 November) virtually guaranteed that the attack would be postponed for the winter.

But the 9th and 10th were both fine dry days. *Ominously* dry days.

Behind the scenes, orders were being dusted out. Artillery preparation was already going ahead for a possible attack on the 13th. On the other hand, other putative attack

British troops in the flooded Ancre Valley. Taylor Library

dates, such as the first and fifth of the month had come and gone, surely this one would also be cancelled…

On the 12th, the Battalion marched back to Bertrancourt, where:

Warlike stores were issued and the men rested until midnight. An additional haversack ration of biscuit and cheese was issued.[11]

The attack was to involve the following divisions from left to right: 31st (south of Hebuterne), 3rd (opposite the sinister strongpoint of Serre), 2nd (on the Redan Ridge), 51st Highland Division (opposite Beaumont Hamel, the place of such disaster on the 1st July), 63rd Royal Naval Division (opposite Beaucourt), and on the other side of the River Ancre, the 39th (opposite St Pierre Divion) and the 19th.

The initial assault on the enemy by 2nd Division was to be done by troops from 6 Infantry Brigade on the left and 5 Infantry Brigade on the right. 99 Brigade was in reserve, with the 22nd and 23rd Royal Fusiliers to move forward and be ready to support these attacks.

At 5 am the siege artillery batteries opened fire, as they had done on the previous two mornings at the same time for an hour: one couldn't conceal that one was going to attack but one could keep the enemy guessing as to when. On the morning of the 13th, however, the assault began at 5:45 am. The divisions attacking to the right of 2nd Division achieved most of their objectives. Thus Beaumont Hamel was in Scottish hands (51st Division) by the end of the day after difficult and costly fighting, while the 63rd Division had pushed up close to Beaucourt (taken the next day), the 39th Division had stormed into St Pierre Divion and the 19th Division had smartly taken its modest objectives on the extreme right flank. The newspapers loved the stories about the hundreds of prisoners in the deep caverns at Beaumont Hamel, and the galleries at St Pierre Divion:

The foulness of the atmosphere, in the St Pierre Divion tunnel especially, is ascribed to the bad condition of some of these stores – of the German war bread in particular, which is said to become most energetically offensive when mouldy.[12]

On the left of 2nd Division, 3rd Division had suffered a disastrous day. The Germans at Serre, on a knoll looking down on the attackers and possibly above the thickest part of the fog, appeared to be expecting an attack here and were very alert,[13] while the mud here (formed of a very clingy loam as opposed to the chalk further south) prevented any quick movement by the attackers. A few determined men got into and even beyond the German front lines, others stayed in shell-holes all day. Many on the right (8 Brigade) blundered into the territory of 2nd Division's 6 Brigade area, while some of the latter also drifted into 8 Brigade area with much mutual recrimination.

In any event, there was no progress on the 3rd Division front, and this affected what happened on either side of the division: on their left, the 31st Division had made some lodgements in the enemy line but had to withdraw again; on their right was the 2nd Division. On the left of the 2nd Division area, on 6 Brigade's front, the 2nd South Staffs and the 13th Essex struggled amid thick fog, uncut wire, and fire from a German strongpoint called the Quadrilateral (and later from Serre, once the attacks there had failed). On the brigade right the attacking troops did get into the German lines, but for all but 100 men on the extreme right, the attackers were so weak in numbers that they could not hold onto their gains. On the brigade left, the confusion between the troops from 6 Brigade and 8 Brigade meant that the barrage soon left them behind.

In contrast, on 2nd Division's right, on 5 Brigade's front, the 24th RF and 2nd HLI made good progress, keeping up with the barrage and taking many prisoners, and at one stage were ahead of the 51st Highland Division on their right. The two units were in touch with each other on the first objective, the Green line, by the end of the day, but the left flank of 5 Brigade's front was 'in the air' and needed reinforcing. This would be the 22nd Battalion's job. First they needed to move up to the trenches.

Captain Roscoe, commanding A Company, left an evocative description of the scene:

> *The time is midnight and the night November* [12th/13th]; *a pale and watery moon throws its light in fitful gleams on field and village shrouded in an autumn mist which drifts on the light breeze, sometimes thickening and sometimes lifting. In an orchard near to a village is a camp of wooden huts, built under the trees and surrounded by thick and sticky mud, where in spite of the late hour men are moving to and fro restlessly, carrying stores and ammunition or walking up and down to keep warm. Presently there is a sign of general activity: men come out of the huts fully equipped and pass along the narrow lane leading to the road. Here they group themselves, and soon the companies are fallen in and ready to move away into the mist and the unknown happenings of the approaching day. Not many men are in a talkative mood and as the column moves away at a slow, easy pace an almost complete silence broods over them, broken by an occasional remark or the humming of a tune. The roads are silent and empty, and save an occasional passer-by there is no sign of the usual roaring stream of waggons which fill the night with their ceaseless clatter. On through the sleeping village goes the creeping column of men towards the quiet empty wilderness where lie the trenches wrapt in mist, and silence broken only by an occasional gun firing with a hollow boom that echoes away to silence again. Soon they reach another village* [Mailly Maillet] *which shows by its deserted and war-scarred houses that the trenches are now not so far away.*
>
> *Presently they halt, and from a small field by the wayside men emerge carrying heavy sacks of bombs and ammunition, and machine guns. These join the column, which here splits up into companies and again moves slowly on up the road, and after a little while the column pauses, and stringing out into single file they pass from the road into a deep narrow trench* [Sixth Avenue] *which will lead them with many windings up towards the very front of all.*
>
> *After seemingly endless moving up this trench the leading men halt and whispered instructions are given to lie down and wait. In the cold of the early morning this is no pleasant time to sit in an open trench feeling the cold grip one's toes and fingers and gradually creep all over one; and the men mutter and stamp their feet, shaking the drops of water from their clothes. For the mist is thicker now, and lies like a heavy wet blanket over all the earth, so that it is impossible to see more than a few yards ahead.*

It is very quiet now, and the guns seem to be resting and taking breath before the mighty hurricane which they will pour out in a few minutes time. One can almost picture the gunners sitting by the guns, with ammunition piled all round then on every side snatching a last few minutes rest before the strenuous work ahead of them.

All attention is now fixed on the watches of those who know the exact hour at which the battle will commence, and as each minute goes by a wave of excited expectance goes down the trench; men get up, and stand whispering together.

One minute more! As the hands of the watch draw towards that the end of that last minute a faint murmuring is heard far away to the right, which comes rapidly nearer, swelling to a mighty volume of sound which is taken up by the guns behind us, and with huge deafening roar, the battle has begun. Away up the trench stagger the men with their burdens, eyes smarting and grope their way through the thick fog of smoke mingled with the mist away into the unknown chances of war.[14]

At zero hour, 5:45 am, the Battalion took up positions in the old British support line and remained there all day, seeing both prisoners and wounded British soldiers stream past them.

They all moved forward again in mid-afternoon when C, B, and D companies, under Major Adams, were called forward to form a defensive flank for 6 Brigade (to whom the Battalion now reported for the duration of the battle) to cover the left flank of 5 Brigade's advance.

The mud was awful for officers and men alike:

The squelching, glutinous, knee-deep mud, through which after dark we tried to find an appointed headquarters in a dug-out which proved to be brimful of other headquarters [Royal Berks] and stragglers, and which had acquired such a foul atmosphere that B.B. nearly fainted half way down the stairs and had to be helped to the surface by the doctor and myself; the calamity of our invaluable mess-sergeant wounded just outside the dug-out as he arrived with the rations; and the move at dawn after a night on the dug-out stairs to another dug-out in Valhade, where for the rest of the fight we sat cramped on the floor, writing messages and telephoning, and getting an occasional mug of soup or cocoa from time to time through the day and night.[15]

Nevertheless, Colonel Barker's orders to Major Adams and the three companies were crisp and clear:

1. *to cross 'No Man's Land' by Companies, place their right on Green Line* [where 5 Brigade had reached], *and left on 'No Man's Land' and advance due north*
2. *to take up a position with their Right in vicinity of Lager Alley, and left on K.35.c.4.7* [southern base of the Quadrilateral]
3. *from this position to throw out Strong Points well in advance and at once get in touch with enemy by patrols.*
   I placed the Operation under Command of Major Phythian-Adams, my 2nd in Command
4. *I kept 1 Company in Reserve in my own hands near Buster in old British line[16]*

Several hours passed with no news coming back. One can imagine the anxiety in the overcrowded Battalion HQ dugout. One report at around midnight suggested the leading company was still a long way away from its destination. In fact C Company made their way into the old German front line, where disaster struck: Captain Gell, in charge of the company again after his recent illness, and considered by Colonel Barker to be his 'finest fighter and company commander' was wounded in the knee. On the other hand Second Lieutenant Kelly seized the opportunity to prove himself a more than capable deputy. Kelly and his men attached themselves to the left hand side of 5 Brigade's attacking troops, thus lengthening the front. This was around 2 am. He then sent out a patrol to investigate positions and started establishing the flank out to the left towards the Quadrilateral.

Meanwhile, B Company, for the same reasons as had affected many other units, lost their way and only reported back some hours later. D Company may also have had some navigational problems, but did manage to join the flank to the left of C Company. In his report later Colonel Barker noted that

> Two companies had got lost, but were in position before dawn, thanks to the skill, courage and most able leadership of Major Adams.[17]

A Company was pushed up to replace B Company somewhere around 4 am and joined to the left of the line of posts, closest to the Quadrilateral. Sometime just after A Company had linked arms with other British troops, Saki (Lance-Sergeant Hector Hugh Munro – who had rushed back from hospital to take part in the battle) met his end. His friend Corporal WR Spikesman tells the story:

> It was a very dark winter morning, but after much excitement we were hailed by voices and a figure rose to the top of the trenches in front of us and shouting greetings to the Company Commander (one Captain Roscoe, one of the finest of fellows…) engaged him in conversation. A number of the fellows sank down on the ground to rest, and Hector sought a shallow crater, with the lip as back-rest. I heard him shout, 'Put that bloody cigarette out,' and heard the snip of a rifle-shot…It was some time later, about an hour, when a fellow came up to me and said, 'So they got your friend.' My feelings then I cannot describe, but I knew I had lost something inestimable, the friendship of a man whose ideas and thoughts I tried to emulate, someone whom I loved for his being just 'Saki'.[18]

The men had been exhausted by their journeys. Some of the worst 'going' in the area – with mud up to waist high – was just south of the Quadrilateral. Nevertheless, by early in the morning of the 14th all three companies were in position (with B Company in support), and the flank consolidated:

> The picquets were posted well in advance, touch was obtained with the enemy, and Lewis and Vickers Guns placed in good positions.[19]

During 14 November the line was consolidated further, taking advantage of the KRRC and Royal Berks attacking on their right (through 5 Brigade area) to try and get to the second objective, the so-called Yellow line. The attacks were not particularly successful - the battalions were required to attack over ground they were unfamiliar with, in poor visibility, and the KRRC soon lost direction and drifted into 51st Division territory. The

Berks, on the other hand, although losing many men to the British barrage, did take part of Serre Trench. This was on high ground overlooking part of the Quadrilateral, and they reported seeing some of its defenders running away afterwards.

Amid this confusion, the 22nd Battalion were able to do some good work. Men like Second Lieutenant Leon Simons had been busy:

> *He organised and pushed forward his strongpoints with great courage and skill under very heavy fire. He set a splendid example throughout.*[20]

By noon the flank was a fairly continuous line and was supported by ten Lewis Guns and four Vickers Guns, while A Company, on the left, had created a strongpoint on the southern point of the Quadrilateral itself.[21]

The Battalion were supported by parties from a variety of sources: 13th Essex

The Battle of the Ancre in summary

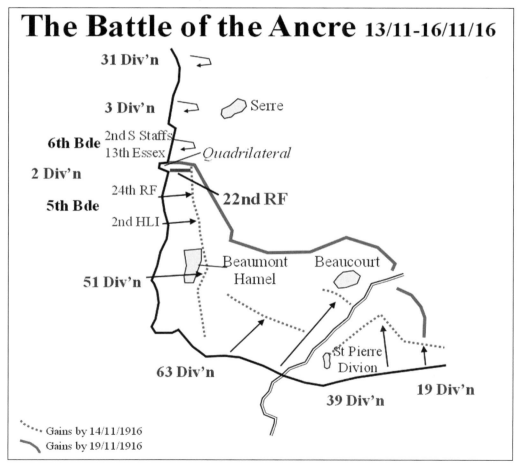

153

(whose CO, Colonel Carter, fed parties of men forward to Major Adams, and had a new communication trench dug into the German front line south of the Quadrilateral with a post just short of the old German line adding to the threat against the German defenders in the Quadrilateral), 1st Kings (operating as a combined unit with the 13th Essex), 2nd HLI, 23rd and possibly some 24th RF, all carefully put in position by Major Adams. On the 15th a party of fifty men from the 4th RF were added to it. Indeed it could not be called the 22nd RF any more, and was renamed Barker's Mixed Force, now perhaps 450 strong.

For Major Adams to handle a body of men of known abilities in his first big battle in such terrain would have been difficult enough, let alone handling an unwieldy combination of men from a variety of units, yet he seems to have taken it in his stride. We hear of him the next day, under shellfire, but adamantly refusing the offer of artillery support until he was absolutely certain about the position of all his men, and warning that progress would take much longer because of the terrain.[22]

On the other hand the 22nd Battalion HQ was a place of great stress and anxiety: the messages received there were incomplete, out of date, and sometimes contradictory, and there was little you could do to react quickly if your men were in trouble. To cap it all, someone had reported in on the afternoon of the 14th that one of the 22nd companies was miles away, mixed with the KRRCs. Despite a very favourable report from Major Winter of the 23rd RF, searching for lost 23rd men, that he had found Major Adams, and that the defensive flank did exist,[23] there was still mistrust and confusion for a while. Major Adams sent out Captain Walsh to check. The latter's report has just a touch of irritation about it:

W.r.t. Batt HQ message SS27 and your message to Lt. Powell, I have made a personal reconnaissance from your [Adams'] HQ as far as the Green Line. Lt Powell had already established a liaison with the 13th Essex. Their left flank does not extend in front of our line, i.e. the defensive flank put out by us completely defends the left flank of all troops of 5th and 6th Bdes in front line. All dispositions have been made by Lts Powell and Kelly with great skill. I can place none of the K.R.R. anywhere near us. I suggest they have confused the 22nd RF with the 24th RF.[24]

On the other hand, the news coming into 2nd Division HQ from the northern flank on the 14th was sufficiently encouraging that 6 Brigade were asked to develop the situation. Colonel Norris of the 1st Kings had suggested that it might be better to tackle the Quadrilateral from the south than trying to attack it directly again. This meant it would fall into the province of Barker's Mixed Force. Consequently Colonel Barker ordered Major Adams to attack the Quadrilateral at dawn next morning, by pivoting on his right and swinging his left though the Quadrilateral. Two tanks were to be supplied for the attack.

The dashing Captain Jameson of the 1st Kings was asked to take some men and guide in the tanks. Needless to say the tanks soon bogged, one in the British front line and one a little further forward in no man's land. Evidently not one to miss a scrap[25] Captain Jameson collected a mixed Essex/Kings party and went forward to join

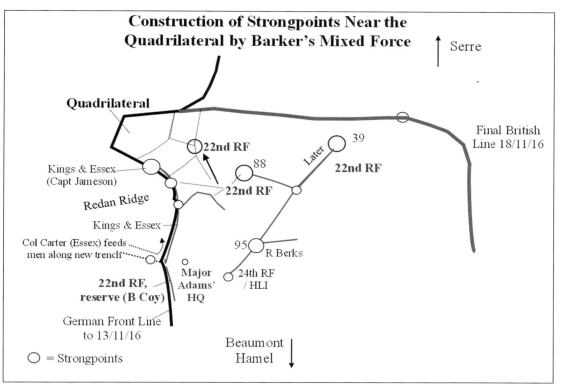

Construction of Strongpoints Near the Quadrilateral by Barker's Mixed Force

Serre

Quadrilateral

Final British
Line 18/11/16

22nd RF

Kings & Essex
(Capt Jameson)

Redan Ridge

88

39

22nd RF

22nd RF

Kings & Essex

Col Carter (Essex) feeds
men along new trench

95

R Berks

Major
Adams'
HQ

24th RF
/ HLI

22nd RF,
reserve (B Coy)

German Front Line
to 13/11/16

Beaumont
Hamel

○ = Strongpoints

The fight for the Quadrilateral.

Barker's Mixed Force. Meanwhile, aware that there were attackers to west, south and east of them, and perhaps aware of the sound of tank engines, the Germans had abandoned a machine gun post at the southern edge of the Quadrilateral that had been causing problems to Major Adams' men.

This was just what the attackers needed. B Company, aided by parties from 6 Brigade (one led by Captain Jameson), drove north/north-west along the old front line trenches on the western side of the Quadrilateral, meeting little resistance, and getting up and over the 140 metre contour (the high point). Parties from A and D companies, on the eastern side of the Quadrilateral struggled forward through deep mud, but managed to establish a strongpoint plumb in the centre of the feature, and another one to the east of it (point 88) also roughly on the crest of the ridge. By noon, therefore, elements of Barker's Mixed Force occupied half of the Quadrilateral and overlooked the rest of it with Lewis and Vickers Guns. Colonel Barker ordered another advance, up Serre Trench in a north-east direction to form another strongpoint (at point 39) to negate a machine gun hindering their advance forward from point 88. Enough leverage had been created and shortly afterwards the Germans evacuated it.

Later in the day the force was still advancing satisfactorily when Colonel Barker received orders to halt and consolidate on the high ground, ready to be relieved, rather

Major [Phythian-]Adams, now second-in-command of the Battalion; and cool and confident in charge of all the troops in Barker's Mixed Force.
(Phythian-Adams papers)

than get into less defensible positions down the northern slope.

The absence of enemy defenders meant that enemy artillery could concentrate on the area and the men were subject to very heavy shelling almost all day, with at one stage a whole post of C Company's being blown up. Nevertheless the mixed force held on stoutly, despite shortages of food and water, until relieved in the early hours of 16 November. Colonel Barker was full of praise for Major Adams' work:

No one could have handled the situation in the German lines in a more capable manner than Major Adams did, and I have placed his name in my recommendation for honours.[26]

Life changed at the moment of relief. Christopher Stone recalled:

But the misery of it all ended at dawn on the 16th when B.B. and I sallied out into the open air, clambered out on to the top and walked back to Mailly Maillet, revelling in the perfect freshness of that November morning and full of the unspeakable relief of feeling that the show which we had been regarding with apprehension for six weeks of urgent suspense was over and done with. B.B. was grey and haggard, the deep lines of his face deepened by the strain of mental and physical over-exertion; but we both felt new life coming to us as we stretched our limbs and set out through the long grass towards a warm billet, a stunning breakfast, a divine bath and bed. Great days, those, in retrospect.[27]

Captain Roscoe had his own unique perspective:

The time is early morning, and the scene an old trench. Daylight is just showing in the sky, and round the entrance to a deep dug-

Second Division.

No. **552**

Name. **Sgt. J D F Tilney.**

Regt. **22nd R. Fus.**

Your Commanding Officer and Brigade Commander have informed me that you have distinguished yourself by conspicuous bravery in the field on **13/16 to Nov 1916** I have read their reports and, although promotion and decorations cannot be given in every case, I should like you to know that your gallant action is recognised and how greatly it is appreciated.

H.J. Walker Major-General, Commanding 2nd Division.

Date **5-12-16**

Sergeant Tilney was commended for Redan Ridge – as he was for the September 15th raid
(courtesy Arturo E Goodliffe)

out stands a group of men – haggard and filthy, with a three-days beard on their blackened and mud-streaked faces. Presently, from below, an officer appears, hardly less dirty than the men.

'Any sign of that relief yet?'

'No, sir,' answers one of the men: and they wait again in silence.

Soon, however, parties of men start to arrive, some up the trench, others across the top; and after some little time the whole of the relieving party is collected and slowly and painfully they move off towards the posts where the old defenders of the position are stationed.

When all are gone the officer comes up again, this time with the equipment and orderlies, and taking up his position on then fire-step he surveys the scene. Daylight is strengthening rapidly and the sky, without a cloud in sight, gives promise of a fine day to come. It is bitterly cold; a thick white frost lies over the ice-bound ground, and he stamps about to keep warm. More parties of men are still arriving to relieve different parts of the line, and a number of these have lost their way and find themselves on the top in a very exposed position. Those he directs on their way and hurries them across the exposed point – none too soon, for almost as they go several Hun shells whizz up and burst maybe 50 yards away.

After what seems to him a long time he sees some of his company coming down the trench, and hailing them asks if the relief is going alright. Slow but sure is the method of relief, and as each party is relieved at its post, the men come down and are despatched by the Company Commander across the top towards our old front line with instructions to go straight down to the first village, where they will find all ready for them.

Later he starts out himself across the top with his orderly and Sergeant-Major. By now the sun has risen, and a gold and sparkling world spreads out before them after days of mud and darkness. Never has it seemed so good to be alive before; and away they stride towards the village. Arriving there he finds all ready for the company, who are by now nearly all in their

Signallers' work was often unseen, but the contribution of Sergeant Keeble was recognised with the DCM for displaying 'great courage and skill in maintaining communications under very heavy fire. He set a fine example to his men.'
(Keeble papers)

billets, asleep, rolled in their blankets, or eating the first good hot meal they have had in several days.

Further down the street is his servant waiting to guide him to the billet, and there he finds a sumptuous meal prepared, and a bed, with clean clothes and hot bath already; and he feels that after all a battle is worth going through to realize the comforts of 'ordinary war.'[28]

1 *RBB*, 1/10/1916

2 *RBB*, 12/10/1916

3 Interview with ex-Sergeant Roland Whipp, 18/11/1983

4 *RBB*, 20/10/1916; Mufti, October 1920, 2, No 5 p1

5 *Mufti*, Spring 1928, 10, No 1, pp 6-7; one of those killed was a Private Russell-Davies, a company sanitary-man, who left a valuable collection of ironwork to the South Kensington Museum

6 *RBB*, 23 and 29/10/1916; Letter from JPC Sankey-Barker; 11/2/1986; name slightly obscured, probably F.H. Wardale

7 22nd RF *History*, op cit, p39 and *RBB*, 24/10/1916

8 Temperatures from *The Somme, The Day-By-Day Account*, Chris McCarthy, 1993, pp 142-3; See *Sheffield & Inglis* p71 and 73

9 22nd RF War Diary, *WO 95*/1372, 30/10/1916 and 2/11/1916

10 Interview with Ex-Corporal George Challis, 1984

11 22nd RF War Diary, *WO 95*/1372, 12/11/1916

12 *The Times*, 17/11/1916

13 See 8 Brigade report and reports from the COs of the 2nd Royal Scots and 1st Royal Scots Fusiliers, WO 95/1416

14 *Mufti*, 2, No 7, January 1921, pp 3-4

15 *B.B.*, p7; Dugout at Egg/Vallade intersection

16 Taken from Colonel Barker's report, 6 Brigade War Diary, WO 95/1355

17 *Ibid*

18 *Biography*, p102. also see *Sheffield & Inglis*, op cit, p75.

19 Colonel Barker's report, op cit. The worst areas for mud tended to be those that had received the most artillery attention, and those tended to be the enemy strongpoints

20 Second Lieutenant, later Captain Simons's MC citation, *London Gazette*, 13/2/1917

21 Message received at 5 Brigade (*WO 95*/1344) at 2.45 pm, sent 1.45 pm, that '22nd RF hold another post at base of Quadrilateral'

22 6 Brigade message folder, RBB to 6 Brigade, 12.20 pm, 15/11/1916

23 Major Winter's Reconnaissance Report, 23rd RF War Diary, *WO 95*/1372, 16/11/1916

24 Captain Walsh to Major Adams, 14/11/1916, 5.45 pm, 6 Brigade message pocket, *WO 95*/1358.

25 Stuck against uncut wire at the Quadrilateral on the 13th, he then escorted wounded men back to British lines, then went forward on the 14th with 25 men to report to Colonel Carter, whence he escorted the tanks in and became part of Barker's Mixed Force, *WO 95*/1355

26 Colonel Barker's Report, op cit, *WO 95*/1355

27 *B.B., p7*

28 *Mufti*, February 1921, 2, No 8, p2

Chapter Seven

Christmas At Yvrench

COLONEL BARKER summarised the Ancre battle as follows:

The ground absolutely beat us and exhausted the men. Many of them were absolutely stuck and couldn't get out. The fighting men, the real stuff were indescribably magnificent. How they endured the hardships and awful fatigue caused by the mud I don't know. If it had come off in July or August we should now be in Berlin. They were very different Huns to fight than the Delville Wood lot. Boys like Billa and oldish men.

Stories abounded of German 'kamerads' with their bags packed just waiting to be overrun. Indeed, Ollie Berrycloath, sent to escort seven prisoners to the rear, found that the seven had become eight:

One of the Jerries had got through our lines and when he saw us coming along he [just] fell in. When we reported eight prisoners they said where did the other one come from, we said 'he must have grown!'[1]

Some Germans might have been kamerads, but after the first day German resistance stiffened almost everywhere. What is true is that he 22nd Battalion emerged from the battle with great credit. They had achieved their objectives with skill, determination and sheer doggedness. They had suffered a considerable number of casualties, certainly, but less than half of those at the taking of Delville Wood. They were fortunate to have been allotted a task under their own control. Brigadier-General AC Daly, commanding 6 Brigade, wrote Colonel Barker a very generous letter of thanks for the 22nd Battalion's assistance:

My dear Barker,

I must just write you a few lines to express, as well as I can, my thanks for and admiration of the really splendid work of your Battalion during the last three days. I really don't know how we should have got on if I had not had the good fortune to be lent the 22nd Royal Fusiliers. As you know, at the time you joined us, 6 Brigade mustered, for fighting purposes, at the most some 600 rifles, and we should have been sorely put to deal with the Quadrilateral situation. In fact, I doubt if we could have done anything of an offensive nature. My most grateful thanks (in the name of the whole Brigade) to you and Major Adams and, if your Brigadier has no objection, would you take steps to convey my statements of esteem and admiration to all ranks of the battalion. I hope your casualties were not very heavy. I hope to see you soon and thank you in person.

Yours very sincerely,

(ad) A.C. Daly[2]

In total, 19 other ranks had been killed, with 56 wounded and 7 missing, while one officer, Second Lieutenant Fitton (leading a contact patrol out from one of the posts), had been killed, and four others wounded. Second Lieutenants Hutcheson, and Gell were more seriously wounded, while Doc Miller and Second Lieutenant Parkes were both slightly wounded, but still at duty. This time Colonel Barker wrote off to the Mayor with the list of casualties on the 17th of the month, so letters from the latter would almost certainly have arrived before any official War Office correspondence.[3]

Although Doc Miller initially stayed at duty, he was soon obliged to leave the Battalion for good. His principal helper Sergeant WH Metcalfe recalled him:

> *Every man will remember his short sturdy figure with the rather large head crowned with a disreputable service cap pushed well back, his rolling walk and his blue eyes, which could be like steel when he was wiping the floor with you, and extraordinarily soft and winning at other times.*[4]

Christopher Stone, who had shared many a dugout with the doctor, highlighted:

> *His sly Scotch mischievousness which would make him put a hedgehog in the Padre's bed; and perhaps one ought to add his deliciously entertaining rebelliousness.*[5]

The men marched back from the line with plenty of souvenirs acquired from prisoners to Mailly Maillet, where rum and a hot meal was waiting for the men. Some got more rum than others, especially the Lewis gunners:

> *Some…may remember the double ration of rum (two jars) and grub scrounged from every cooker in the battalion, when they came back to Mailly Maillet after the commencement of the Ancre scrap, when they, or most of them, got full and very festive, and poor old [Sergeant] Hennessy sang love songs in Spanish and poor 'Bri' [Sergeant Brierley] gave a dissertation on cricket at the same time.*[6]

The Battalion moved further back on the 19th, to Gezaincourt. The next day they were visited by Sir Douglas Haig, just back from the Inter-Allied Conference at Chantilly, where the victories (Beaumont Hamel, Beaucourt etc) had helped strengthen his hand in arguing next year's strategy. He too was in generous mood:

> *In the afternoon the men were drawn up outside their billets and inspected by the G.O.C.-in-C., who warmly congratulated Company Commanders and the Commanding Officer on the good work done by the battalion.*[7]

Major Adams was presented:

> *The Brigadier was kind enough to lavish some very complimentary remarks on me, and I had a short conversation with the 'Great Man'. Individually he asked me what the behaviour of the Huns was like and I told him that whenever threatened by a decent number of our men they hurried to their dugouts and 'packed up their kits for London'. He seemed amused.*

Indeed General Haig wrote down almost the exact phrase in his diary.[8]

Christopher Stone, on the other hand, tried not to catch the C-in-C's eye, but did:

> *He brushed Adams aside and held out his hand to me. 'My Adjutant' said Adams. What do you think the great man asked me? 'How long have you been soldiering?'! However I wasn't taking any, so I said 'Since the beginning of the war, sir, I began as a private. 'Splendid, splendid. And where did you win that?' 'At Delville Wood, sir.' 'Very fine; you must have had a very hard time there. Well', he held out his hand again, 'I'm proud*

to shake hands with you.'

The Battalion moved further and further away from the line and arrived at their destination Yvrench (about 16 km from Abbeville) on 27 November. They were now in divisional rest, and would be able to rest and refit for some weeks. Colonel Barker went off on leave sick. He struggled back, still not completely well, on 8 December, but immediately had to go off to command the Brigade. Meanwhile drafts started arriving: 346 men and officers between 27 November and 14 December. Drafts in these sorts of numbers would have been more than useful some time in October, before the fight, but they were welcome now. Colonel Barker thought that the new drafts contained 'splendid looking men'.[9]

As a new 'Sig', Private 'Lively' Gladwin, who joined just before the battle, needed a gentle lesson from his upstanding Signalling Sergeant Fred Keeble:

...In nineteen sixteen I joined the 'old Batt.'
With Collins and Lampshead and Wright,
And one or two others whose names I forget
But I know it was quite late at night.
We had walked many miles, were hungry and cold
Went into a trench, and there in the mud
Were inspected by Sgt A Keeble.
Now he looked at me, and I looked at him
We didn't think much of each other.
Said he, 'Follow me, and do as you're told,
And I'll treat you just like a brother.'
He gave me a flag, a lamp and some wire
And loaded me up like a camel.
Issued instructions, and off we went
Up the line. To Beaumont Hamel.
Now that was a scrap I shall never forget
It was my baptism of fire.
Up came Keeble. That was my lot,
'Cause I'd dumped the lamp and the wire.
'You ain't done that old chum,' said he
In a voice severe and kind.
Well 'xxxxx' find it and don't be long
There's a good chap. Do you mind?
I hung my head in shame and remorse
And went searching for that which I'd dumped.
Hooray, I found it, and hurried straight back.
The battalion had moved. I was stumped.
I staggered along with my weapons of war
Just like an innocent child
Then I met Keeble. He just looked at me,

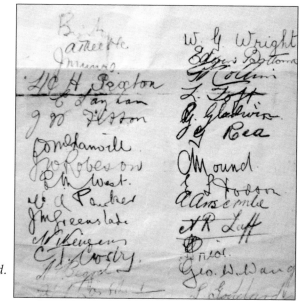

These signatures were done at the Signallers Christmas Dinner on 9/12/16, when Fred had long since forgiven Gladwin.
(Keeble papers)

161

And I looked at him. We both smiled.
I deserved a court martial. Of that there's no doubt.
In those days I cared not a fig.
But now years have flown, I feel very proud
That I was a 'Kensington' Sig.[10]

Little did Gladwin know that his Signalling Sergeant was a big softie at heart:

My Dear Darling Sweetheart Edie,
Very many thanks for Letter and Photo received today. Darling Edie, really my Dear it's the Sweetest thing I have received for many a month…
Your Ever Loving Boy, Fred xxxxx. [11]

The picture of Edie that kept Fred sane through 1917.
(Keeble papers)

He carried that picture around with him for the rest of the war.

Meanwhile Henry Lea, the mad inventor, had been regaling Mayor Davison with his war-winning suggestions. He created something called Rolling Cover that looked like a man carrying an inverted canoe on his back. Lea ought to have been whisked off to some idea factory, there to debate and refine his ideas. As it was:

When the men of my own Trench Mortar Battery saw a tank in action for the first time they yelled: 'Look! There's old Lea's Rolling Cover!'

Yvrench was remembered by the men most for its Christmas celebrations, about which

It would be eminently portable…
(From Henry Lea's *A Veld Farmer's Adventures*)

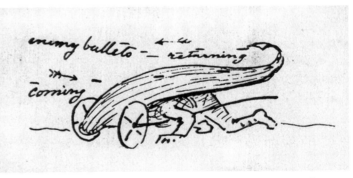

Henry Lea's Rolling Cover – designed to deflect German bullets back to their sources, and it could be carried on one's back.
(From Henry Lea's *A Veld Farmer's Adventures*)

more anon, but also for the excellent baths that Sergeant McGowan constructed from scratch, which Christopher Stone describes:

> We took a tumbledown shed; paved the floor with rubble from the road, dug a trench and two soak pits…bunged up the draughts with sacking; 'acquired' three barrels which were sawed into 6 tubs, borrowed some boilers which had been thrown away as useless by the villagers, and when I went in there this afternoon there were 20 men bathing, scrubbing each other, putting on clean underclothing, hunting for small game, and thoroughly enjoying the steam and warmth.

Ralph Durand was in charge of the Regimental Canteen. At Yvrench he was able to acquire some beer and a ruined cellar. What it really needed was some form of heating and firewood was in short supply:

> One day, after dark, a man – I won't say who – came and offered to sell us coal. There was an A.S.C. coal-dump in the village and my conscience would not allow me to be mixed up in the theft of property belonging to His Majesty's Army, so I pushed off, leaving the canteen-sergeant to grapple with the problem, but when I came back and found men drinking their beer over a roaring fire, I did not challenge the item in the canteen cash-book, 'one sack of coal - one franc.' After all, this man may have come by the sack of coal honestly. His aunt may have sent it to him for a Christmas present.[12]

Training was undertaken and lectures attended, but there was still plenty of time for entertainments like cinema and concerts, football and boxing tournaments. The regimental canary ('Dicky' Bird) did his single-handed best to entertain the men by singing *Egypt* a number of times nightly between 6 and 8 pm. Much home leave was given at his time also, but it soon dwindled into a memory, as Paul Destrubé commented:

> Alas!, my leave, for which I regarded as being the crowning compensation for this tedious and monotonous existence, is now but a dream, a thing of the past. What would I not give to have it come over again?[13]

The next thing was to make it a Christmas to remember. The Mayor of Kensington did his best to support the men by sending over 2,300 candles and 230-250 pairs of socks in early December, but his main Christmas presents to the men were pipes (800 sent) and cigarettes (820 boxes of fifty cigarettes). Mrs Barker sent plum puddings and £5 per company, meanwhile her husband asked Ralph Durand to spend the profit from the Regimental Canteen, about 2,000 francs, on buying extras for the Christmas dinners. Durand bought pigs from a farmer:

> A Coy came to fetch their pig this morning. The pig knew he had his orders to 'go over the top' & instead of taking it like a man, squealed the whole place down. The pigs have no discipline at all.[14]

A Christmas revue was being prepared for the Battalion's amusement. It was set in a Conscientious Objectors Tribunal, where a Mr Maconochie was defending himself. He argued that as he supplied eatables to the armed forces he was exempt, but it all hinged whether what he produced could be called 'eatable'.

The men, with the aid of the pioneers, had transformed their cow houses and

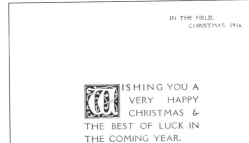

IN THE FIELD,
CHRISTMAS, 1916.

ISHING YOU A
VERY HAPPY
CHRISTMAS &
THE BEST OF LUCK IN
THE COMING YEAR.

From . .

DELVILLE WOOD

Inside of 99 Brigade 1916 Christmas Card featuring a picture of Delville Wood, but one's eye is drawn to the fatalistic 'best of luck in the coming year'. (Phythian-Adams papers)

broken down barns into fairy grottoes with Chinese lanterns, unlimited cotton wool from the aid post and some bought-in paper decorations, plus holly and other greenery. When the contents of parcels from home were added in, there were some pretty impressive spreads.

Colonel Barker and Captain Stone (Major Adams was on leave) took nearly 1½ hours to tour around the various parties, with lots of cheers and speeches and rounds of 'For he's a jolly good fellow'. Colonel Barker's plan for a trouble-free day had been lots of food, unlimited (weak) beer, but limited whisky. One of the company parties seems to have been the sort of restrained adult affair that the Colonel was intending:

> *By judicious expenditure of francs and with the help of generous parcels from Blighty we were able to load the tables with cakes, oranges, Christmas cheer and dainties of various kinds and the mess tins were loaded with helpings of beef, pork and vegetables.*
>
> *The barrel of beer rapidly yielded up its contents, but the men 'carried on' with gusto. The C.O. and the Adjutant gave us a look-in, and we exchanged the compliments of the season.*
>
> *There was plenty of cheer and plenty of festivity and we finished up late at night with carols round the fire of logs.*[15]

The Lewis gunners' party was believed to be rather less restrained. There were no arrests, as the divisional police had been invited in to share the banquet. Some undeniable damage was admitted:

> *We had no cases of Orderly Room except Father Xmas. He, apparently, in full costume fell through an estaminet window at 11 p.m. on Xmas night. As he offered to pay for all the damage I let him off. They are all dears, just a pack of humorous children.*

If Christmas had been one of the most pleasant days, Boxing Day had one of the least pleasant events. At 7:08 am on the 26th, Private CWF Skilton was shot for desertion, after a Field General Court Martial on 9 December.[16] The picture of Skilton that comes through from the words of his accusers (he did not defend himself or request a prisoner's friend) is of a skiver - phrases like 'always endeavouring to shirk fatigue' and 'unreliable and useless' were used about him. There was strong suspicion – but insufficient evidence – that Skilton had deserted on the day of the Delville Wood attack and within the last six months he had been sentenced to Field Punishment Number One and Number Two for absence from fatigues and parades. In peacetime the Army and Skilton would surely have been separated by less extreme means. The present crime related to absence for the whole Ancre battle. Major Adams reported that only three men failed to reach the German lines. One was acquitted and the second one was given two years imprisonment with hard labour.

The third one was Skilton, who had been told by Sergeant Pearson to reconnoitre along a particular trench to see if it would be safer for B Company (then being heavily shelled). This was at 10 am on 13 November. He was next observed, and put under arrest, at 7:30 am on 16 November at billets in Mailly Maillet, having rejoined the Battalion when it was being relieved. He claimed that someone – possibly Second Lieutenant George Evans – had told him to mind a bomb store. Under cross-examination he added that he had not been aware that the Battalion had all moved forward a few hours later, even although they would have passed within twenty yards of him. And no one had come for bombs all the time he was there. Evans said that he had not given any such order, and that there was no bomb store where the accused had described it. The problem, as seen by Adams, Barker and Walker, was that the high standard of discipline in the Battalion needed to be maintained, and this soldier had a *consistently* poor record, hence the proper penalty for this offence ought to be imposed.[17]

On the 27th the officers learnt that the divisional general Major-General WG Walker had returned to the UK and been replaced by Major-General Sir Cecil Pereira, a Guardsman. Colonel Barker hoped that there wouldn't be any change in the 'united happy and gentlemanly way' they soldiered. On the other hand, when General Pereira did come down to the 22nd Battalion to inspect billets he was very complimentary, and Colonel Barker soon warmed to him.

By the end of the month the first awards of medals concerning the Ancre battle began to arrive. Brigadier-General Kellett received the CMG, while Colonel Barker (and Sergeant-Major RD Burgess) would soon find that they had been Mentioned In Despatches. Major Adams, Captains Simons and Roscoe were given MCs, while Sergeant Keeble got a DCM, and there were a number of MMs: Sergeants Hennessy, Guy and Smith, Lance-Sergeants Palmer and Gimson, Lance-Corporal Ayres, Privates Garman, Porker, Stewart, Turner and Wagland. The Colonel was a little disappointed for Major Adams that he had only got an MC instead of the DSO he felt he deserved. Nevertheless, it was prompt recognition for his determination and coolness under fire and his citation included the following:

He displayed great courage and initiative when in command of advanced battalion headquarters, and took up a defensive flank. He has on many previous occasions done fine work.[18]

Back in Kensington, the Mayor had been making a seasonal appeal for soldiers' knitted

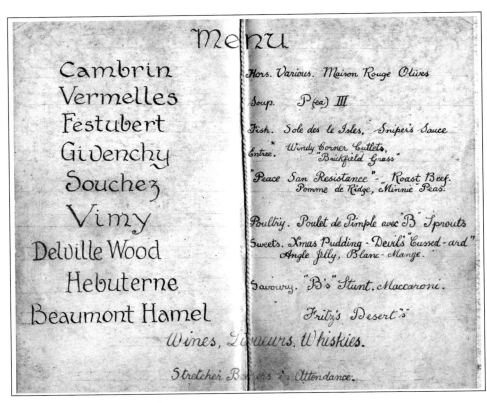

B Company's Christmas Lunch menu (courtesy Mrs B Sutcliffe)

comforts. In a rich borough like Kensington, the tone of the Appeal was somewhat different from the norm:

> *Dear Madam…I am told that in a number of houses the maids have lent valuable assistance in knitting comforts, the wool being provided by their mistresses, a joint present to our men at the front being thus given by the household. I hope this suggestion may commend it to you.[19]*

The Mayor's reply to a Mrs Schruter of Rutland Gate included the following:

> *Will you also kindly convey my thanks to your servants for having made the articles with the wool which you were good enough to provide.*

As the year ended, there was great competition between the battalions about which one was to demonstrate an attack to the Army Commander. Colonel Barker used their successful raid in Hebuterne as their attack, but with live ammunition instead of the usual blanks. First the 22nd Battalion, featuring a platoon under Lieutenant GH (George) Evans, were chosen as the battalion to represent 99 Brigade. The platoon practised several times before performing before the Divisional General who said 'he would pay £10 in London to see it'. It then competed with the chosen representatives of the other brigades in front of the Corps Commander, who picked the 22nd Battalion's platoon – a performance of 'great éclat and noise'[20] – as the chosen one. More practices followed, then it was played to the Army Commander with great success on the 5th January. The platoon received some choice rewards:

> *The platoon which did the Army Comdr show today were all bathed and given new underclothes and uniform and a jolly good tea, with plum-pudding and cigarettes.*

The 22nd Battalion's standing was again high on the 8th when the Corps Commander picked out their Transport as 'standing out alone' above other Corps transport units. The Battalion's long spell of rest was nearly over – the division was ear-marked, it was rumoured, for one of the worst spots in France. On the 9th, on a somewhat cold day, they set off on a fourteen mile march to Candas, with the men carrying full packs, steel helmets, gas masks, iron rations etc. It was the beginning of a sustained spell of very cold weather, with lots of snow and ice, for the next month, with temperatures of twenty below freezing being common. On the 20th they reached billets in Bouzincourt (a few miles north-west of Albert) which was where the 'Decca' gramophone arrived in the Battalion HQ mess. Christopher Stone wrote:

> *Our beloved colonel, the famous 'B.B.' … was quickly converted to the Decca, and in his autocratic way began to insist on hearing his favourite records every evening, till our music became as much a matter of routine as the evening report from the orderly room, or the last whisky and soda before bedtime.*[21]

Or, one should add, of the pre-dinner bridge sessions, with five people playing so that one player could drop out each rubber and write his letters.

The too-efficient 22nd Battalion casualty communication system had fallen foul of the authorities, who were not at all keen to see either the Colonel or Mayor Davison creating an *unofficial* system to rival their own. Although the Colonel had told the Mayor that he must on no account show the list of names in any public place, the Army Council refused to budge; it was the Adjutant-General's policy that commanding officers were prohibited from giving out unofficial casualty lists.[22]

99 Brigade was reserve brigade in the division at this time, so they were not among the first battalions to face the awful trench system in the Courcelette area. This was all ground wrested from the Germans after huge bombardments and much exploding of mines, so it consisted of a mass of mine craters, shell holes and wire entanglements. There were no trench lines as such, just widely-separated posts. Nor were there any communication trenches leading up to the posts, so all movement was at night on duckboard tracks.

The Destrubé brothers had been considering applying for commissions. Colonel Barker, who called them 'the two bravest men in the Battalion'[23], was in favour of them becoming officers, but not yet. He had work for them to do.

On the 28th January the Battalion moved to freezing Nissen huts at Wolfe Huts, sending working parties forward. A Company was first to experience the front line post system, followed on the 1st February by the remainder of the Battalion. Posts were held by two companies, with the companies relieved by the other two companies in the Battalion after two days.

On the 3rd Colonel Barker had a disturbing message:

> *Just had a wire handed me that Roscoe has had his leg blown off. He is my very very best*

officer. I don't know what I shall do without him. He was splendidly brave & as clever as a man of 40, although just 20. He is now my senior Captain & one in whom I had the most implicit confidence. I do hope he pulls through but the wire sounds bad. What a beastly vile thing this war is. I saw him last night in the front posts, so cheery & bright. He was just being relieved & coming back here with his company. Having suffered every possible discomfort & danger for 48 hours, he returns to comparative safety [his company HQ] *& then gets it.*

Captain Roscoe, one of the few original officers left from 1914, was mortally wounded by shellfire while he was asleep in A Company's HQ post. Doc Coad and a party of stretcher-bearers made a hazardous but successful journey over the top in daylight to bring back his body, but he could not be saved and died on the 4th. He was buried at Contay on the 6th February, with a large attendance not just from the Battalion as a whole, but from across the whole brigade. The War Diary said 'his sterling strength of brain and character had played a very notable part in the training and history of the regiment', while George Challis told us Roscoe:

…was loved. Very much a soldier. Not everyone who can accept responsibility & be nice too. He was only a young man. I'm pleased to have met him.[24]

In the early morning (3 am) of the 5th there was a very successful raid from the Battalion area, but carried out by the Royal Berks, with all the attackers dressed in white for camouflage in the snow, on a vulnerable enemy salient called 'The Nose'. They isolated the salient with accurate Stokes Mortar fire followed by a box barrage around the area, and then moved forward to trap a party of 65 Germans. They killed fourteen and took two officers and forty-nine men back to the British lines as prisoners.[25] This had the effect of shaking up the area; there had been something of a live and let live atmosphere because of the conditions. Now enemy shelling became much severe on the dumps and the brushwood tracks that served as roads up to the posts. Fortunately for the 22nd Battalion, they were relieved on the evening of the 5th, although they did suffer eleven casualties.

The freezing weather continued: the Colonel's moustache froze solid on eight consecutive days; Perrier bottles froze and burst; eggs froze hard (but made reasonable omelettes), while bread had ice crystals in it. Wells also froze, so there was a general water shortage. One man was found outside his billet at Bouzincourt on the 7th February, having died of cold and exposure. It was said he had been suffering from agonising toothache and went outside to walk around.

On the 12th of the month the 2nd HLI were raided by the Germans and a corporal and six men were taken prisoner.[26] The relevance for the 22nd Battalion is whether or not any of these captured men gave any secrets away about forthcoming operations. German prisoners often did, in many cases without realising it. At about the same time, on the evening of the 12th/13th, a Second Lieutenant FC Lockyer, visiting the DCLI (2nd Division's Pioneer battalion) for the first time, in the communication trench called Ironside, was spooked by some close-bursting shells and disappeared. It was thought that he had run off, but no one knew in what direction.

On the 11th there had been a conference of senior officers at II Corps (involving 2nd, 18th and 63rd Divisions) to discuss details of the proposed attack on the high ground (Hill 130) just in front of Petit Miraumont.

As 99 Brigade would be undertaking the 2nd Division attack, Colonel Barker, at Brigade because of the illness of General Kellett, was busy making plans. There is a draft plan dated 9 February, and a fully fleshed out and revised version dated the 13 February at 9 pm after all the battalions in the brigade had practised this attack on the 12 and 13 February.

It seems unlikely that a copy of the minutes of the Generals' meeting, or 99 (or 6) Brigade attack plans could fall into the hands of a corporal or a windy sub, but strange things happen in warfare. Some German unit histories claim a copy of future British operations in this area fell into their hands a few days before the attack.[27]

On the 16th the Battalion moved to battle positions between the East and West Miraumont Roads. Major Adams was in command of the Battalion, as Colonel Barker was still at brigade HQ. The initial attack would be done by the KRRCs on the left (next to the 6th Northants from 54 Brigade, 18th Division, who were attacking on their left), and the 23rd RF on the right (next to the 2nd South Staffords of 6 Brigade). Two platoons of B Company were given over to C Company of the KRRC for mopping-up duties (the other two platoons being used for carrying parties), while D Company would accompany the 23rd RF and seek to make a defensive flank on the right wing of 99 Brigade attack, from the Old British Line to the first objective. A and C Companies would take over from the KRRC and 23rd RF at the second objective and attack the third objective.

The author(s) of the plans had tried to cover off almost all eventualities, and tried to put into process lessons learnt from recent battles. A page was devoted to making the defensive flank on the right (D Company of the 22nd Battalion from the Old British Line up to first objective, and the 23rd RF from there forward up to the second objective). The artillery would be using a new form of barrage with less weight on the creeping part (which particularly affects getting to the first objective, usually achieved in set-piece attacks), and more firepower on objectives in the rear (where attacks run out of steam for lack of support).

The barrage would begin at 5:45 am, when the troops began the advance, while the speed of the creeping barrage had been set for rapid progress over firm ground (100 yards in three minutes up to first objective, thirty minute pause, then in four minutes thereafter).

Unfortunately there was a great thaw on the 16th; too late to change arrangements, so it was sticky slush underfoot, not solid ground. Despite last-minute panics, the men formed up in time and lay and waited until zero hour. They were completely out in the open, because the frozen ground had prevented trench-building. Their protection was silence and surprise. To prevent coughing noises, 99 Brigade had been issued with 4,000 pieces of chewing gum.[28]

1 Interview with Ollie Berrycloath, 15/1/1984

2 Preserved in a number of places: *RBB papers*, 22nd RF War Diary, November 1916: *WO 95/1372*, *Broughshane*, VI:26

3 RBB to Davison, 17/11/1916, *Broughshane*, VI:25

4 *Mufti*, Spring 1926, 7, No 1, pp 5-6

5 *Mufti*, Autumn 1925, 6, No 3, pp 3-4; ADMS is Assistant Director of Medical Services

6 AJL Tottenham, *Mufti*, Summer 1927, 8, No 2, pp 6-7

7 22nd RF War Diary, 20/11/1916: *WO 95/1372*

8 WJPA to his mother, 20/11/1916, *PAP. Douglas Haig War Diaries And Letters 1914-18*, Eds Gary Sheffield and John Bourne, Weidenfeld & Nicolson, 2005, pp 257-58

9 22nd RF War Diary, *WO 95/1372*

10 GH Gladwin, *Mufti*, December 1950, 30, No 116, p4

11 Fred Keeble to his future wife Edie, 22/12/1916

12 Ralph Durand, *Mufti*, Xmas 1921, 3, No 3 pp 3-4

13 *Broughshane*, Destrubé Letters, 2534, 18/12/1916

14 *Mufti*, Xmas 1921, 3, No 3, p4. But Durand himself collapsed and was invalided back to the UK; *RBB*, 22/12/1916

15 *Mufti*, Xmas 1935, 16, No 4, p2 (One thinks of the religious group in B Company)

16 Court Martial: *WO 71/531*. Sentence confirmed by 'D. Haig, Genl' on 23/12/1916. Ollie Berrycloath worked after the war at the cemetery close to where Skilton's mother lived. At the foot of her gravestone was her son's name and the words 'Died of gunshot wounds'.

17 *Ibid* and *WO 93/49*; see Gary Sheffield's paper 'A very good kind of Londoner and a very good type of colonial' in *Look To Your Front*, Brian Bond et al, BCMH, 1999.

18 WSCT, 24/2/1917, p3, quoting from the *London Gazette*

19 *Broughshane*, reverse of 8765, undated (probably late December 1916), reply 8751

20 *PAP*, John (Major Adams) to Grace, 8/1/1917

21 Christopher Stone, *Mufti*, Xmas 1923, 4, p6; BB's son told us that his father had very catholic musical tastes from classical to Ragtime or Music Hall (letter 29/2/1984)

22 *Broughshane*, 8573, Davison to RBB, 19/1/1917, also see 8567 and 8568

23 *Broughshane*, Destrubé Letters, 2534, 30/1/1917

24 *WO 95/1372*, 6/2/1917, also *Mufti*, Xmas 1938, 19, No 91, p8; Interview with George Challis, 1984

25 Also see Trevor Pidgeon's very useful *Boom Ravine*, in the *Battleground Europe* series, Leo Cooper, 1998, pp 38-42.

26 2nd HLI War Diary, *WO 95/1347*, February 1917; also see *RBB* 13/2/1917

27 All spare copies of 'future operations' at the Brigade office, apart from Colonel Barker's own set, were accidentally burnt on the 10th by Captain Allfrey leaving an unattended candle on the table; *Pidgeon*, op cit, p 133-39 mentions the German units, also *Official History*, France & Belgium 1917, pp 76-7

28 2nd Division A & Q diary, *WO 95/1309*, 15/2/1917

Chapter Eight

Miraumont

THE FIRST UNPLEASANT SHOCK to the waiting attackers was very heavy enemy shelling along the whole attack front at 5 am (particularly bad just west of and just east of the East Miraumont Road, ie in the D Company/23rd RF and 2nd South Staffs waiting areas). The shelling also took out the ammunition for the trench mortars, so there would be no support from the latter. The next was machine-gun fire at 5:30 am, coming from areas where none were thought to be: the front right area, east of the East Miraumont Road. A Vickers Gun was hurriedly moved up to accompany D Company. It was as if the enemy had been forewarned.

In fact a deserter had given the Germans about five or six hours advance warning of the attacks. The Germans had some clues from analysing the changes in British artillery firing patterns. They may also have acquired a map and a version of the attack plans.[1] If it had been a copy of 99 Brigade plans these talked only about 'X' (eve of attack) and 'Y' (attack) days, but in one version of them someone had left in a '(15th Feb)' besides 'X-day'.[2] The most detailed information the Germans acquired – the fact that convinced them that the intelligence was trustworthy – was from the deserter on

The promised land: Miraumont from the German side in 1916.
(From *An Der Somme*, courtesy EB Furmston)

The German 1916 caption simply says Bei Miraumont, but it looks like the sunken road on the West Miraumont Road. (From *An Der Somme*, courtesy EB Furmston)

the eve of the attack; they learned from him the probable time of it (between 4 and 6 am, with others claiming 5:15 am). In his diary afterwards, General Pereira believed the deserter had come from the South Staffs, where the enemy shelling was heaviest.

To their great credit, the Germans had hurriedly brought forward extra men and machine guns and made available special counter-attack units, rich in machine guns and skilled marksmen, while they kept up a strong barrage on British lines and forming up areas, especially between 5 and 5:30 am.

At 5:45 am the attacking parties moved off, some of them considerably weakened by the German bombardment. Buff Whitehouse of B Company, among the KRRCs on the left, was one of the early casualties:

> As if he was aware of us, Fritz was shelling us quite heavily. When our bombardment of the enemy commenced the noise of many hundreds of shells, screeching, groaning and passing over our heads, was deafening. A number of German shells seemed to drop into every hole except the one we were in. Our attack began at 5:45 am and my Gun Team hadn't gone more than a dozen yards before a Howitzer burst to our left wounding the No. 1 and myself.[3]

Despite their casualties, the initial attack on the left by the KRRC's A and C companies (containing the two platoons of the 22nd Battalion's B Company, under Second

172

Lieutenants Burgess and Perraton) went well. They kept direction along the West Miraumont Road, despite a thick mist and poor visibility, and the mopping-up parties were soon said to be doing good work in at the junction of this road and Boom Ravine (the first objective was just beyond this).

The barrage moved too quickly for most units because of the thaw, with the thirty minutes pause at the first objective being much too short for reorganisation, as sub-units tended to become separated from their colleagues and inter-mingled with others because of the mist, while delays were also caused by finding ways around enemy resistance. Many of the units involved said the barrage felt thin, and that enemy machine guns were able to continuing firing through it.[4] The barrage carried on uselessly into the horizon with only tiny pockets of men able to follow close behind. There seemed to be a lot more defenders than had been anticipated. Almost all the odds were against the attackers now: no surprise, numerically strong enemy, poor terrain.

As in November, men attacking in featureless terrain in darkness or poor visibility (it was still dark at 5:45 am and the light would remain dull much of the day), lost direction despite the use of tapes and luminous signs to get around the problem. There were also what might be described as 'normal unexpected events.' Thus some of the KRRC B and D companies, due to leapfrog their A and C companies and go to the second objective, South Miraumont Trench, may have been pushed to the right by the 6th Northants. Some of the latter when faced with the natural barrier of the Boom Ravine, and badly cut wire, had side-slipped to their right over West Miraumont Road to get around it, before going left back on track. (Others may have still carried on going in a north-eastern direction).[5] Thus many of the KRRC men drifted half right, some going as far as the East Miraumont Road, where they were severely handled by the German defenders and driven back.

On the left of 99 Brigade, the 6th Northants from 54 Brigade had pressed on well despite losing many casualties, including most officers, to the initial bombardment; they had captured Boom Ravine by 6:30 am, and after a pause for reorganisation, pressed on to occupy the high ground between first and second objectives, with scattered groups making it into the second objective, the South Miraumont Trench. The other troops from their brigade (the 11th RF on their left) had a tougher time but fought through to just short of their second objective. Further to the west, the attacks of 53 Brigade and the 63rd Division on the extreme left, which had suffered less from the initial German bombardment, had been successful.

The 22nd Battalion's A and C Companies, whose original job had been to advance from second to third objective, crossed Boom Ravine but drifted to the north-west.

AJ Newton, C Company stretcher-bearer said:

My platoon (No. 10) were right over on the left and before we could reach them we were shelled all over the place. I thought my time had surely come. It seemed to me that we were being surrounded, which I think must have been the case, as the late Capt. Simons and, I think, Sgt. Herbert was with him, were right in the front.[6]

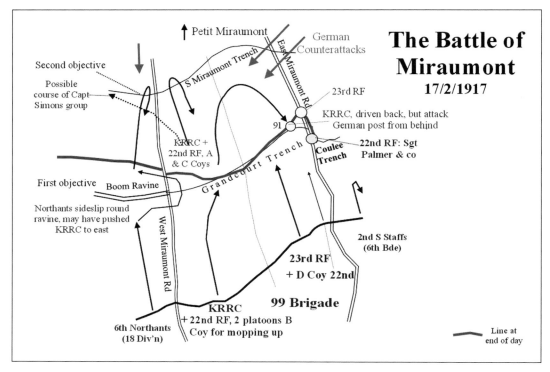

The Battle of Miraumont
17/2/1917

Petit Miraumont

German Counterattacks

Second objective

Possible course of Capt Simons group

S Miraumont Trench

East Miraumont Rd

23rd RF

91

KRRC, driven back, but attack German post from behind

KRRC + 22nd RF, A & C Coys

Coulee Trench

22nd RF: Sgt Palmer & co

Grandcourt Trench

First objective   Boom Ravine

Northants sideslip round ravine, may have pushed KRRC to east

West Miraumont Rd

2nd S Staffs (6th Bde)

23rd RF + D Coy 22nd

99 Brigade

6th Northants (18 Div'n)

KRRC + 22nd RF, 2 platoons B Coy for mopping up

Line at end of day

The Battle of Miraumont (Boom Ravine to 18th Division)

He was then wounded, sent back to Contay Casualty Clearing Station and eventually arrived at the 24th London General Hospital.

Captain Simons and Second Lieutenant Ellison of C Company, along with most of 9 Platoon (the other platoons of the company had become separated, or had been informed of their error), carried on going north-west until surrounded by a large party of Germans somewhere just short of the second objective. After a half-hour gun battle in which Captain Simons was killed, the remaining survivors (Second Lieutenant Ellison and about 10 men) were forced to surrender (possibly around 7:30 am). Almost all of them were wounded according to Ellison and Sergeant Maloney.[7]

These were the first men from the Battalion known to have been taken prisoner.

A Company were originally situated just to the right of C Company. Both veered off to the left but Captain Powell of A realised his mistake and managed to correct his direction – keeping to the right of the West Miraumont Road - on behalf of himself and his company, and then corrected the direction for most of C Company (possibly with the help of Sergeant-Major Phillips, whom Newton met in hospital later):

And I may tell you that he [Phillips] *saved a good many of the boys of 'C' coy., for he told them what had happened and which way to go.*[8]

Captain Powell then advanced on up the West Miraumont Road, a very good natural landmark. He seems to have become a casualty just short of the second objective at around 7.50 am. Two wounded sergeants from his party said they had been close enough to Petit Miraumont (third objective) to describe details of particular houses.

Sergeant WG Ford of A Company was also in his party and was sent to join a mixed group of men at the sunken road (West Miraumont Road just south of the South Miraumont Trench). A sentry told him that he thought he had seen Germans moving. Ford looked up and was wounded in the shoulder. The Germans now made a determined attack:

> 'They are coming over!' someone cried. I scrambled up the bank and we opened fire but it seemed to make no impression. I received another packet in the arm.
>
> I have a hazy recollection of seeing, when I came to, heaps of the boys dead and wounded. Picking up my arm I began to stagger back but a Gerry sent me about 110 yards into Boom Ravine [he means South Miraumont Trench].

Next morning the Germans carried him off to a ruin in Petit Miraumont to await an ambulance.[9]

Another small group from A and C companies had the following experience:

> Petit Miraumont was sighted at about the same time as a party of about a dozen, with an officer, of another Battalion of the same regiment [presumably the 23rd RF], were wandering across the front.

These men were incorporated into the C Company group but little further progress could be made:

> Fifty yards further, and the men ran into such a hail of bullets that it was impossible to press forward, and the men lay down in the shell holes to return the fire of the enemy who were found to be not 20 yards away.[10]

On the other hand, those parties of 6th Northants who progressed as far as the second objective said they saw a number of British troops forward to their right. Their Narrative said the following:

> On the whole the number of 18th Divisional troops in South Miraumont Trench was

Miraumont water mill in March 1917 after the artillery duels of the previous month.

small whereas the trench E of the W Miraumont road was fairly thickly occupied by
British troops.

Some of Captain Powell's men may have been among these, perhaps in combination with KRRCs and 23rd RF men, and there was one German report[11] that some British troops had reached the very northern boundary of Petit Miraumont.

Turning to the attack on the right, the men in 22nd Battalion's D Company faced very heavy shelling and immediately had problems both from uncut wire – Lance-Sergeant A Mobley was later given the DCM in part for 'forcing a gap in the enemy's wire at a critical time'[12] – and a hostile machine gun at Coulée Trench which may have been one of the new guns that the enemy had brought up overnight, or may simply have been missed by the artillery bombardment.[13] Many men were casualties. Captain George Evans and Second Lieutenant Fuller are believed to have been wounded early on, but not before Captain Evans had done some good work, as part of his MC citation says: 'He rallied the men and led them forward to the attack under very heavy fire. He was wounded'.[14]

Sergeant RP 'Micky' Brown was in charge of 20 men, including Lance-Sergeant Garvey and Corporal Woods, forming the advanced bombing party for D Company, due to go over the top with the third wave of the 23rd RF. His party were divided into two shell-holes, with himself and half the men in one hole and the remainder in the other one.

When it came his turn to advance he turned around, but only Lance Sergeant Garvey and Corporal Woods were behind him. They went on and battled their way to possession of about 30 yards of German Support Line trench. After realising they were isolated they decided to go back:

We came back and after crossing the German front line I found 'D' Company in shell holes in no man's land.

Knowing that if the frontal attack [by the KRRCs and the 23rd RF] *had succeeded the right flank was open I went from shell hole to shell hole shouting to the men to follow me forward.*

Major Walsh got out of the shell hole and asked me who I was.

'Sgt. Brown,' I replied.

The following conversation then took place:

Major Walsh – What's up, Brown?

Myself –The whole flank of the division is in the air, sir. We must go forward.

Major Walsh – How do you know this?

Myself – I and two others have been forward into the German support lines but we could not hold it by ourselves, so came back. There is not a man of 'D' Company the other side of the wire.

Major Walsh – Are you sure of this?

Myself – Yes, sir. Give me some men and I will take them forward into the German support lines and form a block.

Major Walsh shouted to the men to follow and I led them forward again.[15]

Sergeant Palmer (top right) and six of his pals (in the *Daily Sketch*, which added, more dubiously, that this was 'after a successful trench raid')

As they travelled back up to the lines, they took two prisoners and sent them back to the British lines after disarming them. Unfortunately Major Walsh was shot just in front of the German support line. Brown pulled Walsh into a shell-hole and began the assault on the trench:

I stood above the trench bombing the Germans, who had re-entered it.

His actions then inspired someone whose deeds would become legendary:

Sergeant Palmer jumped into the trench and shouted for me to lead a mad dash along the trench. I entered the trench again for the second time that morning and led the party. We pushed forward without any opposition for about fifty yards when I came to a traverse which was blown in. I decided to form a block here.

It was now getting light and we could see the Germans reinforcing the trench away to the right. As we had very little ammunition I left Palmer and the rest of the party (Corporal Carr, Lance Corporal Ward and two privates out of 15 platoon, their names I cannot remember) and came back along the trench to find out who was holding the

Sergeant now Second Lieutenant FW Palmer VC.

trench on the other side of the footpath.

I got in touch with a young officer of the 23rd R.F. and told him how we were placed. He said he would try and get over to us with bombs and ammunition.

The officer and several others tried to get across to me but as soon as they left the trench in the embankment they were shot down.

It was hopeless to expect any help and I started back along the trench determined to hold on at all costs and trust to luck that the Germans would not counter-attack.

While talking to Ward I was wounded in the stomach and went down. I felt my number was up and shook hands with Ward and wished him good-bye.

He told me not to be a fool and that I would be all right.

Palmer then came along the trench and asked me to give him a hand as he had got a nasty packet.

I answered: 'I cannot help you, Fred; I am done for.'

L/Cpl. Ward picked me up and helped me along the trench till we came to the dug-out a few yards from the foot path. He carried me down the entrance of the dug-out and ripped off my tunic to dress my wound.

While he was dressing the wound I saw Cpl. Carr and the two privates rush past the entrance to the dug-out and the next minute the Germans were there.

They formed a barricade of trench boards across the trench and threw two bombs down the dug-out.

L/Cpl. Ward was killed instantly. I never received a scratch.[16]

The other two D Company officers, Captain Evans and Second Lieutenant Fuller, had been wounded earlier, so Lance-Sergeant Palmer took control of the situation. He and six men cut the wire and burst into the enemy trench (Coulée Trench), dislodging the machine gun that had been causing many of their problems, and then made a block at the trench, perhaps 50 yards east of the East Miraumont Road. They made another post to the west of the first one, at the junction of the road and Coulée Trench. The enemy, attacking from further down Coulée Trench, made seven different attempts to dislodge his team (by now reinforced by men from other battalions) in the next three hours, but his party withstood them all.

Other parties from D Company made three other posts on the East Miraumont Road south of their position, ie between the Old British Line and the hostile wire. The 23rd RF were believed to have made another post slightly north of their position. The defensive flank was now almost made, if they could just consolidate it, but, their bombs exhausted, and with Palmer gone to Battalion HQ to get some more, the Coulée Trench team were driven back over the East Miraumont Road to the west side of it. This was somewhere around 9 am. On his return, Palmer, despite being a) dazed by a rifle grenade and b) exhausted, rallied the team and they were able to make a successful stand, with the aid of a Lewis Gun from the 23rd RF, and this prevented the Germans from using the road.

The reason that the fate of Lance-Sergeant Palmer's team was so critical was that the attack on their right by the 2nd South Staffs had been a failure: the shelling on the men in their assembly places had been possibly the most vicious and accurate here, while the Germans in the area to be attacked had been greatly reinforced, so that any South Staffs men making lodgement in the German lines were soon ejected.

German machine guns that would have been tied up by the South Staffs attack were free to take a heavy toll of the 23rd RF attack (just to the left of the 22nd Battalion's D Company). The 23rd RF had also been severely affected by the initial bombardment. They got to their first objective, but were not going to get any further. (One of their companies was reduced to just 12 men; out of 14 officers that went into action only 2 were still unwounded by late afternoon). Their war diary says little about their achievements that day (which often happened in cases of very heavy casualties: no one

When Gary Sheffield and I conducted a search for Boom Ravine in 1986 we could not find it at first because a rubbish dump blocked off our view of it from the road.

Once we had climbed the dump it became obvious, and still contained military detritus.

is left to write the story), but as mentioned earlier, they are believed to have made and held a strongpoint slightly to the north of Lance-Sergeant Palmer's block.

At 8:30 am, approximately, the Germans counter-attacked in some force, particularly from the north-east (from the other side of the high ground around Hill 130). Although General Pereira at 2nd Division had been informed by 54 Brigade about this attack, he was reluctant to sanction any artillery support on the area of the 130 contour for fear of shelling his own men. We know *now* that the German attack was about battalion strength and might well have been broken up by artillery fire.

Information reaching higher officers about 99 Brigade progress had been very slow and scanty all morning: all sorts of catastrophes had happened to their communications systems.[17] In fact few snippets of information were being received at 99 Brigade HQ (and hence at 2nd Division HQ), other than from wounded men. Even pigeons were taking a long time to report in because of the fog, while aeroplanes could see nothing. Colonel Barker said he did not receive any sort of reliable message of progress at Brigade until 10:15 am, by which time this attack had run its course.

It was up to the men in their intermingled and scattered units. A variety of confused and bloody actions happened in and around the area of the 130 contour. We do know that the Germans had the advantage of numbers and materiel, and that many of the British rifles and Lewis Guns had become clogged in the mud. Fearing being outflanked and surrounded, the remnants of the 22nd Battalion's A and C companies gave ground slowly, exacting considerable casualties from the German attackers by virtue of Corporal Wilmott's Lewis Gun fire (Wilmott was the sole survivor of his team and would later receive the MM).

In the same way, those forward elements of the KRRC also withdrew. Possibly their B Company (under the inspiring Second Lieutenant Keevil) had been well advanced, but as they came back southwards they were able to attack from an unexpected direction the enemy strongpoint that had pinned down elements of their (KRRC's) D Company. This was at point 91, close to the East Miraumont Road and perhaps 100 yards north-north-west of Palmer's group.

The 6th Northants also withdrew in a controlled manner in response to this attack (seen by them as coming from their north-east), with a weaker one also coming from their north. Their Colonel, Lieutenant-Colonel Meyricke, was killed as he and his Adjutant moved forward to rally the retiring men. The Adjutant, Lieutenant TR Price DSO, helped them set up a defensive line facing north-east towards the German attack (around 9 am). They then found themselves fired on from the left and behind (this was from the continuation of South Miraumont Trench further over to the north-west). Under fire, Lieutenant Price wheeled them around so that they were facing north. All of the groups found themselves just beyond Boom Ravine, along with the KRRC mopping-up parties, which had lost almost all their officers and NCOs.

All of the 22nd men (from A, B and C companies) were collected into one party by Second Lieutenant Perraton. He too was given a MC for his work that day, part of his citation reading:

He rallied and reorganised elements of three companies, and rendered valuable assistance in repulsing a strong enemy counter-attack. He set a splendid example of courage and determination.[18]

This group of men, under Perraton, then reported to the KRRC. It was the latter (notably Second Lieutenant Keevil) who were most responsible for joining up the British line from West to East Miraumont Roads just beyond the first objective. Later in the day the 6th Northants managed to push out posts to regain some more of the high ground, but at the 120 metre contour rather than the 130 one. Colonel Barker had prepared a new 99 Brigade attack to regain the 130 contour, using the Royal Berks and the 17th Middlesex, but this was overruled by higher authority.

By the late afternoon the German counter-attacks had been contained. On 99 Brigade front the new British line was just in front of Boom Ravine, with a pointed salient sticking out where point 91 (KRRC) was, plus the 23rd RF post at the apex, and Lance-Sergeant Palmer's block just south of it. We have no first hand reports of other units of the 22nd RF's D Company, of how they made and held the posts southwards towards the British line, but we do know that the defensive flank succeeded in holding onto its ground. In the evening of the 18th the Battalion was relieved by the 13th Essex and went to Ovillers Huts.

We know that 12 out of 17 officers were casualties, with Major Walsh mortally wounded, Captain Leon Simons believed killed, Second Lieutenant JHE Ellison wounded/captured, Second Lieutenants SF Boulter (died of wounds), WH Payne and EA Burgess all killed. Second Lieutenants GTFF Fuller, GH (George) Evans, Fred Pignon, HP Lawrence and ST Goodman were among the wounded, along with Captain Powell. It had been the most costly action that the 22nd Battalion had been involved in, yet no list of Other Ranks casualties for the Battalion is extant for this battle.

We do know the figures for the other units of 99 Brigade and we have an overall total for the brigade: 42 officers (of which 18 were killed) and 733 other ranks. If we subtract the 227 for 23rd RF, the 186 for the KRRC, the 32 from the 99th MGC and the 12 from the Royal Berks we end up with a figure of 276 other ranks for the 22nd RF. There might have been the odd casualty from the 99th Trench Mortar

The French 1914-18 memorial at Miraumont. One feels as if it also stands for the efforts of 2nd and 18th Divisions

Company included in the Brigade total. Call it 270-275. This is by far the heaviest number for any of the battalions involved in 2nd Division (the 2nd South Staffs, whose attack was virtually broken up by shelling before it started, had 109).[19]

As far as **fatal** other rank casualties are concerned, if we cross-check the names given in *Soldiers Died in the Great War* (which has dates) with those given in the Roll of Honour in the *History* (listed by year and by company) we get 94 names, with another 8 very likely (listed in the former but not in the latter).[20]

We can count the numbers by company for the 94: A 25, B 31, C 16, and D 22. It looks as though the most lethal role to be was in the mopping-up parties with the KRRC (two platoons of B Company), although the two B Company platoons involved in carrying ammunition for the 99th MGC might also have been sucked into the fight.

It was however even more dangerous to have been a member of a Lewis Gun team, whatever the company. These would have been particular targets of the German counter-attackers and their very accurate snipers. Perhaps as many as three-quarters of their men became casualties, but they did manage to bring 8 out of their 14 guns out of the fight. 'Tot', the unofficial historian of the gunners, gleaned the following sad story from Captain Pimm (the Lewis Gun officer) and Vincent Plummer (a Lewis Gun team leader):

At Miraumont 'Plum's' team were posted in a shell hole under Capt. Pimm and Sgt. Brierley.

They saw dear old Axtens wounded by a sniper and then killed by a second shot, while trying to crawl towards them, Brierley got out of the shell hole and fell back dead into Plummer's arms, shot through the head by the same sniper. Guy Destrubé was the next victim and when his brother Paul rushed to his aid he was also killed. The brothers were found clasped in death. They now lie in one grave in Serre Road British Cemetery No. 2.

Sgt. Hennessey and Lance-Corporal Squibb (last of his team) took a gun out to try and help Captain Simons and fifty men of C Coy who were surrounded by Germans and Hennessey was shot through heart.

Squibb, with a broken arm, was taken prisoner together with some of C Coy.

Out of the sixteen guns in action only Capt. Pimm some seventeen men and nine guns returned and one of these was out of action. Plummer was one of the very few team leaders to bring his gun and team out intact. The gunners had suffered 75 per cent casualties – many killed.[21]

Doc Coad had brought in Major Walsh after dark, but the latter's

John Walsh's grave looks out over such a lonely and beautiful spot that one can't help pondering on the futility of war.

stomach wound was too far gone and he died on the 19th. Christopher Stone spoke for everyone when he wrote in the war diary:

> *He had commanded both B and D Company, and had won from all ranks an unstinted admiration for his fine qualities as a man and as a leader of men.*[22]

In the *Illustrated London News* a few weeks later, both Major Walsh (looking sensitive, noble and somehow tragic) and Lieutenant-Colonel Meyricke of the 6th Northants (compact, energetic and driven) were pictured together.[23]

At noon on the 21st Major Walsh was buried in Ovillers Cemetery in front of a large number of officers and men from the brigade. Shortly afterwards, the Battalion pioneers commemorated all the 22nd RF men who had fallen in the battle by erecting a huge wooden cross over Major Walsh's grave with the names of the 80 or so men others known at that time to have died.[24]

Later, however, it was discovered that the information on the cross wasn't completely accurate. Alice Moody informed the Mayor that Sergeant J Smith Wilson, who had been billeted on her in Horsham, had survived his chest wound, had survived two days lying in a shell hole and was a prisoner in Hannover. She wanted to know how to get food parcels to him.

Micky Brown, down in his dugout, had also been given up for dead:

> *When the German who took me prisoner, came down the dug-out and reached young Ward's body, which was huddled up about four steps above me, he started to go though Ward's pockets and then looked towards me. I said: 'All right, Jerry, I am beaten.'*
>
> *He was so surprised to hear me speak that he turned and dashed up the steps of the dugout.*
>
> *A few minutes later he returned with two other Germans. They beckoned me to come up and when they saw that I was badly wounded they came down and helped me up into the trench.*
>
> *They took me along to their officer who greeted me in perfect English with 'Good morning, Tommy: you caught a nasty packet.' After dressing my wound he gave me a drink from his water bottle and then sent for a stretcher party to take me back.*
>
> *I take my hat off to those Germans who held that trench. They treated me with kindness itself.*

He was taken away on a stretcher, and then on in a horse-drawn wagon. The jolting made him pass out. He was operated on at a casualty clearing station without anaesthetic and passed out again Eventually he was taken to a hospital in where:

> *I was taken into a room and laid on a table naked. A German orderly held me by the feet and another by the head while two German officers started messing about with my wound while questioning me about our lines.*
>
> *All kinds of questions they asked me but my answers were the same: 'I don't know.' They kept on tormenting and jeering at me till at last I told them that if they wanted to know they had better go up to the front line and they would soon find out.*
>
> *This so angered them that one of the officers stabbed me in the side with a knife saying 'This is what you suffer for England you English dog.' I was taken back to my bed where*

I lay for a fortnight during which my wounds (I had two now) were only washed and dressed and dressed once.

He then endured another nightmare journey to get to Mulheim-an-der-Ruhr, where he was taken to a prisoner of war hospital. He had to endure some more rough treatment until his case came to the attention of the senior doctor, believed to be Dr Kulhatt, who operated on him (with an anaesthetic), and he received very good post-operative care thereafter. When he improved sufficiently to have his tubes removed, he had enough returning spirit to refuse to be put to work like a common private – and to be backed up by the Commandant. In May he was transferred to Dülmen Concentration Camp – where he was reunited with Squibb and Maloney, thence to Minden on June 6th.[25]

When Colonel Barker had time to dash off a letter to his wife on the evening of the day of the battle on the 17th, he was very depressed:

Things have not gone well. No one is to blame…Everyone fought splendidly, but they were too strong & prepared for us…It was not an absolute failure we got half of what we wanted.

Soon the Corps Commander wanted to see senior officers and the divisional general called a conference of COs. What had gone wrong? Why didn't they make the second and third objectives? Whose fault was it?

Clearly it was not a victory. Yet by the 19th opinions had begun to change:

It's all so humorous. No one had made up their minds (or dared to do so) that we had brought off a big success. The Divl Commander had to find out what the Corps Comdr thought, & the Corps Comdr what the Army thought. The wires of congratulation are now coming in!!![26]

A couple of days later it was in the newspapers:

We all read the accounts of the battle with great excitement. It seems to have been a glorious victory!! It would be all amusing if it wasn't so tragic.

Colonel Barker had great regard for the professionalism of the German opponents on this occasion:

They were a fine lot of Huns & quite equal to the Delville Wood lot. As one prisoner said 'We still have a few soldiers left in Germany'. They fought cleanly & were at us unceasingly, never giving us a moment. Much different to what we had to deal with on the Ancre.

On the 24th February, Brigadier-General Kellett returned to duty, so Colonel Barker returned to the Battalion, which had moved to Bruce Huts that day, then back to Ovillers and Wolseley Huts on the 26th.

On the 24th came a different sort of news: the Germans were retreating from the Miraumont-Pys area. The Germans were known to be preparing lines in the rear of the Somme battlefield, but were believed not to be intending to withdraw into them before mid-March. It seems that the Miraumont attack – half success-half failure that it was - had produced an immediate result. The Germans did not simply retire, but left booby traps (such as pressure-sensitive handrails leading down stairs in dugouts which were connected to mines) and poisoned the water wells as they went.

One practical result was that leave for senior officers was cancelled in case there should be any pursuing required. On the 26th Colonel Barker, probably succumbing to a dose of trench fever, had his leave warrant in his pocket but was stopped from going. After one look at him, Brigadier Kellett sent him to bed and argued for his leave all the way up to Corps. When the Colonel arrived back in Wales at the end of the month, his wife was shocked by how frail and worn out he was.[27]

The Battalion, now very weak, were reorganised into three companies on the 3rd March, with A and B combined into one under Captain Martin, and with Captain Kelly commanding C, and Lieutenant TH Evans, who had been a Liaison Officer during the battle, commanding D. The battalion began to obtain a few officer reinforcements, such as Captain JD Scott, the architect, and Captain de Wet, nephew of the famous Boer guerrilla leader, but no sign of any men.

Meanwhile, plans were afoot to interfere with the German plans for slow and deliberate withdrawal by ejecting them from some more territory. For 99 Brigade this meant attacking Grevillers Trench on the 10th of March. The KRRC attacked on the left and the Royal Berks on the right, with one company of 23rd RF being employed on the far left to capture a long ravine, which from its shape, had been given the name of the Lady's Leg Ravine. The 22nd Battalion's role was a modest one: one 'company-sized' carrying party for each of the two main attacking battalions, plus the third (the 'double' company) to support the attack with 8 Lewis Guns from Grundy Trench. Knowing they would be shortly abandoning their positions, the Germans were much less keen on repairing all the wire-cutting damage done by the 2nd Division guns, and the latter appeared to gain the strategic ascendancy very quickly. As with Miraumont, this was a very well-planned affair, but there were no deserters this time, while communications worked perfectly. The result was a spectacular success, with the Germans driven out of Grevillers Trench all the way along the line, and with 18th Division (attacking on the left) taking Irles. There were fewer casualties in the whole of 99 Brigade (200) than there were prisoners taken (227), plus many enemy killed and wounded.

The 22nd Battalion carried out their limited role with some distinction: all dumps in enemy trenches were stocked up within an hour of zero (which was 5:15 am), and the carrying parties continued to carry materials forward until dusk. The stretcher-bearers were also said to have done good work. Four Lewis Guns were called up to support the KRRC, and two went in support of the Royal Berks.

Overall the Battalion suffered 1 officer (Second Lieutenant Done, a recent arrival) and 5 other ranks killed, with 17 other ranks wounded.[28] The Battalion now moved to billets in Albert.

The KRRCs were very grateful to the 22nd RF in their War Diary:

> *I have great pleasure in bringing to your notice the excellent work done by the Company of the 22nd Bn. Royal Fusiliers, under Lieut. Evans. They did all one could possibly want, working with great energy and cheerfulness under a heavy barrage, and supplies reached the front line very quickly.*[29]

First announcements of medals for Miraumont came in: the MCs for George Evans and Second Lieutenant Perraton have already been mentioned, along with Sergeant Mobley's DCM. Corporal JW Carr also won the DCM.[30] He was in Freddie Palmer's team, most of whom were decorated with MMs, so his contribution was particularly recognised ('He rallied the men under heavy fire and materially assisted in the success of the operations. He set a splendid example to all ranks'). MMs were won by Sergeant GC Moon, Corporals CJ Cole and PE Wilmott (the Lewis Gunner), Lance-Corporals CF Martin and R Hawes, and Privates J Gullen, A Burgess, LJ Brown, JT Murton, AP Hepburn, GM Temple, WB Taylor, and A Stroud. Later in the month Sergeant EC Guy was given a bar to his MM.

On the 14 March, Sergeants Freddie Palmer and J Steele, along with Corporal Carr, were given commissions in the field. Four more second lieutenants arrived for duty, but this time there was a draft of 100 other ranks.

Colonel Barker returned for duty 16 March. Practically his first task was to write off to Mr Destrubé, the father of the three boys:

> Both your boys were buried on the battlefield, with many of their comrades, by the Chaplain. A cross has been erected at Ovillers to all the gallant men of the Regiment who fell in that action. They were both killed in the way they would have wished – 'Fighting their gun to the last.' The Germans made a heavy counter-attack and, if it had not been for their gallantry, also Sergt. Brierley's, a very serious situation would have arisen.
>
> As you know of old, I had always the greatest admiration and affection for your three boys. They were simply splendid, full of humour, always cheery, and burning for a fight. I had only three days before the action recommended them for Commissions. I think we always understood each other, and had therefore the mutual confidence which a Commanding Officer always tries to get with his men![31]

The Battalion travelled between Albert, Ovillers Huts and Bruce Huts until the time came to move out of II Corps area into XIII Corps (Lieutenant-General Congreve) on 25 March. This meant several long marches, first away from the line, arriving at Fiefs on 30 March and staying in this quiet rural area a week, then northwards via Le Thieloye (reached 7 April) to the Arras/Vimy Ridge area, where some large-scale plans were brewing.

The Battalion was desperately short of men: 'If only we had some men!! & the ones we have aren't properly trained as all the specialists were shot.' On the 19th they received 'A draft of 128 untrained men and 44 returned wounded, sick etc.' [32] A few days later the Colonel returned to the same theme: 'I hardly know a man in the Regiment and we are hopelessly weak'.

Trained recruits in decent physical condition were few and far between in Britain at this time and medical boards were busy trying to comb out any likely lads who had escaped the net first time around. As long ago as last November Major Powlett, now second-in-command of the 27th RF, the 22nd RF's feeder battalion in Edinburgh, had been bemoaning the tendency to reclassify category C men (very poor physical specimens) as Category A so they could be sent abroad as reinforcements.[33]

While Christopher Stone was away on a morale-boosting short leave to Paris, his Adjutant duties were taken over by Captain Scott:

> So I have Scott the Architect as adjutant he is now designing me a house…He is a nice person & I fancy in first flight at the game, he drew Adams a War Memorial for Regents Park 300 feet high!!![34]

Captain Scott's combination of great ability and considerable self-belief inspired Major Adams to verse:

The Paragon

First verse:

> *Ambitions of a baser kind,*
> *The lust for lucre, greed of gold,*
> *Improper instincts, nasty mind,*
> *Are human failings we are told,*
> *But these we never could connect*
> *With J. B. Scott the Architect.*

Last verse:

> *This marvellously model man,*
> *Of startling grace and stately movement,*
> *Was built on an heroic plan,*
> *And given to us for our improvement.*
> *'What' we exclaim in wonder, 'WHAT'*
> *ARE the defects of J. B. Scott.*[35]

On 3 April, the Battalion received excellent news: Fred Palmer had won the VC for his actions at Miraumont. Everyone was excited for him and the citation for the award quite captured the popular imagination, with headlines like 'Sergeant's Three Hours of Heroic Leadership', 'Bravery That 'Cannot Be Overstated', even 'Resisted Nine Attacks and Averted a Possible Disaster'. Mayor Davison was one of many to congratulate Fred. He wrote back:

> I feel a very proud chap at the distinction conferred on me, not only for myself, but for the reputation of the Battalion in which we all pride ourselves so greatly.[36]

Two days later came what appear to be decorations for the Grevillers Trench attack, with Captain TH Evans (much praised by the KRRC) getting the MC[37], plus a DCM for Lance-Corporal FG Miles and an MM for Lance-Corporal Fahey.

Meanwhile, the Rev St John left the Battalion for a calling in Mesopotamia. He had been with the Battalion almost the whole time it had been in France and had done a fine job for them.

In the *History of the 22nd* it describes his legacy succinctly:

> The memory of [St John] goes back to many services in France, before battles, in sheds and barns and huts or in the open air; services which for their poignancy can never be repeated, nor for their simple and appropriate surroundings. We were very lucky in our Padre, whose sense of humour was as large as his heart.[38]

1 See *OH*, 1917, p77, note 1. *Pidgeon*, op cit, Chapter 11, pp 133-139 devotes some pages to trying to find out the identity of the deserter. Also see *WO 95/2042*, 1369, 1356; 1362, 2044, 1371, and 1372, plus 1289 for General Perreira's diary

2 *WO 95/1369*, plan dated 9 pm, 13/2/1917. This was Staff Captain Allfrey's first plans: Colonel Barker said that young Allfrey was keen, but made lots of mistakes, so he had to redo almost everything

3 *Mufti*, Summer 1976, 56, No 167, p15 and March 1920, 1, No 5, p2. Buff was a B Company Lewis Gunner, and almost certainly with the KRRCs.

4 *OH*, 1917, p77 note 2

5 See 99 Brigade No 3672 (*WO 95/1295*). Also see *6th Northants Narrative, WO 95/3044*

6 *Mufti*, Summer 1930, 11, No 2, pp 8-9

7 Trevor Pidgeon, *Boom Ravine*, op cit, p82; Sgt J Maloney (Minden POW Camp) to the Mayor: *Broughshane*, 8661. Names of people taken prisoner on this day who are mentioned in Kensington records, or *Mufti*, are 2nd Lt Ellison (C), Sgt Ford (A), Sgt Micky Brown (D), Sgt Wilson (A), Pte H Morris (B), Cpl Squibb of the Lewis Gunners (D), Sgt Maloney (C), L/Cpl C Madden (C), L/Cpl GA Strevens (C), Pte E Moore (C). A Sgt Baker was mentioned by Maloney.

8 Colonel Barker to Lt-Col Deedes, GSO1 at 2nd Division on 20/2/1917, *WO 95/1295*, also the report by Major Adams of the 22nd RF activities on 17/2/1917, *WO 95/1372*

9 *Mufti*, Summer 1930, 11, No 2, pp 8-9

10 *Mufti*, February 1920, 1, No 4, p3; this may be the same group mentioned earlier

11 Cited by *Pidgeon*, op cit p84

12 L/Sgt Mobley's DCM citation, *London Gazette, 17/4/1917*. It went on to describe how he continued encouraging the men, although wounded

13 Pidgeon, op cit pp 130-132 shows how easily the machine-gun could have been missed by the artillery

14 *London Gazette, 17/4/1917*

15 *My Story of Miraumont – I, Mufti*, Summer 1937, 18, No 85, pp 5-6

16 *My Story of Miraumont – II, Mufti*, Autumn 1937, 18, No 86, pp 5-6

17 See *WO 95/1295* and 1369.

18 *London Gazette, 17/4/1917*

19 See *WO 95/1296* & 1369. Incidentally, the 6th Northants and 11th RF in 54 Brigade suffered about the same level of casualties as the 22nd RF (*WO 95/2041*)

20 *Mufti*, February 1921, 2, No 8, front page. *Soldiers Died in the Great War, Part 12: The Royal Fusiliers*, 1921, reprinted in 1989 by JB Hayward.

21 *Mufti*, Summer 1943, 24, No 102, p5. Notes: *Corporal* (not L/Cpl) Squibb. Also *WSCT, 7/4/1917*. And the Colonel had recommended the Destrubés for commissions

22 *WO 95/1372*, 19/2/1917

23 *Illustrated London News*, 10/3/1917

24 *Mufti*, Summer 1962, 42, No 135, p12

25 *Miraumont to Germany – IV, Mufti*, Spring 1938, 29 No 88, pp 6-7. *Prisoner in Germany – V*, Summer 1938, 19, pp 4-5; POW interview, WO 161/1003021/pp 4040-41, preferred for names and dates. (In it he said he wanted to sue the Germans for £1000 for their initial misconduct to him)

26 *RBB*, 19/2/1917

27 *RBB*, 28/2/1917 and note by his wife

28 The casualties numbers vary: I have quoted the figures in the *22nd History*, p45

29 KRRC report on operations, March 1917, *WO 95/1371*

30 *London Gazette, 17/4/1917*

31 RBB to Mr Destrubé, 16/3/1917, *Broughshane*, part of *Destrubé Letters*, 2534

32 Also a problem with the KRRCs: see KRRC diary, 19/3/1917, *WO 95/1371*

33 *Powlett Diary*, 11/11 and 4/12/1916. By the end of the year the 27th RF had been renamed the 103rd Training Reserve Battalion in a reorganisation of home-based RF battalions

34 *RBB*, 18/3/1917

35 *Mufti*, December 1951, 31, No 118, p 12, (WJ P-A)

36 Fred Palmer to Mayor Davison, 9/4/1917, *Broughshane*, VII: 15-16 (cuttings) and 18; 8566

37 *London Gazette*, 11/5/1917 – the citation is less inspiring than the heartfelt KRRC report

38 *History*, op cit, pp 63-64

Chapter Nine

Oppy Wood

O N THE 9TH THE INITIAL NEWS of the Arras/Vimy Ridge offensive was very good, with the Canadians storming almost all of the ridge on the first day, while British units attacking from the Arras area also achieved some pretty impressive performances:

> *Isn't it ripping. We hear that we have now captured 10,000 prisoners and 100 guns. This was told me in best authority. Anyhow one thing I do know for certain is, that we have captured at one place the whole of the German first defences viz about 2000 yards in depth. The next line is about a mile or so off. How I know this is that we go up tomorrow to take it over & will doubtless push on later to the 2nd line.[1]*

On 11 April, 1917 the Battalion moved forward to relieve the 1st/6th Gordon Highlanders in the old German Support and Reserve lines. On the 13th, they moved

Following the fighting at Arras, lightly wounded Highlanders are served refreshments from RAMC personnel before going on to a Casualty Clearing Station. (Taylor Library)

to front line positions opposite Gavrelle, where they could see the promised land:

At the moment we are in an old German gun-pit with good dug-out attached; and from it we get the most wonderful view over the valley in front of us for the first time that I remember...And behind them [German lines] *miles and miles of the plain with villages in full swing, factory chimneys smoking and a great big town on the horizon* [Douai].[2]

There were a couple of cryptic sentences in Colonel Barker's daily letter to his wife on the 13th:

We were to have attacked a certain place at dawn tomorrow, but the Bosche skipped out of it at lunchtime and has now been shelling it since!

It began with the Divisional General doing some personal reconnaissance around the new front line. He found some very sloppy work going on: poor positioning of men and posts, bombs and ammunition lying all over the place, even in the mud. One can just feel this ex-Guardsman's hackles rising:

No salvage work, no cleaning up, no burying, absolutely nothing was doing and the men were being allowed to deteriorate in the mud. Not a latrine in the place. These coys belonged to the 60th [the KRRC], *I found them and fairly put it about them and I am considering whether a Court Martial would not be most salutary.[3]*

Later he was more mollified:

My visit to the 60th had a marvellous effect as one Coy Comdr that I dropped upon for not having sent out any patrols immediately got busy about it after my departure, one of his patrols [under Second Lieutenant GH Lee DSO] *got down to Bailleul station found it unoccupied and he immediately sent down parties and occupied the line of the railway and sent his patrols further afield. They got into Bailleul which last night was occupied by the Boche by riflemen and M.G.s.*

This meant that Bailleul was taken by the KRRC without the need for the normal heavy preparatory bombardment, with the 34th Division on the left taking Willerval and the 23rd RF getting Hill 80 on their right. General Pereira congratulated the KRRC on their 'bold and rapid advance' – a far cry from the Court Martial he had been considering earlier. While the KRRC were having fun, the 22nd RF weren't strong enough to hold the line on their own:

At about 4:30 pm [on the 14th] *Lieut. Col. Barnett Barker commanding the 22nd Bn. Royal Fusiliers arrived* [at KRRC HQ] *to arrange about the relief. The 22nd being considerably weaker than ourselves had been organized in two Companies. It was therefore decided that 1 Company 22nd R.F. should hold the front line, with the other one in support and that our C Company should be attached to them to act as Company in reserve, for the time being.[4]*

This was a time when mules were in common usage for transportation. Norman Tasker was with a fatigue party employing them:

I was one of a carrying party told off to accompany some of Sgt. Mark Neyland's limbers laden with some trench stores. We were to carry the stuff from where it was deemed unsafe to risk the lives of valuable animals![5]

Even so, the mules weren't always looked after:

Sharing the dangers: mules being loaded with supplies for the trenches. (Taylor Library)

I met fifty mules on my way, calmly coming down from the top of the hill. I ran like blazes off to the left of them. Of course they were shelled and scattered. I met the officer in charge of them at the bottom of the hill and told him what I thought of him. Fritz will stand a good bit these times, but the worm turns at anything too ridiculous.[6]

There was a strong sense that the Bosche was on the move, Colonel Barker:

By the time this reaches you our troops should have Lens, as he is blowing it up and of course the Vimy Ridge commands it. Everything seems to be going well as we are pushing everywhere.

Everyone recognised that there was a very strongly held position ahead, the Méricourt-Arleux-Oppy line, but perhaps the Germans would skip out of this one too now that they were on the run. In fact the Germans had a completely different outlook. They had adjusted to the loss of the Vimy Ridge, had voluntarily given up hard-to-defend villages at the bottom of the ridge and were now back in their prepared positions (the Oppy-Méricourt Line) having no intentions of giving any more ground.

191

They had a new 'elastic defence in depth' to counter the all-powerful Allied artillery. Their front line was only lightly held, but covered by concentrated machine-gun fire. The idea was to take the sting out of the attack and at the same time lose the minimum amount of men. Most of the defenders were kept much further back. They would then counter-attack the invaders from front and flank once they had become winnowed down and the 'oomph' of their attack had declined. Even these techniques might not produce a successful defence against a completely determined force which broke through their lines with dash and in sufficient numbers to resist counter-attacks (such as in the initial stages of the Arras/Vimy Ridge battle). It would however prove to be very successful against units under strength *and* determined. On the 14th the Germans made very successful use of this technique, as the Royal Newfoundland Regiment and the 1st Essex, after brushing aside token early resistance, both penetrated deep into enemy territory near Monchy-le-Preux only to find that they had been sucked into a trap. Both battalions were practically wiped out.

On their way out of the line on the 17th they met Field Marshal Haig's car in a narrow lane. Colonel Barker halted the men and took them off the road to let the C-in-C past:

> He put his head out and thanked me very much. He looks very much the same as he did in the old days…I really think now, for the first time, that if we don't make a mess of things and uselessly sacrifice men, we have the Hun beat to the world.

Initial news about the French attack, which began on the 16th, was positive in terms of guns and trenches taken, but so much had been expected from the attack that this felt like failure. For the time being, the British would have to keep attacking to divert attention and reserves away from them.

For once, the men were disappointed to be coming out of the line:

> We didn't a bit want to come out, as we had most exciting things on & the men, though suffering discomfort were as keen as mustard. They were in fact quite annoyed to be sent out.[7]

They had been out in the open for a week, had been shelled heavily, but had not had any chance to 'get a bayonet into a Hun, [and taken] no prisoners except half baked deserters'.

They moved back into the front line opposite Oppy Wood on the 25th/26th[8], and again help from the KRRC was 'on call' to them if they needed it. During the day times the front line was evacuated to allow the heavy artillery to cut the enemy wire opposite (around 250-300 yards away). In the night and early morning of the 27th/28th they were relieved by the 17th Middlesex, who took up battle positions for an assault on Oppy Wood and village on the 28th. The Battalion moved back to Gin Trench and Kleemans Stellung.

General Pereira had chosen to attack with his two numerically strongest brigades, 5 and 6. 5 Brigade would attack north of Oppy Wood and on their left the Canadians would be assaulting Arleux. 6 Brigade would be attacking from in front of Oppy Wood and just south of it, while the 63rd Division would be attacking further south and

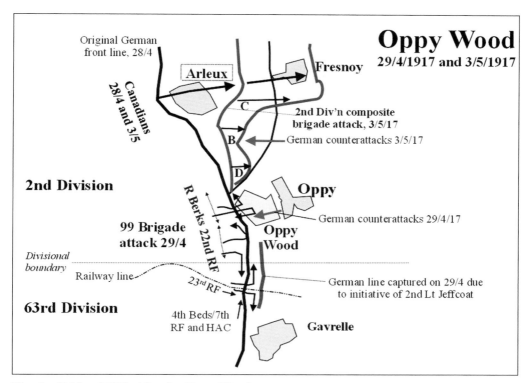

The April-May 1917 battles for Oppy Wood

would provide flank defence to 6 Brigade.

The Canadians successfully stormed Arleux. The local German commander decided not to counter attack here because although there was a loop of the main Oppy-Méricourt line in front of Arleux, the main defence line passed behind it (and just in front of Fresnoy; it was more important to protect the latter).

5 Brigade was not quite so successful; it had had most success on the left where the 2nd Ox & Bucks were in touch with the Canadians, least on the right of the 2nd HLI just north of Oppy Wood.

In 6 Brigade area the 17th Middlesex drove into Oppy Wood and beyond it with great determination, despite facing a stiffening resistance with fewer and fewer troops. Unfortunately they were facing a skilful enemy (the 1st Guards Reserve Division), confident in the use of the new flexible defence in depth technique, who first made and then exploited the gaps between the Middlesex and the HLI, and between the left and right wings of the Middlesex. Next, he drove their left flank back to the old German line, then drove it all the way back to their starting point. He did the same with the right of the Middlesex attack. A less determined battalion might not have got so far, yet it was that determination that sowed the seeds of their own annihilation.

On the right of the Middlesex, the 13th Essex had also started well, but the German

99 Brigade officers watching the passage of the 99th TMB – an original Henry Lea sketch.
(Phythian-Adams papers)

defenders were able to attack them on the right flank because the 63rd Division attack on the extreme right had been a failure. As the enemy forced back the Middlesex, they were able to threaten the left flank of the Essex. Thus the Essex men were also driven back to their starting points; they had experienced heavy casualties, but by no means as severe as the 17th Middlesex.

New units would have to take Oppy. 99 Brigade were called back and given the 6 Brigade task. They would attack at 3 am on the 29th. There was no time for proper reconnoitring, or patrolling to find out where the gaps were, or even of formulating subtle and cunning plans to succeed with fewer men than the battalions which were decimated the night before.

On the left just north of the Wood would be the Royal Berks (less one company that had been employed in the previous day's fighting), on the right would be the 22nd Battalion (around 240 would go into battle, arranged in two companies: B/C under Major Gregg, and D/A under Captain TH Evans), reinforced by one officer and fifty men from the KRRC. Two parties of one officer and fifty men from the KRRC would be used as carrying parties, one for each battalion attacking. There was also one company of the 23rd RF as a common reserve between the two battalions.

Colonel Barker got back to his HQ at 7:30 pm after the conference at Brigade outlining the attack. He had to brief his officers quickly as the Battalion was due to pass the starting point at 9 pm on its way to the jumping-off area. This they did, only to find that the attack had been put back an hour until 4 am. Unfortunately someone had told the brigade transport officers (delivering rations) not to set out until 11 pm, so they had no food apart from their emergency rations and any water that was in their water bottles.

When the 22nd Battalion arrived at their battle HQ at 3 am:

> Lieut-Col. Martin, Essex Regt. informed me (a) That there were no bombs, tools, S.A.A. etc. in any of the trenches (b) that the dump at Railway Truck had been heavily called on the day previous, and (c) that the GERMAN WIRE ON THE FRONT OF THE SECTOR I HAD TO ATTACK WAS BADLY CUT AND IN FACT NOT CUT AT ALL ON THE PORTION FACED BY MY RIGHT COMPANY. On the receipt of this information, I at once informed Brigade H.Q.s and my 2 Company Commanders (See R.B.B. 22, 23, 24 (1) (2) (3).) I made suggestions to the Coy. Commanders as to how to meet the difficulty and to confer together if time allowed.[9]

The Battalion set off in good order as soon as the six-minute barrage lifted. Inevitably the attackers found themselves greeted with uncut wire. The difficulties of finding what gaps there were in two belts of wire in the dark meant most people were trapped between the first and second belts when the barrage moved on. The helpless men were simply mown down by rifle and machine gun fire.

Not everyone was lost, however.

On the left, Platoons 14, 15 and 16 of D Company appear to have been cut to shreds, with Second Lieutenant Palmer one of very few survivors, and obliged to spend the day in a shell hole. Second Lieutenant Parks and the only remaining three Lewis Gunners retired to the old British line to take up a position there. 13 Platoon at the extreme left managed to side-slip through the two lines of wire into the German trench. They formed a block on the right and bombed down to their left to meet up with the Royal Berks, whose fate they shared.

The Berks attack, on the other hand, went well initially. There had been a number of gaps in their wire on the left hand side and the attackers poured into the German trench. Within a quarter of an hour they had taken a good chunk of German front line in front of Oppy Wood. They pushed out patrols into the Wood itself and captured three machine guns which they then turned against the enemy. With just a little luck this would have been a great success story. Unfortunately the Berks were isolated on both left (less critical) and right, for beyond 13 Platoon there was a huge gap. German defenders attacked the Berks five times from the right. They were repulsed four times but on the fifth time the Berks had run out of bombs. They began to give way – only to come across a store of German bombs. Using these, and attacking 'furiously', they won back all the ground they had lost. Yet the enemy attacked again.

Eventually the Berks, now less than half their initial numbers, were obliged to retreat. Their left company, only thirty-five in number, taking its wounded and the three captured machine guns, went all the way to the left until they got in touch with

5 Brigade's line. The remainder of the Berks (and 13 Platoon) force were obliged to go back to the old British line, reaching it somewhere around 9:15 am. Some seventy prisoners had been captured and sent back to British lines. Lance-Corporal James Welch was one of many Berks men who performed extraordinary deeds of courage and was later awarded the VC.

Turning now to the Right Company, on the right of 22nd Battalion front, Major Gregg and all the officers barring two were casualties almost immediately. Second Lieutenant Steele lost his whole platoon apart from one man and these two survived the day in a shell hole. Second Lieutenant Jeffcoat found a gap in the second belt of wire, along with CSM Hogan and about a platoon of men. They jumped into the enemy trench. CSM Hogan, attempting get in touch with the Left Company, began bombing left, while Second Lieutenant Jeffcoat attempting to get in touch with the 63rd Division, bombed down to the right. They did take some prisoners as they went along, but as the *Narrative* of the battle said:

> *'The fighting was very desperate and 2/Lt Jeffcoat informed me* [Colonel Barker] *that no quarter was asked or given and many Germans were killed.'*

Jeffcoat and his party managed to get to within 100 yards of the railway (some 400 yards outside 2nd Division's boundary) where he got in touch with the 4th Bedfords of 63rd Division.[10]

CSM Hogan bombed left about 100 yards, made a block in the trench and travelled down to the right upon hearing that Second Lieutenant Jeffcoat was under attack. Once this emergency had been passed he returned back down the trench only to find that his block had been driven in and, their bombs exhausted, his sixteen men had retired to the old British line. Nothing daunted, he went after the men, organised them for an immediate counter-attack and sent a message back to Battalion HQ. Jeffcoat also set up a stop in the trench and sent a message back to HQ. Hogan would win a DCM for his efforts on this day, as did Lance-Sergeant CE Fidler, whose citation suggests he was part of the Jeffcoat-Hogan attack:

> *For conspicuous gallantry and devotion to duty during a hostile bombing attack, when he took charge at a critical moment, and by his determination and courage repulsed counter-attacks on both flanks. When eventually relieved he and a private were the only survivors of over twenty men.*[11]

Meanwhile, anxious that he had heard little news, Colonel Barker had sent his Intelligence Officer, Second Lieutenant Hudson, forward to find out what was happening. Hudson was himself wounded but sent back news (received at 7 am) that there was great need for bombs. Colonel Barker sent forward half (two platoons) of the reserve company of 23rd RF under Captain Taylor to carry as many bombs as could be found and to garrison the old British line. He then added a third platoon of the 23rd RF. Captain Taylor arrived in time to stop CSM Hogan making a further attack – likely to be both costly and fruitless.

News arrived from Second Lieutenant Jeffcoat at 9:20 am stating:

> *That (a) He was in touch with Bedfords (b) That I could dribble up men to him via the*

railway and (c) That if I sent him reinforcements and plenty of bombs, he could attack
again and probably capture the line.[12]

Colonel Barker proceeded to do just that, sending at 10 am around 100 men of the 23rd RF, under Captain Bowyer, well supplied with bombs (which had hurriedly been brought up from 99 Brigade HQ). Captain Bowyer and his team reached the German line via the railway line with very few casualties. Here they appear to have met not only the Jeffcoat force but men from a variety of 63rd Division units: 4th Bedfords and 7th RF (these being part of a composite battalion) and the Honourable Artillery Company (alias the 'HAC' - on the right of the composite battalion).[13]

They immediately started bombing left towards Oppy. Christopher Stone recalled in 1920 that:

> *With his medley of men – Bedfords, H.A.C., from the 63rd Division, a few of the 1st*
> *K.R.R.C., some reinforcements from the 23rd R. Fusiliers – and a nucleus of B and C*
> *Coy. men, he* [Jeffcoat] *fought his way towards Oppy, hand to hand, bombing from*
> *traverse to traverse, jumping on the top, cheerful, glorying in the excitement of it.*[14]

The KRRCs were presumably part of the company sent to reinforce the 22nd Battalion, and whose original role was that of making a defensive flank. They made a strongpoint between British and German lines down close to the divisional boundary between 2nd and 63rd Divisions. Thereafter a number of their men were sucked into the fighting in the German line, where they 'were of the greatest assistance' according to the official *Narrative*.[15]

Captain Taylor sent patrols over to the German line to keep in touch with the attackers there and feed them with more bombs and ammunition. As the bombing force proceeded north (leftwards), so the left-most company of the HAC extended its front further left, with other companies of the HAC filling in the spaces, rather like the wriggling of a snake sloughing off its skin. The combined force eventually stopped 200 yards before Oppy Wood because of a healthy respect for the garrison there (which had in fact created a strong block south of the Wood) and their own small numbers. The HAC, very enthusiastic participants, were given a northern limit to their line-acquisition:

> *General does not want your left flank to rest any higher than B24 b 3.5. You must build*
> *a block there and leave the manning of the trench to Bedfords and Fusiliers.*[16]

Colonel Barker and the Colonel of the Bedfords had met and agreed to cooperate fully, as their men were already doing. As a result of this cooperation, and men like Captain Bowyer, Captain Taylor and Second Lieutenant Jeffcoat, about 1,000 yards of German trench was handed over that evening.[17] Plans were afoot for this *impromptu ad hoc* force to throw out patrols and posts towards the enemy, especially as a rumour had spread that the Germans were retreating from Oppy, but this was probably no more than ration parties going back to rear lines.

Afterwards, Colonel Barker was very generous in his official report:

> *I wish to place on record the splendid gallantry of Second Lieutenant Jeffcoat…It was*
> *entirely owing to the excellent report he sent me on the situation that I was able to push*

up the 23rd R. Fus. and so capture practically the whole of the objective given me.

The OC Bedford Regt gave me most excellent advice and assistance and our co-operation together was everything that could be desired.

I cannot speak too highly of the valuable services of Capt. Bowyer and Capt. Taylor, 23rd R. Fusiliers. The success of our counter attack and the gaining of our objectives was greatly due to their excellent leadership and gallantry. The information they gave me, placed me in a position to give them the assistance they required. It would be impossible to say enough about all the officers and men of the 23rd R. Fus. who came under my command. They were ready, eager and prepared to move at a moment's notice, quickly understood their orders and carried them out to perfection.[18]

One would like to report that Second Lieutenant Jeffcoat survived and got the VC. Neither of these things happened. Perhaps the latter was because there were already three VCs in this area around this time: two to members of the HAC at Gavrelle - Second Lieutenant Haine on the 28th (involved in taking a German strongpoint at the railway line) and Second Lieutenant Pollard on the 29th (the inspiration for the HAC re-taking the German strongpoint) – plus the already-mentioned Lance-Corporal Welch of the Royal Berks on the 29th.

Oppy Wood during the fighting.
(Taylor Library)

In fact Jeffcoat was mortally wounded after he had given the information that enabled Captain Bowyer to do his fine work. Doc Coad, and his assistant, Lance-Corporal Parkinson of the golden tooth, went off in brilliant sunshine to try and bring in Jeffcoat.[19] The latter survived long enough to see his CO:

The gallantry of Jeffcoat and the men cannot be adequately described. He was running about on the trench, throwing bombs and encouraging the men, till he fell blown to bits. They brought him to my Headquarters. He had one leg blown off and the other half off. Half his face was gone and one eye. Poor poor fellow. He was quite conscious, and in no pain. I told him I would move heaven and earth to get him a V.C. He died like an absolute hero, without a squeal or a grumble, and telling me how pleased he was he had satisfied???? me.[20]

Doc Coad, and others, had made great efforts to care for the wounded. Conspicuous amongst the others was Sergeant TE

McGowan, the sanitary sergeant. His DCM citation shows the conditions the medical services and stretcher-bearers had to operate in:

> He has continually displayed the greatest fearlessness in collecting and attending to wounded under heavy fire. He took a stretcher party through intense barrage to rescue a wounded officer, and when all were killed but himself, he remained with the officer until a fresh party arrived.[21]

In his short time with the Battalion, Captain de Wet had made a big impression on it – and it on him:

> I joined the 22nd – a wild youngster straight from the Kalahari Desert – a journey of some 7-8,000 miles. I had not been with you a week when I felt I had friends and comrades of the right type around.
>
> I was made welcome from gallant B.B. to the youngest Rookie in my Company.
>
> One of the bravest acts I have ever seen was the manner in which the 22nd faced that withering fire in Oppy Wood.[22]

When he was being brought back wounded he insisted on seeing the Colonel:

Captain de Wet came to the HQ dug-out wounded and bandaged up, and said to the Colonel: 'Sir, before I go I want to say something. I came here with [-out] a very great idea of the Englishman as a fighting man. But I am sure I have fought in the finest Battalion a man could wish to fight with.'[23]

Not everyone could be brought in and that night the Germans saturated the area of attack in front of Oppy Wood with gas. Anyone wounded lying out in no man's land having lost, or unable to get their gas mask on, would have been in great danger.

The remains of the 22nd Royal Fusiliers were relieved after dark that night by men from the 11th East Yorks (31st Division), and went back to Gin Trench and Railway Cutting. Colonel Barker wrote almost immediately, in a rather shaky hand (two days without sleep, most of it in the grip of battlefield tension), to Mayor Davison:

April 30

My dear Willie

Only a line. I will write when I have time. Got safely out of battle this morning. The Regt doesn't now exist. Only 40 men returned with me, but I hope to find about another 60 or so which got mixed with other units. Palmer VC the only officer returned except Hdquarters. Dear old Gregg I am afraid got a mortal one. They fought and died as heroes.

The old Regt can't be rebuilt, so if I have time I shall have to make a new one. It was a glorious end of the old regt...I feel as if I never want to see or hear of a battle again – it's all very beastly and I am very very depressed at losing all my gallant friends

PS They put the gas on us last night for 6 hours to add to our many discomforts. Poor poor wounded lying out.[24]

Battle casualties were as follows, officers: Second Lieutenant Wardley killed, Second Lieutenant Jeffcoat died of wounds, Second Lieutenant Perraton, Second Lieutenant Saword and Stevenson missing (ie killed); wounded officers: Major Gregg (who survived the loss of a leg), Captain TH Evans, Captain de Wet and Second Lieutenant Hudson. Of the officers said to have gone into battle, only Palmer, Steele and Parks escaped injury. As far as other ranks are concerned, out of around 240 attacking, the war diary gives nineteen dead and forty-eight wounded, thirty-one wounded and unaccounted for, forty-six unaccounted for, and nineteen 'more or less extremely gassed'. These figures amount to 163: over two-thirds of the attacking force. The German intention of drenching the area with gas might not have been to kill off the wounded, but the latter is the picture that keeps coming to mind.

Just as Colonel Barker had added in his own hand 'Only Hd Qtr officers + 40 marched out of the action' to the 22nd RF war diary before signing it, so did the CO of the Royal Berks, Colonel Harris, add a comment in their war diary on their casualties of fifteen killed, eighty-nine wounded and forty-seven missing, totalling 151: 'Out of the 250 who actually attacked.' Two fine battalions destroyed through ill-conceived, sloppy, rushed attacks. One looks around in anger, seeking to point the finger of blame. Most of all the cause lies in unwarranted overconfidence among senior officers from underestimating the enemy's resilience and professionalism. In fact no one would take

Oppy village until the last months of the war, but Oppy Wood was taken by a much more limited operation at the end of June. Five reasons were put forward for the success of the June attack:

1. Sufficient time for preparation
2. Adequate force of artillery and infantry
3. Careful arrangements of all details by the Brigade
4. Excellent barrage and effective counter-battery work
5. Energetic and rapid consolidation owing to the troops being fresh

Almost every single one of these reasons did *not* apply in 99 Brigade's attack. One might also add that the June defenders were not as strong, and that the attackers had one or two innovations, such as Artillery Boards erected by artillery liaison officers to show the line held by infantry, while there was also Thermite, whose effect:

Was excellent. The garrison of the trench appeared to have fled incontinently.[25]

Hardly had the survivors of 99 Brigade's attack reached their billets, when news came over that 2nd Division was required to make one more attack in the Oppy area. Words like crowning insult and last straw come to mind. The Division was now so weak that instead of having twelve battalions it had just enough troops to make a Composite Brigade under General Kellett, made up of four weak composite battalions, each one to consist of four companies of at least three officers and 100 men.

5 and 6 Brigades got away with just supplying one composite battalion each, while 99 Brigade, the weakest of the three, supplied two. In the absence of any evidence, one suspects that this is due to lion-hearted General Kellett never ducking a challenge. C Battalion consisted of two companies of Royal Berks and two of 23rd RF, while D consisted of three of the KRRCs and one from the 22nd RF. The 22nd could just about supply 100 men, having about eighty survivors from the last attack plus about forty men left out of battle. Second Lieutenants Palmer, Holmes and Carr were the officers selected for the 22nd RF's contribution. The 22nd Company would be under orders of the KRRC, but be in close support of C Battalion (commanded by Colonel Vernon of the 23rd RF) on the left of the attack.

This time the Composite Brigade would be attacking north of Oppy, with the Canadians attacking Fresnoy to their left, and 31st Division attacking at Oppy Wood on their right. At least there was a day or so to reconnoitre the area, as the attacks (which extended right down to Bullecourt in the south) were to be on the 3rd May in order to draw attention away from a major French offensive planned for the 5th May.

The attacks began badly before they started, with a huge row about start times and an unsatisfactory compromise resolving it. So the start was neither the night time desired by the Australians in the south, nor the daylight hour wanted in the northern sector. It was at 3:45 am, which meant that as the attacking troops formed up, they were illuminated on the skyline by the setting full moon. Any element of surprise was lost .

Up and down the line it was a tale of disaster; for example the 31st Division attacking Oppy Wood were spotted forming up and were shelled to pieces before they started; some brave survivors made it as far as Oppy village before they were ejected. Even the ever-reliable 18th Division had a bad day at the office, as did one of the Australian brigades, but another Australian brigade performed great heroics. There was one big exception - the Canadians. Despite being shelled by an alert enemy in their forming up trenches, *despite* the enemy being gathered together in Fresnoy to launch their own attack, the Canadians defeated them *and* carried the village.

Returning to the Composite Brigade, they were all moving up to their taped out areas at 9 pm when an unexpected Chinese (feint) barrage from 2nd Division artillery hit the German front line trenches. Maybe this was some subtle double-bluff: something so obviously a feint that the Germans would immediately dismiss any thought of an attack here. Well, the Germans took it seriously and immediately shelled all the British lines of approach, causing great confusion to the attacking units, and delays to the bringing up of rations and ammunition. The Germans also laid down barrages on the forming up areas at 1:30 am, 3 am and at 3:44 am, one minute before zero. The artillery and machine gun fire (much of it from Oppy in the south) seemed strongest in the southern part of the attack.

The party from the 22nd set off on the night of the 1/2 May. The guides were poor, resulting in the party being broken up into two groups and spending much of the 2nd trying to get in touch with the correct units. The KRRC narrative commented:

> The Coy. of the 22nd Royal Fusiliers was very scattered. Eventually 2nd Lieut. Palmer, V.C. collected his men but he was now placed under the orders of Lieut. Col. Vernon D.S.O. [the CO of the 23rd RF].[26]

It reads as if he couldn't wait to get rid of them, but it was sensible for the 22nd Company to be under orders locally, and it meant that the three companies of the KRRC could act as a cohesive whole in the southern (right) part of the battlefield.

C Battalion (the 23rd RF and the Royal Berks) was next to the Canadians. They got away well and captured their objectives. On their right, B Battalion (troops from 6th Brigade under Colonel Norris of the 1st Kings, the latter providing the two outer companies) had a much tougher time: the two inner companies of their force weren't ready at zero and when they did arrive they caught the full force of enemy retaliation, and could not get forward. Both 1st Kings Companies performed very well, but Germans coming up from Oppy were soon attacking right in the middle of the Composite Brigade, threatening to roll up the British line from the right. The British forces were obliged to give up much of their gains in the centre. The left of C Battalion held firm, and was in touch with the Canadians, while the KRRC stoutly defended a series of strongpoints south of B Battalion's right hand side, in which they were given good assistance by the 99th Trench Mortar Battery, under Second Lieutenant F Canter, under attachment from the 22nd RF.[27]

We know very little about what the Company of 22nd men did on the 3rd May but we do know that, guided in by Major Winter of the 23rd RF, they constructed and held the strong point at Y (right in the centre of the new line, where the sunken road running south-east from Arleux comes above ground) on the night of the 3rd/4th. The

23rd RF had this to say about them: 'This strong point was formed by a party under Lieutenant Palmer who worked magnificently after dark and made a good job of it.'[28]

In the end not much ground had been gained by 2nd Division, but it had at least protected the gains of the Canadians on their left. Most of the ground gained and held was due to 99 Brigade units – and of course most of the casualties had been theirs too. Out of a casualty total of nineteen officers and 498 men for the division as a whole, the share of 99 Brigade units was fourteen officers and 321 men, with the hard-fighting 23rd RF (seven officers and 122 men) and Royal Berks (six officers and 116 men) suffering most of all. Despite their stern defence of a number of strongpoints, the three companies of the KRRC only suffered one officer and fifty-nine other ranks casualties. Fortunately for the 22nd Battalion their losses were the lowest of any of the 99 Brigade units at just twenty-four (six killed, twelve wounded and six missing) out of the 100 men supplied.

The 22nd Company returned to the rest of the Battalion at X Camp, Ecoivres during the night 4th/5th. The 22nd were no longer the weakest Battalion in 2nd Division, with nine officers and 150 other ranks.[29] That was now the doubtful privilege of the 23rd RF (down to ten officers and 108 other ranks), with the Royal Berks not much stronger than the 22nd RF because of their heavy losses on both 29 April and 3 May.

One thing was certain: the Division would be unfit for major fighting for weeks, maybe months to come.

1 *RBB*, 10/4/1917
2 *CRS*, 14/4/1917, also *Sheffield & Inglis*, op cit, p90-91
3 General Pereira's Diary, *WO 95/1289*, 13/4/1917
4 KRRC diary, *WO 95/1371*, 13-14/4/1917
5 Norman Tasker in *Mufti*, June 1954, <u>34</u>, No 123, p5
6 *RBB*, 14/4/1917
7 *RBB*, 16/4/1917. The Barker letters stopped on the 18th April.
8 Their new Chaplin, the Reverend Charles Earle Raven, arrived, plus a draft of 24 men
9 *Narrative of Attack*, appendix to the 22nd RF war diary for April 1917, *WO 95/1372*, also see KRRC diary for same time, *WO 95/1371*
10 In fact it was a composite battalion of the 4th Bedfords and the 7th RF, commanded by the OC of the Bedfords
11 *London Gazette*, 27/7/1917
12 *Narrative of Attack*, op cit
13 Note in the HAC diary at 7:54 am says that they had been in touch with the 22nd RF (and the Bedfords) and were planning to occupy the German line north of the railway: *WO 95/3118*, 29/4/1917
14 *Mufti*, April 1920, <u>1</u>, No 6, p2. Stone may have conflated two different phases.
15 *Narrative of Attack*, op cit, There was also a KRRC carrying party under orders of Captain JET Kelly of the 22nd
16 *WO 95/3118*, 29/4/1917, 12:50 pm
17 General Kellett in his report (*WO 95/1369*) says 1100 yards, but 800 yards in document 'ROK 21'
18 Narrative of Attack, op cit, *WO 95/1372*
19 *Mufti*, Xmas 1938, <u>19</u>, No 91, p8

20 *RBB* to Davison 2/5/1917, *Broughshane*, VII: 39-40. Stone said that the recommendation was backed by an HAC officer; Captain AO Pollard *Fire-Eater*, pp 214-24; reprinted by the *N&M Pres*)

21 *London Gazette*, 26/7/1917, also in *Daily Graphic*, 28/7/17; his name is spelt McCowan here

22 *Mufti*, June 1955, 35, No 125, p4

23 *Ibid*, Summer 1937, 18, No 85, p2

24 *Broughshane*, VII: 35-36, 30/4/1917

25 XIII Corps diary, *WO 95/896*, reasons for success of 28/6/1917 action.

26 KRRC diary, *WO 95/1371*,

27 99 Brigade diary, *WO 95/1369*. The 99th TMB supported posts A and B and 'materially assisted the defence of the R. flank'

28 All the deaths in *Soldiers Died* were listed on the 3rd May not the 4th; 23rd RF war diary, May 1917, *Narrative of Action*, *WO 95/1372*

29 Numbers produced by subtracting the 22nd battalion's 24 casualties from the figures given in *History of the Second Division*, op cit, p444, note 2, for trench strength on 1/5/1917– ditto for 23rd RF'.

The Cross is very faded now, but one can just make out the word Oppy

As they did at Miraumont, the pioneers built a cross to commemorate those who had died (many others were missing and are not recorded on the Cross). The Oppy Cross was brought back to England in 1929 and used as the centrepiece of OCA services in the 1930s. It now resides in St Mary Abbots church in Kensington *(Mufti)*

Chapter Ten

Starting Again

AFTER THEIR EFFORTS THE BATTALION might have anticipated a goodish spell away from the line. They had just a few days in rear areas, before spending the next fortnight staying in bivouacs near Écurie, training and providing working parties on the roads.

Bombing, Lewis Gun and Signalling were the principal classes, but a Divisional Riflemen's School was formed this month in Magnicourt under Captain Gore, a Canadian trapper, expert in ground concealment. This was General Pereira's initiative in response to the way that the enemy had been able to infiltrate in and around British positions and cause panic, whereas a few well-trained enemy snipers had kept British heads down in similar situations. General Pereira's idea was that Gore could make the men not just good shots but also 'keen and cunning'.[1]

Signalling Sergeant Fred Keeble described a typical day's training to his wife-to-be Edie:

I started off about 9 AM training my men in the Latest Ideas of Signalling and of course training them to perfection so that they can gain self confidence in whatever means of signalling they may have to lay their hands to. In the afternoon I carried out the same performance, at 6 PM I was at an open air service and now it's about 7 PM and here I am writing to you my Darling.[2]

Great efforts were made by the Division to provide services to the soldiers in and around Écurie. There was a coffee bar, a barber's shop, a library and a theatre that also showed cinema films. There were baths, including some of the new 'spray baths'. You could get new clothing and boots, and have the old ones recycled, but not if you had used too much Harrison's Pomade (against lice) because it stained the clothing too much.

With Colonel Barker at Brigade (as General Pereira was on leave), and Major Adams also on leave, the Battalion had a new CO until 20 May, Christopher Stone – a circumstance that must have seemed very remote when he was a plump and unmilitary private in the 16th Middlesex in 1914.

Reinforcements started arriving within a few days, with the first 118 appearing on the 7th; not necessarily fully trained, and not necessarily fit: the 22nd war diary mentions that the first three to arrive were sent to the Corps Rest Camp.[3] Colonel Barker was very pessimistic in his letter to Mayor Davison:

As we have no men to fight except an untrained draft of 190 men we may anticipate being put into a fight. I have sixteen bombers in the regt. – last year I had 480 – I suppose someday we shall be sent back and allowed to reorganise and make a new regt., but it seems all very hopeless.[4]

Corporal Roland Whipp missed some of the biggest battles by a combination of illness, injury or training. Some awful event happened to him as soon as he got back. Oppy was no exception. He had just rejoined his team when he was buried by a heavy shell that destroyed his gun and killed the two men next to him.

99 Brigade officers in the summer of 1917. In front from the left we have Major Adams, Colonel Barker and General Kellett. Behind them are Captain Murray and Captain Stone. The other officers are mainly from the 23rd RF (whose Colonel Winter is next to Kellett).
(Phythian-Adams papers)

Sometime just after the battle Ollie Berrycloath came across a stray horse. It became called 'Oppy' of course:

> *I said to my mate 'This horse's lost'. I goes out, spoke to him, took hold of him and led him back. That horse was with us until the end of the war. In the History it says where it came from no one knows – but it was ME... He was a good old pony.* [5]

Norman Tasker fills out the story:

> *Thin to the point of emaciation, the poor devil had apparently been turned loose, sick, by some unit on the move. We brought him back to the 22nd lines, and the section kicked in with a franc or two each to buy oats and fodder. Never mind where from.* [6]

The horse 'Oppy' – described as *"the narrowest quadruped in the world"* in the *History* [7] –

pulled a truck containing all the tools and bits and pieces of Sergeant Lindsey and Sergeant McGowan, the Sanitary Sergeant and all-round odd-job man.

The Battalion was fortunate that, back in England, it had someone with the authority and know-how of Mayor Davison. He could be a conduit for anxious relatives about whether so-and-so was ever going to get any leave, or comfort the relatives of men taken prisoner that they would begin to receive regular food parcels, or even correspond with the prisoners directly. [8]

Back in France reality, in the form of going back to the trenches, followed on the 23-28 May, with the Battalion taking over very battered trenches – more a collection of posts that connected lines – in the Arleux Loop, north of Oppy. In the three weeks since they had been away, the Germans had regained Fresnoy (and those elements of Fresnoy Trench so painfully won on 3 May) on 8 May, but the area had been fairly quiet since then.

As all the battalions in 99

Brigade were still very weak, they were organised as two companies. In the case of the 22nd these companies were commanded by Captain ER Orme (an ex-Lovat Scout) and Captain Scott. Despite the new recruits, the 22nd Battalion was weaker than it had been before the Oppy battles. Its collective level of experience and know-how were correspondingly lower.

Patrolling started almost immediately. Private Place was part of an officer's patrol that went out on the evening of the 24th. The enemy was alert, and the patrol was fired upon. Most of its members made it safely back to the British lines. Five of the men got lost, and strayed behind enemy lines. They were challenged in German and broken up into two groups. The two-man group managed to make it back to the British lines on the *next* night.

The ordeal of the three-man group had, however, just began. They were bombed out of their original trench/hole, but lay undisturbed all day on the 25th almost right under the high enemy parapet. Private Place took charge of the group and insisted that they continued with their observations about enemy movements. At night they made another attempt to escape, but went too far north, and had to spend another day in a shell hole, with the same happening on the 26th/27th. At last on the night of the 27th/28th they moved off in the right direction and got back to the British lines, with much useful information, and all safe and well despite three days without food and water. Private Place was later given an MM.[9]

Lieutenant WA Murray, newly returned to the Battalion after seven months away with his second wound, was getting into bother while on patrol on the night of the 25th/26th. A bombing fight with a German patrol developed and he was wounded and captured, but managed to wrest himself free and dive into a trench. It wouldn't be his last wound with the Battalion.[10]

Second Lieutenant Fred Palmer with his medals: the VC on the left and the MM on the right.

Robert Wright, wounded at Delville Wood with the 23rd RF, now arrived to join the Battalion:

> At Ternes [sic] *we had lunch at the Officers Club and when it was known that we were on our way to join the 22nd we were told that we should all get M.C.'s as the adjutant was a novelist.*[11]

Fred Palmer, on other hand, was released from hospital for his VC investiture. He was not looking forward to it, as he explained to Mayor Davison:

> *I have just received official confirmation from the War Office that I have to attend the Investiture at Hyde Park on Saturday 2 June. I am tremendously nervous about the whole affair, but I can see no way of avoiding it. There are some things in England a little worse than a German barrage, and this most certainly is one of them.*[12]

Fred received his award from the King. Hammersmith – emphasising that he was born and educated in that

Borough – was very proud of its VC-winner and in July asked him to sign the Borough Roll Of Honour – an honour hitherto reserved for crowned heads, ambassadors, and the like.[13]

A battalion 'good news story' from the *Daily Mirror*, about the way able men could be promoted from the ranks.

For those who had been with the Battalion for a long time – men like Christopher Stone or Fred Keeble – the period after Oppy was a very depressing one. The Vimy-Arras offensive had built up such hopes, and now the war was again endless. All that was left was to put one's head down and carry on. Stone was fortunate to be on leave for the last fortnight in May, but down in the dumps thereafter, while Fred Keeble was considering whether to apply for a commission (which would mean time at home). He wanted to put out of his fiancée Edie's mind this awful idea she had of getting herself posted to France. Even so, taking a commission would feel like a betrayal of his men.

The Battalion had a few days in rest billets at St Aubin, did four days in the Arleux Loop trenches, going to Bray on the 14 June to recommence training.

Presaging a busy summer for subalterns in the Battalion, Second Lieutenants Feord and Holmes were out raiding the enemy on the 9th, with Feord returning with just one other rank the next night, invading the enemy's line but sparing the life of a sleeping German sentry. Meanwhile, Captain Orme obtained a loan of Brigadier Kellett's giant telescope and with it acquired some very useful information about the enemy's wire and defence set-up in the Oppy Wood area.

There was however a very important event on the 9th – the Brigade Horse Show at Écurie. The Battalion's turnout (featuring one cooker, one water-cart and two limbers), plus the Light Draught Horse qualified for the next stage, the Divisional show. Christopher Stone commented:

> We won the Brigade competition hands down, and our men, limbers, cookers, horses and mules were perfect – 238? marks out of a possible 250. We hope to win the divisional competition tomorrow, and after that the Corps and finally the Army! We are ambitious, you see. The pains the men take are incredible; they even sent home for ribbons for the horses' tails, and the cooker was hidden in a shed so that competitors should not see our preparations. We won the light draught horse competition too, with full marks.

The Divisional Show was on the 12th and the Battalion turnout duly won by 23 points from the 2nd HLI, with the Light Draught Horse also prevailing. Major Adams wrote

> When we came to France our least candid friend would have called our Transport the worst in the country. This reflects untold credit on our transport officer, an old Cavalry Sergeant-Major.[14]

At the XIII Corps Show on the 20th, the Battalion turnout was pipped by the offering from the 10th DCLI, but the Light Draught Horse marched on and was entered into the First Army show, but it failed at the final hurdle.[15]

Some decorations for the Oppy battles had come in, mostly in 2nd Division Routine Orders. There was an MC for Doc Coad (bringing in Jeffcoat), DCMs for Sergeant McGowan and Lance-Sergeant Fidler, with MMs for Sergeants White and Peatfield, Corporals Dennis and Moore, acting Lance-Corporal Faux, and Privates Downing, Wilkinson (a Bar), Kirkby and Wratten.

For Colonel Barker there was a mounting series of recognitions. On the 5th he received a Brevet Majority, on the 12th was Mentioned in Despatches, but on the 17th came the honour he deserved above all, a Bar to his DSO. His citation was in no way over-written:

> For conspicuous gallantry and devotion to duty. During an assault his battalion was compelled to withdraw from its objective owing to heavy casualties and to its flank being unsupported. At this most critical moment he reorganised and rallied all the men of his brigade who were within reach, and by his promptitude and fine leadership won back most of the objective, and maintained it until relieved.[16]

The Battalion got the reward it needed too: on the 18th it received orders to move to the Bethune area (XI Corps), where 'We found beautiful green fields, with grass growing in nearly all the shell holes; duck-boarded trenches and a peaceful enemy.'[17] On the 21st they went into support trenches at the Village Line, Cambrin Section – almost exactly where their trench life in France had begun in November 1915.

The return to the Bethune area was probably the shot in the arm that convinced Fred Keeble to stay where he was, particularly as it seemed that he would get some leave within a couple of months. He raised the stakes and Edie backed down. She told us:

> When I told my fiancé he said that if I went to France I'll have nothing more to do with you. That put paid to that![18]

Colonel Barker went back to Brigade so that Brigadier Kellett could go on leave. New 'subs' continued to swell the number of officers, but very few other ranks appeared. General Pereira, having motored over to GHQ to investigate policy with regards to reinforcements, found out that divisions not about to go into attack would be kept at 10,000 men, not at their establishment of 13,000. This meant that battalions would stay somewhat under strength but there was a particular problem with Royal Fusiliers:

> All our Royal Fusilier battalions are permanently weak owing to the large number of Fusilier Battalions to be kept up.[19]

On the 27th they moved into the front line at Cambrin: it felt rather a large expanse of front line for their current numbers, but in contrast with the Arras/Vimy area, full-scale attacks and counter-attacks were rare. Raids, releases of gas and patrols were not. Front line spells were generally six days rather than two to four. Conditions were perfect for young officers who enjoyed patrolling, and in the next few months the Battalion war diary is full of reports of night patrols, generally carried out by an officer and one or two men if they were looking to gather information stealthily about the

The Trench Gate, something that could be lowered to make a block in the trench if the enemy was to attack along it. It was devised by Major Adams in the Annequin area, and put together by 'my Pioneer Sergeant' - probably Sgt McGowan, a resourceful handyman.
(Phythian-Adams papers)

enemy. Particularly distinguished were Second Lieutenants Feord, Bird, JH Davies, Blommy Blomfield, Jimmy Carr DCM and the extraordinary Frank Kiteley.

Lieutenant Ross was promoted to Brigade Transport Officer, Lieutenant Murray (just back from hospital) became a captain, Second Lieutenant Parks a full Lieutenant, and Second Lieutenant Duff qualified to wear Captain's rank while commanding a company. Second Lieutenant Canter, after doing well with the 99th TMB was now officially posted to them.

Wire-cutting began on the 12th for a planned raid by the 23rd RF on the 20th. On the evening of the 19th it was time for the Battalion (then in Support) to provide a feint for the raid. Second Lieutenant Feord and nine other ranks carried a giant Bangalore Torpedo up to the enemy line, with the purpose of exploding it under the enemy wire and making a passage through it. Christopher Stone must have heard Feord report, as his account is both vivid and authoritative:

One of our subalterns did a very fine thing last night. He and a party of about eight men carried a long torpedo, 20 ft long, across No Man's Land in the pitch darkness and the rain, and pushed it under the Boche wire: then he sent all the men back and tried to light the fuse which was only a 45 second one. He failed with the port fuse twice, so he lit a fusee which of course sparked up. He was immediately shot in the shoulder by a Boche who was about seven yards [away] but he lit the fuse all right and managed to fall back into a shell hole before the thing exploded with a perfectly terrific detonation. It stunned him a bit, but he managed to crawl back through the machine gun fire and when he reached our wire he called out and men came out and dragged him in.

Edie (top left) and her QMNY pals at the
Canadian Convalescent Home in Wokingham
(Keeble papers)

Feord was given the MC for his work here, while Corporal Woodward and Private Herrington were given MMs.[20] The procedure did work as a diversion: as soon as British artillery shelled the area near it, German artillery was very active on the passageway through the wire created by the torpedo.

The next night the 23rd RF raid involved a new invention: burning oil, sent over in canisters. A number of Germans were killed, much damage was done, but no prisoners were taken as the enemy had retired. Next morning General Pereira was greatly amused when one of the raiders paraded in his pants, his trousers having been left on the German wire. Unfortunately, the Battalion suffered some casualties from the enemy retribution, two men killed on the night and four others on the 22nd when they went back into the line.

In the north the Third Battle of Ypres had begun on 31 July, but for the Battalion it was simply back to the front line 2 August. This was in fact a very quiet tour, with just one other rank killed and one wounded in the six days.

In their next spell in the front line (14-20 August), Second Lieutenant Davies went out patrolling four nights in a row. On at least two of these occasions he was bombed and machine-gunned, and presumably had to spend a considerable amount of time lying down on the ground or in shell holes. It's perhaps no surprise that he was evacuated sick to hospital on the 21st. Second Lieutenants Bird and Kiteley (each with one man) went on hazardous daylight patrols on the 17th. Kiteley even entered the enemy trenches 'obtaining important and interesting information' according to the war diary. The success of daylight patrols showed that the enemy was holding his front line quite loosely.

Meanwhile Fred Keeble had got his long-anticipated leave in August. It sped past. Then there was the anxiety waiting for the first post-leave letter from his Edie:

> *Very many thanks Edie Darling for your sweet letter just received...I've read it through and through, till practically every word and sentence has pierced my brain...I can tell you that I've hardly done a stroke since I've been back, because I haven't got over my leave yet, but I suppose I'd better soon.*[21]

Training became more intensive in September until they went back to the trenches on the 7th, with parts of the Portuguese contingent on their left and 5th Brigade on their right. The Battalion lost Doc Coad, as his contract had come to an end.

On 9 September Second Lieutenant Kiteley transferred to the 17th RF; the Battalion had just begun to be accustomed to his extraordinary boldness, but he had been sent to the 22nd in error and had always been promised to the 17th RF.[22] He did write an amusing memoir of his short time with the 22nd. The CO told him he wanted to inspect the new line to be taken over with himself and one other officer (probably Second Lieutenant HA Lane, who had arrived with Kiteley). The problem was that 'Horses would be provided', and while Kiteley had done some bare-back riding back in Canada when he was a boy, Lane had never ridden before and wished to use a bicycle instead, if the CO agreed:

Fred Keeble near the end of his first leave for a year. No way can he raise a smile.
(Keeble papers)

> *Next morning **outside** the Orderly Room, two horses with shining saddles and one apprehensive second lieutenant. **Inside**, one irate colonel – he had not taken kindly to the bicycle suggestion.*
>
> *... I am pleased to report that the trip went off satisfactorily and on the way back... A dignified mounted Colonel – a rodeo, bare-backed rider and a furiously pedalling cyclist. It only needed a few yapping dogs to complete the picture.*[23]

Christopher Stone returned from leave ('stale and unenthusiastic') the day the Battalion moved into support in its new area, whose place names had been made legendary in 1915 and early 1916 by Bruce Bairnsfather cartoons: Number 1 Company was in billets at Windy Corner, while Number Two Company was at the Marie (and other) Redoubts.[24]

The Battalion marched forward to billets in Beuvry for two nights then into the front line trenches on the 20th. On the 26th they were back in Beuvry. Unfortunately that was just in time to be involved in 'Roger' fatigues, ie carrying up gas cylinders to the front line, everyone's least favourite occupation.

At the end of September Second Lieutenant P St L (Laurie) Lloyd joined D Company on his first appointment. D Company's commander at the time was Captain Duff, an ex Lovat Scout like Captain Orme. Duff impressed Lloyd straightaway:

He was a grand character, big in every sense of the word and taking pity on my greenness he arranged very tactfully that I should accompany one of his Subalterns on a working party to the front line and so enable me to get to know our sector and have my first taste of enemy fire without the added responsibility for my platoon.[25]

The Battalion got a new doctor, Captain DFA Neilson, on the first of October, did a spell in the Cambrin trenches from the 2nd to the 5th, then went to a small mining village called Raimbert, north-west of Bethune where they stayed for a month of

The Battalion's MO from October 1917, Captain Neilsen (second left), with his assistant Steve Holliday next on the right. (Courtesy Mrs Holliday & Mrs Dickson)

Sergeant Furmston (centre-right, with relaxed grin) was one of the many who were wounded and returned to the Battalion. Here he looks to be recovering well. It all looks very cushy, until you spot the splint. (courtesy EB Furmston)

intensified training. Reinforcements began flooding in, 258 of them between 3 and 12 October, with another forty-six by the 24th making 304 in total. Both the 22nd and the 23rd RF (similarly reinforced) were still about 250 under the strength they were in December 1916, and lower than the Royal Berks and KRRC.[26] Even so, it would be hard not to combine the arrival of reinforcements with the intensive training and deduce that they were being 'fattened up' for the Third Ypres/Passchendaele offensive that had been raging to the north since the end of July. The 99 Brigade diarist has just the right tone of voice:

> This is the first occasion an attempt has been made to make the Brigade up to strength since its depletion in the fighting against Oppy in April and May last, so that offensive operations in the near future are anticipated.[27]

One of the more interesting inventions at Raimbert was the Tump-Line Platoon under Second Lieutenant Fisher. In almost every battle there was a need to supply ammunition either before or after the battle had started. Normally those who did the carrying were scratch parties of anyone that happened to be available. Much better to train men in the art of efficient transportation – and even better if the men detailed could be those with a lower fighting ability. As it says in the *History*:

> The Tump-liners, mostly older men who had not great combative value, began to display great esprit de corps, and very soon it was difficult to stop them carrying everything they could lay hands on to the front line.[28]

Second Lieutenant Blomfield continued to patrol aggressively and was awarded the MC for his fine work, 'an outstanding example of pluck and good leadership'.[29] As with that other excellent patroller, DF Davies, Blommy's health gave up, and he was evacuated sick to England in November.

On 25 October a Brigade exercise was held, with General Pereira also present, in which the lie of the land looked very similar to Passchendaele Ridge. Despite the units having tried to incorporate the lessons learnt in the Passchendaele fighting, it did not go very well. It was repeated on the 31st of the month 'and by careful attention to the lessons learnt on that occasion, there was a noticeable improvement.'[30]

On 5 November the Battalion moved again to arrive at Herzeele on the 8th, where they would continue training until the 23rd of the month. They were now due west of the Passchendaele battlefield. Unknown to the Battalion, the last acts of this offensive, the taking of Passchendaele village by the Canadians, were already under way.

At Herzeele D Company were doing Company training under Lieutenant JW (Jimmy) Carr (Captain Duff was away). Carr had come through the ranks, being commissioned and given the DCM after Miraumont and was now a full Lieutenant.

This 1917 sketch of Fred Keeble is by Leslie Grimes (a runner at Battalion HQ before he went off to become a fighter pilot), who would become very famous after the war as a cartoonist in *The Star* (Keeble papers)

One imagines that he would be a more rough-tough-up-and-at-'em type of personality than the more sensitive Laurie Lloyd. In any case, Carr was in charge of an exercise about quickly dispersing off the road when marching in the usual column formation and coming under fire. He instructed each platoon in turn, but when he came to Lloyd's Platoon, he gave all his instructions to the Platoon Sergeant, not Lloyd.

It was time for Lloyd to stand up for himself:

> I called my Sergeant who informed me of the orders issued to him. In a voice loud enough to be heard by the platoon I informed him that I was in command and he would make it clear to the men that, in the absence of any orders from me, whatever whistles blew, the platoon would continue to march in column.[31]

Carr then blew his whistle and the other three platoons rushed into the undergrowth, while Lloyd's Platoon carried on marching. After some words between Carr and Lloyd, the exercise was repeated, this time Lloyd instructing his men to move like lightning, which they did. One can imagine the atmosphere in the Company Mess later. Later Lloyd would disobey orders from an even more senior officer (Adams) in favour of contrary ones given by Lieutenant Carr, and so Lloyd and Carr saw eye to eye after that.

Another rumour moved centre stage: that the Division was to go to Italy. Big changes were indeed underfoot for the Battalion, but they came from an unexpected source. Colonel Barker, none too well – 'wretchedly ill and so wracked with rheumatism that he could hardly walk'[32] – went off on leave 18 November, only to be recalled to take command of 3 Infantry Brigade. By the time he had come back, the whole business had rejuvenated him.

In *B.B.*, Stone described the farewell:

There was little time for talking; he was leaving us after two years of constant companionship in France; the tailor was busy sewing red tabs on to his coat, there were battalion matters to settle, and we all felt rather bewildered and distracted. When the car drove off the next day – piled to its utmost capacity with his kit – he turned away. The leave-taking had been too much for us all and the War Lord [Major Adams] *and I went miserably back into the mess.*

He left behind a noble farewell message:

On relinquishing Command of the Battalion I wish to place on record my great appreciation and grateful thanks to all ranks for their unswerving loyalty to me at all times.

I was with the Battalion at its foundation and, in fact, enlisted the first man, and it was my wish to remain with you to the finish – but apparently this cannot be.

You were well thought of at home, quickly made a name for the Battalion in France, and in the fighting line you cannot be surpassed. That is the opinion of not only your near Commanders, but also of the highest. If proof were required (which it is not) our casualties would show that the 22nd, when needs be, can die to a man. You all feel as I do what we owe to our gallant comrades who gave their lives not only for their Country but for the glory of the Regiment. They have made the Regiment famous and I am absolutely confident that you can only add fresh laurels to our already glorious record.

It was my one ambition to make and keep you a happy Regiment, and if I have succeeded in just one item, I shall feel that I have commanded you successfully.

My parting words to you all are, to keep happy and endeavour to make each other merry and bright. Don't forget that we are all comrades in this great adventure, and that our job is to strafe Germans and not each other. An unhappy man can't fight, and if a Regiment is full of imaginary grievances its fighting spirit disappears.

I hand over the Regiment to Colonel Phythian-Adams with the feeling of the greatest confidence. He has been born and bred a 22nd man, and had proved himself to you on the field of battle. I know that you will extend to him the same confidence and support that you gave to me. He richly deserves the great honour of commanding you and can't

Laurie Lloyd as a young subaltern (from the cover of *The Wood of Death*).

be anything but successful.

'Adieu' (I purposely use this word, as 'Goodbye' could never be said between us, as long as any of us exist) my brave friends and comrades. May the God of all battles have you in his safe keeping.[33]

When Mayor Davison heard the news, he managed to be both honest and generous:

My dear Randle, I received your letter of the 21st instant with very mixed feelings. I heartily congratulate you on the already overdue honour which you have received in being made a Brigadier-General, though I need not say how much I regret that this will involve your ceasing to command the 22nd, which you have done with such distinction and success.[34]

On the night of the 20th Colonel Adams was telling his mother the proud news:

A line to tell you that the Colonel has been appointed to the command of a Brigade and that I am now Lt Colonel Commanding of the Battalion. Funnily enough, I still have my first tunic which has now undergone alterations from junior subaltern to Commanding Officer, a record of which I am unaffectedly proud.[35]

There was no doubt that ex-Major Adams deserved his promotion. He had shown by his cool and assured leadership in command of the mixed Barker-force almost exactly a year ago that he could successfully handle large numbers of men in battle.

Stone took over as Second-in-Command, with Second Lieutenant Bexon as acting Adjutant. There was hardly time to digest the changes before the Battalion set off on their travels; they arrived at Achiet le Grand – not Italy – on the 24th with almost ten miles to march before they got to their destination, Barastre, late at night. A new battle was being fought in the vicinity of Cambrai, some fifteen or so miles to the north-east, and the 2nd Division were wanted there.

1 *WO 95/1372*, plus *History of Second Division*, op cit p449
2 Fred Keeble to Miss E Lacey, 13/5/1917, *Keeble Papers*
3 *WO 95/1372* and 1369; 55 of the new recruits were Class II men of lower levels of fitness and health (and the KKRC had 135 of them)
4 RBB to Davison, 11/5/1917, *Broughshane*, VII: 49
5 Interview with Ollie Berrycloath, 15/1/1984
6 *Mufti*, June 1954, 34, No 123, pp 5-6
7 *History*, op cit, p63; 2nd Lt Feord discovered later that it could jump fences
8 *Broughshane*, 8720 9/5/1917, 8683, 14/5/1917
9 Only found in the *History of the Second Division*, op cit, pp 451-2; also see *WO 95/1309* and *WO 372/23*. Several hands did the battalion war diary in May, without any consistency
10 *Mufti*, Summer 1938, 19, No 89, p6. Other details from *History*, p62
11 *Mufti*, Summer 1964, 44, No 143, pp 2-3
12 FW Palmer to Mayor Davison, *Broughshane*, VII: 22-3; he had suffered head pains after Oppy
13 *The West London Observer*, 8/6/1917 and 13/7/1917
14 *PAP*, WJ P-A to his father, 16/6/1917
15 *WO 95/1372*, June 1917 entries; could the horse be Oppy? We have no more information
16 *London Gazette*, 24/7/1917

17 *History*, p53

18 Edie was serving in a Canadian Convalescent Home in Wokingham. Interview with Mrs Keeble 28/5/1984

19 General Pereira's Diary, 2nd Division diary, *WO 95*/1289

20 *CRS*, 19/7/1917, also *Sheffield & Inglis*, op cit, p101-2 ; also see *London Gazette*, 8/1/1918

21 Fred Keeble to Miss E Lacey, 23/8/1917, *Keeble Papers*

22 Personal communication from his widow, Sarah Kiteley, June 1984

23 *Mufti*, Summer 1963, 43, No 141, p4

24 *Ibid*, 12/9/1917, p103

25 *The Wood of Death and Beyond*, Ed RJ Lloyd, Oakham Books, ~1997, p20, hereafter *Wood of Death*

26 General Pereira's diary (*WO 95*/1289) has 99 Brigade going from 1913 men in 29/9 to 2943 in 13/10. Contrast this with the Canadians, able to make up their battle losses almost at once.

27 *WO 95*/1369, 8/10/1917

28 *History*, p 65-66

29 *Mufti*, Spring 1933, 14, No 1, p5, cited the citation in the *London Gazette*

30 99 Brigade diary, *WO 95*/1369

31 *Wood of Death*, p23

32 *B.B.*, op cit, p8

33 *History*, pp 54-55

34 *Broughshane*, 8546, 26/11/1917, 8549, and 8545

35 *PAP*, WJP-A to Mother, 20/11/1917

Chapter Eleven

Cambrai

O
N 20 NOVEMBER THE BRITISH launched a surprise attack from south-west of Cambrai towards the town, with massed tanks and no previous artillery registration to alert the enemy. In the first few days, great advances were made, but the Germans made strenuous efforts to bring up reserves and seal the breach in their lines. Fierce fighting raged in and around the area of Bourlon Wood for some days.

On the evening of the 26th, in a snowstorm and a biting east wind, the Battalion relieved units of 36th (Ulster) Division. They were now astride the Cambrai-Bapaume road, with Battalion headquarters in the Hindenburg Support Line, C and D Companies on the right of the road in Kangaroo Trench, while A and B Companies were left (ie north) of the road and just east of the Canal du Nord.

Next night, a series of 'detached' adventures began for the Battalion, working for many new masters. At 10:30 pm Colonel Adams was summoned to 99 Brigade HQ:

An urgent message to H.Q. brought us stumbling though the dark to a brief interview with General Kellett, a handshake and another half hour of stumbling to the quarters of a new Brigade [186]. There in a few words General Bradford outlined the situation. His men were exhausted and were being withdrawn, and only two dismounted cavalry 'Battalions' remained to garrison the position.[1]

Brigadier-General 'Boy' Bradford VC MC was at 25, the youngest brigade commander in the British army, and a soldier of immense potential. Soldiers from his Division (the 62nd) had made record advances on the 20th November at the outset of the Cambrai battle. Normally, they would have been relieved after putting in such a major effort, but there were few reserves, so 186 and 187 Brigades had been called forward again for one further, futile attempt on 27 November to take the northern parts of Bourlon Wood, and complete the capture of the village to the west. The enemy forces were strong, and composed of fresh men. Not only did they repel the attacks but their counter-attacks threatened to break through the British lines.[2]

Colonel Adams' memoir continues:

My orders were to proceed at once to the Wood, leaving the Battalion to follow at full speed, and to represent to the Battalion Commanders on the spot the need of attacking and capturing Bourlon village by dawn. Back again to H.Q. Company Commanders conference, a bite, and a much needed drink and off to Bourlon Wood.

In fact he found both of the commanders of the dismounted cavalry battalions, whom he met at 1:30 am, very doubtful about the likely success of any such attack. They agreed that the 3rd Dismounted Battalion would send out strong patrols to assess the situation. In case the response was favourable, the 22nd RF (minus B Company) were sent forward into the Wood, to the vicinity of Star Cross Roads, arriving there at 4:30 am.

Christopher Stone had the job of bringing up the Battalion, a none too pleasant task.

A number of the new members of the Battalion would not have seen action before. As they moved forward in daylight and under fire, with shells landing to either side of the road, it would have been easy for panic to spread. To set the men an example, Christopher Stone took off his tin hat and 'walked up and down beside us waving it in his hand.' Almost certainly RSM Rumble was also involved in keeping the troops calm at this time.[3]

The patrols found that the enemy was holding the village in some strength and so the idea of an attack was abandoned. The 22nd Battalion therefore formed up as a defensive flank on the left of the 186th Brigade area.

The Germans shelled the Wood continuously, which affected both the Battalion's move into it and its stay there. The shelling rose to a peak on the afternoon of the 28th, but no more attacks came, and the Battalion began withdrawing at 9 pm to some very uncomfortable billets on the Hermies-Graincourt road.

In the action over the two days, three officers (Captain Parks, Lieutenant Steele and

The 22nd Battalion's part in the Battle of Cambrai where they were given over to other brigades: first in Bourlon Wood (right), then defending against German attacks near Moeuvres (left). Their replacement within 99 Brigade was 17th RF, whose Captain Stone won the VC at The Rat's Tail.

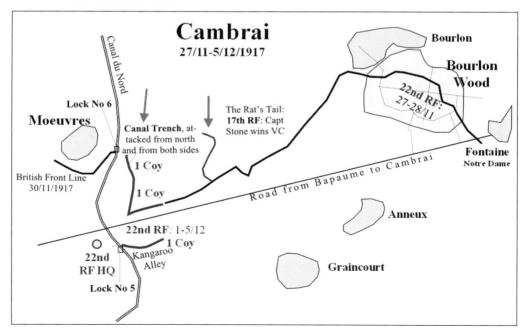

Second Lieutenant Wardell) were wounded, with seven other ranks killed and thirty-four wounded.

The 17th RF had replaced them in 99 Brigade's defensive area, so it was decided to leave them there, and to put the 22nd Battalion under the orders of 5 Brigade *pro tem*.

When the big German attack came on the morning of the 30th, all the battalions then with 99 Brigade performed with great distinction. The KRRC – the King's Royal **Rifle** Corps – showed just what could be done with well-handled rifle fire (presumably some credit must go to the Riflemen's School). The Royal Berks, and the 23rd RF produced feats of extraordinary heroism, but pride of place for sheer self-sacrificial example went to the 17th RF, whose rearguard under a Captain Napoleon Stone fought and died to a man, with Stone later awarded a posthumous VC.

The 22nd Battalion, on the other hand, moved forward through the German bombardment to the Canal du Nord area, and took up positions on the west bank at Lock 6, fortunately suffering only seven casualties in the process. In the early evening they were asked to go further north, and took up a position on the west bank where the Canal and Bapaume-Cambrai road crossed each other, in touch with the 17th Middlesex.

Next morning, when the 17th Middlesex sent up a SOS flare, meaning they were in danger of being attacked, the left company of the 22nd Battalion sent up all the bombs they had spare, plus a Lewis Gun, then the 22nd Tump-Line Platoon got to work and moved 50 boxes of bombs forward in good time.

Shortly afterwards 5 Brigade were in touch, with orders stretching the front held by the 22nd Battalion, and thus the Battalion spent much of the day consolidating their positions.

The 22nd Battalion was then given over to the care of the 6 Brigade Commander, and within half an hour of this order, Captain WA Murray (C Company) received an urgent request from the 1st Kings for assistance. He sent up half of his company – returned to him a few hours later when the panic had subsided. Later the Battalion was asked to relieve the 13th Essex with two companies east of the canal, another company to relieve a company from the HLI in Kangaroo Alley (further back), with the fourth company to stay where there they were.

Of the two companies east of the canal, one was in a 'normal' transverse trench, but the other one was simply a long (300 yards) sap pointing towards the enemy, with a block at the far end, behind which were known to be deep dugouts that could hold many more attackers than they could oppose with defenders. This sap, known as Canal Trench, was also vulnerable to attack on both sides. This was probably the worst spot ever held by the Battalion, and an attack was expected on it on the morrow (2 December).

The 6 Brigade Commander Brigadier-General Walsh came over to personally go over arrangements with Colonel Adams. Overnight the Tump-Line Platoon worked non-stop bringing up some 200 boxes of bombs, rifle grenades and SAA (ammunition). Wire was put out to try and channel any attackers from the north into the fields of fire of the Lewis Guns at the transverse trench. Additional bombing and Lewis Gun posts were put out, both to protect the block and against attackers using the canal bank.

All through the day of 2 December tension rose, with the enemy reported to be massing in the north. At 4:45 pm there was an SOS all the way along the line, with heavy enemy shelling both of our front lines and of our batteries, and the attack came at 5:13 pm. The enemy, using two groups of about 30 men each, attacked down both sides of Canal Trench. The party on the east of the Canal Trench were caught by the Lewis Guns in the transverse trench and dispersed quickly.

Those on the left of Canal Trench were rather more persistent. They stayed at a distance from it, 'vigorously' throwing bombs into it (German bombs could be thrown longer distances than British ones, although the British ones had more destructive power). It took about half an hour's brisk fighting with bombs and Lewis Guns before this group was also successfully dispersed.

Second Lieutenant James Brownlee won the MC here, almost certainly for defending the block at the end of Canal Trench:

> His platoon held a block within twenty yards of the enemy, who were known to have massed in great numbers against this critical point. He was heavily attacked from both flanks simultaneously, and although wounded early in the action, continued to lead his men without losing ground until the enemy were repulsed, refusing to withdraw until the position was secure and his casualties had been evacuated. His courage and example were magnificent.[4]

Sergeant FC Shepard (awarded the MM for his work) recalled two actions: one on the 1st, one on the 2nd. He described the latter to Mayor Davison:

> We were attacked again at 4 pm on the 2nd inst. though stronger in numbers, this time from three sides. An order came to Shepard that the barricade must be held at all cost and owing to having many wounded and his platoon officer getting wounded, he rallied the men and kept hold of his position until reinforcements came up. After holding this barricade never losing ground was congratulated for his work by all superior Officers for presence of mind, bravery and devotion to duty.[5]

All was quiet by 6:30 pm. The Battalion suffered perhaps fifteen casualties as a result of this action. The night was spent in constructing T-heads and wiring around them to strengthen Canal Trench. There was another scare early next morning, but no attack developed.

The Battalion now found itself back under the orders of 5 Brigade again, as the latter had taken over this sector. This time the order was to withdraw from the front positions on the night of the 4th/5th.

Colonel Adams reassured his mother on the 3rd that the danger had largely passed and anyway: 'The work is very exciting and stimulating which contributes to keeping up my vivacity as hard intense work always does.'[6] There was no doubt that Colonel Adams kept a very cool head under pressure.

First the Canal Trench defenders had to face another attack, this time from the saphead itself. Reports reached the 'OC Forward Area', Captain ST Goodman, that the block had been forced by the enemy. Captain Goodman's MC citation makes it likely it was for dispersing this attack:

> He was in command of the companies holding an important position when the enemy attacked in force. His dispositions were made with such judgment and his supports so carefully organised that the attack was driven back with heavy loss and the position was held intact. His courage and unflagging energy in difficult circumstances were mainly responsible for the success achieved.[7]

During the night the withdrawal went off very well. Lieutenant Bird and A Company, plus two Lewis Guns from D Company, had been designated as the rearguard – about sixty men in all. After the others had withdrawn the rearguard followed them, blowing up dugouts containing surplus ammunition and covering the entrances with blankets to stop them being seen. Finally Lieutenant Bird and a few men remained behind to blow up the last dugout, the one that had been Forward Headquarters, and then they too withdrew. It had been perfect, with no casualties. After counting, however, there was one man missing. Private Metcalfe had been one of the D-Company Lewis Gunners posted on the east bank of the canal. He had fallen heavily and had lost sight of his colleagues. He moved into Canal Trench by accident, got buried there by an explosion but eventually broke free, then faced his own personal shelling by the Germans (about to occupy the deserted territory) before managing to scuttle back into the British lines.

Overall, from 30 November onwards, the Battalion had suffered four officers wounded in action: Captain WA Murray, Second Lieutenant Brownlee, Second Lieutenant Park, and Second Lieutenant Lloyd. Six other ranks were killed, seventy wounded and one was missing. This time WA Murray's injury, his fourth (sniper-shot in the head, but the bullet had been slowed down by his steel helmet) was his most serious. In 1938, after a glittering golf career, he said that he had undergone sixteen operations on what he called 'his bunker'.[8]

Richard Deville (C company) remained a private, but the chevron on his left arm denoted two years good conduct and the three vertical stripes show he was wounded three times (Courtesy G Deville)

Laurie Lloyd recalled that Murray had been given up for dead but that his batman went out looking for him, against orders. He found Murray, covered up his head wound with a coin, and dragged him back to the British lines. Lloyd himself had a great slice of luck; he was taken to the Acheson Hospital (for officers) in St Johns Wood where many of the VADs were Society Belles.[9]

In his Observations, Colonel Adams particularly praised the Tump-Line Platoon:

> *The use of these trained load-carriers is, I consider, indispensable. They have an esprit de corps of their own and can carry more and work harder and longer than haphazard parties collected from exhausted fighting companies…Tump Lines only* [burden straps looping around the forehead, as beloved by the Canadian troops] *were used.*

The great shame – it still bothered him in 1920 when writing a memoir about the actions – was the waste of so much of their efforts when blowing up the excess ammunition when the Battalion withdrew.[10]

Here is Deville (centre) recovering after one of his wounds (*Courtesy G Deville*)

The Tump-liners were very enthusiastic about picking things up and taking them away, but not always out of altruism:

> *On behalf of Lt. Fisher, Tump Line Platoon, the R.S.M. and myself, I wish to thank very heartily the C.O., Lt.-Col. Phythian-Adams, 2nd in Command, Major Stone, Captain and Adjutant Bexon, and, I believe, the M.O., for the odd bottle of Scotch and sundry Perrier Waters we waylaid and halted on their way to H. Q. Mess through the trenches outside that grim Canal du Nord. I would add that we never touched a drop without solemnly rising to our feet and sincerely toasting 'The H.Q. Mess.'[11]*

Colonel Adams summed up the actions:

> *At Moeuvres our part was not a minor one: we had the hardest task of any, to manoeuvre under another command after*

days of shelling and fatigue, from which our comrades were exempt, to move here or there, wherever we were most wanted, and finally when endurance seemed no longer possible, to enter the front line and, at the eleventh hour to come to grips with the enemy.[12]

The Battalion moved back to the Old British Line east of Hermies, working on establishing a new front line, and on the 6th they went right back to a tented camp near Haplincourt, where they rested for a few days.

On the 11th an anxious Mayor Davison, having seen accounts of the recent fighting in the newspapers, wrote to Colonel Adams, enquiring about casualties, and there was also the matter of Christmas presents:

I hope to send you out next week 800 copies of the Soldier's Notebook and Diary with special greeting for Xmas and the New Year on the outside from the Mayoress and myself and Friends of the regiment in the Borough.

Colonel Adams wrote back saying the men would really appreciate the gift. As for numbers: 'Our ration strength is much less than 800 – I do not know what our depot is doing.' It was true that all through 1917 the Battalion had been low in numbers, usually just lower than the 23rd RF Battalion, and almost always significantly worse than the Royal Berks and the KRRCs – even when they were 'fattened up' in October.

On the 13th they moved to the Hughes Switch line on the right bank of the Canal du Nord where, early on the 15th, the enemy made a bombing attack, preceded by rifle grenades, on one of the Battalion's advanced saps, but the attack was beaten off with heavy casualties to the enemy.[13] Newly promoted Sergeant Roland Whipp was in the front line in the immediate area:

*And our fellows round in the sap were cooking their bacon – there was a lovely smell of bacon from there – and over came the bombs instead. But I was round the corner, not in the sap. Bombs were dropping all over the place…After it had been going on for some time I heard the sounds of the wounded chaps on **both** sides – for our side were throwing things back.*

A young somewhat shaky officer came along and Roland calmed him down by showing no fear, despite the rifle grenades falling all around them, and by joking about the danger – which maintained morale in the immediate area and the officer recommended him for an MM. Gradually the noise slackened off, while rifle-grenadiers from our side now lobbed grenades against any Germans left in the sap, and the survivors fled.[14]

Later on that day, an officer's patrol investigated the area. There were no German bodies – these must have been dragged away – but much evidence of a fight such plenty of blood and battle debris. (Sixty-six years later, Roland remembered a figure of thirteen helmets – virtually the same as the official report of eleven rifles and two helmets!)

On the 17th they went back into Support, followed by moving into huts near Barastre in reserve on the 21st. Whereas Christmas 1916 was a very festive occasion, the celebrations in 1917 were more muted. There were a number of possible reasons:

Eric Stevens' 1918 diary, the Mayor's 1917 Christmas present.

muddy Barastre was not a patch on Yvrench; the Battalion had suffered so many losses in 1917 the social glue was not as strong; while winning seemed just as far away as ever.

From the 26th to the 30th they were back in the line, this time on the west bank of the Canal. News began to come in of awards won by the Battalion in the Cambrai series of actions; most of these awards were omitted from the battalion history for reasons that will become clearer later. Colonel Adams was given a DSO, with MCs to Hon Lieutenant and QM RW Burgess, Captain ST Goodman and Second Lieutenant J Brownlee, with RSM WA Rumble winning the DCM. As was customary, there was a longer list of MMs: Sergeant CW Lindsey of the Tump-Line Platoon, Corporal (Lance-Sergeant) V Plummer, Corporal R Whipp (our friend Roland), Lance-Corporals J Beaty, A Carter, FC Shepard and WJ Cooper, and Privates JW Becks, L Warwick, W Glover, B Chennell and WC Fletcher.[15]

The Battalion went back to brigade reserve in Hermies on the 30th, thence to the hutted camp at Barastre where they stayed throughout most of January.

Stone took over as CO again, with Colonel Adams going off on some richly deserved leave. The Battalion moved straight into the right section of line opposite La Vacquerie. The trenches were wet and muddy but life appeared quite peaceful: enemy artillery seemed directed towards rear areas, not the front line.

The winds of change were afoot. Brigadier Kellett was home on leave, but his health was failing:

> There is a rumour that Kellett is not coming back to the Brigade and and of course we are hoping wildly that if he doesn't Barker will get it.[16]

General Kellett had served 99 Brigade very well. His infectious 'can do' enthusiasm impressed almost everyone. Corporal George Challis recalled him with great affection seventy years later:

> Our Brigadier...Kellett...he was loved, no doubt about that. He'd talk to you. He

wasn't afraid, he'd come up the line of an afternoon.[17]

The rumour was true and an excited Brigadier Barker, who did not enjoy his time at 3 Brigade, wrote off to Mrs Stone:

Isn't it all too wonderful!!! It is a direct answer to prayer. The old triumvirate is never to be separated. I believe we shall all die together or get through it…I feel in a trance as it's the only job I wanted bar commanding the dear old Regt.[18]

He arrived at 99th Brigade HQ on the 24th.

Major Stone felt very reassured to have his old friend General Barker close at hand to ask for advice. He began to plan a scheme to take place in their next period in the line. This began 29 January and continued until they went to Metz-en-Couture on the 1st February. It may have been connected with the DCM won by Sergeant L Hawthorne, who brought back valuable information about an enemy post and rescued his comrade although both were badly wounded.[19]

Other, much larger schemes overtook it. The British Army had become very short of men. From being the junior partner to France in 1914 and 1915, it had been moving nearer the centre stage through 1916 and 1917, accordingly suffering increasing numbers of casualties. Now it was very difficult to keep units up to scratch. The War Cabinet preferred the solution of keeping the number of divisions and brigades the same, but reducing the number of battalions in them. Thus there would now be nine battalions instead of twelve per division, three battalions per brigade not four. Divisional commanders were given some general principles such as not to disband regular battalions, and to keep lower numbered service battalions rather than late-formed ones. In the case of 2nd Division, where half the battalions were regulars and half were service battalions, it meant losing three service battalions out of six.

It seems to have been quickly decided that the 13th Essex and 17th Middlesex (despite their wonderful Cambrai performances) would go, and one of the four Royal Fusiliers battalions. General Pereira wrote in his diary on the 19th January:

It was left up to me to decide which R. Fusilier battn was to be broken up but I could not bear to be personally responsible for doing away with any of them and so I went to Corps Hqrs and got the Corps Comdr to draw lots. The 22nd R.F. drew the unlucky number.[20]

It has to be said that, after its mauling at Miraumont, and the loss of two-thirds of the remaining effectives at Oppy Wood, the 22nd Battalion was always struggling for numbers. If the thirteen battalions (ie including the DCLI Pioneers) were ranked in order of their numbers, all four Royal Fusilier battalions tended to be near the bottom, but the 22nd Battalion was often in 1917 the weakest battalion of all. A civil servant, knowing only numbers and nothing about the spirit of battalions, would have picked out the 22nd for disbandment. The Third Army Commander, General Sir JHG Byng arrived on the 31st to have a short conversation with General Barker. One can imagine some last-minute special pleading; if so it was to no avail.[21] Colonel Adams returned from leave on the 31st January to find a *fait accompli*. He wrote off to Mayor Davison in admirably restrained tones:

Colonel Adams (front row, fourth left) and others at the 2nd Army School at Wisques
(Phythian-Adams papers)

231

I believe you have heard from General Barker the fate which has befallen the 22nd.

It is not my place or duty to comment upon it nor is it of any use to question the policy which underlies this move.

What it meant to me – on my return from leave – you can well understand and I need not describe my feelings. The 23rd and 24th Bns will get my men and I feel sure that we shall be able to make some arrangement for keeping in close touch with them and caring for their future and their kinsfolk now and after the war as we have been trying to do heretofore.[22]

On 2 February Brigadier Barker did his best to capture the right note in his message of farewell to the Battalion:

Since November 1915, under the able leadership of our Beloved and Gallant Brigadier, Brigadier-General R. O. KELLETT, C.B., C.M.G., we have fought together in the following actions: Delville Wood, Vimy Ridge, Ancre, Miraumont, Grevillers Trench, Oppy and Cambrai in every one of which the 22nd Royal Fusiliers played a conspicuous part.

The mention of these important actions, in which we have added fame to the 2nd Division, is sufficient to prove the magnificent part you have filled in making the History of 99 Brigade.

We all understand with what feelings you must view the disbanding of your fine Battalion. We know full well, your splendid esprit de corps *which engendered your fine fighting spirit.*

We know of the N.C.Os. and men still with you who gave up their all in 1914 to join you. Nor can we forget the many heroes who died for you and us all.

Knowing full well all this, we can truly offer you our heartfelt sympathies in your day of trial.

The 22nd Battalion Royal Fusiliers never lost a yard of trench or failed their comrades in the Day of Battle. Such is your record and such a record of you will be handed down to posterity.

All of you, I am thankful to say will remain in our famous Division and 300 of you in the Old Brigade…

As one who served with you from the day of your foundation to your disbandment (except for two months) I know full well what this step means to you all.

I know that though the 22nd Royal Fusiliers has ceased to exist as a Unit, you will not forget that we are all Englishmen fighting Germans, and that the fine indomitable spirit of the Battalion will still carry you on until the One Red and Two White Stars are inscribed on the Forts of the Rhine.

R Barnett Barker
Brigadier-General,
Commanding 99 Infantry Brigade
2/2/1918[23]

The 5 February was the designated day for the disbandment. The day before was a massive booze-up. Roland Whipp remembered it as only the second time he had ever been drunk:

> *The last day when the 22nd was broken up. That was an event! All the sergeants and officers together joined up together in the hut* [the Sergeants' hut] *where they had masses of whisky from the Officers Mess.*
>
> *Everyone got drunk and then lay on the ground until they were sober enough to start drinking again.*[24]

It took some time to sort out which men would join which units. Eventually some fifteen officers and 309 men (including most of the original 'K' men) went into the 23rd RF (the 22nd *History* commented 'received with the utmost consideration'), while fourteen officers and 274 men went into the 24th RF.

Perhaps it was because the 24th were in a different brigade with a different attitude to life, but the marriage with the 23rd Battalion went rather better than with the 24th. Roland Whipp, recently made a Sergeant, found himself reduced back to Corporal when he joined the 24th because they had too many sergeants. This may have been true, and his new company officer taking an instant dislike to him may have been bad luck (he said the men in the 24th were 'just like us'). On the other hand Syd Rogers enjoyed his time in the 24th, and expressed admiration for its CO Colonel Pipon.[25]

For Ollie Berrycloath, on the other hand: 'Our section went straight into the 23rd Sportsman's Battalion…They were a good lot'. For Robert Wright, who had trained with the 23rd RF, it was a simple choice; he returned to his old unit.[26]

Back in Kensington Mayor Davison was not taking the disbandment of his Battalion lightly. On the 6th February he sat down, pen afire, in the first of a number of pleas: 'Dear Sir Douglas Haig, In consequence of rumours which had reached me…' – and he adduced a number of powerful reasons why the 22nd Battalion should be kept alive, but it was already too late.[27]

Of course, the day after the Battalion had been disbanded a parcel of comforts arrived:

> *We got 18 bales of stuff today including 993 pairs of socks, 1300 pairs of mittens etc!! Marvellous organisation. Of course these things have been sent to be distributed among our fellows in their new battalions.*[28]

Brigadier Barker did his best to take as many of his veterans onto the brigade staff as possible. Major Stone followed him as a learner under the Brigade Major (really intended for someone of more junior rank). For Colonel Adams the thought of commanding strangers must have seemed repugnant so he chose the chief instructor's job with the Second Army School. Captain Goodman, Second Lieutenant Vaughan and Second Lieutenant GL Pargeter applied to the RAF,[29] with Pargeter later winning the DFC. Major Scott also went to teach at a school at Lucheux, to help corporals and lance-corporals to smarten up their ideas.

In 1923 Stone was still pessimistic about it:

> *We know that for us the great days were over with the passing of the 22nd; that whether we 'retired from the war' or carried on in new surroundings with a dismal loyalty to the broader esprit de corps, we should never recapture the glories of the old*

comradeship, never find elsewhere the love of our devoted leader…it is still but the afterglow of a sun that has set, the echo of a voice that is forever silenced.[30]

And yet, as predicted by Colonel Adams in his note to the Mayor, and greatly encouraged by Christopher Stone, that same spirit would reappear after the war.

1 *Bourlon Wood and After, Mufti*, May 1930, 1, No 7, p6 (also *Royal Fusiliers in the Great War*, pp 401-2)

2 Unfortunately General Bradford only had a few more days to live before being killed by a shell

3 *Mufti*, Summer 1974, 54, No 162, p4; RSM WA Rumble won the DCM in one of the Cambrai actions, and the citation talks of 'When a very heavy barrage was in danger of disorganising the troops and causing heavy casualties, he showed most …marked courage in rallying the men and disposing of them in places of comparative safety,' *London Gazette*, 30/4/1918.

4 *London Gazette*, 16/7/1918

5 *Broughshane*, 8825, Shephard to Davison, 3/3 /1919 and 14/3/1919. Shephard was having his MM presented to him by the Mayor and was attempting to recall the citation for the latter's benefit.

6 *PAP*, WJP-A to Mother, 3/12/1917

7 *London Gazette*, 16/7/1918.

8 Figures from the *Narrative* (WO 95/1372), December 1917; *Mufti*, Summer 1938, 19, No 90, pp 6-7

9 *Wood of Death*, p49 and pp 44-46; (Murray misremembered as 'Gibson')

10 WO 95/1372, December 1917; *Mufti*, May 1920, op cit

11 GL Pargeter, former Intelligence Officer to the Battalion, *Mufti*, December 1954, 34, No 124, p11

12 *Mufti*, May 1920, op cit

13 WO 95/1372, 15/12/1917, *History of the Second Division*, p cit, p519

14 Interview with Roland Whipp, 18/11/1983

15 WO 95/1310 and 1372. Also a Corporal SH Wright insisted he had been awarded the MM for his work on the 2nd December but it did not appear in the lists above

16 CRS, 20/1/1918, also *Sheffield & Inglis*, op cit, p112

17 Interview with George Challis, 1984

18 *Sheffield & Inglis*, op cit, p112, RBB to CRS, 23/1/1918

19 *London Gazette*, 20/4/1918

20 General Pereira's diary, 19/1/1918, WO 95/1289, retold by the General in *Mufti*, Summer 1923, 4, No 2, pp 2-3 (except he said that it was the GOC Vet Corps who drew the lots).

21 WO 95/1369 and 1372

22 WJP-A to Davison, 2/2/1918, *Broughshane*, 8888

23 99 Brigade diary, Appendix 2, February 1918; The red and white stars were the divisional symbol

24 Combination of two separate interviews with Roland Whipp in November 1983

25 *Mufti*, Xmas 1976, 56, No 166, p13

26 Interview with Ollie Berrycloath, 15/1/1984; *Mufti*, Summer 1964, 44, No 143, p3. Unfortunately he lost a leg on the 6th March

27 *Broughshane*, 8885 ,8881. Ironically, Colonel Innes was being invalided out of the army at this time.

28 CRS, 6/2/1918, also *Sheffield & Inglis*, p114

29 Private communication with Henry Phythian-Adams; *Mufti*, Summer 1932, 13, No 2, p3

30 *History*, p61

Chapter Twelve

To The End of the War

A) The March Retreat

IN THE SPRING OF 1917 THE AMERICANS had entered the war, but it would be a year, perhaps eighteen months, before they had amassed together and trained an army of significant size. On the other hand, the Russians were effectively out of the war. By the end of 1917 many battle-hardened German divisions, accustomed to being victorious on the Eastern Front, were now available to the Germans in France and Flanders. The British had exhausted themselves with their offensive at Third Ypres/Passchendaele. Their limited offensive with massed tanks at Cambrai had been promising, but there had been no reserves with which to exploit their success, and the ferocity of the German counter-attack – using tactics perfected on the Eastern Front – had shocked the British.

Now the stakes were raised. The manpower equation was now temporarily in favour of the Germans. The latter needed to attack and win the war outright before superior American manpower won it for the other side.

On the British side, the big shortage of manpower meant that the number of fighting battalions was cut down from twelve to nine per Division. The 22nd Royal Fusiliers had been just one of 141 battalions disbanded. Another big change was the (tentative) adoption of the German style of defence in depth, with one's main defensive punch further back, rather than the old method of cramming one's front trenches with troops to stop an enemy making any penetration at all.

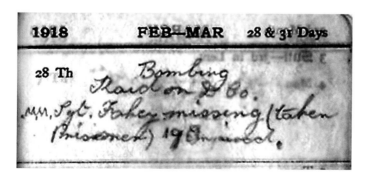

After the disbandment of the 22nd, Eric Stevens went into the 24th RF, as did Sergeant Fahey. His 1918 diary records that his unlucky comrade - without having had a scratch in his service in the 22nd - was taken prisoner just three weeks after reaching the 24th.

Transport Sergeant Furmston (in the cab, to the right), pals and lorry, with his friend Sergeant Wm Hayward standing at the front. (A 1919 signed photo of Sergeant Hayward says 'Wm A Hayward'; there was a Sergeant Wm J Hayward in the Battalion, so this is probably after the disbandment). (Courtesy EB Furmston)

In early 1918 much digging of defensive lines went on well behind the British front line, but lack of resources meant that even in mid-March 1918 some of the areas were simply lines on a map. It was hard to shift one's mindset from attacking to defending.

2nd Division was in V Corps along with 17th, 63rd and 47th Divisions. V Corps was the right hand corps of Byng's Third Army, with the left-hand unit of Gough's Fifth Army (9th Division of VII Corps) to their right. Areas at the junctions of command units are traditionally weak spots, particularly here, as Fifth Army was a much weaker force.

The area of line held by 2nd Division (and the rest of V Corps) was the Flesquières Salient, ground won at great expense in the Cambrai battle, and sticking out from the British lines like an upside down soup plate. The British divisions in V Corps were all solid, reliable, battle-hardened ones that had worked hard on their defences and were confident of resisting any direct attacks from the Germans.

The Germans, on the other hand, simply drenched the defenders of the salient with gas day after day in mid-March: particularly with mustard gas, which was highly persistent. It attacked any available skin part, so masks themselves were not totally effective. It lay in wait in shell holes or dips in the ground. Wearing a mask for many hours at a time was itself very tiring, and one would be suffering from sore eyes and a loss of voice at the very least. In the middle part of March, 99 Brigade had so many gas casualties (around 800 out of around 2000 effectives) that it had to be taken out of the line on the 19th.

The rest of 2nd Division was taken out of the line just before the German attack began on the morning of the 21st March. The Germans did not attack the point of the salient (where 47th Division had relieved 2nd Division) but made very strong attacks from the north (faced by 51st Division) and east (faced by 9th Division, Fifth Army). Evidently, they were going to attempt to 'pinch out' the salient and surround the defenders.

On the night of the 21st the 47th Division withdrew a mile or so to Highland Ridge. Behind them 2nd Division withdrew also. If one looks at the shape of the front line on a day by day basis, one sees that, despite the withdrawal, the Germans were making so many inroads into the British lines to north and south that the salient now stuck out much more than before. The whole Corps was in grave danger although it had hardly been drawn into the fighting as yet.

Heavy German attacks on the 22nd meant that 2nd Division's brigades were used to support other units: 5 and 6 Brigades were attached to 17th and 19th Divisions respectively, while 99 Brigade, under General Barker, was already attached to 47th Division and receiving a stream of orders and counter orders. It was essential to keep touch between Third and Fifth Armies and the latter were retreating much faster than the former. 99 Brigade's job was to try and plug the gap. It was a hopeless task. On the 23rd March all the battalions in the Brigade ended up fighting desperate rearguard actions, extricating themselves in the nick of time from being surrounded when units on the left or right of them withdrew. The 23rd RF was more exposed than the others and suffered very badly on the 23rd and on the 25th. Somehow a big gap grew between the KRRC on the left and the other two battalions. It was a hugely anxious time for General Barker, convinced he was going to lose all his battalions.

The following comes from the 2nd Division *Narrative* to give some flavour of the period. It refers to the 23rd March:

> So the dogged, undaunted troops fell back from ridge to ridge to the Red Line which is in most places no more than a mark on a map. It afforded no resting place for the exhausted and dwindling platoons, but only a pause for breath before a further retirement to the Bapaume-Peronne Road now almost emptied of its colossal stream of traffic of the previous crowded hours…A grim and exciting spectacle to the observer, the battle field spread out like chess-board on which the pieces moved at random, troops of several Divisions inextricably mixed, with here a salient and there a gap, but all drifting westward with the waves of the enemy close at their heels… Captain Duff of the 1/Kings hurries to and fro, as he has been doing all day, re-organising the stragglers as they arrive and putting them into fire positions with the word that cheers and steadies. And

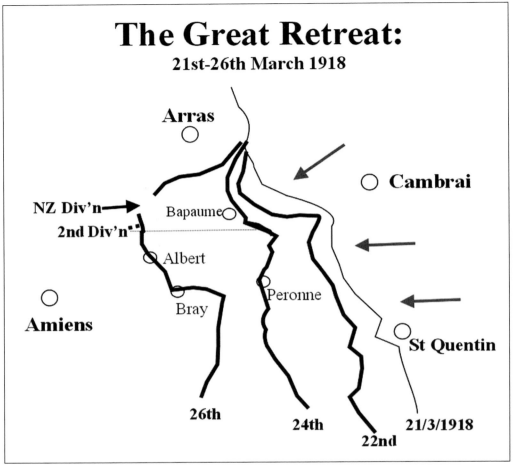

The Great Retreat:
21st-26th March 1918

Arras

Cambrai

NZ Div'n→

Bapaume

2nd Div'n

Albert

Peronne

Amiens

Bray

St Quentin

26th

24th

21/3/1918

22nd

Showing the stages of the great retreat, as 2nd Division, especially 99 Brigade, tried to fill the widening gap between Fifth Army (south of 2nd Division) and Third Army (north), leading to the miraculous appearance of the New Zealand Division in the nick of time on the 26th of March

> *on all sides as far as the eye can see is the battle – broken ground, derelict camps and smashed property, forsaken horse lines, crippled lorries, dead horses – all the flotsam and jetsam of modern warfare.*[1]

On the 24th and 25th March it was the turn of 2nd Division's other two Brigades, 5 (with the 24th RF well to the fore) and 6, to undergo a fighting retreat: pulling away and then stopping and fighting, preparing a defensive line only to find they had to move away in conformity with the retirements of other units, all the time looking for somewhere that one could just make a proper defensive position and make a stand.

On the 26th the crisis came. All three brigades of 2nd Division, very much reduced in numbers, were seeking to make a stand near Auchonvillers in the old British 1916 lines. For once they had managed some sleep the previous night; they had food, plenty of ammunition and a defensible trench line. The enemy in front of them was not harrying them with the same vigour as before; probably it was equally exhausted.

Yet there were no units on the left of 2nd Division, where the enemy was trying to get around behind them, and two battalions could be seen massing for an attack. Surely this time their luck had run out?

New Zealanders and, later, a number of Whippet tanks (their first appearance in action[2]), appeared on their left almost by magic. The New Zealand Division was one of the most professional units on the Allied side. It was well rested and in peak condition, had come down from the Ypres area with instructions to fill a huge gap in the British lines as quickly as possible. As transport facilities were a complete mess, its men were arriving and then being pushed forward piecemeal. They were very surprised to find any 2nd Division troops *in situ*. The New Zealand unit War Diaries talk only of finding war-worn remnants: thus in *The New Zealand Division* 1916-1919 it states:

> Elements of the 2nd Division were located astride the road from Hamel to Authonvillers…they were in no condition now to withstand further pressure … In and about the left of our line were handfuls of very weary troops of all brigades of the 2nd Division, about 80 men in all. These were withdrawn in the evening.[3]

The New Zealand Division filled the gap, pushed back the enemy and relieved 2nd Division, which moved back to Mailly Maillet Wood.

Roland Whipp (now with the 24th RF) remembered this day. It was when he went into action three times in twenty-four hours: first retreating, then checking the enemy, then advancing: after which he never took a backwards step again.

The first incident was an undignified scurry out of some trenches in the morning, as the enemy was pressing hard:

> I was the last man out and they were almost in the trench when the call came from behind to get out…They were so close 20 yards or less than that, and strolling along as if unaware of our existence.

He couldn't make a pioneer 'cigarette drooling out of his mouth, not aware of the war' see the urgency of the situation, and had to leave him behind. Afterwards he felt 'thoroughly cross' about being bundled out of the trench.

So when some New Zealanders appeared later he was quite keen to get one back at the enemy. He saw the opportunity to take out a gun and cover the right flank of the New Zealanders' attack. As a mere Corporal he didn't have the authority to do this, so he asked a nearby Sergeant:

> Sergeant, I was wondering if I should volunteer - I was thinking of just myself alone of offering to go on the right flank of their attack with a Lewis Gun.

The Sergeant replied: 'I wouldn't mind going out with you.' He in turn felt obliged to contact the Sergeant-Major, Rosie Read. He said 'I'll go too,' and went off to get it confirmed with their Captain, who made the offer to the New Zealand Captain. The latter was delighted. The Sergeant-Major decided that they would need a volunteer to carry spare ammunition up to their position. A young chap volunteered and they set off to find a good position:

We got quite close to where they were in action and an MG caught us…They must have seen us…Anyway it killed the volunteer stone dead…and he fell right over the gun into the muddy ground… it wouldn't have fired – a very delicate mechanism, covered in mud.

Whipp wasn't simply going to give up his scheme, so he went back to the front line, and decided to 'play Colonel':

There was a man opposite me. I said, 'This gun's useless, take it and get another one for me.' And he did, somehow.

He went back with the new gun.

Just ahead of me I could see this German officer – a brave man – standing up, revolver in hand, boldly meeting the advance. I let fire one burst with the Lewis Gun. I couldn't see what happened. By that time I couldn't get in another burst cos by that time the New Zealanders were there. We just waited on for a bit to see that it was over…they'd won.

Later on they retired to Mailly Maillet Wood. Next morning there were shouts that the Germans were putting on an attack, but Rosie Read told him that it was us who were attacking, in fact there would be a 'general advance'. Rosie Read, Roland Whipp and his brother Leslie advanced though the wood. An accurate burst of fire from a machine gun brought them quickly to earth, shooting away Roland's ammunition pouches and bits of Leslie's gun, but they got up again and carried on going forward, and never took a backwards step until the end of the war.[4]

Whipp was right; for the exhausted remnants of 2nd Division, the crisis was over for them on the 27th March. It was then back to trench warfare until the summer, when they started moving forward again in the advance to victory.

Looking wider, the front of the Third Army (containing the New Zealanders, 2nd Division etc) solidified on 26 March, although the Fifth Army continued to be driven backwards for another week or so. Once the German attacks had been contained in this offensive, they attacked again at Arras, where they were repulsed, and in the Ypres area, where their attack was menacing for a while, and most seriously of all, in the Chemin des Dames where they gained huge amounts of territory, even threatening Paris. On the Allied side was the conviction that if these attacks could be contained, then the Germans would have lost their gamble, and it would just be a question of time before the Allied side prevailed.

In July the French began regaining some of the territory recently captured by the Germans, and the Americans made a first successful attack as a separate army in September, but the most dramatic success was the British Fourth Army attack on the 8th August with massed tanks, including the new Mark Vs and the faster Whippets, east of Amiens, spearheaded by the Australians and Canadians. Third Army (including 2nd Division) made a very successful attack a fortnight later and thereafter the Allies kept moving forward until the Armistice on November 11. From August onwards, British and Dominion forces captured roughly as many guns and prisoners as all of the French, Belgian and Americans forces put together.

Going back to the Great Retreat, there had been many casualties amid all the hurrying and scurrying. For 2nd Division there were around 2,600 casualties in March, about 1,500 of them 'missing' (some killed, but most were probably taken prisoner).

Ex-22nd RF officers JW Ireland and N Thornhill both went missing on the 23rd (Ireland was taken prisoner), while Second Lieutenant Coppack (attached to the 24th RF) died on the 24th. Second Lieutenant DF Davies (with the 23rd RF) survived the Retreat but died a few weeks later. Second Lieutenants Brownlee, GRS Fisher, Guy, Franklin and Hope were wounded and/or gassed while with the 23rd RF, and Second Lieutenants Fair and Bird with the 24th RF. A number of others were simply not identified by name.

For the men it is impossible to disentangle the casualties for ex-22nd RF soldiers. We can hazard a guess at what they must have been like from the total casualties. For the 23rd RF, there were eleven officers and 240 other ranks gas casualties in mid-March. They then had a fighting strength on 20 March of twenty officers and 350 men, and suffered a further twenty officers and 290 men killed, wounded or missing in the period 21st-31st March. Thus there could only be about sixty unwounded men left – so a former 22nd man in the 23rd RF was very likely to have been taken prisoner, wounded or gassed. For the 24th RF the numbers were much less severe, eleven officers and 127 men from 21 March until the end of the month,[5] so an ex-22nd man would have had a fair chance of avoiding being a casualty.

There was one particular casualty in the March Retreat of especial interest to ex-22nd men. Christopher Stone was close at hand when it happened:

In the confusion caused by attachment to strange Divisions – now to one, now to another – he [General Barker] *had to act very largely on his own initiative, and all his gifts as a tactician were put to the test. He got no sleep, his meals were precarious, and, worst of all, he ran out of cigarettes.*

On the morning of the 24th [actually the 23rd]*, when our headquarters in a hut in Manancourt first came under machine gun fire, he realised that the gap between the two armies was widening, and had sent his third battalion to help the other two in their desperate task of keeping touch on either flank. 'I shall lose all three of them,' he said; 'I don't see how they can extricate themselves.'*[6]

By evening some 300 or so men had arrived, but the KRRC was still out of touch. Next morning General Barker, Staff-Captain Bell, Major Stone and staff moved off early in the morning to Geudecourt. Stone again:

Exhausted troops lay basking in the sun by the roadside, and I was detailed to maintain the steady current of wagons and carts and limbers through the village, while B.B. sat on a mound and wrote his orders for the defensive positions to be taken up by the heterogeneous troops at his disposal. No headquarters could be found for him, but Colin B- [Bell] had a tent put up by the roadside on the west of the village and there was a camp chair for him to sit on near by...Suddenly a 5.9 shell burst about four hundred yards to our left beyond the village. A ranging shot said B.B., and was anxious because

At the furthest west point on Geudecourt, where the road points towards Le Sars, was where BB (and Captain Bell) were killed by a stray ranging shell 24 March 1918. I imagine BB and Bell standing at the extreme left of the picture (or just outside it) and Stone putting BB's last message into an envelope over to the right, near where I am standing (1986 picture).

> it implied that when the enemy attacked he would probably put down a barrage across the west of the village. Just then two generals came up, and persuaded B.B. that it was useless to defend the village if both his flanks were exposed, and he sat down and wrote a message to the officer commanding the troops in front of the village [Colonel Winter, of the 23rd RF] telling him to retire at his discretion when his flanks were in the air, and added that brigade headquarters were moving back a mile. That message was timed 5 30 p.m., and he handed it to me to put into an envelope. While I was doing this another single shell fell just in front of me. When I went forward to the spot I found B.B. and Colin B- [Bell] and the latter's servant lying dead close by the tent. They were hit just as they were starting out for our new headquarters, and the shell had burst at their feet, and they were lying on their faces, almost like men asleep; but they were quite dead. No more shells fell near the spot for some time.

The 99 Brigade war diarist said:

> As Commanding Officer of the 22nd Royal Fusiliers he won the respect and affection of everyone in the Brigade and when he succeeded Brigadier General R.O. Kellett C.B. C.M.G. in command of the Brigade it was with the happiest auguries for the future.[7]

Mayor Davison was of course heartbroken, but hinted at a moving underlying story of loyalty:

> He was certainly a fine soldier and a splendid man in every way…Stone and some men of the old 22nd who were on the spot took the bodies by hand and car to Albert and

242

buried them in the British Cemetery there... As far as he himself is concerned we need not mourn, as it is the death he would have desired – to go without pain or illness, when he was commanding his men in the field of battle.[8]

It was indeed old 22nd men that took his body for burial, led by Sergeant TE McGowan: Sanitary Sergeant, odd-job man, and loyal friend:

It was to this spot on the main road [Destremont Farm] that his body and Colin B-'s had been carried along in the never-ending stream of tangled traffic on the evening of March 25th [24th]. Shoulder-high on stretchers they went, carried by Sergt. McC [McGowan] and his faithful men, through mile after mile of the old Somme battlefield now covered, as far as the eye could see, with moving troops and lines of transport...Divisional headquarters were at Destremont Farm, in a couple of tents, and here Sergt. McC laid down his load and decided to await a lorry. At 8 p.m. three lorries turned up - against the stream of traffic – full of ammunition, which was unloaded by the side of the road. 'Where have you come from?' 'Albert.' 'Ah, ah! Do you know that I've been waiting for you since ten o'clock this morning? Where have you been all the time?' 'What for?' 'Why, for these two generals' bodies, of course. Didn't you get your orders?' 'No; never heard -.' 'Well, don't stand there arguing. Turn your lorries round, and we'll get loaded up quick.'[9]

And of course the lorry driver was persuaded to take them back to Albert.

Next morning they dug two graves, got someone to conduct a service over them,

Albert Communal Cemetery Extension. BB and Captain Bell are both buried here (gravestones close to the wall).

and even acquired and inscribed some slabs of stone from a mason's yard. Christopher Stone commented:

> *Sergt. McC, with his light blinking eyes and unquenchable energy and humour, was a great favourite of B.B.'s, and there is no one that he would sooner have chosen to bury him.*[10]

At the end of Christopher Stone's memoir of Barnett Barker is quite the most eloquent picture of him at battalion HQ circa January 1917:

> *When I recall him to my mind, it is generally to see him in the intimate little circle of the mess, reading a novel in front of the fire, in a brown leather waistcoat with slippers on his feet and a cigarette in a long holder in his mouth: getting up to put his writing-pad in his special corner of the mantle-shelf and to slip his fountain pen into its cardboard box; cutting bread from the loaf and toasting it himself; sitting down to bridge with the doctor and old man G----* [Captain Gregg; lost a leg at Oppy Wood] *and poor S-----* [Captain Simons] *who was missing at Miraumont; listening to his favourite Faust records on the gramophone; writing voluminously to his wife; having his glass of sherry and bitters before dinner, or looking at his watch at 10 p.m. and then at the War Lord* [Major Adams], *whose duty it was to mix the evening drink at precisely that hour; ragging everyone, laughing at everything, making the world every minute of the day a little bit better because he lived in it; the gallantest, cheerfulest, finest fellow that a man could ask to have for a leader and a friend.*

B) Prisoners of War

The Battalion might have been disbanded, but the prisoners remained.

The Germans had little food to spare for prisoners, mainly black bread and thin soup, but Hugh D Hughes didn't even get soup:

> *At the Prison Camp at Graudenz on the Vistula* [a region given over to Poland after the war] *the rations deteriorated and for 6 months (until parcels arrived from England) he faded to nothing on half a turnip a day. Hunger is a desperate condition that one can never forget, especially with 30 degrees of frost as an aperitif.*[11]

Food parcels were a very real necessity for prisoners' survival. After a delay of a month or two for the paperwork to be processed, prisoners would begin to get their three-times-a-fortnight food parcels regularly, although receipt could be complicated by the German tendency to shuffle men around between camps.

There was of course 'leakage' between initial despatch and receipt by the individual addressee, and it probably depended on the regime in each camp whether you were allowed to receive anything like a reasonable proportion of your quota of parcels. If one could look forward to say a parcel a week of these, then one would live quite well, even if one was sharing with a chum.

For longer term prisoners, their clothing and boots would start to disintegrate. The arrival of clothing parcels seemed to be less certain. In December 1917 Sergeant Maloney wrote that he had regular food parcels but not the clothing he had asked for. By next March his co-prisoner Corporal Squibb was writing:

Sergt. Maloney has not yet received any clothing, and if the rain continues he will not have any boots to put on.[12]

Several ex-22nd RF men were taken prisoner with the 23rd RF on or around the 23rd March, mostly going to different camps: Lance-Corporal A H Hall and Private T Fitzgibbon to Gustrow, Corporal H Margetson to Netochke, and Joe Goddard (housed near a coal mine near Essen), plus Corporal SH Wright and Cyril Grigg (camps not given). Sergeant WJ Fahey, who went to Minden, was the only one identified as coming via the 24th RF.[13]

Sergeant Fahey was particularly unlucky:

Well, Sir I was with the Battalion when it was formed in 1914 and went through every engagement with it, without a day's illness, and when returning from my second leave I was informed that I had to join the 24th RF, and [in] *my first tour in the trenches with them I was captured.[14]*

The news of General Barker's death had reached Brown, Maloney and Squibb in Bohmte (Hameln 17, Hannover):

We are very sorry to hear such sad news about Mr Barker, would you kindly tender our deepest sympathy to Mrs Barker in her sad bereavement.

There are only a few of the old Roffey Boys left now who remember him [then]*, but everyone who has served under him, can't help admiring him as a Soldier and as a Gentleman. We had a good time in England with him and an equally good one in France, & he was more than pleased when he saw his Lads do that which was prophesised by him in the early days.[15]*

Sergeant Micky Brown had originally been having quite a pleasant time at the British NCO camp at Minden. All this changed when they were sent to Bohmte camp. The Commandant there wanted them to work on tilling the waste ground around the camp. As NCOs they refused. This was a high risk strategy:

'Our punishment was to stand all day long on the camp parade ground. All our parcels and mail were to be stopped.'

The stand-off went on for eleven weeks. Eventually the cunning Commandant tapped into the British sporting instinct:

He allowed us to drain some waste land just outside the camp and lay out a football pitch. This took several months to do but when finished we were allowed to play there twice a week. On these afternoons we were on our honour not to escape. Nearly the whole camp used to turn out to watch the matches not once did we give the Germans any trouble.

In mid-1918 the prisoners could see the shift in the fortunes of war reflected in their captors:

In the early summer of 1918 the change in the German personnel became quite noticeable. Nearly every fit German left the camp. They were replaced by old men and young boys or wounded who were unfit for active service.

Their uniforms were ragged and patched and they looked anything like soldiers... Then late in July two severe frosts ruined their crop, and we could see they were having a rough time. Later rumours began to get about the camp that the Germans were cracking and that they had asked for an armistice. At 10 p.m. on November 11 we got the news that the armistice was signed. The war was over. How we cheered and sang!

One of the conditions of the armistice was an immediate release of allied prisoners, but as no one wanted long lines of prisoners walking all the way back to Holland or France, the prisoners were to stay put until transport could be found for them. The problem was that food parcels stopped with the armistice, and the Germans had no spare transport.

Some men could wait no longer, and Sergeant Maloney, accompanied by a Middlesex Sergeant, made a break for it. He wrote from Holland on the 10th December:

I have the pleasure to inform you that I crossed the frontier about midnight on the 3rd inst after escaping from Bohmte whilst attending the burial of two Belgians.

He reported that 'although wet through, footsore and weary,' they 'had cheered themselves hoarse when challenged by a Dutch patrol.'[16]

The rest of the Bohmte camp followed on three weeks later, and in an extraordinary feat, walked the 130 miles in about four days. The Dutch offered them every kindness and put them aboard a boat that began its voyage home about midnight on Xmas Eve.

---

1 Presumably this is the same Captain Duff who had served in the 22nd; *The 2nd Division on Welsh Ridge, WO 95/1299*, p18: written by Christopher Stone as one of his first jobs at 2nd Division HQ

2 *OH, 1918, The German March Offensive and its Preliminaries*, 1935 (reprinted by IWM/The Battery Press), p526

3 *The New Zealand Division 1916-1919*, Col H Stewart, 1920, p344 and 346; see also 2nd NZ Brigade Diary, *WO 95/3696*

4 Interview with Roland Whipp, 18/11/1983; he hinted that the action went on rather longer, but felt too responsible for the boy's death to claim any credit for himself

5 *WO 95/1349 and 1311. The 23rd (Service) Battalion Royal Fusiliers*, op cit, p60 says that they marched into Mailly Maillet Wood with just 4 officers and 70 men

6 *B.B.*, op cit, pp 20-23

7 99 Brigade war diary: *WO 95/1370*. Obituaries, eg *The Times* 4/4 and 5/4/1918; the *Abergavenny Chronicle* courtesy 5/4/1918, the *West Sussex County Times*, 6/4/1918.

8 Davison to BF Woods, 5/4/1918, *Broughshane*, 8538

9 *B.B.*, op cit, pp 10-11 (24th not 25th)

10 *Ibid*, pp 11-12 In fact the graves were blown up when the Germans briefly captured Albert. Now they say 'known to be buried in this area'

11 *Wheel and Woe, Mufti*, Xmas 1930, 11, No 4, p4

12 *Broughshane*, 8655, 8656, 8651, 8650, 8647, 8653, 8651, 8647, 8648, 8645, 8643, 8692. More clothing was sent out

13 Ibid, 8811, 8805, 8712, 8715, 8710, 8700-02, Goddard wrote his memoir in *Mufti*, eg Summer 1932, 13, No 2, p8

14 Ibid, 8703, 8701. Private EA Stevens joined B Company of the 24th RF and we have his 'Kensington' 1918 diary; on the 28th February: 'Bombing raid on D Co. Sgt. Fahey M.M. missing (taken prisoner) 19 injured.'

15 *Broughshane*, 8643

16 Maloney to Davison, 10/12/1918

Chapter Thirteen

Après La Guerre

INFORMAL TALKS about arranging a reunion began as early as the Spring of 1919. Soon Sir William Davison MP[1] was brought in, and an Old Comrades Association (hereafter OCA) was inaugurated in June, with the first reunion taking place on the occasion of the Borough of Kensington's Peace Celebrations on 26 July 1919. At roughly the same time as they were being asked about their interest in reunions, ex-members were being canvassed about whether they wanted to march in the Battalion contingent at the *Triumphal March of London Troops* on 5 July. The efforts on both fronts reinforced each other, as on the *Triumphal March* the Battalion was believed to have produced the largest New Army contingent, while on the 26th: 'About 500 turned up and thoroughly enjoyed a day of glorious sunshine and crowded rejoicings.'[2]

Considerable unemployment and hardship was emerging, with the result that welfare became a central concern of the OCA, as can be seen from its aims:

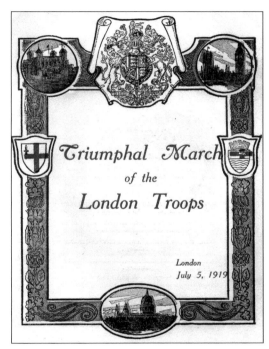

Triumphal March
of the
London Troops

London
July 5, 1919

Although the 22nd suffered from a very low level of reinforcement, and was disbanded in early 1918, it had one of the largest representations of any Kitchener battalion at this event.

1. *To enable all members to meet their comrades regularly in some central place which will be found shortly*
2. *To assist any member out of employment*
   The Association has already been the means of helping many members so placed. We have not many openings on our books, however, so I ask all members who can give or obtain employment of any kind to other members to write to me stating the nature of such employment. I have had several letters from members asking if I can help them, but not stating what kind of work they can undertake. This is most important, so will every member who writes to me for help getting employment please give

247

me all particulars.

3. *To investigate any complaints about pensions.*

Members of the Army clerical staff are on the Committee and will institute enquiries in all cases which may be put to them.

4. *To hang together and help each other*

Come to the meetings and see your pals. Pay what you can afford, remembering that anything you give will help one of the old battalion; may possibly set him on his feet again. If there is anything you are in difficulty about, anything you want to know or anybody you want to get in touch with, write to me, and the Old Comrades' Association will be able to give you the answer you want.[3]

One very important decision was to start up an OCA magazine. This was called *Mufti*. Receipt of a magazine is a tangible benefit, and *Mufti* would play an increasingly central role over the years in keeping members in touch with each other, especially those living far from London. It would allow members to share wartime reminiscences, it was where forthcoming events could be advertised and then reported on, and in its pages the OCA could both chronicle what it was doing and reinforce the spirit of comradeship.

Mufti's first edition, 12 pages long, was brought out by JM Greenslade and Fred Pignon in November 1919. Sir William contributed an introduction and the *Mufti* editors reminded everyone of wealth and conscience that the magazine was being produced on a shoestring. Christopher Stone gave the justification:

And herein lies the test and proof – that although the Battalion was disbanded in February, 1918, and the remnants of it scattered here and there all over the battlefields of the world, yet this magazine is a response to an insistent demand that we should keep in touch with each other and should pick up again in peace time the threads that bound us together in the days of warfare. It is the spirit of comradeship and loving-kindness, the memory of great adventures, of gallant leaders and friends, and the consciousness that we not only cannot but do not even wish to blot out the last five years from our recollection – it is these impulses which have drawn us together round the

The cover of the first edition of *Mufti*, the magazine of the OCA.

Fred Keeble was one of the first of the old 22nd men to get hitched. He married his Edie, 22nd September 1919, and they would remain happily together until his death in 1966. (Keeble papers)

altar-fire of our brief history, to fan the flames in reverence for the departed, and into cheerful warmth for the living.[4]

Mufti reported on of the July reunion and on 13 Platoon's annual dinner. 13 Platoon had managed to meet every September throughout the war, although the 1918 one was just a chance meeting of four colleagues. Their first peacetime dinner, in Holborn on the 27th September 1919, had 24 attending.[5] *Mufti* also had a page of snippets of gossip about members, while three whole pages were taken up listing the names of members, so that Bill could see if his old mate Bert had signed up or not, and perhaps get in touch with him through the pages of *Mufti*.

In the second edition was a report on another event destined to become an annual occasion: the Memorial Service at Horsham. This was conducted by Padre St John in a Horsham Parish Church 'filled to overflowing', followed by a procession from the church to the Cenotaph near the Carfax where Major Christopher Stone laid the wreath 'before a vast and sympathetic crowd'.

At the Annual General Meeting in 1920, WH Metcalf, the Hon Secretary, described a year of endeavouring to trying to find work for those without it (successful in around 80% of cases), and of giving grants of money in special cases. Sir William brought good news: the profits of the Peace Celebrations the previous year had been some £400, and the 22nd RF's share was to be £190.[6]

The OCA held a memorial service at Padre St John's parish church (in Kennington) in January 1921 – something else that became an annual event.

There was still the problem of trying to balance the books, so that *Mufti* did not drain the coffers of monies wanted for welfare work. Friends did their best to help out. Thus Mrs Barker sent a very

---

"13"

PLATOON
22nd Service Batt. Royal Fusiliers
(KENSINGTON)

VICTORY DINNER

5th ANNIVERSARY
Saturday, September 27th, 1919

ENGLAND	FRANCE	ENGLAND
1914	1915-16-17-18	1919
WHITE CITY	VIMY RIDGE	HOLBORN
HORSHAM	DELVILLE WOOD	RESTAURANT
CLIPSTONE	BEAUMONT HAMEL	
TIDWORTH	MIRAUMONT	
	OPPY WOOD	
	BOURLON WOOD	
	CAMBRAI	
	METZ	

"CARRY ON THIRTEEN"

H. J. THOMPSON
President

S. J. UPTON   S. A. GORDON
Vice-President   Hon. Secretary

"FOR AULD LANG SYNE"
All the Profits from this Booklet and any Thirteen "Do" to be handed over to the O.C.A.

First of a long series of post-war 13 Platoon reunions that would go on until 1971.

welcome £31 that she and Mrs Powlett had raised from a Cake Fair and *Thé Dansant*, 13 Platoon ran Whist Drives and Sir William more than once made considerable personal donations.[7] A number of schemes were tried, including advertising, but from 1922 onwards *Mufti* became a quarterly publication – probably the right frequency in terms of filling the pages with good 'copy'.

More stories and vignettes appeared, stimulated by incidents in *Mufti*, or people met at reunions – very important for those who had returned abroad, or had emigrated, such as Fred Palmer VC, EC Rossell (the Battalion's first MC) and Marjorie Edwardes (the former cub reporter of the *West Sussex Gazette* and now Mrs Marjorie Hay) who had gone off to the Malay States.

The OCA began a new service to members in 1922: treats for the children of 22nd men. The first one was on January 14th 1922, and again in July as a Children's Summer Fete with Punch and Judy show, games, tea and so on. Some 120 children and 38 adults attended the event, which ended with presents:

> *Near closing time a rush was made for the presents and with a struggle each child managed to get one.[8]*

In 1921 and 1922 the *History of the Second Division* and *The Royal Fusiliers in the Great War* were published. Both had considerable input from the 22nd Battalion. Three of the nine stories that featured in the Appendix of *The Royal Fusiliers in the Great War* were about 22nd Battalion actions, and had been taken from *Mufti*.

In early 1923 it was the turn of the 22nd Battalion. *The History of the 22nd (Service) Battalion (Kensington) Royal Fusiliers* was privately published by Harry Rosewarne for the OCA. Sir William Davison wrote the Foreword, JM Greenslade wrote the first chapter from their beginning until they went to France, while Colonel Adams contributed a brief Epilogue, but Stone wrote everything in-between. He achieved the extraordinary feat of cramming an enormous amount of detail into 42 pages, while maintaining a lightness of touch and an easy readability.

The early twenties produced the first private battlefield visits. JB Morton gained a great thrill in 1924 when he identified Braddel's Point, a former strong point on the La Bassée Road, where he would have been based in early 1916. He walked on a little, his senses heightened:

> *As I stood by an estaminet window, looking out across the fields, I heard the laughter of the people in the room behind me. Some of them were singing. I could see figures moving down a lane in the windy dust. And suddenly they were unreal. The laughter and songs were unreal. All these living people were unreal. For a moment my mind was a blank, and then a terrible reality darkened it. I strained my eyes, gazing across the fields, and I saw men in mud-stained clothes; I saw their young faces: I heard the thuds of their feet.*
>
> *And the ridiculous music-hall song they sung was like a scourging wind across the soul.[9]*

From the mid-twenties obituaries became an increasing part of *Mufti*. One of the earliest was Major 'Doc' Miller, the lion-hearted medical officer in 1916, who succumbed in 1925 to the effects of buried pieces of metal and glass under the skin.

Looking down the Carfax to Horsham Parish Church after an OCA annual service. Picture is undated but probably late 1920s from the clothes and sheer numbers attending.
(courtesy EB Furmston)

Major Gregg, hero of Vimy Ridge, who lost a leg at Oppy Wood, died in May 1929. Christopher Stone found ennobling words:

> *That was the man we all loved. Sturdy of build, with thin light reddish hair and dropping moustache, a ruddy countenance and the bluest of light blue eyes, he was not only one of the most genial and lovable men, with all Ireland in his voice and gurgling laugh; he was also – and even more notably – one of the straightest men I have ever met. He had the strength of his convictions, he loved an argument and a fight, he was the champion as well as the leader of his men, and he had all the quiet, unassertive, steel-like courage of the genuine hero.*[10]

It was the late twenties before AJL Tottenham discovered the OCA for the first time. He had stayed behind in France to work for the Imperial War Graves Commission. 'Tot' was soon regaling readers of *Mufti* with a stream of articles about his time with the Battalion, and this encouraged others to write down their stories.[11] Straightaway he became the man who encouraged the gunners to come to reunions (there were markers for each of the Companies now: ex-Sergeant[-Major] E Phillips for A, ex-Sergeant CE Fidler DCM for B, the esteemed Smith Brothers for C and WH Metcalfe for D, while Fred Keeble rounded up the Signallers). In fact the annual dinners had become quite noisy affair by the mid-1920s. The 1924 one was so wild that *Mufti* wrote an apology in its pages, fearing that Sir William Davison:

> *…must have been a trifle dazed by the vigour of the rejoicing at the festive board, at this*

year's annual dinner, which in number and boisterousness, broke all records.[12]

In November 1927, 125 turned up to the Annual Reunion, rising to 150 in the 1929 one at *Molinari's* in Frith Street. The guest list included General Kellett, Colonel Adams (now Reverend Phythian-Adams in his new career), and Sir William Davison. The problem was that only eighty-five tickets for dinner had been sold and 145 wanted to eat. There were too many people for the dining room booked and so C Company were placed upstairs in a room on their own. That was no great hardship to them – 'Judging from the hilarious sounds that reached us, they were quite happy' and they had the first of a regular series of reunions on their own some four months later.[13]

Downstairs General Kellett was being introduced:

None of us had seen General Kellett since he handed over 99 Brigade to the late Colonel Barnett-Barker. Here he was among us again, his kindly, well-remembered face wreathed in smiles, his eyes twinkling behind his glasses.

"They became suffused – they betrayed his emotion when we rose to give him musical honours with a fervour that there was no mistaking.[14]

On 6 April 1930 the newly acquired original wooden cross from Roclincourt (carrying the names of 22nd men who fell in the Oppy Wood battles) was dedicated in a moving ceremony at Padre St John's new church (St Andrew's in Stockwell) in front of at least 120 men, friends and family from the 22nd Battalion, plus a full congregation of

The 1930 Pilgrimage Tour Party. Brigadier-General Kellett is at the rear right with white hair, while Fred Keeble is just behind and to the right of the central figure at the front.
(Keeble papers)

Brigadier-General Kellett placing a wreath on BB's grave in the 1930 OCA Pilgrimage visit to France. (Keeble papers)

parishioners.[15]

On 18 April the first OCA Battlefields Pilgrimage set out for France, with twenty-two in the party, and headed by General Kellett. They stayed in Albert, which had been extensively rebuilt – the restored cathedral even had a Madonna on it. They were able to lay a wreath at the grave of General Barker in Albert British Cemetery, which commemorated all the fallen of the 22nd Battalion and Captain Kellett, the General's son, killed at Coigneux in 1916.

On 12 November 1931 General Kellett – Major-General RO Kellett CB CMG – was killed from a fall from his horse while out hunting. Colonel Adams wrote:

> *The compelling voice, the quizzical glance and smile, the force and fire of an indistinguishable ardour, those you could always count upon to inspire your courage and revive your flagging enthusiasm. Only men who fell badly short of the soldier's standard knew the sterner side of him, the whips of scorn and anger which could lash without mercy.*
>
> *A man so simple of heart, so single of mind, so utterly determined to do his damnedest, had no time to waste on the slacker, the scrimshanker, and the coward. He just went berserk and the culprit wilted away.*
>
> *So he is gone as he would have wished to go, with the Irish wind in his face and a good horse under him. Loyal and well-tried comrade, brave leader, great and gallant gentlemen, we bid you with aching hearts – Hail and Farewell!*[16]

A successful small voluntary organisation needs a core of people who believe in their cause and are happy to put themselves out for it – year after year. Often there are too few people willing to do the big jobs like Chairman, Secretary and Treasurer, and when

the first office-holders get worn down by the effort required, the organisation begins to falter. The 22nd Battalion OCA was very fortunate this way. If one looks at the officials listed in 1921 and 1931, the OCA still had many people still doing the same jobs, so it's not surprising that the OCA reached peak popularity in the nineteen thirties. In 1933 a record 170 members attended the Annual Dinner, but it reached a peak of 250 in 1935 at the *Empire Restaurant*. 13 Platoon had a record twenty-five at their 1935 dinner, while over 250 children and parents attended the Children's Party in January 1936.[17]

The day after the 1935 reunion was the Service of Remembrance at Padre St John's latest church, St Matthew's in Westminster. For many of the men attending it would have been their first chance of hearing their former Colonel, now Canon Phythian-Adams of Carlisle, actually preaching. He had been appalled by the way fighting in the Great War had been 'rubbished':

> We are a little tired, we who fought in the Great War, we who were told loudly and constantly that we were heroes – although we had sufficient sense of humour to know that that was not true – of being told now that we were doing the Devil's work out there and that we were the instruments of the powers of evil in Europe.
>
> That is a charge which we ought not to pass by in silence, for it dishonours not only the living, but the dead.[18]

Nearly 100 members, plus another 300 parishioners, attended the annual Remembrance Service in Horsham in July 1935. After the laying of the wreath there was a slightly unusual feature:

> After the solemnity of the service was over, with a suddenness that was almost an outrage, there was thrust upon one's notice – the penalty of fame. Major Christopher Stone, who had read the Lesson in the church, was bombarded even to the point of evoking the writer's sympathy, by photographers and autograph hunters.[19]

Stone had of course become a very familiar voice since his radio programmes began in 1927.

Reg Abbott couldn't really believe his eyes when he looked at the signature on one of his 1937 Children's New Year Treat acceptance forms: it said 'Uncle General Pereira' with the comment 'I propose to look in'. The former commander of 2nd Division was as good as his word. It would not be his only visit to an OCA children's party (he was back in 1938), and he also came to the 1937 annual dinner.

The numbers of guests at the dinners multiplied: besides the current Mayors of Kensington, Paddington, Fulham and Hammersmith, all the local MPs, people from the Horsham and South Kensington British Legions and the Royal Fusiliers

Association, there were representatives from other OCAs, such as the 17th, 23rd and 24th RF, the 1st Royal Berks and the KRRCs, plus their old friends the 13th Kensingtons.

By the summer of 1939, twenty-five years since the Battalion was formed, *Mufti* was anticipating breaking all records at the annual dinner. Unfortunately World War Two intervened and it would be several years before the OCA had a mass gathering. 13 Platoon did manage to squeeze in their annual dinner in October at George Evans' *Cock Tavern* in Great Portland Street, but the main topic of conversation was what their sons were doing in the war effort.[20]

Many of the OCA members, let alone their sons, were desperate to get back into uniform. There was a slight problem. A chap who had been one of the younger soldiers – say twenty years old in 1914 – would be forty-five in 1939, while an older soldier – say thirty-five in 1914 – would now be sixty. Nevertheless, one gets the impression of the 22nd men straining their backs getting up into the loft to look out their old uniforms. Most of them realised that their ages militated against front line service, but their past experience did count for something. For many this

Another war, for another generation, but many ex-22nd men wanted to do their bit

became the Home Guard, formerly the Local Defence Volunteers, whose London commander was none other than General Pereira.

OCA business changed with the onset of war. There would be no Children's Parties now, and help to the disadvantaged would be money rather than parcels because of rationing. *Mufti* was reduced to two issues a year because of paper shortages. In 1940 13 Platoon had what might be called a 'virtual' reunion: they were each asked to sing the platoon grace (*Tee Latsi Bah*) at 7:30 pm on 11 November, wherever they might be.

In August 1941 the OCA arranged a reunion of sorts at George Evans' *Cock Tavern* (about forty turned up). Cheese and sausage were served and he had kept back some

JM (Jack) Greenslade, well-known newspaperman and editor of *Mufti* from 1919 until his death in 1944.
(*Mufti*)

beer for the occasion. Similar 'austerity' reunions were also held in 1942, 1943 and 1944. The *Cock Tavern* also became the place where the monthly committee meetings were held, so it had quietly become the spiritual home of the OCA.

Although there were few deaths of OCA men on active service (Micky Brown being an exception), natural wastage continued to operate. Probably the biggest blow to the OCA was the death of its long-term *Mufti* editor, Jack Greenslade, in September 1944. Fred Pignon took back the editorial reins that he had first shared with Greenslade in the 1919 days when the two of them were known as 'Pork and Greens'.

It was not possible to hold a reunion in 1945, but there was better news in 1946. BF Woods used his considerable charm on the management of the *Tavistock Restaurant*, who agreed to provide for up to 150 people. Many more tickets could have been sold.

The representative of the 13th Kensingtons OCA, Mr GS White, put into words what many other guests must surely have felt:

It is a source of wonder to me that you are still able to meet in a gathering of this kind. You have no home, as we have, you have no new blood, as we have, and yet year after year, you renew the spirit of the battalion in which you were proud to serve, with

HOW RIGHT WE WERE TO WAIT FOR THE O.C.A. DINNER — !

Because of shortages no Battalion-sized reunion was possible until 1946, when the sequence would go until 1977. The caricature is of course that of Christopher Stone and the cartoonist is another 22nd man, Leslie Grimes.

Ex-Sergeant B Furmston's menu card for the 1951 Battalion OCA reunion dinner. Apart from Tommy Atkins (A), the signatures are well-known names from B Company.
(courtesy EB Furmston)

Baron Broughshane was buried in Kensington Cemetery, Gunnersbury. (He married Louisa after divorcing Beatrice in 1929).

an annual reunion.
13 Platoon also met in 1946, with nineteen attending. It did not take long for the same special atmosphere to be recreated.[21]

Padre St John went to Alderney in the Channel Islands, but the Oppy Cross was brought back to Kensington, and it now resides in the Lady Chapel of St Mary Abbott's Church.

In the fifties, the lists of those having died grew noticeably: 1953 brought with it a number of blows. Baron Broughshane (Sir William Davison) died aged eighty, followed a day later by Padre St John, with (Captain) WE Murray and Major Powlett not long afterwards. There was neither the space in the magazine, nor obituary writers who knew them well to accord them the same honour as those who had died earlier.

Marjorie Hay and her husband returned from life abroad, and Marjorie began to make a number of contributions to *Mufti*. 13 Platoon became famous in 1958, when the BBC filmed their 44th reunion.[22]

Fred Pignon had a very difficult job to make *Mufti* interesting in the 1950s – those meaty series of memoirs that had graced issues in the 1930s were no more. He died in February 1960, just two years after retiring from his job of golf correspondent of the

13 Platoon's 1953 reunion. At bottom left Syd Rogers, then going along the back row: WH Metcalfe, JJ Munro, SA Gordon, F Hylands, F Bull, SJ Upton (the famous Claude); standing C Farrar, W Alley, T Heck; front row from right LM Friend, T Hughes, HD Hughes, WW Clark (Baby), WJ Stone and SB Robertson, with P.E Green at the very front. (courtesy WW Clark)

Within the menu image:

"*Answer your names*"

Claud

1914 1953

"13"
PLATOON
22ND (SERVICE) BATTALION
ROYAL FUSILIERS

39th Anniversary
DINNER
at
THE MUSEUM TAVERN
on
Saturday, 17th October 1953

Carry on Thirteen!

"*They Can't Get Us Down*"

Daily Mail, which he had held since he had managed the British Ryder Cup team in 1931.

The first *Mufti* of 1960 – entitled 'Memories 1914-18' – differed radically from its predecessors. Whereas Fred Pignon had eschewed using his own reminiscences (with one glorious exception about his first experience in the trenches[23]), the new editor, Claude Upton, filled the magazine with his. He justified it thus:

Attending my first committee meeting of the O.C.A. after an absence of several years I felt almost ashamed, for here were five or six men, all of advancing years – one was blind as a result of the First World War, another was slowly recovering from a severe stroke which had left him void of speech and unable to read. But here they were, on a very wet night, in a half-darkened room, met together with one object – 'To see how they could best help their less fortunate comrades of the 1914-18 War.' For while they have done so much in the past, I have done so little...

How better can we keep the spirit alive than by reviving memories of the past? In this issue I hope to call to mind the days of 1914-18.

The issue took the reader right through from the White City through

Fred Pignon, editor of *Mufti* in its early 1919 days and again in 1944-60. *(Mufti)*

Horsham, Clipstone and Tidworth to first days in France. Each section had a few paragraphs of Claude's recollections, but each paragraph was headed with the words 'Do you remember'. As a result, in the next (Christmas 1960) issue were nearly three pages worth of memories from ex-Sergeant JR Walker; a vivid word-picture of life on exercise in Salisbury Plain in 1915 from FJ Harriss and a short humorous vignette from HD Hughes. By the Summer 1962 edition – probably the most historically interesting *Mufti* – Claude had enough material to run a potted history from contributed memoirs (twelve different people were credited), covering stories and vignettes from arriving in France to Cambrai in November 1917.[24]

The OCA had found a splendid Padre in the Reverend Canon Peter Gillingham, who seemed to catch just the right note with his sermons, and also joined the men at the reunion dinners.

The Colonel of the Royal Fusiliers, Major-General 'Cosmo' Nevill, was also often seen at the reunions (as was the Regimental Secretary, Colonel CAL Shipley). He was also keen to attend a 13 Platoon reunion, but that was invitation only, with rank counting for nothing. He got his wish in 1964:

Canon Gillingham was an excellent and sympathetic padre for the OCA for their Horsham services from 1960 until the very end. (courtesy Mrs Keeble)

> *The General in his reply* [to the toast by Syd Rogers] *said it was the very highest honour to be asked to attend the 50th Anniversary of the 13 Platoon's Dinner, although he felt that he was a self-invited guest, for he had expressed a wish to attend and had been told only last year by the Chairman* [presumably OCA Chairman Robert Wright], *that he could not come until he was invited. However, he was delighted when he received an official invitation for he regarded it as a much greater privilege than to attend one of the sumptuous City Dinners. He was sure it must be an occasion unique in the history of the Royal Fusiliers and indeed of the Army. He wished to convey the greetings and congratulations of Lieutenant-General Sir Kenneth Darling, the Colonel of the Royal Fusiliers, and also on behalf of the whole Regiment. It was indeed an inspiration and made him proud to be a Fusilier. He thanked the 'Boys' of '13' Platoon for a truly wonderful evening, which he would never forget.*[25]

The June 1965 *Mufti* was another excellent issue, with several pages of Claude Upton's wartime memories. The next two editions had a number of contributions in response, but by Christmas 1966 Claude was asking for 'copy' in his editorial. He tried again in Summer 1968, but there were few answering contributions this time. Simply put, numbers were coming down sharply. From 349 old comrades listed in *Mufti* in 1951, there was a steady decline of about 4% to 5% per year through 203 in 1962, to 152 in 1967, but by the next list of members in 1975 there would only be fifty-two left alive. Some of those who died in the mid-sixties were: General Barker's widow, who had been very generous to the OCA with her fund-raising; WH Metcalfe, the OCA's first Secretary/Treasurer back in 1919, and Christopher Stone.

Stone was the man who most ensured though his *History* that the men of 22nd Battalion would continue to be proud of their achievements and, through his efforts and vision, that there would be an OCA. Through his humanity, he made others human; through his acuity of vision and the power of his prose he ennobled others.

Fred Keeble had died in 1966 and in 1967 Colonel Adams' long and full life had come to an end. He had been the only officer to serve from first moments in the White City through to the disbandment, which had been a shattering blow for him.

There were getting to be as many senior officers at 13 Platoon's reunions as members: in 1970 both Major-General Ransome (as the 'one and only' official guest) and Major-General Nevill (as the 'one and only' self-invited guest) attended, plus Colonel Poulton of the Royal Fusiliers Association, while there were at least six former members of the platoon: Claude Upton, Syd Rogers, Baby Clark, Punch Robeson, WW Carr and Charles Tourney.[26] It was down to four in 1971 (the other seven were either too ill to come, or too frail to travel). Understandably, this was the last one.

Even in the 1970s there were heart-warming letters from comrades receiving help from the OCA:

> *Thank you kindly for nice letter and money. My Doctor found it on the mat when he came to see me, and said 'I hope it is a fortune for you'. When I opened it I said 'By Golly Sir it is' and he said 'They must be a lot of lovely lads after all these years'. I said 'Yes Sir, I wish I knew some better words to thank them'. The lady next door will post this for me.[27]*

Unfortunately the rest of the news was of illnesses and resignations. Secretary GL Pargeter DFC was a 1972 casualty, with Roland Whipp taking over his post. Shortly afterwards Reg Abbott, one of the originals, could continue no longer. Before he was taken to hospital, he persuaded broad-shouldered Roland Whipp to take on this post as well. Claude Upton was both Chairman and Editor of *Mufti*. For the last few years he had been helped to produce *Mufti* by his daughter Joan,[28] but he was now too ill. George Challis agreed to take over *Mufti* and the Chairmanship. The Registrar, PH Spowage had also died by 1974, but his wife agreed to carry on doing the work.

The 1974 reunion was the 60th anniversary of the founding of the battalion and the 53rd actual reunion; it had also been sponsored by Charles Wheeler. For the first time it was a Luncheon not a Dinner, and there were ladies present: many of the attendees needed a helper, and Mrs Spowage now was a Committee Member.[29]

The question was now of ending things in a dignified manner.[30] It was agreed that

The pilgrimage to Horsham in July 1973. Standing second left (beside her grand-daughter) is Mrs Edie Keeble (widow of Fred), with her daughter Gwen Stokes besides her. Next are Mrs and Mr Jack Holliday. Next but one is Syd Rogers and next but one to him are Percy and Doris Spowage, while the modest Roland Whipp is trying to escape from the picture. It also looks very like George Challis at the back (second left).
(courtesy WW Clark: picture from *West Sussex County Times*)

the Christmas 1977 *Mufti* would be the last one and the OCA would then close down at the end of 1977. The Royal Fusiliers Association agreed to give consideration to all former 22nd OCA members seeking assistance, while all remaining credit balances at the dissolution of the OCA were to be given to The Royal Fusiliers Aid Society.

The final OCA reunion was the AGM and Luncheon at the Tower of London on the 29 September 1977. For the AGM it was simply a question of going through the motions of the final acts. It was soon time for the Luncheon. Some forty-eight sat down to eat, including ten veterans of the 22nd. The final speeches were Roland Whipp proposing 'The Chairman' and George Challis replying. After the applause for George Challis had died down, the emotion of the event produced something unrehearsed: Marjorie Hay

...stood up suddenly and lustily sang our Marching Song 'We are the Kensington

Battalion of the Royal Fusiliers.'[31]

All the others joined in:

So, with many thanks to the Songsters, our successful and very happy 56th Re-union came to a close.[32]

Almost as if they had been freed at last, a number of the stalwarts died within a month or so of the final reunion.[33] George Challis and Roland Whipp brought out the last *Mufti* in early January 1978.

The final act was an exhibition of 22nd Battalion material, shown at Kensington Town Hall and Kensington Public Library, in the early spring of 1978.

The exhibition at Kensington Library in 1978. George Challis is on the left, with the Mayor next and Roland Whipp in front of the Mayoress. Sid Rogers is next, with Colonel Chard, secretary of the Royal Fusiliers Association, at the extreme right. (courtesy WW Clark)

Epilogue

When we first started researching the 22nd Battalion in 1983, there were about ten old comrades left alive and we met everyone who was willing and able. We became great friends with Roland Whipp, whom we met at the *Halfway House* at Rickmansworth. Roland, then ninety-three, used to walk down the big hill to the pub, and afterwards we would drive him up the hill to his house. He still went to the annual Royal Fusilier luncheon in September for all WWI service battalions of the Regiment. The year before (1982) the average age had been eighty-eight. One of the very few who went there without needing an escort, he was treated with great honour:

> *The General of the whole lot; he insisted on me coming and sitting with him. We just chatted. I didn't feel any different from anybody else. I've been a civilian now since 1918 – I had nothing to do with the Army except for 3½ years.[34]*

We were charmed by Mrs Keeble in Horsham and by Mrs Palmer in Lymington. We had fruitful correspondences with the sons of General Barker and Colonel Adams, and the relatives of Major Powlett. Many others passed us on vignettes and copies of *Mufti*. The Rev Peter Gillingham, himself a veteran of the Second World War, took the annual Horsham Remembrance service for the OCA every year from 1960 till the last one in 1977. Right from the start he clicked with members. He shared this with us in 1984:

> *Names of OCA now escape me. I only remember that remarkable sequence of services, and the spirit which kept them going for so long. It was a spirit which belonged to the 1914-18 war, more than the Second World War – for although this also had its reunions, these have never had the same spiritual ethos of the First. It was a compound of a close-knit, simpler society, moulded by common religious bond. 'Abide with me' sung at the Cup Final, was a simple expression of it. The present generation sing it as part of a tradition – but they could never have invented it!*
>
> *But also it sprang from the sheer horror of the casualties and life in the trenches. One may question to-day the theology of the hymn 'O Valiant Hearts.' But hearing these veterans sing it, makes you realise it grew naturally out of their world and their belief. It rang true for them.*
>
> *Among their contemporaries, there was something special about the 22nd Battalion Royal Fusiliers that you better than I can pin-point. It was a privilege to have known them.[35]*

It seems right to give the last word to Mrs Keeble:

> *I have the Book relating to Col R. B. Barker with his photograph inside the Cover. The Commanding Officer was loved by All his Men. True comradeship prevailed, as per the Book.[36]*

1 Now ex-mayor but knighted in 1918 and MP for Kensington since the 1918 election

2 *Broughshane*, <u>8909</u>; also *Daily Sketch*, 7/7/1919, for photos of marchers (p12); *Mufti*, November 1919, <u>1</u>, No 1, p2

3 WH Metcalfe, *Ibid*, p7

4 *Ibid*, p4

5 61 out of 75 original members had survived the war; unfortunately Captain Jimmy Carr MC DCM became a victim of the influenza epidemic just a few days after the Armistice

6 *Mufti*, August 1920, <u>2</u>, No 3, pp 5-6; this fund would last almost twenty years.

7 *Ibid*, May 1921, <u>2</u>, No 11, p5

8 *Mufti*, Spring 1923, <u>4</u>, No 1, p7

9 *Ibid*, Summer 1924, <u>5</u>, No 2, pp 2-3; reprinted from the *Daily Express*

10 *Mufti*, Autumn 1925, <u>6</u>, No 3, pp 2-4, Spring 1926, 7, No 1, pp 5-6 for Major WA Miller DSO MC RAMC; obituary of Major RH Gregg DSO MC *ibid*, Summer 1929, <u>10</u>, No 2, pp 1-2; HE Harvey also lost his fight against his gassing in 1929

11 *Ibid*, Summer 1927, 8, No 2, pp 6-7 and others in 1928 and 1929

12 *Ibid*, Xmas 1924, <u>5</u>, No 4, pp 1, 3-5

13 Albert and his 2 brothers. In September 1931 12 Platoon (that of Albert Smith) held its only reunion: *ibid*, Autumn 1931, <u>12</u>, No 3, p6

14 *Ibid*, Xmas 1929,10, No 4, pp 2-5

15 *Ibid*, Summer 1930, 11, No 2, pp 1-2; we heard no more about the Miraumont cross

16 *Ibid*, Xmas 1931, <u>12</u>, No 4, pp 2-3

17 *Ibid*, Xmas 1935, <u>16</u>, No 4, p12 and Spring 1936, <u>17</u>, No 1, p12

18 *Ibid*, Xmas 1935, <u>16</u>, No 4, pp 3-6, longer excerpt in the Preface. See also Autumn 1936, <u>17</u>, No 3, p4 for Canon Adams on the same theme

19 *Ibid*, Autumn 1935, <u>16</u>, No 3, pp 2-3

20 *Ibid*, Xmas 1939, <u>20</u>, No 95, p12

21 *Ibid*, Xmas 1946, <u>27</u> No 109, pp 2-5

22 *Ibid*, December 1958, <u>38</u>, No 132, p9

23 *Forty Years Afterwards*, *ibid*, Xmas 1956, <u>36</u>, No 127, pp 12-iii

24 Issue called *Fragments From France 1915-18*, <u>42</u>, No 139

25 *Mufti*, Xmas 1964, 44, No 135, pp 10-11; General Nevill used almost exactly the same words to us in 1984 (personal communication 2/7/84)

26 *Ibid*, Xmas, 1970, <u>49</u>, No 155, pp 10-12; the 6 above were named, there might have been others

27 *Ibid*, Summer 1970, <u>49</u>, No 154, p2

28 Personal communication from his daughter Mrs Joan Farrar, 1984

29 *Ibid*, Xmas 1974, <u>54</u>, No 164, pp 9-10; the write-up was supplied by their good friend Douglas Sherwood of the 24th RF OCA

30 WW 'Baby' Clark said he had put forward the fateful suggestion to wind things up

31 Letter from Roland Whipp, 15/12/1983

32 *Mufti*, Xmas 1977, <u>57</u>, No 179, pp 20-23

33 *Mufti*, Xmas 1977, <u>57</u>, No 170, pp 20-23; Captain GH Evans, OCA President, whose pub became the spiritual home of the OCA in WWII, was one of a rare number of men with a DCM and the MC.
Marjorie Hay, the cub reporter who had chronicled the Battalion's deeds in 1914-15, was much missed in her village of Burpham near Arundel, where the path to the local church was named after her.
Stan J Upton, alias Claude, was the guiding spirit of 13 Platoon, a fine Chairman of the OCA, but above all a wonderful editor of *Mufti* from 1960-73; without him, many of the incidents used in this book would simply not be chronicled.

34 Interview with Roland Whipp, 18/11/1983; we presume he is talking about General Nevill

35 Letter from Rev Canon Peter Gillingham, 2/7/1984

36 Letter from Mrs Edie Keeble, 5/3/1984; the Book is of course Stone's *History*.

Appendix A

Casualties and Honours

1) Casualties

In Stone's 1923 *History*, he mentions total casualties of 90 officers and 2,230 other ranks. Are these high, low or typical? The 23rd RF is the most obvious example for comparison.[1]

Total Casualties	22nd RF (Nov 15-Feb 18)	23rd RF (Nov 15-Mar 20)
Officers	90	128
Other Ranks	2230	3113
Total	2320	3241

The 23rd RF carried on through 1918, a year at least as heavy in human cost as 1916 and 1917, so we would expect its casualties be about a third higher than the 22nd RF, which is what we find.

If we confine the information to those who lost their lives on active service then we can make comparisons from *The Royal Fusiliers in the Great War* with other Royal Fusilier service battalions. Confining ourselves to Other Ranks deaths we get:

23rd RF (served till the end of war)	723
24th RF (served till the end of war)	534
17th RF (served till the end of war)	519
22nd RF (disbanded Feb 1918)	440
20th RF (disbanded Feb 1918)	566
12th RF (disbanded Feb 1918)	443
32nd RF (disbanded Feb 1918)	403

Evidently deaths on active service in the 22nd RF are comparable with other service battalions.

Different sources give different figures for Other Ranks fatalities: the figure above for the 22nd RF (440) differs from summing up the names listed in *Soldiers Died in the Great War (The Royal Fusiliers)*, which comes to 436, while the number of deaths listed in Stone's *History* is 399. Some of the differences are due to error (eg under-representing deaths for Oppy Wood in the *History*), but others may be due to different interpretations of transfers.

The following lists of Other Ranks fatalities for the Battalion use both sources:[2]

Total Fatalities Month	22nd RF (History, Mufti)	22nd RF (SDGW)	Actions
December 1915	5	5	
January 1916	1	1	
February 1916	5	5	
March 1916	3	3	
April 1916	5	5	
May 1916	17	18	Vimy Ridge
June 1916	14	15	(spread through month)
July 1916	79	73	Delville Wood (1)
August 1916	20	20	Delville Wood (2)
September 1916	2	3	
October 1916	6	6	
November 1916	28	29	Ancre (Redan Ridge)
December 1916	1	0	
1916, not identified when	4	0	
January 1917	2	2	
February 1917	100	112	Miraumont
March 1917	12	14	Grevillers Trench
April 1917	27	56	Oppy Wood (1)
May 1917	15	18	Oppy Wood (2)
June 1917	3	4	
July 1917	12	11	(spread through month)
August 1917	4	4	
September 1917	5	6	
October 1917	0	0	
November 1917	10	10	Cambrai (Bourlon Wood)
December 1917	12	13	Cambrai (Moeuvres)
1917, not identified when	5	0	
1918 (Jan/Feb etc)	0	3	Disbanded Feb 1918
Total	399	436	

Total Fatalities	22nd RF (As listed in History)	22nd RF (Common to SDGW and History)
1915-1916		
A Company	35	32
B Company	64	58
C Company	54	48
D Company	37	36
Total	190	174
1917-1918		
A Company	36	34
B Company	89	84
C Company	39	39
D Company	45	45
Total	209	202

In most cases the numbers are close. The biggest discrepancy is in April 1917, when the Battalion lost the highest proportion of its fighting strength at Oppy Wood. B Company appeared to be in the thick of it in all the battles, especially Miraumont, Oppy Wood and Cambrai in 1917 – and of course their own Vimy Ridge adventure in May 1916.

Using *Soldiers Died, the History* and names listed by month in Mufti in 1921, we can make our best estimate at a more complete roll of honour for the Battalion:

Roll of Honour for the 22nd Battalion: Other Ranks
A) Names Listed Both in *Soldiers Died* and in 22nd Battalion *History*

Name	Rank	Number	Company	Died
Adams, J	Private	976	C	17/2/17
Akhurst, AH	Private	61526	B	23/2/17
Alp, FHB	L/Cpl	1028	C	24/5/16
Amor, GF	Private	25229	A	17/2/17
Andrew[s], H	Private	4326	B	19/10/16
Andrews, HM	L/Cpl	4930	B	22/7/17
Ansell, GF	Private	1358	B	21/7/16
Archer, JH	Private	51000	B	17/2/17
Arthur, RWH	Private	7601	C	9/6/17
Ashton, JGR	L/Cpl	996	D	6/2/16
Aston, JE	Private	7115	B	17/2/17
Atherton, T	Private	15629	B	13/11/16
Avery, H	Private	41666	A	17/2/17
Axtens, HM	Private	1097	D	17/2/17
Ayling, GP	Sgt	937	C	14/7/16
Bailey, S	Private	1806	D	28/8/16
Baldwin, TC	Private	409	A	24/5/16
Banfield, TS	Private	1292	C	3/8/16
Banks, WJ	Private	61530	C	17/2/17
Bannerman, J	Private	23657	B	3/5/17
Barber, HB	Private	571	A	17/2/17
Barcham, F	Private	397	B	26/7/16
Barden, H	Private	20967	B	28/7/16
Barnes, CJ	Private	20664	B	29/4/17
Barnes, FC	Private	61531	B	16/2/17
Barnes, W	Private	2073	A	25/7/16
Barnett, A	Private	443	C	28/7/16
Barnsdale R[3],	Private	61500	A	17/2/17
Barrow, W	Private	48445	B	4/12/17
Bartlett, AG	Private	47580	A	26/4/17
Bartlett, RLW	L/Cpl	51986	A	17/2/17
Barttelot, RW	L/Cpl	61505	A	18/2/17
Barwise, LW	Private	210(?)42[4]	B	27/7/16
Bascombe, W	Private	1432	A	27/7/16
Bateman, Lord R	Private	1620	B	17/2/17
Batte, G	Private	5921	B	29/4/17
Bear, HA	Private	14271	B	3/5/17

Bedwell, R	Private	21167	A	7/9/16
Belton, J	Private	119(?)	C	30/5/16
Bennett, L	Private	527	B	28/7/16
Berry, RH	Private	346	B	13/4/16
Bestal, AH	Private	20834	C	17/2/17
Blackstock, J	Private	58901	A	4/12/17
Blackwell, H	Private	2055	A	17/2/17
Bonner, HJ	Private	51988	B	17/2/17
Booker, GL	L/Cpl	4515	B	19/10/16
Boraston, JP	L/Cpl	49393	B	13/8/17
Bowden, WJ	Private	7772	B	27/7/16
Brackenberry, JH[5]	Private	982	C	29/7/16
Brewer, W	Private	14554	B	4/2/17
Brickell, PH	Private	23473	B	29/4/17
Brierley, MR	Sgt	1208	B	17/2/17
Brough, RA[6]	Private	46345	B	17/2/17
Brown, EE	Private	599	D	26/7/16
Brown, FE	L/Cpl	608	A	14/11/16
Brown, J	Private	6436	D	29/4/17
Burge, SHO	Private	560	D	25/2/17
Burnham, SG	Private	51176	D	17/2/17
Burton, W	Private	25234	A	2/8/16
Cane, JM	L/Sgt	513	A	2/8/16
Carrack, CJ	Private	49388	B	17/2/17
Carter, R	Private	20960	B	17/2/17
Chandler, J	Private	6283	B	1/5/17
Chesworth, A	Private	14334	C	29/4/17
Chilvers, FG	Private	40401	B	27/11/17
Christian, OM	Private	492	A	29/7/16
Clark, ER	Private	654	D	13/11/16
Clark[e], C	Private	832	C	28/7/16
Clarke, J	Private	3256	C	28/7/16
Clements, CJ	Private	G/50992	A	12/5/17
Cohen, D	Private	192	B	3/8/16
Collins, WT	Private	1033	C	2/8/17
Cook, HW	Private	1522	B	21/4/16
Coombs, W	Private	748	B	19/11/15
Cooper, H	Private	61540	C	17/2/17
Copeland, FA	Private	1653	A	17/2/17
Copelstone, EA[7]	Private	1066	C	20/7/16
Corbett, H	Private	1937	B	27/7/16
Corcoran, J	Private	9829	B	28/7/16
Corsi, FD	L/Cpl	60892	B	9/12/17
Cotton, C	Private	948	A	28/7/16
Craft, C	Private	61503	B	30/11/17
Craib, JE	Cpl	753	D	27/7/16
Crondace, H	Private	47864	B	17/2/17
Crosby, CT	Private	786	D	29/4/17
Curson, FW	Private	10269	D	17/2/17
Cuthbertson, FJ	Private	1122	D	28/7/16

Darrington, WA	Private	25247	C	27/7/16
Davi[e]s, F	Private	968	C	28/7/16
Dearden, AJ	Private	1909	C	28/7/16
Destrubé, CJ	L/Cpl	1236	A	17/2/17
Destrubé, PJ	L/Cpl	24	A	17/2/17
Devil[l]e, A	Private	21249	C	10/3/17
Dillon, JF	Private	1344	B	23/7/16
Dix[s]on, G	Private	140	D	20/7/16
Drew, R	Sgt	543	B	24/5/16
Dryden, G	Private	49313	D	17/2/17
Duncan, FW	Private	51989	C	11/3/17
Durber, E	Private	9455	B	29/4/17
Easton, W[8]	Private	1256	A	17/2/17
Ecob, H	Private	51959	A	17/2/17
Eden, T	Private	58916	B	15/12/17
Edgeller, AFC	Private	633	D	3/8/16
Edgington, AJ	Private	1357	B	5/12/15
Ellis, J	Private	12848	B	13/11/16
English, G	Private	1436	C	30/5/16
Escudier, H	Private	769	D	28/7/16
Evans, CWH[9]	Private	23270	C	17/2/17
Evans, JE	CQMS	138	C	3/8/16
Evans, PJ	Private	52021	D	18/3/17
Exeter, FE	Private	L/16587	C	29/4/17
Farley, R	Sgt	1255	C	26/7/16
Farnes, A	Private	5370	A	8/3/17
Farrell, TW	Private	2173	C	6/3/16
Farrimond, T	Private	51024	B	27/11/17
Fidler, J	Private	4918	B	13/11/16
Field, H	Private	2103	B	20/9/17
Finer, HJ	L/Cpl	1372	A	27/4/17
Fitt, [J]C	Private	6876	C	17/2/17
Forecast, C	Private	43591	B	3/5/17
Gallagher, JA	L/Cpl	6909	D	3/5/17
Gallop, AJ	Private	13911	B	27/7/16
Gardener, CH	Private	1333	D	14/11/16
Gardner, LU[10]	Private	257	B	24/5/16
Garman, V	Private	1322	C	24/11/16
Garston, SH	Private	689	D	14/11/16
Garvey, J	L/Sgt	52009	D	17/2/17
Gibson, B	Cpl	6974	B	3/5/17
Gilbert, C[A]	Private	1886	B	27/4/17
Gi[l]es, AT	Private	51961	A	20/2/17
Ginsberg, S	Private	2102	B	2/8/16
Goodhall, CR	Private	9844	D	10/3/17
Goodhew, J	Private	3363	A	28/7/16
Gore, AS	Private	63051	B	16/12/17
Gould, A	Private	1405	B	27/7/16
Gould, JB	Private	1540	A	2/8/17
Goulding, P	L/Cpl	7203	A	17/2/17

Grant, J	Private	5903	A	18/11/16
Green, GL	Private	47101	B	17/2/17
Greene, FG	Private	26	B	11/6/16
Griffiths, JF	Private	32808	B	13/8/17
Grigg, AJ	Private	722	C	28/7/16
Grover, EB ('Dad')	Private	690	D	28/7/16
Guest, A	Private	7466	B	25/5/16
Guiland, MA	Private	10691	C	24/7/17
Hackett, CF	Sgt	52006	B	3/5/17
Haddock, W	Cpl	663	D	27/7/16
Hallum, EJ	Sgt	51982	C	17/2/17
Halstead, FFR	Private	1342	B	25/6/16
Harbour, I	Private	1786	C	17/2/17
Harding, ES	Private	43434	B	22/7/17
Harding, WC	Private	1008	D	27/6/16
Hardy, RW	L/Cpl	1332	B	27/7/16
Hare, JP	Sgt	9507	A	17/2/17
Harrington, W	Private	1860	A	28/7/16
Hawkes, CW	Private	62496	D	17/2/17
Hay, AE	Private	1851	B	20/7/17
Hayes, FA	Private	14147	C	28/7/16
Hearn, RP	Private	522	B	28/7/16
Heath, SW	Private	6699	A	6/10/16
Hedges, AJ	L/Cpl	1624	C	19/4/17
Henness[e]y, HW	Sgt	1233	A	17/2/17
Hennessey, JM	Private	812	B	28/7/16
Herbert, AT	Sgt	975	C	3/5/17
Herbert, E	Private	13878	B	28/7/16
Hicks, FB	Private	51962	C	29/4/17
Higgins, A	Private	1147	D	14/11/16
Hinchsliff, G	Private	20743	B	17/2/17
Hine, AC	Private	25220	C	25/7/16
Hitchcock, FC	Private	949	C	24/7/17
Hoare, SP	Private	1411	D	5/2/16
Holden, F	Private	38541	B	17/2/17
Holmes, HH	Private	61504	A	17/2/17
Hood, HC	L/Sgt	694	D	1/11/16
Hore, SJ	Cpl	562	B	17/2/17
Howes, JW	Private	42602	D	26/2/17
Hudson, A	Private	1986	B	28/7/16
Huggins, T	Private	195	C	28/7/16
Hughes, RV	Private	25941	B	1/12/17
Hulyer, EA	Private	61524	B	3/5/17
Humphrey, J	Private	1450	A	1/6/16
Irving, F	Private	49419	B	14/4/17
Isaac, B[J]	L/Sgt	61541	D	10/3/17
Jackson, H	Private	1549	B	13/11/16
Jackson, WJ	Private	51163	B	17/2/17
James, F	Private	60897	C	29/4/17
Jarm[a][i]n, R	Sgt	61495	C	29/4/17

Jeffery, HA	Private	1562	C	17/3/16
Johnson, GH	Private	2179	B	27/7/16
Jones, GAH	Private	1268	C	14/2/16
Jones, T	Private	300	A	1/6/16
Judge, G	Private	904	C	24/5/16
Keates, WM	Private	826	C	26/8/16
Keen, FW	Sgt	728	D	28/7/16
Kellern, H	L/Cpl	10106	A	19/6/16
Kelly, EJ	Private	843	C	20/4/16
Kench, SJ	Private	2045	B	24/5/16
Kendall, WD	Private	51168	C	26/5/17
Kessell, FH	Private	25269	C	27/7/16
Kelminster, JW[11]	L/Cpl	2883	A	13/11/16
Kingsland, FW	L/Cpl	150	A	2/2/17
Kirkland, R	Private	4043	B	17/2/17
Knight, WC	Sgt	22093	C	17/2/17
Knight, W	Private	35455	D	9/6/17
Landman, KE	Private	1894	B	31/3/16
Lambrick, SW	L/Sgt	51940	C	17/2/17
Larner, AJ	Private	L/16094	A	1/3/17
Lawton, C	L/Sgt	59	B	28/7/16
Leppard, P	Private	1294	C	28/7/16
Levens, JS	Private	835	C	28/7/16
Levey, J	Private	1547	A	3/8/16
Lindsay, AE	Private	3279	A	27/7/16
Lingwood, WJ	Cpl	292	B	29/4/17
Livingstone, D	Private	1235	D	19/6/16
Lowry, HA	Private	25218	B	22/7/17
Lovendahl, W	L/Cpl	985	C	13/11/16
Luke, J	Cpl	9214	B	5/11/16
Lyall, G	Private	50601	C	17/2/17
Lyon, CC	Private	6484	B	30/11/17
McGrath, WE	Cpl	4927	C	17/2/17
McGuinness, HR[12]	Private	12304	C	27/7/16
Mallett, JF	L/Cpl	1319	D	17/2/17
Manning, FJ	Private	766	D	20/9/17
Mardell, PW	Private	60901	D	13/3/17
Markie, J	L/Cpl	517	B	26/7/16
Marks, JH	Private	20448	D	17/2/17
Martin, GP	Private	L/16493	D	20/9/17
Mash, H	Private	81179	B	5/12/17
Measures, AE	Private	1613	D	19/1/16
Meeds, EJ	Private	61502	A	27/2/17
Merricks, S	Private	1390	B	4/1/17
Merriott, CW	Private	48448	D	11/7/17
Meyers, EJ	L/Cpl	1094	A	21/10/16
Miles, G	Private	1433	D	20/9/17
Milne, J[WH]	Private	51966	A	17/2/17
Minter, FS	Private	60899	D	10/3/17
Minty, WL[13]	Cpl	312	D	27/4/17

Monahan, D	Private	1374	A	26/5/16
Moore, HJ	Private	24467	C	29/4/17
Morris, C	L/Cpl	10(?)0(?)9	D	29/12/15
Morton, AV	Private	472	B	12/5/17
Mortimer, AJ	Private	19140	B	24/8/16
Mountier, AA	L/Cpl	558	A	18/6/16
Moxon, G	Private	2180	B	17/2/17
Munro, HH ('Saki')	L/Sgt	225	A	14/11/16
Murton, AS	Private	1197	A	4/6/16
Neale, HD	Private	1267	B	25/12/15
Neale, HC	Private	25539	C	17/2/17
Negus, J	Private	900	C	25/7/16
North, WG	Cpl	1025	D	11/5/16
O'Donnell, J	Private	43538	B	26/5/17
Orders, A	L/Cpl	34737	B	29/4/17
Outram, AR	Private	51968	A	17/2/17
Page, RAP[14]	Private	68760	B	27/11/17
Palfrey, W[G]	Private	60905	D	17/2/17
Passfield, W	Private	1959	C	19/10/16
Patching, CJ	Private	68765	B	27/11/17
Payne, CR	Private	61516	B	17/2/17
Pearce, AE	Private	3453	B	1/8/16
Pearce, BS	L/Cpl	369	B	24/5/16
Pearce, G	L/Cpl	L/12189	C	29/4/17
Penn[e], W	Private	2074	C	14/11/16
Penwarden, J	Private	1121	D	28/7/16
Perkins, T	Private	50047	B	17/2/17
Perry, A	Private	2118	C	27/7/16
Pescud, AJ	Private	1455	B	11/2/16
Petch[e]y, J	Private	2059	B	22/7/17
Peverill, T	Private	718	C	25/7/16
Phillips, AHP	Private	48394	B	1/7/17
Phillips, E	Private	25498	C	14/11/16
Phoenix, A	Private	1463	B	2/8/16
Pilkington, RD	Private	7708	B	13/11/16
Powell, HW	Private	51949	A	25/3/17
Pratt, HJ	Private	61547	D	29/4/17
Price, F	Private	50260	A	4/8/17
Pritchard, G	Private	1878	C	28/7/16
Purver, LA	Private	61546	B	15/12/17
Pyke, C	Private	1395	D	24/6/16
Ramsay, RC	Private	41459	D	11/3/17
Ransom, JF	Private	545	D	27/7/16
Reid, RA	Private	93	A	29/7/16
Richards, FW	Private	498	D	27/7/16
Richardson, E	Private	3042	D	6/2/17
Robinson, RL	Private	8941	B	17/2/17
Roe, AJ	Private	2259	B	14/11/16
Rogers, LA	Private	68777	B	30/11/17
Rose, JA	Private	G/49006	B	4/12/17

Ross, JT	L/Cpl	47699	A	17/2/17
Rowland, A	Private	51181	D	17/2/17
Rush, W[A]	Private	51995	C	17/2/17
Russell-Davies, LG	Private	27161	B	19/10/16
Salter, AR	Private	23390	C	10/3/17
Sarsfield, FP	Private	674	C	3/8/16
Sayers, R	Private	20718	D	23/11/16
Scarrold, GH	Private	20617	B	27/7/16
Scott, GA	Private	733	D	28/7/16
Senior, JW	A/Cpl	49468	D	29/4/17
Shephard, HA	Private	81146	B	28/11/17
Shock, AE	Private	61550	D	17/2/17
Singleton, W	L/Cpl	1323	D	17/2/17
Slade, AE	Private	50274	A	17/2/17
Smith, F	Private	1490	C	14/2/16
Smith, FWJ	Private	24480	D	3/8/16
Smith, Thomas	Sgt	413	B	17/2/17
Smith, Thomas	Private	46666	B	19/12/17
Snell, JH	Private	50303	B	20/7/17
Southcliffe, CW	Private	61552	D	17/2/17
Speakman, J	Private	1483	D	17/2/17
Springall, WG	Private	2086	B	14/11/16
Stanborough, EG	Sgt	483	C	17/2/17
Stannard, GM	Private	6527	B	24/5/16
Staples, AH	Private	1601	B	17/2/17
Stark, FC	L/Cpl	20(?)869	A	27/7/16
Starkey, E[A]	Private	51996	B	17/2/17
Stevens, C	Private	35228	D	9/6/17
Stewart, JF	L/Cpl	412	B	27/7/16
Steward, WJ	Sgt	1138	C	14/7/16
Stokes, W	Private	24473	D	4/8/16
Stow, ET	L/C[pl	51955	C	1/3/17
Stratton, CE	Private	4688	B	9/3/17
Such, S	Private	435	A	27/7/16
Sykes, S	Private	47863	C	18/8/17
Symonds, WJ	Private	2020	A	17/2/17
Talkington, W	Private	36779	B	19/2/17
Taylor, J	Private	7877	A	13/11/16
Thurston, R	Private	46114	A	17/2/17
Timms, EW	L/Cpl	1315	D	13/6/16
Tomlinson, JE	Private	49469	D	17/2/17
Tong, AE	Private	2177	D	19/6/16
Tonge, AE	L/Cpl	237	A	17/2/17
Towndrow, A	Private	48295	D	1/5/17
Trafford, TJ	Private	50(?)316	B	29/4/17
Tromp, H Van	L/Cpl	256	B	24/5/16
Tubby, CG	Private	1649	B	17/2/17
Turner, AE	Private	48456	A	14/11/16
Turner, BP	Private	50(?)318	D	29/4/17
Ulph, W	Private	1129	D	9/7/16

Vango, TL	Private	956	A	25/12/15
Vasse[y], WA	Private	81151	B	28/11/17
Verrall, PR	Private	41811	B	17/2/17
Vickery, AE	Private	497	B	27/7/16
Walder, A	L/Sgt	1262	C	3/5/17
Walsh, W	Private	878	B	17/2/17
Walters, JH	Private	47111	B	17/2/17
Walton, AE	L/Cpl	89	D	29/4/17
Ward, FG	L/Cpl	678	D	17/2/17
Ward, FJ	Private	1592	B	24/5/16
Ward, J	Private	1470	A	13/11/16
Ward, LJ	Private	51253	A	17/2/17
Watson, R	Private	533	C	24/5/16
Waugh, GW	Private	4520	D	17/2/17
Weedon, R	Private	1631	C	24/6/16
Webb, AJ	Private	68607	B	29/11/17
Webb, J	Private	11075	C	13/7/17
Wells, MGL	Private	1565	B	25/5/16
Westland, NG	Private	1398	A	28/7/1
Whibley, A	Sgt	677	D	17/2/17
Whitchurch, A	Private	487	D	17/2/17
White, CE	Private	792	B	13/11/16
Whitlock, HE	Private	836	C	1/6/16
Widowson, B	Private	1547	C	9/7/16
Wiles, F	Private	49819	B	17/2/17
Williams, FF	Private	11387	B	17/2/17
Williams, GA	L/Cpl	787	D	14/11/16
Williams, SJ	Private	29425	C	26/5/17
Williams, WFD	Private	49820	D	19/2/17
Wilson, WJ	Private	917	C	23/4/16
Wilson, WR	Private	17727	C	17/2/17
Winsbury, J[15]	Private	2171	D	27/7/16
Wood[s], A	Cpl	1269	D	17/2/17
Woodward, AW	Private	51950	C	26/4/17
Woolford, SA	Private	2121	B	29/4/17
Wright, A	Private	2000	D	13/11/16
Wright, WP	Private	49878	B	17/2/17
Youels, HA	Private	1149	C	24/5/16

We get the rank and regimental number from *Soldiers Died* and the company from the Roll of Honour in the *History*, and we can generally cross-check the date of death from *Soldiers Died* and the month/year of death from the Roll of Honour listed in *Mufti* in 1921 (which formed the basis of the names listed in the *History*).

B) Names Listed in *Soldiers Died* but not in 22nd *Battalion History*

Name	Rank	Number	Company	Died
Allen, E	L/Cpl	47858	NA	17/2/17
Armer, C	Private	1508	NA	18/12/17
Batting, HJ	L/Cpl	48283	NA	29/4/17
Benn, GV	Private	16856	NA	29/4/17

Birch, GR	Private	60889	NA	19/9/17
Blundell, G	L/Cpl	684	NA	29/4/17
Bond, GW	L/Cpl	17587	NA	28/2/18
Bright, AG	Private	16614	NA	17/2/17
Brinklow, CF	Private	35021	NA	13/11/16
Brittain, E	Private	50961	NA	29/4/17
Bryan, A	Cpl	25005	NA	29/4/17
Burchardt-Ashton AE	L/Cpl	8219	NA	11/7/16
Carpenter, DT	Private	1381	NA	21/8/16
Carroll, J	Private	66	NA	18/9/16
Chittenden, ES	Cpl	48365	NA	29/4/17
Clarke, FG	Private	48546	NA	24/4/17
Cole, CV	Private	41291	NA	29/4/17
Crane, E	Sgt	717	NA	29/4/17
Deeks, VA	Private	61510	NA	8/11/18[16]
Downs, JH	L/Cpl	47482	NA	29/4/17
Durrant, EF	A/Sgt	7743	NA	29/4/17
Evans, EA	Sgt	11805	NA	29/4/17
Fuller, W	Private	61537	NA	27/2/17
Goodwin, F	Sgt	1305	NA	29/4/17
Guilford, W	Private	15368	NA	29/4/17
Hardy, WJ	L/Cpl	53098	NA	29/4/17
Harrington, D	Private	6	NA	8/2/17
Hollwey-Miller WGE	Private	43722	NA	29/4/17
Jackson, A	Private	51993	NA	29/4/17
Johnson, JW	Private	5330	NA	13/4/17
Jordan, A	Private	2158	NA	27/7/16
Langley, JH	Private	4575	NA	29/4/17
Larkin, T	Private	47001	NA	20/4/17
Legrove, EC	Private	62490	NA	17/2/17
Leney, NA	Private	61542	NA	29/4/17
Loker, A	Private	3325	NA	17/2/17
Lovett-Janison, PW	Sgt	527	NA	2/8/16
Lucking, GE	Private	27895	NA	3/5/17
Madden, EM	Private	371	NA	1/9/16
Manchester, PF	L/Cpl	6014	NA	29/4/17
Massey, FJ	Private	1636	NA	24/8/16
Middleton, B	L/Cpl	49387	NA	29/4/17
Moody, WA	Private	61544	NA	14/2(?)/17
Palmer, T	Private	68582	NA	20/12/17
Proctor, A	L/Cpl	7663	NA	14/1/18
Regan, WD	Private	5575	NA	29/4/17
Rogerson, RH	L/Sgt	G/1556	NA	29/4/17
Sadler, J	Private	28438	NA	28/2/17
Smith, J	L/Cpl	53092	NA	29/4/17
Stewart, LT	L/Cpl	1594	NA	3/5/17
Stride, WO	Private	46716	NA	3/5/17
Tarr, JR	Private	51978	NA	17/2/17
Turner, A	Private	48456	NA	30/12/17
Turner, JH	Private	9578	NA	29/4/17

Veglio, PR	Private	770	NA	29/4/17
Walker, LB	L/Sgt	1666	NA	17/2/17
Walton, F	Private	48291	NA	29/4/17
Watts, H	Private	60202	NA	8/6/17
Wood, HAL	Private	1354	NA	21/5/16
Wright, SA	Private	47857	NA	17/2/17

Both the list of names of deaths for April 1917 given in *Mufti* in April 1921, and the Roll of Honour in the *History*, appear to be deficient in deaths for Oppy Wood (29/4/17). There is such a high proportion of deaths for this date in the list above, that we feel confident that that the great majority of the names above are genuine omissions from the first list. Also, men missing on 17/2/17 and 29/4/17 were only reclassified 'presumed dead' many months later e.g. for Lance Sergant LB Walker (above), it was January 1918 before it was announced. (see www.ewhurstfallen.co.uk/.../walker.htm)

C) Names Listed in 22nd Battalion *History* but not in *Soldiers Died*

Name	Rank	Number	Company	Died
Ashton, AEB	NA	NA	A	July 16
Davies, H	Private	2934	A	2/8/16[17]
Stevens, HG	NA	NA	A	September 16
Wharton, H	Cpl	NA	B	28/7/16[18]
Janison, PWL	NA	NA	B	August 16[19]
Miller, EH	NA	NA	B	July 16
Taylor, GH	NA	NA	B	September 16
Finlayson, RI	NA	NA	B	? (poss Oct 16)
Basnett, J	NA	NA	B	? (poss Oct 16)
Wiles, C	NA	NA	C	? (poss July 16)
Foster, G	NA	NA	C	August 16
Yeoman, JF	NA	NA	C	? (poss Nov 16)
Taylor, H	Na	NA	C	? (poss Nov 16)
Randall, WL	L/Cpl	1295	C	5/12/16[20]
Wood, H	Private	1863	C	28/7/16[21]
Stacey, RFW	NA	NA	D	July 16
Garner, J	NA	NA	A	February 17
Arnell, E	Private	22241	A	26/4/17[22]
Wales, WJ	NA	NA	B	'1917'
Spatcher, CP	NA	NA	B	'1917'
Frampton, WJ	NA	NA	B	'1917'
Curley, J	NA	NA	B	'1917'
Farr, C	NA	NA	B	'1917'

Probably, many of these men fought beside 22nd RF comrades but were only 'attached' to the Battalion, not transferred into it. The same thing applied in reverse to men like Randall and possibly Wharton, both of whom died serving in the 99th MGC.

There is also a Private Edwardes, not in either of the above sources, but listed in AJL

Tottenham's Roll of Honour of the Machine Gun and Lewis Gun Section, as having died 20/1/1916 (and cited by him in Mufti as having been the first casualty in the unit).[23]

Roll of Honour for the 22nd Battalion: Officers

Here we have an easier task: to record those officers who died while serving with the Battalion, whatever the paperwork. We have included two exceptions: Captain CB Grant, a 22nd man who was attached to the 99th Machine Gun Company, and was killed at Delville Wood while leading the Company, and Brigadier-General Randle Barnett Barker, who was killed when commanding 99th Brigade. It would be unthinkable to exclude the father of the Battalion.

Name	Rank	Died	From	Age	Notes
Fowler, CJ	2nd Lt	1/6/16	Weybridge	28	d.o.w. from Vimy Ridge
Black, GDA	Captain	21/6/16	Richmond	20	
Grant, CB	Captain	27/7/16	Warnham	22	Commanding 99th MGC
MacDougall, A	Captain	3/8/16	North Uist	30	Delville Wood
Fisher, PW	2nd Lt	12/9/16	Stratford	34	DCM
Fitton, N	2nd Lt	14/11/16	NA	NA	7th RF, attd 22nd; Ancre
Roscoe, RL	Captain	4/2/17	Hampstead	19	
Simons, L	Captain	17/2/17	NA	NA	missing, Miraumont
Payne, WH	2nd Lt	17/2/17	S Croydon	21	Miraumont
Burgess, EA	2nd Lt	17/2/17	NA	NA	Miraumont
Boulter, SF	2nd Lt	18/2/17	Wanstead	21	Miraumont (d.o.w.)[24]
Walsh, J	Major	19/2/17	NA	34	Miraumont (d.o.w.)
Done, NS	2nd Lt	10/3/17	Groombridge	35	5th RF attd 22nd RF, Grevillers Trench
Wardley, ME	2nd Lt	29/4/17	NA	28	Oppy Wood
Saword, R	2nd Lt	29/4/17	Woldingham	26	missing, Oppy Wood
Perraton, FM	2nd Lt	29/4/17	Plymouth	20	MC, missing, Oppy Wood
Stevenson, F	2nd Lt	29/4/17	NA	NA	missing, Oppy Wood
Jeffcoat, SF	2nd Lt	29/4/17	NA	NA	Oppy Wood
Barker, RB	Brig-Gen	24/3/18	Abergavenny	48	Commanding 99 Brigade, Geudecourt

Details are taken from War Diaries, local newspapers, references in *Mufti* and mentions of place names in letters such as those from Stone and Barker.

Second Lieutenant JHE Ellison[25] was originally listed as missing believed dead at Miraumont in the *History*, but was afterwards discovered to have been captured and to have survived the war.

A number of officers passed through the 22nd RF and were killed in service with other units (like Major Boardman), or were killed in 1918 after the 22nd had been disbanded like Second Lieutenant Coppack (24th RF), Second Lieutenant DF Davies (23rd RF),[26] and Captain Jimmy Carr (dying of influenza a few days after Armistice Day), but discovering where each person went afterwards is outside the scope of this exercise.

2) Decorations and Awards

Victoria Cross
Palmer, FW

DSO
Barker, R Barnett –
and Bar
Adams, WJ
Phythian-
Gregg, RH
Miller, WA (RAMC)
Stone, CR

MC
Adams, WJ
Phythian-
Blomfield, AJ
*Brownlee, J
Carr, JW
Coad, CN (RAMC)
Evans, GH
Evans, TH
Feord, A
Gell, EAS
*Goodman, SJ
Gregg, RH
Martin, WJR
Miller, WA (RAMC)
Orme, ER[27]
Perraton, FM
Roscoe, RL
Rossell, EC
St John, Reverend EP
Simons, L
Stone, CR
(Spear, JC)[28]

DCM
Baker, FR
Brierley, MR
Carr, JW
Evans, GH
Fidler, CE
Fisher, PW
Harvey, HE
Hawthorne, L
Hogan, LU
Keeble, AT
McGowan, TE
Metcalfe, WH
Miles, FG
Mobley, A
Rumble, WA
Robinson, R
Webb, G
Wheeler, CA

MM
Guy, EC – and Bar
Leonard, J – and Bar
Wilkinson HV
– and Bar
Ayres, G
Baldwin, J
*Beaty, J
*Becks, JW
Blundell, T
Bone, CC
Booth, H
Brown, L[J]
Burgess, AF

Cannot, PA
*Carter, A
*Chennell, B
Cole, C[J]
*Cooper, WJ
Crane, E
Dennis, HG
Downing, JT
Duke, R
Fahey, WJ
Faux, CY
Fitton, JW
Fletcher, WC
Garman, V
Gent, F
Gimson, SG
*Glover, W
Griffin, E[W]
Gullen, JBW
Guyatt, G
Halstead, H
Hawes, R
Harrington, HV
Harvey, HE
Hennessey, HW
Herrington, HV
Hepburn, AB
Keeble, AT
Kirby, FD
Lindsey, C
McGowan, TE
Martin, C
Martin, R
Moon, GC[29]

Moore, HJ
Murton, JT
Palmer, FW
Pearson, CE
Peatfield, W
Petchey, J
Place, FC
*Plummer, V
Porker, LH
Richardson, H
Rogerson, RH
*Shepard, FC
Shoreman, LE
Smith, T
Stroud, A
Stewart, LT
Taylor, E
Taylor, WB
Temple, GM
Turner, W
Vaisey, JC
Wagland, P[V]
Ward, R
*Warwick, L
Wharton, WH
West, EM
White, WJ
*Whipp, R
Wilmot, PE
Woodward, E
Wratten, S
*Wright, SH[30]

MSM Turney, C

Belgian Croix-de-Guerre Amery, TA

Mentioned in Despatches
Barker, Lt-Col R Barnett (at least three times
while Colonel)
Walsh, Major J
Ross, Lt J
Roscoe, T/Lt RL
Burgess, Sgt-Major RD
Hartley, Sgt-Major GH
Brierley, Sgt MR
Butcher, Cpl WJ
Dennis, Cpl HG

Act of Courage Woolford, Pte HW: supplied
22 fluid ounces of blood for transfusion

** Not listed in
History, mainly
because the actions
involved were those
at Cambrai, just
before the Battalion
was disbanded.*

278

1 Major Lewis, *History of 23rd (S) Battalion R.F. (Sportsman')*, p12, 1920, from The Million Book Project online. I arrived at totals of 32 officers and 688 other ranks killed in action

2 Roll of Honour in *History*, pp 74-78, cross-checked with Mufti 1921 in which the names were listed by month

3 Barnslade in *History*

4 The reprint of *Soldiers Died* had evidently been photographed from an original in which the strokes of the 6 and 9 were becoming faded and can be taken for 0s, so 21042 could be 21942 or 21642. The worst examples are marked '?'.

5 Ending in -ury according to *History*

6 Brough, E in the *History*

7 *History* has it as Coplestone

8 The *History* has H

9 EWH in *History*

10 LV in *History*

11 Kilminster in *History*

12 Just one initial, J, in *History*

13 The *History* has WE

14 Page, ARP in *History*

15 The *History* has Winsburg

16 Not marked 'k in a,' or 'd of w,' but simply 'd' for died – possibly in captivity

17 Listed in *Soldiers Died* as from the 27th RF – the feeder battalion which stayed in the UK (probably the paperwork hadn't gone through)

18 Information from Tot's *MG & LG Section Roll of Honour* handwritten, in author's collection

19 News from local Horsham newspapers (*WSG*, 17/8/1916, *WSCT*, 19/8/1916)

20 Information from Tot's *MG & LG Section Roll of Honour*

21 Listed in *Soldiers Died* as from the 27th RF – the feeder battalion which stayed in the UK

22 Listed in deaths for 32nd Battalion RF, from where he had been attached to the 22nd Battalion

23 *Mufti*, Spring 1928, 9, No 1, pp 2-3; Tot's Roll of Honour of the MG and LG Roll of Honour:

24 In CWGC list as London Regiment Cyclist - 25th Battalion; d.o.w. = died of wounds

25 Ellison's Circumstances of Capture document (*WO 374/22611*) appears as an illustration in Trevor Pigeon's *Boom Ravine*, op cit, p82

26 2nd Lt Thornhill went missing from the 23rd RF in the Great Retreat, as did 2nd Lt JW Ireland (attached 23rd RF, attached the 99th TMB) on 25/3/18. The latter was repatriated in December 1918

27 Some doubt as to whether this was earned with the 22nd RF

28 *Ditto*

29 *History* has GJ

30 From correspondence with Mayor Davison

Appendix B

Sources

Primary/Key Sources

Barnett Barker Papers, privately owned, also at RWF Museum, Caernarvon

Christopher Stone Papers, owned by Mrs Anthea Secker, now at IWM

Phythian-Adams Papers, owned by Henry Phythian-Adams

Keeble Papers, privately owned

William-Powlett Papers (Diaries of Barton William Powlett), privately owned

The Broughshane Collection (Second Series), 7 Volumes, Kensington Central Library, Local History Section

Broughshane: 22nd Battalion Cuttings Book, Kensington Central Library, Local History Section

Mufti (22nd RF OCA Magazine), 1919-1977, collections (incomplete in all cases) at Kensington Central Library (Local History Section), Imperial War Museum and in author's possession

Interviews with veterans 1983-5:

Roland Whipp, George Challis, Olly Berrycloath, Mr J Farnsworth (thanks to Glenys Hogan), WW ('Baby') Clark and Mr Pumphleet.

Interviews with veterans' families: Mrs Edie Keeble (widow of Fred), Henry Phythian-Adams (son of Canon Phythian-Adams), Mrs Doris Palmer (widow of Fred), Jean Rossell (wife/widow of Colonel Rossell), Mrs Rawly (daughter of Chris Wakelin), Mrs Stevens (widow of Eric Stevens), and Oliver William-Powlett (grandson of Major William-Powlett).

Written correspondence with a large number of other veterans' families and others who knew them, notably Valerie Ames (friend of George Stribling), DC Bone (son of CC Bone), Mrs I Braham (widow of AH Braham), J Burchill (nephew of W Burchill), Mrs Comerford (widow of LB Comerford), G Deville (son of R Deville), Elizabeth Dodson (daughter of Steve Kempsell), Alice Dyson (daughter of Sir George Dyson), Katharine Ehle (friend of WB Boulter), Joan Farrar (daughter of Claude Upton), Tom Foster (neighbour of Mrs Futers who left a memoir of her long-term neighbour Captain Robinson), Mrs Holliday and Mrs Dickson (widow and daughter of Steve Holliday), Mrs Ena Franklin (wife of Major AV Franklin), EB Furmston (son of B Furmston), Arturo E Goodliffe of Buenos Aires, (brother-in-law of JDF Tilney), AS Kempsell (son of Steve Kempsell), Sarah Kiteley (widow of Frank Kiteley), Miss P Lacrotelle (daughter of FE Lacrotelle), Jim Lissiman (son of HC Lissiman), A McCowan (son of Sergeant McCowan), Hilda Marshall (daughter of LG Lewis), J Metchear (daughter of Mr Metchear, who died just before we could see him), Mrs Ena Nutt (daughter of G Edmands), Elizabeth Oakley (granddaughter of Mr Benwell), Edith Parsons (daughter of John Mitchell), BE Pearse (son of G Pearse), Esther Ratcliff (daughter of Richard Barnard), Mrs Sutcliffe (widow of T Sutcliffe), Peter Whipp (son of Roland Whipp), Mrs L Watkins (daughter of JJ Watkins), Hetty M Wickens (daughter of WJ Wickens), RA Wilkins (son of Mr Wilkins), Lady Woods (widow of Sir John Woods). Other helpful providers of information: WL Binns (archivist at Christs Hospital), Brian Dowling (information on Henley Park), Rev Peter Gillingham (conducted OCA Horsham Memoriam Services at Horsham for many years), Elspeth Griffiths (archivist at Sedbergh School – BB's old school), Bill Kirby (former pupil at Christs Hospital from September 1914), Stanley Malone (Master at Christs Hospital), Major-General CAR Nevill CB CBE DSO and Mr & Mrs Wally Soffe.

National Archives at Kew

War Diaries: (*WO 95* series unless stated otherwise) 2nd Division: HQ 1288-1304, A & Q: 1306-1312, also CRA and associated artillery brigades; 99 Brigade 1368-1370; 22nd and 23rd RF 1372; 1st

KRRC and 1st Royal Berks 1371; 99th MGC and 99th TMB 1373; other neighbouring and higher units as required. The battalion War Diaries cited above, ie 1371 and 1372, are now available online. Other National Archives: RP Brown POW report *WO 161/100/3021* (pp 4140-41), Court Martial Report *WO 71/531, WO 93/49*, Medal Rolls *WO 372 (accessible online)*, Second Lieutenant Ellison's Circumstances of Capture document *WO 374/22611*.

General Pereira's Diary is contained in 2nd Division War Diary, *WO 95/1289*

London Gazette (in National Archives Library) for medal citations, various editions between 1916 and 1919 (also accessible online)

Imperial War Museum

Diary of Sir Henry Wilson, IWM
Documents concerning the Writing of the History of the 22nd RF Battalion, Dept of Printed Books, IWM
Farley Papers, Dept of Documents, IWM

Newspapers

Especially those local to Horsham and West London:
West Sussex County Times,
West Sussex Gazette
The Kensington News And West London Times
West London Observer
Also cited:
The Abergavenny Chronicle, Camberley News, Cardiff Times, Chiswick Times, Daily Sketch, Evening Standard, News of the World, South Wales Weekly News, The Daily Mail, The Daily Mirror, The Edinburgh Evening Dispatch, The Evening News & Evening Mail, The Haddingtonshire Courier, The Mansfield and North Notts Advertiser, The Porthcawl News, The Richmond And Twickenham Times, The Surrey Herald, The Times, Westminster Gazette

Magazines

Victoria University College Review
The Tatler
22nd Batt. Royal Fusiliers' Fortnightly Gazette, various editions 1915, Horsham & Clipstone: Kensington Central Library, Local History Section and IWM
The magazine of New College Oxford (loose pages in the Phythian-Adams Papers)
Sedbergh School: *The Sedberghian, Sedbergh School Register, Rouge Et Noir* (house magazine)

Books – Specific to the Battalion or its Members

Major Christopher Stone (Ed), *History of the 22nd (Service) Battalion Royal Fusiliers (Kensington)*, 1923
Christopher Stone, *B.B.*, 1919
GD Sheffield & GIS Inglis (Eds), *From Vimy Ridge to the Rhine, The Great War Letters of Christopher Stone DSO MC*, Crowood, 1989
Ralph Durand, *The Steep Ascent*, c 1931
HE Harvey, *Battle-line Narrative*, 1928
AJ Langguth, *Saki: A Life of Hector Hugh Munro*, OUP, 1982
Henry Lea, *A Veld Farmer's Adventures*, 1936
RJ Lloyd (Ed), *The Wood of Death and Beyond, The First World War Recollections of Major P. St. L. Lloyd O.B.E.*, Oakham Books, ~1997
Saki, *The Square Egg and Other Sketches With Three Plays*, (currently reprinted by Kessinger Publishing as *The Biography of Saki*, nd, as an extract from The Square Egg)

Official and Semi-Official/Unit Histories

British Official History, Military Operations, France and Belgium, 1916 Vol I & II 1938; 1918, *The German March Offensive and its Preliminaries*, 1935; also 1917 (3 volumes); and T*he Occupation of the Rhineland 1918-29*, HMSO, 1987

Jack Alexander, *McCrae's Battalion*, Mainstream Publishing, 2004
David Bilton, *Hull Pals*, Pen & Sword, 1999
Cyril Falls, *The History of the 35th (Ulster) Division*, Constable 1996 edition
General Sir Martin Farndale KCB, *History of Royal Regiment of Artillery: Western Front 1914-18*, 2007(?) Henry Ling Ltd reprint of 1986 RAI original
Jill Knight, *The Civil Service Rifles in the Great War*, Pen & Sword, 2004
Major Lewis, *History of 23rd (S) Battalion R.F. (Sportsman's), c 1920*
WC O'Neill, *The Royal Fusiliers in the Great War*, 1922, (reprinted by N&M Press)
Statistics of the British Empire, HMSO, 1922
Col H Stewart, *The New Zealand Division 1916-1919*, 1920
Soldiers Died in the Great War, Part 12 (The Royal Fusiliers), The War Office, 1921, (reprinted in 1989 by JB Hayward & Son)
E Wyrall, *History of the Second Division*, 1921, 2 volumes, (reprinted by N&M Press)
The 54th Infantry Brigade 1914-18, Gale & Poldon Ltd, 1919
A Short History of the 55th Infantry Brigade in the War of 1914-18, nd, (~1919)
Alex Weir, *Come On Highlanders: Glasgow Territorials in the Great War*, Sutton Publishing, 2005

Battles and Campaigns
Malcolm Brown, *The IWM Book of the Somme*, Pan 2002
Christopher Duffy, *Through German Eyes: The British on the Somme*, W & N, 2006
AH Farrar-Hockley, *The Somme*, Pan, 1966
JP Harris & Niall Barr, *Amiens to the Armistice*, Brasseys, 1998
Peter Hart, *The Somme*, Weidenfeld & Nicolson, 2005
Peter Liddle, *The 1916 Book of the Somme*, Leo Cooper, 1992
Chris McCarthy, *The Somme, The Day-By-Day Account*, 1993
Lyn Macdonald, *Somme*, Michael Joseph, 1983
James McWilliams & R James Steel, *Amiens 1918*, Tempus 2004
Jonathan Nicholls, *Cheerful Sacrifice: The Battle of Arras*, Leo Cooper, 1993
Alistair McKean, *Vimy Ridge*, Pan, 1968
Martin Middlebrook, *The First Day of the Somme*, Allen Lane, 1971
William Moore, *A Wood Called Bourlon*, Leo Cooper, 1988
Ian Passingham, *Pillars of Fire: The Battle of Messines Ridge June 1917*, Sutton, 2004
Robin Prior & Trevor Wilson, *The Somme*, Yale University Press, 2005
Gary Sheffield, *The Somme*, Cassell, 2003
Jack Sheldon, *The German Army on the Somme*, Pen & Sword, 2000
Jack Sheldon, *The German Army on Vimy Ridge 1914-1917*, Pen & Sword, 2008
AJ Smithers, *Cambrai, The First Great Tank Battle*, Leo Cooper, 1992
Peter Weston, *Redan Ridge: The Last Stand*, P Weston, 2005
Herbert Fairlie Wood, *Vimy*, Corgi, 1972
Battlefield Europe Series, Pen & Sword/Leo Cooper:
    Jack Sheldon, *The Germans at Beaumont Hamel*, 2005
    Jack Horsfall & Nigel Cave, *Bourlon Wood Cambrai*, 2002
    Jack Horsfall & Nigel Cave, *Flesquières Cambrai*, 2003
    Kyle Tallett & Trevor Tasker, *Gavrelle Arras*, 2000
    David Bilton, *Oppy Wood Arras*, 2005
    Nigel Cave, *Delville Wood Somme*, 2003
    Nigel Cave, *Beaumont Hamel Somme*, 1994/2000
    Nigel Cave, *Vimy Ridge Arras*, 1996/7
    Jack Horsfall & Nigel Cave, *Serre Somme*, 1996
    Michael Renshaw, *Redan Ridge Somme*, 2004
    Trevor Pidgeon, *Boom Ravine Somme*, 1998

Collections of Papers

Ian FW Beckett & Keith Simpson (Eds), *A Nation in Arms*, Tom Donovan, 1990
Brian Bond et al, *Look to Your Front: Studies in the First World War*, BCMH, 1999
Brian Bond & Nigel Cave (Eds), *Haig: A Reappraisal 70 Years On*, Leo Cooper, 1999
Paddy Griffith (Ed), *British Fighting Methods in the Great War*, Frank Cass, 1996
Gary Sheffield & Dan Todman (Eds), *Command & Control on the Western Front*, Spellmount, 2004

Memoirs/Autobiographies/Biographies/Collected Letters

John Baynes, *Far From a Donkey: The Life of General Sir Ivor Maxse*, Brassy's, 1995
Major-General Sir CE Callwell, *Field-Marshal Sir Henry Wilson His Life And Diaries*, Cassell & Co, 1927
Keith Jeffery, *Field Marshal Sir Henry Wilson: A Political Soldier*, OUP, 2006
Ernst Jünger, *Storm of Steel*, (first pub 1920) Penguin, 2004
Ernst Jünger, *Copse 125*, Zimmerman & Zimmerman, 1985
John Lee, *The Warlords: Hindenburg and Ludendorff*, W & N, 2005
Prince Lichnowsky, *My Mission to London 1912-14*, Cassell & Co, 1918
Compton Mackenzie, *Gallipoli Memories*, (first pub 1929) Panther 1965, p9
Sir Frederick Maurice, *The Life of General Lord Rawlinson of Trent GCB*, Cassell, 1928
Svetlana Palmer & Sarah Wallis, *A War in Words: The First World War in Diaries and Letters*, Pocket Books, 2004
Captain AO Pollard, *Fire-Eater*, first pub 1932, reprinted by N&M Press, nd
Robin Prior & Trevor Wilson, *Command on the Western Front*, Blackwell, 1992
Major William Redmond, *Trench Pictures From France*, N&M reprint of 1917 original
Walter Reid, *Douglas Haig: Architect of Victory*, Birlinn Ltd, 2006
Gary Sheffield and John Bourne (Eds), *Douglas Haig War Diaries And Letters 1914-18*, W & N, 2005
Herbert Sulzbach, *With the German Guns: Four Years on the Western Front*, (first pub 1935) Leo Cooper 1998

Prisoners of War

HG Durnford, *The Tunnellers of Holzminden*, CUP, 1930
Hugh Durnford and Others, *Tunnelling to Freedom*, Dover, 2004 (was John Lane, 1932)
AJ Evans, *The Escaping Club*, (first pub 1921), Florin (Jonathan Cape), 1936
Robert Jackson, *The Prisoners 1914-18*, Routledge, 1989
Michael Moynihan (Ed), *Black Bread and Barbed Wire*, Leo Cooper, 1978
Gunther Pluschow, *Escape From England*, (first pub 1916), Rippingyarns.com, 2004
Geoffrey Pyke, *To Ruhleben – And Back*, Constable & Co, 1916
Barry Winchester, *Beyond the Tumult*, Allison & Busby, 1971
Richard van Emden, *Prisoners of the Kaiser*, Pen & Sword, 2000

General

Max Arthur, *When This Bloody War is Over: Soldiers' Songs of the First World War*, Piatkins, 2001
Tony Ashworth, *Trench Warfare 1914-18: The Live and Let Live System*, 1980
Brigadier CN Barclay, *Armistice*, JM Dent & Sons Ltd, 1968
Shelford Bidwell & Dominick Graham, *Firepower: The British Army Weapons & Theories of War 1904-45*, (first pub 1982) Pen & Sword, 2004
Vera Brittain, *Testament of Youth*, Fontana edition, 1979 (first published 1933)
Hugh Cecil & Peter Liddle (Eds), *The Eleventh Hour: Reflections, Hopes & Anxieties at the Closing of the Great War 1918*, Leo Cooper 1998
Cathryn Corns & John Hughes-Wilson, *Blindfold And Alone, British Military Executions in the Great War*, Cassell, 2002
Gordon Corrigan, *Mud, Blood & Poppycock*, Cassell, 2004
Cyril Falls, *Was Germany Defeated in 1918?*, Oxford, 1940

Niall Ferguson, *The Pity of War*, Allen Lane/Penguin, 1998/1999

John Fox, *Forgotten Divisions in the First World War: From Both Sides of No Man's Land*, Sigma Leisure, 1994

Andrew Green, *Writing the Great War: Sir James Edmonds and the Official Histories*, Frank Cass, 2003

Paddy Griffith, *Battle Tactics of the Western Front*, YUP, 1994

Major H Hesketh-Prichard, *Sniping in France*, BCA (Leo Cooper), 1994

Richard Holmes, *Acts of War*, (first pub 1985) Cassell 2004

Tonie & Valmai Holt (Eds), *The Best of Fragments From France*, Milestone Publications, 1978

John Horne & Alan Kramer, *German Atrocities 1914, A Century of Denial*, YUP, 2001

Derek Hunt & John Mulholland, *A Party Fit for Heroes*, N&M Press, 2007

Richard K Massie, *Dreadnought: Britain, Germany and the Coming of the Great War*, Pimlico, 1991/2004

Charles Messenger, *Call To Arms*, Weidenfeld & Nicolson, 2005

Martin & Mary Middlebrook, *The Somme Battlefields*, Viking, 1991

Laurence V Moyer, *Victory Must be Ours: Germany and the Great War 1914-18*, Leo Cooper 1995

Robin Neillands, *The Great War Generals on the Western Front, 1914-18*, Robinson, 1999

Gerard Oram, *Worthless Men: Race, Eugenics and the Death Penalty in the British Army During the First World War*, Francis Boutle Publishers, 1998

Albert Palazzo, *Seeking Victory on the Western Front (The British Army and Chemical Warfare in World War I)*, University of Nebraska, 2000

Ian Passingham, *The Life and Death of the German Army on the Western Front 1914-18*, Sutton Publishing, 2003

Joseph E Persico, *11th Month, 11th Day, 11th Year*, Arrow Books, 2005

John Ramsden, *Don't Mention the War: The British and the Germans Since 1890*, Little, Brown, 2006

Andrew Rothstein, *The Soldiers' Strikes of 1919*, MacMillan, 1980

Gary Sheffield, *Forgotten Victory: The First World War Myths and Realities*, Headline, 2001

GD Sheffield, *Leadership in the Trenches*, MacMillan Press, 2000

Peter Simpkins, *Kitchener's Army: The Raising of the New Armies 1914-16*, MUP 1988, reprinted by Pen & Sword, 2007

Andy Simpson, *Hot Blood and Cold Steel*, Tom Donovan, 1993

Andy Simpson, *Directing Operations: British Corps Commanders on the Western Front*, Spellmount, 2006

AJ Smithers, *The Fighting Nation: Lord Kitchener and his Army*, Leo Cooper, 1994

John Stevenson, *British Society 1914-45*, Penguin, 1984

John Terraine, *The Smoke and the Fire*, BCA 1981

John Terraine, *White Heat: The New Warfare 1914-18*, BCA 1982

George Malcolm Thompson, *The Twelve Days*, Hutchinson, 1964

Tim Travers, *The Killing Ground*, Allen & Unwin, 1987

Tim Travers, *How the War was Won*, Routledge, 1992

Ray Westlake, *Kitchener's Army*, The Nutshell Publishing Co Ltd, 1989

Stanley Weintraub, *A Stillness Heard Around the World*, Oxford, 1985

Maps

Old London Ordnance Survey Maps from Alan Godfrey Maps,

Trench maps: within *WO 95* documents and augmented from ghsmith.com

Mrs Pope-Hennessy, *Map of Main Prison Camps in Germany and in Austria*, IWM 2000

INDEX (Illustrations in bold)